It's Not In The Genes

Mary Dalton

Author's Note: This book is autobiographical. Some names and places have been changed to protect the people involved.

ISBN 978-0966136005

Boo's Publishing Co.
1915 31st Ave. S
Seattle, WA 98144
www.it'snotinthegenes.com

Printed in the United States of America

To receive a discount on orders over 10 books, please contact:
boo_dalton@yahoo.com

For my children,

Maria, Joe, John, Tony, Christopher, Anne

Forward

I believe that our children can grow up without being abused or becoming the abuser. My parents weren't bad people; they just didn't know any better. I refused to believe that abuse was in the genes, and chose instead to believe in the law of nature and that what we feed grows. Refusing to believe the "in the genes" theory meant accepting the responsibility for how my children would turn out. It was the greatest decision I've ever made as well as the most unbelievable challenge! I wanted to prove that "the hand that rocks the cradle rules the world."

I believe that we are inadvertently harming our kids. "Good mothers" have become America's tragedy: we overextend ourselves trying to be perfect while unwittingly creating a generation of children who feel entitled. What's more, we live in a nation that doesn't consider it a crime to allow psychiatrists to drug our children, blaming our challenges on hormones or physiology.

This has nothing to do with being good or bad parents, good or bad teachers. It has to do with a lack of understanding. We have not yet learned how to replace the old parenting and teaching methods that do not work in today's world. It is simply because we, as a society, just haven't learned another way.

In the seventeenth century, kind and caring doctors and nurses did not know that they were carrying germs from one patient to the next because they did not wash their hands between patients. Semmelweiss discovered that patients were actually being nursed to death because of this ignorance. Our situation with today's parents and teachers is similar. It is our responsibility to take care of our children, but without knowledge or intention, we are often the ones who hurt them most. We need to re-learn how to raise our children to be competent, caring, responsible and independent adults. We can all learn the art of parenting using common sense, encouragement, natural and logical consequences. We can all learn to throw away the measuring sticks we use to decide who is first and who is best. We could make a breakthrough in parenting and education that is just as revolutionary as Semmelweiss' discovery was for medicine.

The harm of which I speak becomes evident throughout these pages. No matter who you are or where you are from, I hope you will be able to see yourself in me. Our uniqueness as human beings is obvious. However, our similarities as parents and educators are too often ignored. We all make the same mistakes; we have similar problems in our homes and in our classrooms. We have so much to learn from each other. I do not believe that I am any smarter than anyone else, nor am I a better parent. I just learned things – things that anyone can learn.

In our society, we keep searching for the new and undiscovered when what we really want is timeless: mutual respect, kindness, love, a warm home, enough food for everyone, children's laughter, hugs, acceptance, sunshine and rain. The truth is…only you and I can change the world.

"Anything can be anything else."

--Alfred Adler

"Have the courage to be imperfect."

--Rudolf Dreikurs

"It's a law of nature… what we feed – grows."

--my daddy

1

"Not Again! Please! I'm begging you this time—don't make me spank you again." Exhausted, I pulled Anthony close and held him. "Let me see your arm. Oh honey, I know that must hurt really badly! Must you always be such a bully, Joey?"

Had I now become the screaming maniac my mother always said I was? My voice could be heard from anywhere inside our small home. Probably outside, too. Our neighbors sure got an earful with my screaming at the kids every day.

Anthony's big black eyes were full of the tears that always seemed to be dripping from the tips of his long lashes. His face matched his long sleeved red t-shirt when he cried this way. As usual, he wiped his nose on his sleeves.

I saw Joey, his big brother, in my peripheral vision. He stood like a statue, hands in his pockets and his little forehead wrinkled before its time. He was so handsome, that kid. Perfect eyebrows, perfect lips, great smile, and big brown eyes with lashes so long they brushed against his glasses. His one front tooth stuck out and he really worried about "looking funny." But I kept assuring him that it would straighten out. In time. His clothes were pretty clean most of the time and always looked neat. It's understandable how he won the prize in that photo contest. Only thing out of place was the patch he wore on his left eye. Clipped onto his glasses, it was supposed to help his right eye become stronger, but it was always tipped to one side. He thought I didn't know that he pushed it crooked so that he could see out of his good eye.

"See right here, Mommy?" Anthony pointed again to the spot where Joey had punched him.

I held Anthony close and kissed him as he sniffled. He was giving me that pleading look. That look that always tugged at my heart.

"Come here, Joey," I demanded.

Joey sulked toward me with his eyes fixed on my spanking hand. I grabbed his left arm roughly and swung him around to spank him, but he swayed to soften the blow. I barely caught his behind.

"You are such a bully. Must you always beat up on your brother? I'm so sick of it I could die. You're the older brother and you should be setting a good example. Why do you have to be so mean and make him cry?" I was screaming. "How many times do I have to tell you?" I spanked him again. "Now go to your room and don't come out!" He ran to the stairs and started up as fast as possible.

"You bully! You big bully!" I repeated, as if driving in a nail. I started to wonder if I got angrier with Joey because he was his father's favorite kid? He was the only one their father had ever bothered to acknowledge.

What if I began to have favorites? Mother always did. To this day she won't stay overnight at my sister Kathryn's house but will come up here and stay with me for more than two weeks. Through the years she's always had some kind of flimsy excuse. The last couple of years the excuse has been that my sister's bathtub has mold. Says she can't stay there and take a bath in peace. Claims she's worried that she'll get some disease.

I could hear Maria pounding out her piece on the piano without a hint of pleasure, her fingers moving fast. It was loud and full of mistakes. Her long, thick, brown hair was hanging down to her waist with the same perfection it had when I fixed it early that morning. Sometimes it took me half an hour to get it perfect. I hated the fact that I could hear her mistakes on the piano no matter where I was in the house or what I was doing.

"You will practice until you get that piece without any mistakes if you have to stay there the rest of the day!"

She pushed her glasses back up on her nose and kept going.

"Mommy, I don't..."

"Oh, please don't start whining, Maria. I am so sick of your whining. Just practice your piece."

It made me cringe inside when I talked to her like that. Even though I didn't say all the mean words my mother used, I used some of them and my tone was the same.

Her tears began to flood and she stopped playing to wipe them on her sleeve. I stood there wishing I could just slap her and it would all be fixed. Sometimes my screaming felt endless, making me just want to give up. Sometimes I thought about running away, but where would I go? I didn't really want to run away. I just wanted the burdens, the responsibilities, and the challenges to be lighter. Maria was such a responsible kid, and cute as a button, I'd tell her. She was always trying to help me with something. Why couldn't I notice that more? What was wrong with me?

John began teasing Christopher in the other room. I left Maria crying at the piano and trudged into the TV room. Laid down a couple more rules to a couple more kids. Anthony, already reunited with his brother Joey, started screaming again. I went upstairs into my bedroom and closed the door behind me. Felt tears burning my eyes as I started to collect my losses. The palm of my hand was still as bright as a freshly picked tomato from slapping Joey so hard. Little pictures of the children lined the edge of the mirror on my grandmother's old dresser, covering the places where the edge was worn. Maria was taller than Joey, Joey taller than John, John taller than Anthony, and Anthony taller than two-and-a-half-year-old Christopher. That's the way it works when you have babies every year. Each one was just a little taller than the next.

I looked at the picture of Joey dressed up like the Lone Ranger with his arm around Anthony, who was Tonto. It's one of my favorites. They were smiling at each other with those gorgeous smiles and long eyelashes. Anthony had the darkest eyes of all of them. There was quite a bond between those two; the same as there was between Maria and John. Joey and Anthony always stuck together also. How could I get so angry, screaming and spanking all day and then miraculously have it be so wonderful when I read to them each night?

Exhausted and crying, I threw myself across the old white bedspread. The bed matched the dresser. Daddy got both pieces out of the barn, where they had been collecting dust for years, and cleaned them up for me and Joe after we got married and shipped them up to Chicago.

"I was born in that bed," my mother always said when she came to visit, as if it were sacrilegious for me to have slept in it with Joe. But then again, simply having produced children from our marriage was sacrilegious to her. She'd rather pretend that the stork had brought these babies. She could dampen the spirit of any event.

Today's hysterical screaming scene was a rerun of yesterday, the day before yesterday, last week, last month, last year. It had been going on like this for quite some time. Who knows how long? Three years? Four? Obviously it was not getting any better and although I hated to admit it, it was probably getting worse. No matter what I tried, how hard I spanked or how many times I pleaded, the fighting wouldn't stop. I spanked Joey almost every day for being a bully. The kid was only eight years old and already a bully. I hated it when he beat his brother up. And Anthony just seemed to cry louder each time. He definitely had the loudest mouth on the block. Joey said he was just a big crybaby. Sometimes I would say to myself that I was prepared to spank them for as long as it would take. But how long would it take? The instant satisfaction I felt from spanking them only lasted for about a minute. And no matter how much I thought they deserved it, I felt lousy afterwards.

Both Mother and Kathryn always told me I wasn't strict enough. My sister always said she could "get them in line." She told me she could "break them" of a few things if she had them alone at her house for a couple of weeks, and she meant it. That was probably true and it scared me. Often my mother and sister talked of "breaking the kids" of things and it's easy to see that my sister's kids were scared to death of her.

One day when Mother was here to help me after Joey was born, she sent me into my bedroom to lie down and rest. She was alone with Joey in the other room and he was screaming like crazy. I stayed in my bedroom until I couldn't stand it any longer and then went to investigate.

"Go back to your room!" she screamed at me.

But I stood up to her and said I wanted to get my baby. I went to get him out of his bed and found that she had taped an ice cream stick on the inside of his little arm so he couldn't bend it and put his thumb in his mouth. When I started to take it off, Mother screamed, "It would only take a couple of days to 'break him' of thumb sucking! Now you have ruined everything, you big cry baby!"

She loved to call me names but I didn't care this time. Joey was my baby and I didn't want him "broken" of anything. I wondered why she acted so mean. Didn't she know there was nothing in the world I wouldn't do for her? Didn't she know how she tore up my insides, as well as everyone else's in our family? There was no one in this world who could take the place of my mother in my heart. I had stuck by her side my entire life—no matter what. Just because I didn't want to raise my kids the same way she had raised us didn't mean I didn't love her. Couldn't she understand that? I figured I would just have to try harder.

When Kathryn tells her kids to do something, they do it immediately. I have never seen kids "mind" the way her children do. She could tell them to "be like little soldiers" and they would do it. She would say, "I don't want to hear a peep out of you" and they wouldn't move. When she would say, "hold it in," they held their breath as well as their tears. It was true that my kids never "minded" like hers. When she would scream at my Johnny because he was teasing someone, he would just laugh and run away.

"Boy, I'd get you in line if I had you at my house a few days!" she'd yell after him.

It made me cringe when I heard her yell. Nevertheless, almost every day I myself screamed at Maria about how she played the piano. I hated myself for doing it the same way I hated it when my mother did that to me. She has continued to criticize me my entire life. If she couldn't do it in person, she'd get at me through the postal service. For almost eight years now, ever since I left Perryville, Missouri I would get at least one letter every day and sometimes two.

I never believed my sister when she told me that mental illness could strike me down at any time just like it did her. I never believed it *was* "in the genes." Even as a little kid, I thought that my sister got "the way she was" because of how our mother acted towards her. And when she got coal in her Xmas stocking and nothing else, it was devastating. But then I did get weird that summer when I took care of all those kids. But the doctor assured me it was because I had been taking care of nine kids, all less than eight years of age, for the entire summer without help from another adult. He asked me why I would do something like that with no help from anyone around. I explained to him.

It just sorta happened. Kathryn decided she was feeling funny in the head, is the way she always put it, and could I take the kids for two weeks so she could check herself into the hospital for a little vacation. Of course I said yes, but as it neared the end of the two weeks, she called again and asked if I could keep them two more weeks. .... Well, of course I said okay again and that's the way it went all summer. Needless to say, it was totally exhausting and I felt "a little funny in the head" but I just wanted to help her the way she had always tried to help me with things. I wanted her to get well. But the doctor said I was being totally unrealistic and it was more than insane to try and do what I was doing. He said that that would make most people feel like they had gone crazy after the first day or two—much less after the 10 weeks that I had all those kids.

He called Joe into his office and set him straight. I don't know what all he said to him but the kids were sent home immediately and he put me into the hospital for 3 weeks on complete bed rest. I didn't want to see anyone or talk to anyone except Joe and Father Pat, the new priest who had come to the parish.

"Mommy! Mommy! Joey's doing it again! He's hitting me again!" Anthony gulped between his screams as he buried himself in my leg that was hanging off the bed.

"God damn it! This time I'm going to get you more than good, Joey," I hollered as I jumped off my bed and ran down the hall after him. I caught him in his room and started spanking him hard until he began to sob. I could still hear Maria banging the piano downstairs. And John was making Maria scream between notes.

When I got back in my bedroom, I looked to the ugly little clock. It was 7 p.m.--almost time for our story. I went into the bathroom to throw some water on my face.

"Hey you guys, do you want to have our story now?" I called as I walked out of the bathroom.

Like sweet bundles of joy, they all came running towards me as if nothing bad had ever happened between us. We became an entirely different family.

"It's our turn tonight, Mommy. We're supposed to be in me and Anthony's bedroom," Joey's loving tone reflected none of the anger I saw on his face when I spanked him just minutes before. He sounded as if the afternoon had been one big, splendid picnic. He was like that, that kid. They all were. They didn't care about what had happened during the day. Our good times were great and we all loved that about us.

"Okay, Joey, that's fine."

"Yeah, it's our room tonight, you guys!" Anthony yelled as if everyone on the next block needed to be alerted. His huge grin showed that he was proud of his vocal abilities.

My body slid down onto the floor like honey down a sore throat. It was easier than trying to bend. I was completely exhausted. Stretching out my aching legs, there was total silence and peace before I began to read. Another miracle.

"Halfway up Blueberry hill, in a funny old yellow house, lived Little Brown Bear." Joey reached over and kissed my hand. "Little Brown Bear liked to hunt for honey, he liked to sit on the steps of the old yellow house, and he liked to lie in the hammock under the mulberry tree. But he didn't like to hang up his clothes when he went to bed."

Christopher started to slowly move into the middle of the pile of bodies. "Which one are you reading, Mommy?"

"*Little Brown Bear Loses His Clothes*. Is that okay?" I asked, now totally relaxed.

Anthony snuggled into Maria's lap as she tried to pull on her pajama pants. We could all fit in the area the size of a postage stamp. I looked at our bodies all entwined with each other before continuing the story. Anthony was kissing my knee as he hugged my leg. Joey was kissing my right cheek. John was kissing my left arm. The first time I read to them, I had cried because I didn't know one of the words. Back then there were so many words I hadn't known. It was better now. Sure, there were still some I didn't know, but it wasn't as devastating as it was before. Of course, they'd always loved it no matter how much I'd stumbled. In fact, I don't think they ever even noticed. And if they did, no one ever said anything. I leaned back against the bunk bed my Daddy had made. Christopher was now in the middle of all the bodies. He kissed my foot because that was the only body part left unclaimed by loving arms and legs. I felt reassured again that the horrible spankings and screams were already forgotten.

Who were these little people that had come into my life? These little people that I spanked so often and hard during the day, but read to and loved so intensely at night? How could I love them so much and spank them so often? When was that day that I longed for going to come, when I was going to change and actually do things differently than my mother did? I needed answers. I was tired of hearing myself talk about it and not actually do anything differently. Sometimes I got tired of my promises to myself, but that night as I read to them in peace, it seemed to be enough. Often after I had cleaned the kitchen and went to bed, my mind would wander back to my childhood.

The memories of my childhood could make my stomach hurt. I knew that it had been at least ten years since that night my brother Tommy came home drunk, but it felt like it was just yesterday. Tommy had come down from St. Louis that weekend for the Homecoming celebration. Hours after the football game was over he finally showed up at the back door. Looking for something to eat in a house where food was always scarce, he jammed some bread in his mouth before he noticed me.

"Hi Mary Cecile, did you go to the game?"

"Yeah."

"How come you're not at the dance?"

"I wasn't allowed to go."

"Oh yeah, I should have known that. Where's Mother?"

"Upstairs. Lying down," I said as he raced past me into the hallway and took those huge steps two and three at a time. Mother was up. I could hear the bedroom floor creak from her footsteps.

"You've been with your drinking buddies again and you know I forbid you to come here when you've been drinking," she was standing in the hall at the top of the stairs.

"Aw, shut-up will you, old lady?"

"Don't you dare talk to me that!"

"Will you-please-shut-up, old lady?!" He interrupted her before she had a chance to finish.

I couldn't believe my ears. I had never seen Tommy drunk before but, from the little I had overheard through the years, this time was particularly terrible.

"Oh shut-up, will you? Will-you-please-shut-up??" he screamed at her again, as she tried to say something.

My God. I couldn't believe he had said that.

"Don't you have enough to do watching Daddy and Mary Cecile? Do you have to watch met to? Do you??"

She didn't answer. She might have known her control and power were no longer a match for his.

"I asked you a question, old lady. Don't you have enough to do watching

them? I'm sick and tired of you following me around in St. Louis...you and your private detectives...don't you have enough meddling here to keep you busy?" his words slurred together.

"I don't know what you're talking about."

"Right...you don't know what I'm talking about...you've always got your Goddamn nose in someone else's business...that's what I'm talking about."

"You're my son, Tommy, and I love you, but don't think you can come in here and talk to me like that..."

"Oh, the old 'I-love-all-my-children-the-same' speech? You, Goddamned two-faced bitch!" He screamed louder and headed down the stairs. He couldn't see me standing in the back of the hallway. "I'm so sick of you and all your fucking meddling through the years." He started up the stairs again, yelling at a pitch that shook the very foundation of our pre-civil war house. "You mother fucking bitch! Always sending Daddy to do your talking for you!"

"You better get out, Tommy, before..."

"Don't you tell me what to do, you bitch...I'll get out when I'm damn good and ready and I'll never be back. Do you hear me? I'll never come back to this hole. Who'd want to? Who'd want to come here? See any people rushing to get in the doors here? Huh? Who? Name one person."

He was crying. His fists were shaking as he came down the stairs again, each step sounding like a ton of bricks. He stumbled toward me and I saw the tears streaming down his face. His voice and broken spirit echoed in the hallway. Oh, dear brother of mine, I thought, please don't stop. Keep saying it for me no matter how much damage is inflicted.

"You God damn son of a bitch!" He continued. "I'll never come to your funeral!" He was close to me now and I thought his screaming was going to shatter my eardrums. "I'll never come to your funeral, do you hear me, you bitch? I never want to see you again! Do you hear me? I never want to see you again!!"

Tommy's eyes caught mine, but I quickly looked down. I was ashamed and *shocked that I didn't want him to stop yelling at her. I wanted to scream a million dirty words at her too, for all the meanness she inflicted upon us, but knew I would never do it. I would just stay scared and keep it inside as I always did. He stormed outside and started his car, and just that quick, he was gone into the night. He didn't punch me good-bye like he always did. Was he ever going to come back? Oh, Tommy, I thought, please be safe. Be safe somewhere tonight.*

My body shook as I climbed the stairs in the dark. I was hoping I could get to bed without her wanting to talk. I prayed to God that she wouldn't want to talk to me tonight.

"Mary Cecile, is that you?"

She had heard me coming—those stairs always seemed to creak twice as loud when it was dark. She called me in to brush her hair, and acted as if nothing had happened. She thanked me and told me that God would bless her little Buttercup. I hated it when she called me that. I knew I was her favorite and I hated the way that made me feel. I felt bad for her, and yet inside I had cheered Tommy on in his drunken tirade. I thought for sure that my entire soul had been blackened from those thoughts.

"Come on, Mommy, aren't you going to finish the story?" Joey said with an angel's voice. And he acted like an angel sometimes too.

"Of course I am sweetheart, I'm sorry."

He wasn't a bully now—he was rubbing Anthony's back. And Maria wasn't whining now—she was rubbing Christopher's back. I thought that maybe I should start reading to them the minute they walked in from school until they went to bed.

"And by and by Mr. Wind looked in through the window and smiled. He smiled and smiled and smiled. 'Coat, hat and tie hung up with care, what a tidy room for a Little Brown Bear!' Mr. Owl chuckled softly to himself. The End. Come on, everyone is falling asleep. Let me tuck you in."

They all ran to their beds.

"Can I be first, Mommy?"

"Sure, why not. Hop up there Joey and I'll start with you."

I began his backrub by playing with his hair. My sister told me that I always cut their hair too short. But they liked it short and I reminded her that it was their hair, not hers. I touched his little checks. His eyes were already half closed.

"Please don't be mean to Anthony tomorrow, Joey."

"I won't Mommy, I promise."

"I won't spank you anymore, okay? I hate doing that, Joey."

"I know, Mommy." He meant it and so did I. We would never do it again—the fussing part.

"I love you."

"I love you too, Mommy."

"Anthony, still awake down here?" I began rubbing his back and he purred.

"I'm awake Mommy."

"Don't cry and fight and get Joey in trouble tomorrow."

"Okay Mommy I'll try, but sometimes he's mean to me."

"I know, but try not to cry like that anymore, okay?"

"I won't Mommy. Could you scratch right over here under my arm?"

"Here?"

"Ah yes! That's it," he sighed.

"I love you, Anthony."

"I love you too, Mommy. We won't fight anymore. I promise."

"Okay Anthony, good night. See you in the morning."

I gave him a kiss and tucked the covers around his beautiful little head. I took a deep breath and stood up. I wanted to be finished with all these backrubs because I was so tired. But I did love rubbing their backs because it reassured me that at least there was one thing I was doing differently than Mother. All my life, I was the one who brushed her hair, rubbed her back, and gave her a foot massage, whatever she needed. I loved being able to do things for her. The part I hated was that she thought it was part of my duty as her child.

And being "the good kid" in the family, I of course did everything she asked. My brother Paul was the perfect child and he had always " paid his dues," she said. How he got so perfect I don't know but she constantly told us what a perfect child he was. All her children owed her, she said. And because the others—meaning Tommy and Kathryn—did wrong, I had to make up for it.

I didn't want my kids to feel that they "owed" me. I'd rub their backs forever if it meant changing that idea.

"Will Dad be coming on Saturday to take us out?"

"Probably, but let's talk about it tomorrow okay?"

"Okay Mommy. I love you."

"I love you too."

Leaving Joey's and Anthony's room, I took four steps down the hall into Maria's room to continue the ritual. Two down, three to go! I loved the little hallway that was lined with pictures of them. Before it had been so ugly with just beige walls and cheap beige carpeting.

"I'm sorry for calling you a whiner today, sweetheart," I said, sitting down on Maria's bed. She was always ready for her back rub—on her tummy, covers down, and pajamas up.

"It's okay, Mommy."

"No, it's not. I'm not going to do that anymore." I was saying it more for myself than her.

"It's okay, Mommy."

"I know but I'm just not going to do that anymore. Does this feel good?"

"Mmmm hmmm." She breathed deeply, almost off to slumber land.

I kissed her cheek and she was asleep. I eased her long hair on top of the covers and combed it with my fingers. She was the most beautiful little girl in the world - that was for sure. Tomorrow there would be no screaming, no fighting, and no spanking. I felt relief. I was determined to begin again with these beautiful babies and make it different. There would be no alcoholics among my children. I would not call them names like Mother always called me. Tomorrow was going to be the day I would start, for sure!

"I GET FIRST PICK!!" Nothing like having your own human alarm clocks, I thought, as I rolled over.

"Nuhh-uhh, Maria. I was up first!" Not even two layers of pillows covering my ears could drown out their screaming.

"No you weren't, Joey!"

"Yes, I was Maria!"

"You were not, Joey.

"Keep out of it, John."

"I don't have to!"

"It's between me and Maria."

"I get first pick, Joey!"

"No you don't, Maria!"

"Okay, you big bully!"

"That's right, Mother Hen!"

"You're not the boss, Joey!!"

"You're not the boss either, Maria."

"Mom! MOM! Joey's hitting me! He's being a bully again!!"

"Shut up Mother Hen, you're being a bully!"

"Am not! Mom, Joey's hitting everybody!"

It was Saturday morning. 6 a.m. Mother had already left her morning phone message with the usual greeting, "Are you still in bed while those children run wild? I've been up for hours! I sure worry about how those poor children will make it with a father who was thrown out and a mother who sleeps her life away. If you ever get out of bed, call me back!" Click!

Slowly I sat up in bed and let my feet slide to the floor. It was raining outside and their father would not be taking them out. He gave his usual excuse—some important meeting. It was going to be a long, long day for me.

They were fighting over TV programs, but I was not going to let it get to me. And I was not going to let Mother's phone call get to me. Last night, I really meant my promise. I decided that I would just go down there and talk with them. My stomach was hurting again. My back, too. Maybe it was that cheap mattress. I pulled on my jeans, but then quickly took them off, thinking I'd take my shower before going downstairs.

"Mommy, I was up first and they won't let me watch my show! I never get to pick first because Joey is always being a bully!" Anthony was at my side before I could make it halfway down the hall.

"Tell him to leave you alone, Anthony," I said calmly.

"But he won't, Mommy!" he was pleading.

My stomach grabbed me as I took off down the stairs. "Joey, are you hitting your brother again?"

"Mommy, he was..."

I didn't let him finish but just began whacking him across his behind.

"Go to your room right now. You want to start this day off like a bully? I'll start this day off for you."

I ran after him as he went towards the stairs. He was crying and I swung at whatever part of his body I could catch.

"Wanna start the day, Mr. Bully, want to?" We were both running up the stairs now. When Joey reached the top, he ran into his room. I stopped in the hallway.

"Damn, can you believe this?" I said to myself. Surely they would be carrying me off soon. Oh God, how could this be? Joey was crying in his room. Things were quiet downstairs. I went into the bathroom and closed the door. I hated that I could hear my mother's words come out of my mouth whenever I yelled at them.

"I see your eyelids blinking, young lady. You don't fool me."

I was hoping Mother wouldn't check on me that afternoon. It had to have been 100 degrees out in the sun, but I preferred to lay out in the sun rather than upstairs in my bed. She usually only checked my eyelids if I was napping in my bed, but sometimes she monitored me out there in the yard too. Personally, I thought that eleven years old was too old to take a nap, but Mother insisted.

Mother always said that people in the country never just lay out in the sun. They didn't do anything to get tan. She said this was because they were ignorant and didn't know any better. She claimed that I was the first baby ever to be laid out in the sun in Perryville. I liked getting tan, or, as Mother said, "brown as a berry." My best friend from down the street, Ann, was a year older than me. She was tall, really pretty, and always played last in our piano recitals, but she never got any tanner than I did. For some reason, Mother thought that was really great. I never knew what Daddy thought about it because at that point he hadn't talked for about three years. "He's pouting," Mother would say, and never talked except to "say something ugly."

"Hey, Mary Cecile! Has Mother got supper ready yet?"

"I don't think so, Tommy."

I followed as my brother ran down the brick path to the barn to get some chicken and cow grain to eat. He would take huge handfuls and just shove them into his mouth. I knew he was always hungry, although he never complained. He had gotten so big and tall that year.

I thought Tommy was the neatest thing ever. I didn't see him much since he had started high school two years before, except sometimes when we did the dishes together at night. Other than eating and sleeping, he didn't come home much anymore. Mother said he changed after they did that freshman initiation thing his first year of high school. The seniors had cut his new pants off at the knees. His first pair of new pants ever and they had gotten ruined the first day he had worn them. I knew it was pretty hard on him, but I didn't think that could've changed him too much. I heard that everyone at school liked him, and that was certainly understandable considering how funny he was. He was quickly becoming the school's new football hero and it was obvious that girls liked him.

I missed him playing around on the piano like he used to do before Mother told him he wasn't allowed to anymore. Mother said he had wasted time and money on lessons and that I had better not mess around like he did. I wouldn't dare mess around. I was too scared. She got so mad when I would just make a small mistake.

"Mary Cecile!!"

"Yes, Mother?"

"Come in now and practice that piece you couldn't get right this morning until I have supper ready."

"Okay, I'm coming, Mother."

"Oh, Mary Cecile, do that again! Aren't you ever going to get that right?"

I hated it when she would yell at me from the kitchen like that. Even though she was supposedly busy making supper, she was able to hear every tiny mistake I made on the piano. I stopped for a minute to stretch my back and could already hear her coming into the living room.

"You will practice until you get it right, Mary Cecile. I won't allow you to fool around like your brother and sister did. Now do it again. Get it perfect."

She was standing behind me as I played it once again. I was sure it was perfect. I had done it perfectly this time. Tommy would tell me I was good and that I should keep playing even if she was always standing over me. I waited for her response.

"You're just wasting time. Supper's ready, set the table. You'll have to practice longer tomorrow. Maybe you'll finally get it perfect."

At supper, nobody spoke. I looked from Mother to Tommy to Daddy. There was never eye contact between anyone. Everyone was trying to pretend they were concentrating on eating but I honestly believed that everyone hated to talk to each other. As usual, I ate too fast. It was my way of hoping that supper would be over faster. But Mother would never let me leave the table, even if I *was finished before everyone else. She used to let my older sister Kathryn leave and I would not be following in her footsteps, she reminded me daily.*

"Mary Cecile, stop eating so fast. How many times do I have to tell you that? You're not going anywhere anyway, young lady. Besides, that is why you are always belching something awful."

That was it for suppertime conversation. All eyes were resting on their plates. I just wanted to get out of there.

"Mary Cecile, you can clear the table," she said after what felt like hours. That night, it was my turn to dry and Tommy was supposed to wash. We usually switched off every week or so. I knew if Mother could see how he would stick whole handfuls of silverware under the faucet and then shove them towards me, she would get mad. She said we had to wash each piece individually. I looked up at Tommy and he punched me in the arm. He knew I wouldn't tattle on him, but probably just wanted to make sure. The thing was, I always thought it was funny. He threw the last glass towards me and ran to the back door.

"Come on, Mary Cecile! Let's go down to the barn!"

"Don't you leave the property, Tommy!" Mother yelled as I headed out after him.

Less than two minutes later, I looked back to the porch and could see Mother sitting there with some crocheting or something. I was never out of her sight for too long. Tommy would probably sneak out through the other side of the barn to go hang out with his friends at the filling station. She wouldn't notice though. She was busy watching me like a hawk. I pretended I didn't notice her.

Tomorrow, she would yell at him for running off and he would just say he was down the street. "Why can't you be more like your brother Paul? Or tell the truth like Mary Cecile. She always tells the truth." I hated it when she said that. Tommy usually just punched me in the arm and I knew he meant it as a love tap, but boy, my arm would sure get black and blue. Mother was always saying that she loved all her children the same, but I knew that wasn't true.

I could still hear Joey's unrelenting sobs from two rooms away, while I was lying on my bed. Why was that kid such a bully? Was he ever going to stop? Well, I had spanked him hard enough. I hoped I wouldn't have to do it anymore after that whole scene.

By five o'clock, I had spanked Joey four more times.

I had also screamed at Maria—making her stay at the piano for an extra hour. I had spanked John twice. I had sent everyone to his or her room at least once. I had also given out a million sermons. And that all happened before lunchtime. I was not proud of my record. My back was hurting worse. Their father had come by and given me $48. It was supposed to be $60, but he would take out the $12 I got for renting the garage to the woman down the street. That money sure didn't go very far with five kids. Every day, I worried if we'd make it through.

"Mommy, Maria's being bossy!"

"John, please go back downstairs until I finish washing this floor."

"Can't you tell her to stop?"

The phone rang again. I answered it.

"Hello."

No greeting from the other end. Mother never thought she had to say hello, she just started in.

"And if you insist upon divorcing that good man—maybe I didn't like everything he did but he's a good man—you'd better pull yourself together, young lady. Get up out of that bed and take care of those poor children like a mother should. They're just like poor little orphans with no one to take care of them...and another thing, young lady, you stay away from that priest and stop telling him your problems. It will lead to no good, you mark my words."

"I'm up, Mother, and I take care of my children."

"Not from what I see." She slammed down the receiver again.

I didn't know why she was so against Father Pat. He came to see me when I was in the hospital. He was a priest in our parish and that's what priests do.

They visit people in hospitals. I don't see any problem with that. He wanted us to be okay. I realized he was lonesome and unhappy, but he'd been good to us just like some of our other dear friends in the parish.

Well, I've never ever had any friends that she liked, so why would this be any different? Mother couldn't rule me totally anymore with her relentless phone calls and her letter-a-day tirade. The mailman use to tease me, "a letter EVERY day of your life?" But when I listened to the kids play house, it was eerie, especially hearing myself in Maria's voice bossing everyone around. Maria was using my tone of voice when she told her brothers what to do. It was me coming out of her—my exact expressions.

Mother used to dust the top of things with the bottom of her housedress all the time, and now I dusted the top of the chest with the sleeve of my sweatshirt. Was how we dusted "in the genes?" Was I going to have favorite and un-favorite kids like my mother always had? The way I would scream at the kids sure made me wonder about myself. After all of the years constantly repeating that I was going to do it differently, I wondered was it really possible?

Did it really have to do with lack of money, like Mother had said? Wasn't there something deeper that had never been discussed? Why had my father not uttered a sound for seven or eight years of his life? Why didn't anyone ever come to our house to visit? Wasn't there one relative who was good enough for us, or were we really so much better than all that "white trash," as Mother had always called them?

How about my sister—was she really mentally ill just like Aunt Zita? And was my brother going to be an alcoholic just like Uncle Ed? Was that all "in the genes?" It scared me to think that almost everything with my children and me was going to be a repeat of my own childhood. Why didn't I believe it was all "in the genes?" Everyone else seems to believe it without questioning. Was I nuts for believing the cycle of abuse could be broken?

2

I knew it was going take a while for it all to sink in. I had just turned 18 years old, and was here on my own, sitting in my room at the Queen's Daughters in St. Louis, looking at the fall colors. The trees were especially beautiful this year. Well, I was kind of on my own. Mother checked up on me every day so far, but I was definitely not in Perryville anymore. She had gotten me a job at St. Louis University and also had me sign up for some night classes because I was able to get free tuition by working for the University. The Queen's Daughters wasn't a regular dorm but rather a place for mostly older unmarried women with a few students who couldn't get into the dorms. My roommate and I liked each other. She was popular and the boys liked her. I decided that I was going to go out with boys, too. I knew I'd be good like I had been taught and never let any boy touch me, but I was going out with anyone who asked me. Not that I believed that anyone would ask me out, but I hoped they would.

"No you aren't, young lady."

"Yes I am, Mother."

"We'll see about this. Don't you sass me back. I'll send Daddy up there to get you. There's nothing that says you have to stay up there."

"I'm going to marry him, Mother. I've made up my mind and Joe and I are going to get married."

"You will not let some 'dirty dago' from Chicago dictate to me, Mary Cecile."

"He's not dictating, Mother. We love each other and are going to get married."

"I won't sign. You'll need to have my signature and I won't sign. We'll see how far you get. You're not running everything yet, young lady."

"I don't need your signature, Mother. I don't have to be twenty-one years old in Missouri."

She was silent. It was true; I didn't need her signature. And Joe had said he would stand by me; he was strong. I couldn't believe how strong he was. He said that he'd do whatever it took because he couldn't live without me. He said that he really loved me. It was hard to believe how much he loved me. And he wasn't any "dirty dago," as Mother and other people always called Italians. He was a good person.

"You come home here this weekend so we can talk this over, young lady. Do you hear me?"

"Yes, Mother."

"Good-bye." Click.

No, Mother I'm not coming home this weekend, you can't make me! She was mad, but I couldn't help that. I was going to marry him. She could make fun of us all she wanted, but we had already decided to get married with or without her approval. I had never stood up to her before, and I certainly never would have stood up to her if I didn't think Joe would be there by my side.

It was just like a fairy tale. I met Joe Carlotti after being in St. Louis for just two months. He had recently finished his BA degree at DePaul in Chicago last year and had come to St. Louis University to get his master's degree. After just one year at the University, Joe changed his mind and was about to head back to Chicago, his hometown. At the last minute before he was to leave, we met.

We were fixed up by a friend to go to the prom together; it was our first time out. Then after two more dates, we just knew. In my mind I thought it was true love—something I thought would never happen to me. I figured I just got lucky.

Back in Chicago Joe started in some Ph.D. program at Northwestern University. The university was trying something new, he said, and he could get his masters and PhD all in one. I wasn't sure which program it was exactly, but I remember him saying it was something big. Also, he missed

Chicago really badly and wanted to get back home. Our original plan was to get married the following June, but that soon changed because we missed each other so much that Joe came back to St. Louis in October with an engagement ring and we moved our wedding up to two days after Christmas.

After the wedding, and one night in St. Louis for our honeymoon, we went to Chicago. Joe and his brothers built a little apartment in the basement for us to live in. It was really cute, even if it didn't have a toilet. There was a toilet out in the basement.

It wouldn't be so bad. We were together and that's all I cared about.

"Well, Mary Cecile, I just hope it comes late."

"Why, Mother? Why would you want the baby to come late?"

"Mary Cecile, you don't know anything, do you? If the baby is born on time, it will have been exactly nine months since your wedding. People will talk." I hated it when she used her I-know-everything tone. She made it sound like I was some kind of slut or something. She always had been extremely intense about the sex thing.

"Well, Mother," I said, "I never did anything before I was married. I know that and you know that. Who cares what people think?"

"You better start caring, young lady."

Every day I received a letter. Some days I even got two! I wasn't in her house anymore, but she continued to try and forever control me—even if she had to do it through the mail all the way from Perryville to Chicago. I remember wondering if it was always going to be that way.

During that first year of our marriage, Joe decided he was going to quit school. He told me that it wasn't what he needed in order to do what he really wanted to do in life. I had no idea what it was that he really wanted to do, but believed that he was really smart and trusted his decision. Plus, he said we'd need money now that I was pregnant.

It felt like everything was happening really fast. I have heard people say that it's instinct, but when I got home from the hospital, I felt like screaming, "HELP!! What in the world do I do with this baby now?" Even though Mother and Joe never did get along, I was glad she was coming to visit. I knew I'd have to stop smoking when she came, but I'd rather do that than have her get all upset about it.

"I hope your milk lasts, Mary Cecile."

I had no idea what Mother meant by that. Dr. Angelotti only said that some women can breast feed and some women can't. Joe's family doctor was a man of few words.

"Isn't she the most beautiful thing you've ever seen, Mother?"

"Yes, Mary Cecile. A beautiful little 'dago.'"

Mother tried to make me mad by saying things like that, but I didn't let it bother me. I could understand her jealousy of Joe. I just continued to try to let her know as best I could that I loved her. I didn't know what else to do. It was funny though, because Daddy really liked Joe. While Mother called him Mr. Know-it-All, Daddy really thought he was smart. I felt bad that Mother didn't like Joe, and Joe didn't like her, but what could I do about it? He was my husband and I loved him, too. Sometimes when I would look at the two of them together though, I was surprised at how alike they seemed.

"Well, maybe next time it'll be a boy."

I couldn't tell if they were kidding or not, but either way, it didn't feel good. That was what most of Joe's relatives had to say about Maria's birth. I thought she was the greatest, no matter what anyone else thought. Joe hadn't even made an attempt to hold her yet, but when I asked him about it, he said he was afraid of babies when they're really little. I had never held a little baby either, but I learned quickly. Besides, when Joe would get home from work, he would say he needed to unwind, and usually went upstairs to watch TV and get something to eat. Joe's parents always had something good to eat—a big difference from when I was growing up, and definitely something Joe and I didn't have yet.

Actually, everything about life here was different. "Mom" and "Pop" were Catholic like me, but they didn't go to church except on Christmas and Easter. I had never heard of that. I sure hoped they didn't go to hell when they died. And Joe was definitely his father's favorite, as well as the whole extended family's favorite, because he was the first one to go to college. All his brothers and his sister lived upstairs with Mom and Pop. They had disagreements sometimes, but it was a world of difference from the family fights I could remember.

I thought I'd see Joe more, but his schedule didn't allow it. He slept late, went to work around noon, came home late, and stayed upstairs with Pop watching TV until midnight. When he came down to our basement apartment very late, I knew when he got into bed (although I was asleep). That man always wanted to make love. "It's just that I love you so much," he would say.

And I sure didn't know what happened to our money. Joe got a paycheck now, but I just figured he needed it for other things. It was okay with me, though; I really didn't need anything. We had gotten so many gifts for Maria that we had no need to buy anything for her.

I just couldn't imagine loving another baby. It sounds funny to me now and I never would've dared say that out loud to someone, but that's how I felt. It was probably because I knew Maria, and I didn't know the new baby yet. Maria was definitely the neatest thing that had ever happened to me. I was able to make her a dress out of the smallest piece of material. That's something I still think is amazing.

Everyone except for Joe's mom told me that they hoped we'd get a boy the second time. I couldn't figure out why that was so important to everyone. What difference did it make as long as the baby was healthy? I hated it when everyone said that to me but I would just smile and say nothing.

Pop, who was now called "Nanu" because he was a grandfather, said Joe's brother and his new wife were going to move to the third-floor apartment and that Joe and I should move to the second floor. It was a big apartment with three bedrooms. Of course, almost anything would've been better than that basement apartment with no toilet. I kind of wished Joe and I could get our own place, but I knew we didn't have the money. Every Saturday like clockwork Joe would have to borrow the money from Nanu for food and anything else he wanted to get. I felt so embarrassed about this but we never talked about it.

There was no discussion about names. It was a given that his name would be Joe, after his father. That was okay with me; I liked that name. Mother came again to help me. The tension between her and Joe was awful. I was very relieved at the fact that Joe wasn't around so much while she was visiting. I remember that I didn't want Mother to know how poor we were, and I would try to get Joe up early so he could go get money from Nanu for a few groceries. Mother loved to ask questions about food or money. When Mother wasn't visiting, we never really had to go to the store because we ate upstairs at least one meal every day. But Mother never wanted to visit with Nana (Joe's mom) and Nanu because she said it smelled "too much like garlic." The truth was she wanted to have me all to herself when she visited. She liked to own me and all my time and attention.

Mother would say that she had enough on her mind without having to worry about me, too. She would tell me she didn't think Joe treated me very well, but I believed that was because she didn't like him. There were things about us as a couple, however, that did make me sad. We never spent much time together and we never held hands or anything like that. And Joe still hadn't held either of the babies. His new excuse was that he said some people just couldn't hold babies. I believed him, thinking to myself how I had never known that. I must have been good at hiding that it made me sad because Joe's sister told me she could tell that Joe and I were really in love because of the way I looked at him. I loved hearing Joe tell me how much he loved me. No one had ever said, "I love you" in my family.

"You kids sure do have fun together," Uncle Steve said.

"Oh my Goddie!" was all Nana had to say.

Mother just said, "Again? So soon?"

Nanu said, "Good work, Son."

I said I knew I would be busy, but I was glad. And I was. I had fun with those babies. The people at the hospital not only remembered me from the year before, they said, "See you next year!" when I left. They also said that I must've had heartburn because of the mop of hair on my babies when they were born. This baby was blonder, and Nana said he looked more like my side of the family. I picked the name John. Joe said it was fine. I could tell he was proud. "Another boy," he told everyone.

I wanted to nurse that baby longer than three weeks, but Dr. Angelotti said I couldn't. I really wanted to ask him some questions about it, but he got mad if I ever asked anything.

"He's a really good doctor," Joe said, "It's okay if he doesn't answer questions because he knows what he's talking about."

"I know that babies can be fine on the bottle, Joe. It's just that I want to nurse so badly, it makes me very sad."

"Well, he says you can't, sweetheart. He's been our family doctor for years and there's no need to question him."

"I know, Joe, I know," I paused. "Honey?"

"What is it?"

"Well, I just think about how wonderful it would be if we had our own apartment somewhere else."

"Honey, I know it's hard. But we're just going to have to make do for a while. You know we can't afford our own place. We just can't do it right now."

I knew he was right. It was just getting so much harder. Our every movement could be heard downstairs. Nana knew who had been up, who had been crying, and what the time had been. Day or night, she heard everything. I knew she was lonely, but we needed our privacy, too.

"I know."

"Okay, honey. I'll see you later then. Give me a big kiss. What would I ever do without you? I love you so much."

"I love you too, Joe."

I thought it was a funny thing that I didn't feel so loved by him, but I tried to convince myself that it was just my imagination. After all, I did just have a baby. Shouldn't that be proof that he loved me? To me it was so fabulous the way he said, "I love you," every day, and although I loved hearing those words more than anything else, why didn't it feel good on the inside? I'd have shouted to the world from the highest mountain about the great love letters he use to write to me, so why did his words seem empty now?

"My mother thinks we should get another doctor's opinion."

"Honey, we can trust Dr. Angelotti. He really is a good doctor. Besides, how could we afford to go to another doctor with the bills we already have?"

"I know our pharmacy bill is huge, Joe. But that's because Joey's sick every three weeks like clockwork and penicillin is so expensive. Mother just thinks we should ask a different doctor if he should really have his tonsils out. What about talking to the doctor about not charging us so much?"

"I did, honey, and he said he doesn't care how long it takes us to pay the bill. We can take as long as we need."

"Well, Mother is also worried about all the prescriptions Dr. Angelotti writes for me. Whenever I tell him about being tired, he just gives me another prescription. And now that I've thought about it, he does give me a lot of pills. And none of them seem to work. Sometimes it's like I can't get through the day."

"Yeah, honey. I don't know why you're so tired all the time. I sure wish you weren't.

"Nana says I ought to be tired with three little babies and being pregnant again. She says it's too much."

"Nana said that?"

"Yes, she did. I told her it was okay, but I want to tell you something without you getting mad, okay?"

"About me?"

"Yes, you should know why I'm always tired. The truth is night after night I don't get any sleep. I wake up angry and I've finally figured out why. It's all night long. It never stops. You always want to make love."

"Well, I can't help it. I've told you. I'm just always so excited when I get near you."

"Well, maybe if you thought about it less or something. I don't know. It's just that no matter what I do, there you are poking me in the back from the moment you get into bed. And it's not once in a while, it's every night without fail."

"I guess I could sleep on the couch."

"No. I don't want you to sleep on the couch and you know that. It's just that sometimes it makes me cry."

"I'm sorry, honey. It's just that I love you so much. It just happens when I'm near you, I guess. I don't know what to do about it. Did the doctor say anything about your pregnancy?"

"Nothing besides the fact that I am pregnant. He doesn't say too much, you know."

"Yeah, I know. But he's a good doctor and that's what's important."

"I guess so. Well, I'm going to bed. Are you coming?"

"I thought I'd go downstairs and say hello to Pop for a minute. See what they've got to eat. Is that okay?"

"Sure. Goodnight. I love you."

"I love you too, honey."

We had a new baby every year. Because we now lived on the second floor instead of in the basement, Joe went downstairs to spend time with Nanu instead of going upstairs. Other than that, nothing really changed.

"You didn't have to say that to Nana."

"Say what to Nana?"

"That I wasn't there with you."

"Joe, you know I didn't call her for that reason. I called to find out where you were and I thought she might know! Joey had gotten out of surgery and was hemorrhaging all over the hospital room. Blood was spurting out of him like a fountain; I was scared to death. I wanted you to be there with me. You said you'd be there. You said you'd come. But no, you were too tired this morning, and now you'll say it was my fault for not getting you up. But I think you could've gotten yourself up. I had to go to the hospital with your brother. Good thing he was up or else I would've had to take the bus. I'm a wreck that you can never be there. Our child was being operated on. I didn't call to 'tell' Nana that you weren't there. I just called to find out where you were. Just once, you could have been there with me."

"I know, honey. I am sorry. I'm really sorry, honey. I just couldn't get out of this meeting."

"I'm sick of your meetings. Your meetings have always been more important than us. Always. And I'm really sick of them. I probably shouldn't be saying this, but it's true."

"I'm so sorry, honey. Please forgive me. I love you so much. I just can't stand it if you're mad at me."

"Well, I'm not mad at you. It's just that...well...sometimes I could use a little help."

"I know, honey. And I promise you, things are going to change around here. I don't know where my head has been. But just you watch, things are going to change.... Can I have a kiss?"

"He is the most beautiful baby ever. Don't you think so, Mother?"

"Oh honey, you say that every time."

"I know. They're all beautiful, but look at him. Have you ever in you life seen more hair?"

"Well, all your children have had loads of hair."

"I know, but I really mean it. Isn't he beautiful?"

"Yes honey. How many times are you going to ask me? So, do you think you'll be able to nurse this baby?"

"How should I know? I surely hope so. I try each time, you know that."

"Are you still going to that same doctor?"

"Yes."

"Honey, we're living in a time where people go to obstetricians. Why can't you go to one? Everyone does."

"We have a good doctor, Mother."

"You'll believe anything Joe Carlotti tells you. No matter what." I can still see that familiar frown she had on her face.

"He's my husband, Mother."

"I'm going to have Daddy talk to Joe about you having these babies every year. Maybe if he can't leave you alone, you should come down to Perryville for a while. You just can't keep having these babies every year."

"I like having babies, Mother. It's not Joe's fault. Don't blame him. I'm part of it, too."

"But honey, how are you going to manage with all these babies and no help?"

"I'll manage, Mother. It's no problem."

"And he's never around except, of course, to make the babies. There's more to it than making the babies. There's a lot of work after they come into this world. Look at you. You are painfully thin. Are you happy, honey?"

"Yes, Mother. I'm very happy."

"Are you sure?"

"Yes, Mother. I'm sure."

It was true what she had said, though. There is more to babies than just making them. But Joe wasn't into babies. I didn't know if that would ever change. He was busy out in the community. I believed that everyone loved him. He was good to everyone but his wife and children. He would promise me that he would go to the grocery store on Saturday mornings and then watch the kids in the afternoons so I could go out if I wanted to. Being in the house with all these babies all week long, I really looked forward to a little time alone on Saturday afternoon. But he seldom ever actually watched the kids. He would usually sleep the whole day away and then tell me later how sorry he was. But I no longer believed he really was sorry because it never changed.

I couldn't tell that to Mother, though. Not in a million years could I ever tell her how I was really feeling. She would've loved to hear me say something bad about him so she could go off on him. I would've never lived it down. Her solution to everything was my moving back to Perryville with the children and living out a pure life—meaning one without sex. I didn't want to leave Joe and knew I never would, but sometimes I felt so devastated by it all.

I really believed with my whole heart that things were going to get better. Joe started this new job with a salary of $10,000 a year. That was more money than I could even imagine. We bought a little house with help from Nanu, about 10 blocks from where Nana and Nanu lived. We were still in the same parish. We had found a new friend in Father Pat—a priest who came to St. Mark's Church. Maria had started first grade and loved it. Joey was in kindergarten. John was a healthy, happy 4-year-old, and Anthony was toddling. We had a new house and a new baby.

It had been a long time now. It was two and a half years between Anthony and the new baby. Maria said she was going to leave home if the baby wasn't a girl. But the most important thing to me was that the baby was healthy. When Anthony was born, everyone said, "Another boy? Oh, maybe next time you'll have a girl." Everyone had been so disappointed when Maria turned out to be a girl. No matter what the sex, it was always wrong. It began to piss me off.

"Another boy, Nana. Can you believe it? We've got another boy. And he looks like John. His hair is almost blond, like John. He is beautiful. We're naming him Christopher."

"Well, that's a nice name."

"Thanks Nana."

Sometimes I wondered how much Nana knew. I felt like she could see right through me, and the look in her eyes told me she knew how alone I was. Joe's new job didn't really work out like I thought it would, but he was still never home. And although I dreamed and hoped for him to be around, I really had my own life with the children now. Joe and I went to church together on Sundays, but that was just for show. Otherwise, he was not part of our lives.

At least the children and I were happily settled into our little house now, where we could be a family and not worry so much about the noise and disturbing Nana and Nanu. I think I loved our evenings together the best. The children loved those new *Childcraft* books as much as I did. The pictures in them were so beautiful. Mother had always said I was just a big baby myself and I remember thinking that probably was true. When Mother would say that, I knew she meant it as a put-down, but I took it as a compliment.

I began to appreciate, more than I could have ever imagined, how wonderful kids really were. When I began to read to them, it was the first time I had ever really read to anyone. The greatest part was that they didn't laugh or make fun of me. Maria tried to teach me how to sound out words.

I always knew that the one night Joe would be home early for sure was the night after my six-week check-up after giving birth. That was the day the doctor would decide if everything was okay and if I could make love again. It was amazing how it worked. Joe would be really nice to me as if we were on a honeymoon or something. It was the one night when he always told me that everything was going to change. I always went along and did it with him, but this night for the first time I decided to say no.

"So what did the doctor say, honey? Everything okay?" He kissed me as he said it, and I cringed inside.

"He was nasty to me. He screamed at me and told me to put the baby on a bottle immediately. He talked to me like I was shit."

"So what did he say about you? Are you okay?"

"Yeah, I'm okay, Joe. And I suppose you want to make love tonight, right?"

"Who said anything about making love?"

"Joe, the only night in our entire marriage that you come home early is the night of the baby's six-week check-up. I'm not totally as stupid as you think I am."

"Okay, okay, honey. Tell me what he said about the baby."

"He said he hasn't gained any weight and that I should put him on a bottle right away."

"Really? He hasn't gained ANY weight?"

"No."

"Well, you gave him a bottle then, right?"

"Not yet."

"Why not?"

"Hey, I usually take care of these babies, don't I? Has there ever been a time when I haven't taken care of these babies?"

"Well, when are you going to give him a bottle?"

"I haven't decided if I'm going to yet."

"What the hell does that mean? You 'haven't decided?'"

"I'm not sure what I am going to do, but I think I'm going to try and continue nursing this baby."

"Well, if the doctor said to put him on the bottle, then you should put him on the bottle. Don't feel bad, just do it. Obviously you can't nurse. Why make such a big deal about it?"

"Okay, Joe."

The boss had ruled. God had spoken. All I had to do was follow the orders. As usual, I was frightened, but this time I was going to disobey the master. I was going to nurse this baby. I wasn't going to make love with him that night. It would be the first time I ever said no. I was scared but I was gonna do it.

He was pissed as hell. Boy, if I didn't make love when he wanted to (many times I pretended to be asleep when he came up from Nanu and started poking me in the back), he threw a tantrum all night long. He lay down. Got up. Twisted and turned. Sighed. Paced around. Slammed doors. Coughed. Smoked. Knocked into the bed. He did it all near to me to make sure I heard it, too. If he had gone to sleep, I would've gotten it in the back all night long.

It had been years since I'd had a good night's sleep. I had no idea what one felt like. I was so angry on the inside; he had to know that. I didn't care that he wasn't home anymore. I decided long ago these kids were not going to get short-changed because of him.

The next evening we talked again.

"Did you start Christopher on the bottle today?"

"No."

"What do you mean 'no'?"

"I mean, no, I did not start him on the bottle today. I took him to another doctor. Actually, Leslie drove me to a different doctor—a nursing doctor." My heart was thumping so hard I could see my blouse moving when I looked down.

"And what did he say?"

"He said I could nurse him."

"And where do you think we're going to get the money to pay another doctor?"

"I don't know where we'll get the money and frankly, I don't care."

"You just wanted someone to tell you that you were right in nursing the baby. You just wanted someone to tell you what you wanted to hear. Meanwhile, our baby suffers. You've gone crazy."

"I did not go to him because of that," I screamed. "I went to him because my friend Leslie, who cares about me, told me about nursing." Tears sprang from my eyes. "And she took me to a doctor who knows about nursing babies. He's a pediatrician. He was gentle and kind and very caring. He treated me like I was important and special. He thought our baby was special. He gave me a tremendous lesson. He told me that in the last twenty years, doctors haven't even studied about nursing in medical school. There hasn't been a class on it in years," I sobbed. "He told me..."

Joe interrupted, "I really don't care what the doctor had to say. We have a good doctor already. I think it's pretty childish on your part to run off to another doctor. And furthermore, I am not going to pay for another doctor so I don't know how you're going to pay him." His voice was threatening.

"Maybe I'll get the money from Leslie. Who knows? But I am going to this doctor and I am going to nurse Christopher. If I don't do another thing in my entire life, I am going to nurse him. You don't know anything about these babies or me. You're not going to bully me this time. I am not going back to Dr. Angelotti." I tried to make my voice strong. "I've had five horrible deliveries from that pig. And where were you? Strutting your ass around the neighborhood like you're God. You make my skin crawl. And don't come sticking your body into mine every night. I'm not making love with you for a while."

I thought for sure he would hit me now. I turned my back to him and continued through the tears, "That is, if one can call what we do 'making love.' I don't want to get pregnant right away again. I have five little children. And you know nothing about them. You've never been part of their lives except for sticking it in. So just understand that I am nursing this baby and if you want to stop me, you'll have to shoot me. Get that into your head. Otherwise, get off of my back, you phony shit." I closed my eyes as he came toward me.

"I've never forced you to make love," he said, standing on his toes to be taller than me.

"Maybe not, but if I don't, it's like a damn nightmare, to say the least. Don't you think I know all the little games?"

"I have no idea what you're talking about," he said all innocently.

"I'm tired of crying. Please leave me alone, Joe."

"It's my fault you're crying?"

"Leave me alone, Joe."

"Who cares? I've matched my father," he said with cockiness.

"Yeah, I know Joe, Nanu had five kids and now you do too. It's easy to make someone pregnant, but what about after the baby is born? Do you have any responsibilities then?"

He didn't answer, just gave me a dirty look and walked away.

I became more involved with things at the kids' school. Sometimes I substituted in the classroom and church—there was an opening for a church organist to play for a couple masses on Sunday, and I was thrilled. I hadn't played an organ since I left Perryville, where I'd been the fulltime church organist since fifth grade. Playing the organ for mass on Sundays meant getting all the kids ready for church and then walking the seven blocks with them, which left me sweating—even in the middle of winter. And every Sunday after it was all over Joe would ask me in the same pathetic way why I didn't wake him up so he could have helped me with the kids. I no longer begged him to get out of bed. I no longer asked him for anything. Out of the blue, he excitedly announced that he was going to Utah for some kind of seminar for two weeks. I couldn't have cared less where he was going or what he was doing.

"I'm sorry. I'm so sorry, please forgive me." He came in after his two weeks in Utah, threw down his suitcase, and called all of us into the living room of our little house.

"Forgive me, for I do not know my children. I don't even know your birthdays. I haven't been part of your lives here. You must forgive me. I am a changed man. From now on, I am going to spend time here with you and the children. I have learned so much about myself these two weeks in Utah. Things are going to be different from now on. I know I've said that before, but this time I mean it. Oh honey, I love you so much." He wiped his eyes.

I was not impressed. I had heard those words too many times.

Sensitivity training is what it was called. Joe came home every night for a week. It was dreadful. He had no idea what to do and it really threw the kids and me for a loop. He would spend the evenings pacing around saying over and over how he was missing some important meeting. A couple of times, one of the kids would say, "Why don't you go to your meeting, Dad. We're fine here." And that was the extent of the changed man. One whole week. But it was okay with me. I'd actually been kind of busy.

Father Pat had been telling me how he wanted to reach the people in the neighborhood who didn't come to church. We talked it over and realized he had to go to the people, so he rented a storefront in that neighborhood. Working there together with him I gained confidence about my ideas and helping others. I also started feeling comfortable about telling him my problems. He had not hesitated telling me his for quite some time.

For the last two years, before I went to bed at night, I tried to say the "D" word out loud. I'd gotten it out, but only in a whisper. I knew I'd be condemned if I said all my thoughts out loud. What would everyone think? I still "made love" with him, even though I was terrified of getting pregnant again. My insides felt like they were dying. It was the children that kept me alive. People told me that I looked bad, and they were being kind because I looked like shit. I was going to try it again—refusing to make love with him. I just couldn't do it anymore.

At least I was able to share some of these thoughts with Father Pat. Not all of them, though, since he was a priest and all. Of course, that just made it all the more annoying to endure Joe's questions about Father Pat.

"Do you love him like you love John Quinn?"

"Yeah."

"Do you love him like you love Dan Huber? Do you love them all the same way?"

"What does that mean, 'the same way?' I love them, yes."

How much did I love this Father Pat? Every morning and night there was the interrogation. Over and over and over he asked the same questions. I didn't know. I loved him. He was a good friend. I wasn't going to deny that. What was the big deal? I loved lots of people. And I told all of them, too. Just like I said I would when Daddy died. So bug off about this Father Pat thing, I thought. Joe was trying to make something out of nothing. We were friends; he thought I was great.

Joe obviously hated that someone actually thought I was great. I was not going to lose this friend. I had already lost too many over the years. I had always thought it was my fault, too. Well, I didn't anymore. Before they moved away from Chicago, Dan and Diane Huber told me how much they loved me—how they would do anything for me, and the reason they stopped coming around to our house was because they couldn't stand by and watch the horrible treatment I took from Joe. Yet they never would interfere. They gave me their car, just gave it to me, they said I needed a car with all these kids. Said that's the least they could do for me. All those last months they lived in Chicago I thought they couldn't stand me when actually quite the opposite was true: they loved me. What an eye opener Diane was for me—calling and telling me if I ever needed anything not to hesitate to call them. I vowed the day they left Chicago that I would never again allow this to happen to me.

Now Father Pat was a test and I was not going to lose him as a friend. I decided that I was an okay person and a good mom, regardless of Joe. Not only that but he had bullied me for the last time. It was over. I wanted a divorce.

I was in the kitchen and extremely nervous. I had wiped the cabinets until they looked like new. The lamp from the next room shone dimly into the kitchen. I sat at the kitchen table with my back to him as he came through the door. My insides grabbed me.

"Joe, I have something to say to you that I've held inside of me for a long time. I want a divorce." It was almost a whisper.

"Excuse me?"

"Oh, how polite you are. I said I want a divorce from you."

"Just like that? You want a divorce?"

"No, not 'just like that,' believe me I've had this inside for a long time. But I'm getting one." My voice was shaking.

"Does it make a difference what I think?"

"Not really. Not anymore. I don't care what you think." I spoke so softly I could hardly hear my own voice.

This was not a dream. I had actually said it. My insides were jerking. My entire body was shaking. Please leave, I thought. Please.

He pranced, like he sometimes did in anger. I was standing now, leaning against the cabinets.

More prancing, glaring, smoking, then he went upstairs to talk to "his children."

What was I to do now? Children. I had five little children to take care of. Had to get myself together. It was going be okay. Be strong, I told myself. Be cool. Don't act afraid. Don't let him know. I'm going to need money...a job...whoa...a job? Get it together, I said inside my head.

He was coming down the stairs. Leaving now. Walking out the door.... Be strong for the kids. They were peeking around the corner. Divorce, had I actually said that word? I knew they would all disown me. Me, a Catholic, wanting a divorce; they'd say I had shamed them all. I was scared. How was I going to do this?

"I'm leaving now. I've got to think." The door slammed and he was gone. I had to calm down. *He* needed to think? I had no idea how I was going to make it. I was terrified. But then again, I had been scared my entire life. I didn't know how, but my kids and I were going to make it. I told my mother and my sister, Kathryn. Later in the week I told my brother, Tommy. It was the beginning of daily condemning phone calls from Mother and Kathryn. I never heard from Joe's family again.

3

The screaming stopped instantly. Anthony's huge black eyes stared at me as the tears rolled down his red cheeks. His long lashes blinked once, as if in slow motion. The humidity in Chicago was high that day and his little body was covered in sweat. He was dirty, but then again he was dirty most of the time. He was the picture of a "real boy"—a mop of almost black hair, a huge smile, big black eyebrows that didn't stop much in the middle. When we went somewhere as a group and met someone new, he would step out of the group, extend his hand, and say, "Hi, I'm Anthony, I'm the shy one in the family." He'd say it loud, and everyone laughed and loved it. No one noticed that Anthony's clothes might be a mess or that his face was dirty. He wasn't gonna be overlooked in the line-up of these children. Everyone loved him; he was quite a charmer and character.

He slowly raised his arm and, using his sleeve, meticulously smeared a trail of black dirt, tears, and snot across his face to his ear. His eyes remained fixed upon me, as he stood, frozen, waiting for my reaction.

"Really, Anthony, I don't think it's so bad. Come here and let me wipe your face," Roslyn reached out and affectionately cleaned his face with a wet washcloth that had been lying on the edge of the kitchen sink. "There, now you can go back outside and play with the other kids!"

Turning back to the table, Roslyn took another sip from her Coke as she winked and smiled at me. I watched Anthony run outside as fast as his little legs would carry him, picking up in the game, barely missing a beat. I then turned and stared at my friend in amazement. How did she get him to stop crying so quickly? I got up, emptied the ashtray into the garbage can, and wiped it clean with a paper napkin. It was a nervous gesture of mine that I did often.

Anthony was always screaming bloody murder at the top of his lungs. Who could keep count of how many times a day? And I was forever sending Joey to his room after giving him one good spanking after another. There were my endless lectures, day after day and week after week. I was always telling them how they should love each other and not hurt each other. But nothing ever seemed to work. Nothing had ever changed except that the fighting grew more intense and started earlier in the day. It was beginning at 5 a.m. now. Before I could get out of bed, I could feel the knots in my stomach. I thought about starting the day by slapping them good and hard before even bothering to say "good morning." I hadn't tried that yet. I also hadn't slapped their heads like I'd seen other mothers do; I always hoped I never would hit their heads, but at the same moment I wondered if slamming them up against the wall really hard once might stop their fighting for good.

God! That was the worst part—when I slapped them. I usually did it out of desperation. I just didn't know what else to do. I would lie in bed each morning listening to the fights. When I couldn't stand it any more, I would get up and begin screaming and cursing. Each day was the same as the day before. What else was there to do? I wanted to beat them over and over with the hairbrush until I could make them cry like I had cried over them.

Then Roslyn walks into my kitchen, speaks in a soft tone to my crybaby, and he immediately stops crying and carrying on. What did this woman know that I didn't? I wanted to know. I just sat there, amazed. Roslyn pushed her chair back from the table and stood up. Walking over to the window, she looked out before turning around slowly and leaning gracefully against the cabinet. She was so beautiful to look at, I thought, as I watched her. Her years as a model showed. I was hoping she wouldn't get stuck to the counter from some peanut butter or jelly. Roslyn's eyes widened as she began to speak.

"Mary Cecile, your children fight for your attention," she said with total confidence. "That's why kids fight—for their parents' attention."

"I've never heard of anything like that, Roslyn. What do you mean, 'for my attention?' That's the craziest thing I've ever heard." I felt shocked and confused by her words and yet it made me question something inside of me. Roslyn seemed to know stuff when she was around these kids.

"I understand," Roslyn said. "I thought it sounded crazy the first time I heard it, but it's true. Kids fight for their parents' attention and the more the parent gets in on their fights, the worse it gets. So instead of the kids stopping like we want them to, or like we think they should, it gets worse. We make it worse by all the preaching and punishing we use trying to stop it." She picked up her Coke from the table and took a long sip as she stared at me, waiting for me to respond. I kind of wanted to snicker at her, but there was a part inside of me that hoped she could be right.

Our kids were fighting for our attention? That was totally crazy! But I couldn't say that to Roslyn. Yet, hadn't Anthony gone back outside without any more complaints or screaming? And hadn't this been the longest time between fights since Roslyn and I sat down? Could there possibly be any truth in what Roslyn was saying?

"Come with me to the Child Guidance Center at River Park Fieldhouse on Thursday. It's the place I've been telling you about where lots of mothers come to learn. A couple of fathers come, too. Will you come with me and see what it's all about?" Roslyn was almost begging. "I know I've already asked you a dozen times, but please come with me. Just this once?"

"Well, let me think about it a little bit and I'll let you know," I put my glass into the sink full of dirty dishes and nervously ran my fingers through my hair.

My mind started racing. What did I have to lose? Things couldn't get any worse. I was already half crazy from this whole divorce thing. I had five little kids to feed, clothe, and take care of with a measly $60 a week from Joe! That stupid creep! Why did he have to take it out on the kids?

I was always afraid, and I worried that this fear would last forever. At least I was actually going through with the divorce. Last year, I couldn't even say the word divorce. And now, I was getting one, thanks to much moral support from Father Pat and some other good friends.

I looked up and saw Roslyn waiting patiently for an answer. At least if I went, she'd get off my back.

"Okay," I said, "I'll go."

Roslyn yelled "Yeah!" and gave me a hug. Then she picked up her purse and walked to the back door to call her boys. I noticed that when Roslyn told Robert and Richard it was time to leave, both of her children always said good-bye to their playmates without any fuss. And they were only two and four years old! But this was not the first time I had noticed Roslyn doing things a little bit differently from any other mother I knew.

After I got the kids into bed that evening, I started my regular routine of cleaning the house. I had it down to a system. First, I gathered all the dirty clothes from the bedrooms and bathroom, took them down to the basement, and started the washer. I was always afraid to go into that basement at night, but I did it anyway. Clothes had to be washed and I didn't have any time during the day to do it. Then I would go back upstairs and work on the floors—always leaving the kitchen until last. I hated the kitchen and wondered if it had anything to do with the fact that I had never learned anything about cooking.

One good thing about having a small house was that it was easier to keep clean. Everything except the kitchen floor, which seemed to be forever covered with sand from the nearby beaches of Lake Michigan. I think living in walking distance to Lake Michigan and the beach is what saved my sanity. I loved that lake and the beaches more than I could ever put into words—even in the wintertime. It just did something for my insides, hearing the waves, playing all day with the kids on the beach in the summer. It was my favorite part of Chicago, more than downtown and the fancy stores, more than anything I'd ever had in my life. To me, Chicago is the lake, that beautiful lake.

And I swear there was always peanut butter and jelly everywhere. I washed the kitchen floor every night on my knees. It was almost like an obsession with me. I wished that I could skip the ritual some nights. But living in the city, with the soot and all, made for pretty black socks. Socks that had started out white. At least, that was my rationale for repeating the ritual every night.

White socks were supposed to look white. Mother had always said so.

"Honey, look at those children's socks. What did you wash them in, dirt?"

And then she would snicker at me. I hated the way Mother made fun of me, but telling her so that one time had only made it worse. Now it seemed as if she did it more. Why she did what she did was beyond me. I always loved her so much, and there was never anything I wouldn't have done for her. Never!

I made several trips up to the second floor with loads of clean clothes in my arms and always stopped to look at those innocent faces asleep in their beds, shaking my head. They always looked like such angels when they slept. I couldn't say it to any of my friends who had kids of their own, and be one of those braggy moms, but it was obvious that my children had the most beautiful faces in the world. Maria held her favorite doll tight and looked so sweet in her pink nightgown with her long hair all over the pillow. Joey and Anthony were together in the same bed again. Christopher, rolled up at one end of his crib, held tightly to the pillow that John gave him each night. They weren't bad kids, but they sure could make me crazy and I had no idea what to do with them to make it different.

In the summertime we had the beach, but during the winter it seemed like the only time we had fun together was when I read to them at bedtime. I loved reading to the kids more than I could ever explain in words. I knew they loved it, too.

In those moments at night while I was cleaning the house, I had the time and the quiet to really feel the abandonment of my family. All I ever got from them were the badgering, gut-wrenching phone calls when my mother and sister called me a sinner and condemned me to hell forever. The only thing I got from Joe's family was silence. I had never stopped hoping that things would change someday, but I was becoming more doubtful that they ever would.

4

Roslyn and I decided that we would each drive our own car and meet at the Child Guidance Center. Two kids were all Roslyn could handle; she had told me that often. Roslyn waited in the parking lot until I pulled up with my gang. We both arrived with a few minutes to spare. It was a beautiful fall day in Chicago and the trees were just beginning to change. The kids spotted a playground immediately and screamed with delight. I knew that the Indian summer days wouldn't last and that we'd most likely have lots of snow before 1971 brought in the New Year. I was as grateful as a mother could be for any chance to let the kids run off some of their energy outside.

"Can we play over there, Mommy, on those swings?" Maria asked permission for herself and her brothers. She always looked out for them, was always there to take care of them. And she was kind, always kind. She ran off, her long, thick brown hair bouncing on her back. Of course she was the most beautiful little girl in the world, no question about that. Her turned-up nose, her sweet smile, her caring for little baby brother Christopher who she dressed up as a girl (I wondered how long that would last), her dolls that she loved. She was quite the superstar being the only girl. Although she sometimes complained about it, she secretly loved it too. And she was smart. Already she would teach me things she learned in school that I didn't know. I loved that.

"Can me, too?" shouted Richard, Roslyn's younger son.

"May I, not can me," Roslyn always corrected her kids' English. Richard and Robert followed the "big kids," and my kids were always "the big kids." We looked at each other and laughed. "Sure," Roslyn answered. They were off in a second, running to the playground.

"Monkey see, monkey do," Roslyn said, and we chuckled.

I had no idea what I was going to experience once we got to the Center and was anxious, but I trusted Roslyn as my friend. Sometimes it seemed that she was almost secretive about the "demonstrations" and the ideas she was learning at them. Many times I had questioned her about them, and each time Roslyn answered casually, "You'll just have to come and see for yourself. I can't explain it." Then she would smile her beautiful smile, toss her long black hair to one side, and say no more. I had been curious for some time now about these demonstrations and the Center. She seemed so encouraged by what she was learning and about her relationship with her husband that I no longer shared with her my lack of hope.

When I would see my reflection in any window I knew my body showed what my mind and heart felt. Surely she saw my pathetic body and how I looked. All my bones stuck out—from my hips to my jaw. My hair had always stuck out something awful and really was a mess like Mother always said it was. "That girl's hair was sticking out the day she was born. Never could do anything with it no matter how hard we tried. It's always been a mess." My shoulders slumped and I had toothpicks for arms. I was not a pretty sight, not that I was ever pretty because I wasn't, but now I looked worse. I hated passing a mirror. A window was bad enough, but a mirror was murder.

After one of those horrible verbal lashings on the kids, I would go into my bedroom to cry and pray for another way to raise kids. How many prayers would it take? I began to seriously question if prayers were the answer to breaking the cycle because I couldn't imagine praying any harder. Perhaps this demonstration thing would be another empty search, but it was worth a try because if I didn't learn anything at the Center with Roslyn, I had no idea where I might go next. Nothing was black and white in my life now as it has always been before. Getting a divorce was certainly proving that. Now everything looked like a blurred gray.

Roslyn had said more than once that this session would be different than any class or counseling session I had ever seen or heard about. She also told me how important it was to keep an open mind. I was positive that I had an open mind.

I was to listen and take everything in as best as I could, then Roslyn would explain more after the session was over. It was almost time to start, so we gathered the kids from the swings, took them through the field house to the playroom, and deposited them with the director at the door.

Roslyn turned to me, "She gives a report at the end of the session on all the children who come regularly to the Center: how they get along together, how they share, how they treat each other, that kind of report. She has been trained in Dr. Dreikurs' theories, understands behavior, and knows how to redirect the kids' behavior. She's an important part of the whole counseling program. We'll give her fifty cents per child when we pick them up. It's very reasonable for child care, don't you think?" She didn't wait for an answer as she turned towards the door saying, "Let's go in. It's time for them to start."

I quickly followed Roslyn inside the auditorium. We listened to the session as a mother with two small children told of her difficulties with her kids— including the toilet training of one child and the constant whining of the other child. It seemed to me that the counselor answered very sharply, almost cutting. After talking for about forty-five minutes, the mother was asked to leave the room so the counselor could talk with her children alone. The children were very open, matter-of-fact, and relaxed as they talked with the counselor. And they seemed to enjoy being on stage. That's the way kids are if given a chance. Roslyn was right, it wasn't like anything I had ever heard of or experienced or read about in any parenting book. And I didn't like any part of it. The mother talked about her problems with the counselor right in front of everyone as if they were alone in a private room. My upbringing definitely taught me that you don't tell anyone else anything about your problems. Ever. Don't disgrace the family. Always say that everything is wonderful on the outside, even if you feel like you're gonna die on the inside. I'd never do anything like this with my kids. Talk out loud about my problems in front of all these strangers? Not in a thousand years!

Afterwards, we picked up the children at the playroom, paid the playroom director the small fee, and headed for the exit sign. I hoped no one would question me about whether I liked what I had just witnessed.

"Well, what did you think?" Roslyn asked the instant we stepped outside the building.

"Honestly?" I laughed nervously.

"Of course, honestly!"

"Well, it seemed pretty awful to me," my voice was a little shaky. "I just can't imagine talking about my problems in front of a whole crowd of people like this."

"Let's go again next week and see what you think," Roslyn said, totally ignoring my skepticism. "Next week, I bet you'll feel differently. It's just all new to you. It takes a couple times to get used to it. That's exactly how I felt the first time I saw a demonstration. Go with me at least one more time to give it a chance. Did you learn anything today?" Roslyn was excited. I studied her face as she spoke.

"Well, I was surprised when I heard that most of the problems the mother talked about today were some of the same problems that I have."

Roslyn just smiled as she got out her car keys. She was obviously sure that I would change my mind about what I had seen—given enough time. Some questions still lingered in my head; especially the way Anthony had stopped crying the other day. Maybe I would go again, I thought.

"A man called Dr. Dreikurs is coming to Chicago in a few weeks and he'll be doing a family demonstration. He's the one I've been telling you about. The one who wrote the book I want you to read. Loads of people will come to hear him and I want you to come, too. Maybe you and your kids could be the family he works with for the demonstration. Hmm, Mary Cecile?" Roslyn stopped and looked me in the eye, "How about it?"

"Well, I don't know. Let me think it over." I felt nervous and apprehensive yet I could feel myself wanting to learn more. I felt so mixed up and desperate most of the time. Every day the kids would fight I felt a little crazier—a little closer to falling over the edge. Maybe this would be an opportunity for my children and myself.

I agreed to go again and watch another session the following week, mostly because I didn't want to hurt Roslyn's feelings, but also because there could be a slim chance that it might help me with the kids.

The next time the shock and newness was gone, and I was amazed that I shared the same feelings, experiences, and even problems as the mother who was being counseled. She talked about her kids' fighting the same way I had talked about my own children. The only difference was that the mother didn't have five children but two. When she talked about her kids tattling, I could have sworn that she was talking about my kids. But she was from an entirely different background than me and so how could we possibly have the same problems? It sure sounded as if we were making the same mistakes. Could all mothers feel this way? Could all mothers, no matter what their background and education, be making the same mistakes and having the same problems? This session boggled my mind.

After the session, Roslyn stopped for a moment to talk with someone she knew and I waited for her by the door. When we got to the parking lot, she turned to me and asked again.

"Mary Cecile, have you thought any more about what I asked you last week? I need to tell the director by tomorrow if you will be the family for Dr. Dreikurs to work with. Will you do it? I really think you'll be glad you signed up. It's the chance of a lifetime, you know!" Roslyn's eyes twinkled as she spoke. She was very convincing.

"Well, Roslyn, I'll do it." I paused, " I guess."

"Oh that's wonderful, Mary Cecile! You won't be sorry. You have nothing to lose. Nothing!" With that, she quickly got into her car, giving me no chance to change my mind. "Talk to you later!" she yelled, heading out of the parking lot. I got into my car and started for home, too, wondering if I had made the right decision.

I wasn't sure what had happened inside me, or why I had changed my mind and decided to do the session. Although I felt a little nervous, I also felt hopeful about meeting with this Dr. Dreikurs. Like Roslyn said, I really didn't have anything to lose. If nothing else, it would make Roslyn happy—she spoke so highly of this Dr. Dreikurs.

Little did I know at the time that ours would be the last family in Chicago that Dr. Dreikurs counseled before he died. Little did I know how fortunate we were.

5

The routine inside our home was the same that next week. Fighting. Spankings. Sermons. Punishing. Cursing. Fear. Worry. Screaming. I screamed a lot. At breakfast, I could think no further than lunchtime. At lunchtime, no further than dinner. I was consumed by the present moment and felt constant tightness in my stomach. If the kids weren't fighting, Mother and Kathryn were calling to condemn me, or I was worrying about where our next meal would come from. I felt myself hoping that this Dreikurs guy could help me, but I also didn't want to set my expectations too high.

We still had our stories at night, thank goodness. Somehow we still were able to have that peaceful time after a totally crazy day. If part of the day was hell, then nighttime was heaven. It was peaceful, soothing, and fun. And night after night they looked at me adoringly as if I were the greatest mom on Earth!

I didn't say anything to the kids about participating in a family demonstration until the day before. Roslyn's instructions were to make it simple when telling them. So that's what I did. Keeping it simple was easy for me. I had too much on my mind, anyway.

"We're going to participate in the family demonstration at the Center. Just like we went to last month with Roslyn. I am going to talk to a Dr. Dreikurs. Maybe I can learn something new."

"Why? Why are we going, Mommy?" asked Joey immediately as he pushed his thick glasses back up on his nose. All the kids had inherited my weak eyes. Joey, my oldest son, always wanted to know exactly what was happening. .

"'Cause we fight so much, Mommy?" little Christopher sounded intrigued. Christopher was the youngest, blond and cute. Everyone treated him like a prince, sometimes like a baby. All the kids wanted him on their side in whatever they were doing—fighting, playing, or doing their jobs. Christopher watched. He watched everyone and no matter where we were he was always in the middle. He took everything in and didn't miss a trick. He had lots of teachers among his brothers and his sister and he learned from all of them.

"Because you fight so much, yes, all of you fight too much," I answered matter-of-factly.

No one asked any more questions and I didn't say anything else. I didn't have any more answers anyway. I had already told them thousands of times that I was losing my mind with their constant fighting. Why bother saying it again? The only thing I knew for sure in the world was that I was still searching for a way to raise these children differently than my mother raised us. Perhaps tomorrow I'd begin to learn. I still had hope in tomorrow. When I told Father Pat about going to the session, he said I should go ahead and do it if I wanted to. He agreed to be a member of the audience and was supportive of me. Did that ever feel good! At this point I knew he loved me a lot. I didn't know what kind of love he had for me but I knew he loved me. That was a wonderful feeling.

At 5:30 the next night I was already dressed and ready to go. I felt the nervousness taking control of my stomach. The demonstration was scheduled to begin at eight. From our house to the parking lot of the Center it took about twenty minutes. It was going to take me at least 15 minutes to do Maria's hair. I liked getting it perfect. Maria almost always cried when I fixed her hair. I hated that, but I was just trying to do my best.

"Mommy! What should we wear tonight?"

"I already put your clothes out on your beds!" I yelled from my bedroom. That was another advantage of a small home. I could direct traffic from my bedroom if I yelled loud enough.

I put on the only decent dress I had. I called it my "uniform." It was a little navy blue dress with white trim around the collar. I was ready to go, so I lay down on the bed and tried to rest for a minute while the kids were getting dressed. It seemed like I was always tired. As I lay there, I hoped that this Dr. Dreikurs might be able to help me.

Most of the time I felt it was me and my kids against the world. Not that I didn't have friends. Actually, I probably had more friends than I thought. But the only family member who loved me without judgment was my brother, Tommy. Although he said he'd do anything for me, he was an alcoholic and the liquor always came first.

I sat up slowly on the bed, my heart feeling heavy, and swept away the wrinkles in the covers with my hand. It was time to leave. My stomach bubbled and twisted, and I belched loudly as I walked down the stairs. I had been belching loudly ever since I was a little bitty kid.

I took the children out to the Gold Coin restaurant. It was as if I had taken them to paradise. Going out to eat was definitely a rare and special treat. After eyeing the menu for less then a minute, the children were ready to order. Kids are like that in restaurants, I think. No messing around; get those hamburgers ordered.

"Does everyone know what they want to have?" I asked as the waitress waited patiently.

"I do Mommy. I want a hamburger. Can I please?" Joey said immediately.

"Yes, it's okay with me, Joey,"

Everyone else followed suit and got hamburgers. The waitress looked relieved. Five little kids at one table could be a challenge. I watched as Maria helped Christopher scoot up to the table. Joey helped Anthony with his chair. John took Christopher to the bathroom. I had noticed before how they always helped each other. And they did it without me asking.

The waitress brought their Cokes out and the kids started to blow bubbles in them. Joey was first, with John and Anthony immediately joining in. Maria held back, checking to see if I was looking. I closed my eyes, hoping they would remain quiet and that blowing bubbles would be the only "test" in the restaurant. The hamburgers arrived and the kids ate rather quietly, but it wasn't long before someone managed to kick Anthony under the table.

"Cut it out, Joey!" he cried loudly.

I was glad that one kick ended up being the only disturbance. It was nothing really, I thought. The kids were good when I took them out. It was at home that they drove me nuts.

I took them all to the bathroom to use the toilet and wash their hands. When we left the restaurant, other diners smiled at us as we walked by their tables. I felt proud when I walked with my children. They really were very well behaved when we went out. And cute. One was cuter than the other. Their bodies were the same, slender but not skinny, and each just a stair step shorter than the other. They ate it up when people noticed them. They loved being on stage. On the way to the car, John tried to claim the front seat. Joey, with his longer legs, ran past him, yelling, "No way!" Needless to say, Joey won.

Having a car was a new experience for all of us, as was driving in the city. We had always taken public transportation until just a couple months earlier when our friends Dan and Diane Huber gave us this little car. I noticed how Joey always insisted upon sitting in the front seat. I called him selfish for not wanting to give the other kids a turn, but in the quiet of the night I wondered to myself if he was trying to take his father's place? So many times he would step in to help me with little things. He was always there by my side. It felt like he was protecting me, watching out for me, lots of times. But surely he was too young to think about that. I didn't want my children to carry the burdens I had carried for my family.

As we neared the Child Guidance Center, the kids became very quiet. I was apprehensive. Everyone knew something was up but didn't know exactly what. My nervousness increased when I couldn't find the place, but Joey spotted it, "There's the building over there, Mommy." I breathed a sigh of relief.

It was the middle of November in Chicago but I was perspiring under my coat. We hurried towards the door with the lighted entrance. Just as baby ducks follow the mother duck, the children followed me. In situations like this I never had to say, "hurry up"; they stuck to me like glue.

Roslyn had said not to arrive too early. The big clock in the hallway said six minutes before eight. I saw a door marked AUDITORIUM and pulled it open to peek inside. A huge crowd was jammed into the place; there had to have been at least five hundred people there. My knees buckled for a second and my stomach lurched. At that moment I thought about backing out, when I remembered one of Daddy's favorite lines: "We all put our pants on one leg at a time." I smiled, remembering him. My daddy knew things about human beings. He was just "a country farmer" my mother would say, always wanting to put him down. He only went to 4th grade, but my daddy knew stuff. This much I had learned. My daddy would be all for me learning more about kids. He'd say these kids were worth the fear I felt. That was the only part I knew for sure.

Then Faith, a woman we'd met at the previous sessions, told the children to follow her and led them to the playroom. They looked back at me and I reassured them that everything was going to be okay, even though inside I was really nervous now. After she'd settled the kids there, Faith came back and got me, leading me to the stage where there were chairs already set up. I asked her why there were so many chairs? She explained that there was a chair for each of the five children, one for me, and one for Dr. Dreikurs.

A man was sitting in the middle chair, talking to the audience. Immediately I knew that this had to be Dr. Dreikurs. I walked slowly towards him, through the bright lights on the stage. He had a mustache, wire-rimmed glasses, and dark, penetrating eyes. His hair was mostly gray, a little long around his ears, and the top of his head was mostly bald. He was wearing a white shirt with a little red bow tie and I thought he looked very sharp. When he saw me approaching, he stood quickly and extended his hand. We were about the same height. I thought he looked maybe sixty or seventy years old. I didn't know and it really wasn't important. He took my hand inside of his and squeezed it firmly.

"Hello, I'm Dr. Dreikurs."

His voice was strong and deep with a heavy Viennese accent. His eyes seemed to pierce right into me. I was feeling more excited than frightened.

That surprised me. It was now definitely too late to back out! My gut feelings immediately responded positively to him. I really wanted help. As my eyes were adjusting to the bright lights on the stage, I tried looking out into the audience. It was dark and silent but I could still make out the mass of people out there. My heart did a double flip.

"Sit here next to me," he motioned as he let go of my hand.

I sat beside him. He started talking with me immediately. I never thought of the audience again. All of a sudden it was just this man called Dr. Dreikurs and me. No one else in the world. There was no way I could know that history was about to be made.

"I hear that you have been to our sessions before. Is that correct?" his heavily accented voice bellowed for all to hear.

"Yes, I have come to a couple of sessions with my friend," I answered quickly.

"Good! As a rule we do not counsel a mother until she has sat in on at least two sessions. This way you would soon know that other mothers have exactly the same difficulties that you have. Since you have been here before you know that all mothers are in the same boat and make the same mistakes. So now, how do you feel about being here?"

Well, I felt stupid and everyone would see that for sure. How could they not? But I didn't care about that now. I knew I had nothing left to lose. If I didn't get help soon they would probably cart me off to some mental institution. "Go for it!" my insides screamed.

"Okay. I feel okay," I said nervously but with confidence inside. How I looked to others was no longer important. The lives of my children and me were literally on the line.

"Good. Now let us hear about your problems. You have five children, right? He quickly glanced at his five fingers on his left hand for a second as if to set it in his mind.

"Yes, five children," I giggled nervously.

"Tell me their names and their ages."

"Maria is almost ten."

"She is the oldest?"

"Yes."

"And then who comes next?"

"Joey. He's eight and a half. John is seven and a half; Anthony, six and a half; and Christopher is three and a half."

He watched me closely as I spoke. When I finished, he began talking.

"I would like to use my interview with you for teaching purposes. Will you mind if, from time to time, I interrupt interviewing you to discuss some points with the audience?" His right hand motioned toward the audience-filled darkness that I had already forgotten about.

"No, I don't mind," I answered softly. Do whatever you have to do, I thought, just help me please.

He smiled at my willingness and started again.

"Now, tell us about your problems. What is the reason for which you came here tonight?"

He phrased things a little differently than we do, I thought as I answered him. "Well, my friend says that I need help and it's true, I do!" I laughed, a laugh of relief. It was out in the open now and I felt better.

"So, what is it you want me to help you with?" Dr. Dreikurs wanted to hear it from my lips. He leaned forward on his chair and did not take his eyes off mine.

"Well, everything, I guess. Everything, really!" I shrugged my shoulders in hopelessness.

"What is everything? What do your children do that bothers you the most?" His questions came quick.

"Just one thing?" I felt my eyebrows rise. A giggle came from the darkness beyond the stage. I hesitated and took a deep breath.

"Yes, what bothers you the most?"

"Well, they fight all the time. From early in the morning until late at night, they fight. They fight over everything there is to fight over, and if there is nothing to fight over they make something up. I honestly feel like I'm going crazy with all of it."

"And what do you do about it?" I felt the strength in his voice.

"I talk to them about it and tell them they shouldn't fight. I tell them that they should love each other. I tell them how wrong it is to act that way. I threaten them. I punish them and I..."

"YOU TALK!" he said loudly. Then, turning to the audience, "Everywhere mothers talk too much. If we could eliminate most of the talking that mothers do, then mothers would be more successful." He turned back to me. "So, does this stop the fighting?"

"No. And it sounds silly when I say it out loud to you now, but that's what I do." I rolled my eyes. I couldn't believe my own words. "I talk 'til I'm blue in the face and totally exhausted. And no, it doesn't stop the fighting at all. In fact, it has gotten much worse."

"Of course not. Of course it doesn't stop the fighting." Dreikurs turned to the audience again and said, "Isn't it amazing how well children can train their mother? The children fight and mother falls for it. Here we have a typical situation—normal children who are not adjusted. What is so sad is this: you have children who don't behave properly, who need adjustment, and at the same time who are normal. Here is the focus of the problems in this country. Why are these children doing what they are doing? Why are there so many families in this country who wake up fighting and go to bed fighting? Because, in the present time, the vast majority of parents do not have the slightest knowledge of what to do, nor the slightest realization of what they are contributing to the behavior of their children. In this sense, you have normal parents, in the normal predicament of having children fighting. This is the situation in which the vast majority of parents find themselves."

He waited for my response. I tried to digest all he had just said.

"But I really don't know what to do with these kids," I said, sounding desperate.

"You're absolutely right! You can change things if I help you. But by yourself, you can't do it because you don't know what you're dealing with. You don't know your own role in the situation, right? It is very fortunate that you come when these children are young because it becomes increasingly difficult as they get older. The younger the children are, the easier it is to influence them by *changing our own behavior*," he said loudly, dramatically pointing to his own chest. "But you are willing to see what is going on? To learn what you can do?"

"Yes." I smiled at him and nodded my head. "Yes, yes, I want to learn another other way to raise my kids. What I am doing now is horrible!"

"What else bothers you?"

"Well, they don't help me around the house," I answered immediately. It's not like I had to sit and think things up. I had many examples.

"Now, who is tidy and who is untidy?"

"Well, none of them is too neat," I started. "John cleans things up sometimes, but mostly it's me who does everything. They dress neatly, but that's about the extent of it."

"Do you know why the children are not tidy?" His face was eight inches from my own. I was hanging on every word.

"No." Our eyes could almost touch now. "No, I really have no idea."

He turned away from me and talked out to the audience again. I didn't care if the whole world was listening. It was just me and Dreikurs in the whole world, at least for right then. He had captured me in such a short time.

"Now how many of you—please raise your hands—how many of you know why these children are not tidy?" He looked into the audience. There were several seconds of silence.

"Because Mother is too tidy?" A voice came from the darkness.

"Mother is too 'good.' Why would they have to put things away if Mother is already doing it for them?" He shrugged his shoulders as if to say this was common sense.

"But wait!" I waved my hand at him. He surely couldn't understand how much of a mess I was talking about. "If I didn't do it for them, we wouldn't be able to get through the house. I mean it's a pigsty. I'm not exaggerating—there's stuff everywhere when they come home after school. We'd have to walk on coats, hats, everything, really, if I didn't pick it all up. It's horrible."

Dreikurs looked directly at me and said, "There need not be the mess you describe in your home. You can train them. Who trains whom, do you think?" His eyes continued to pierce mine.

"They've trained me?" As soon as I said it, I knew my tone of voice questioned him. "But, how do I change that?" I begged him.

"Ah, we will come to that. But you didn't know any better, and therefore your way of handling it made it worse. Not that it is your fault. I hope you do not have any guilty feelings about it. You must keep in mind that what you are doing is the same as what millions of other parents are doing, too, with the same bad results. Parents don't know any better. Do you understand what I mean?"

"Yes, they're training me," I shook my head as the words came out of my mouth, still dazed at the thought of it. I wanted to think about this for a minute, but he wasted no time and quickly moved on.

"What else?"

"Well, it seems that they are always tattling. Someone is always telling me about what someone else has done to them. I'm so sick of it."

"I'm sure you are. And what do you do about it?"

I noticed he always emphasized what *I* did rather than what the kids did. It's all about me. It's not about 'them.' I'm always blaming the kids, THEY fight, THEY do this, and THEY do that. He wants me to look in the mirror. He wants me to look at me.

"I try to find out if what they said is true and then tell them..."

"Again, you talk! Am I right?" He already knew what I was going to say.

"Yes," I answered.

"Has it stopped the tattling?" he asked with a smile.

"No." I smiled, too, as I moved slightly in my chair.

"When your children tattle to you then you need to look at them right in the face and say, 'Thank you very much for telling me that! I'm sure that you can handle it.'"

I waited for him to say more.

"That's all you say to them. Then go back to what you are doing and let the children learn to work out their own difficulties. They will never learn how to work anything out as long as you continue to do it for them."

"It's so tiring. I get so tired of saying it over and over. 'You should love your brother. You should help him instead of tattling. You should be taking care of him.' Then I end up sending them to their rooms and punishing them," I sighed. I was exhausted.

"Then get out of it!" His voice was loud and confident. He tilted his head, "What else?" He knew we had only just begun.

"I have problems with Maria practicing the piano."

"Oh, what kind of problems? Does she have a piano teacher?"

"Well, yes, I am her piano teacher," I said proudly.

The audience groaned. I sensed immediately that they obviously knew something I didn't. What was he going to say about this?

"*You* are her piano teacher?!" His eyebrows arched and he leaned closer to me.

"Yes." I covered my face in my hands for a moment, embarrassed.

"And how does it go?"

"Well, it doesn't go well at all." I looked into his eyes again. "She is supposed to practice every morning. Sometimes she does and sometimes she doesn't. Then I make her do it over after school. I become so angry. It's just terrible. The whole thing is a mess." I felt like crying and laughing at the same time. I felt so stupid and yet, somehow, I knew that this man was not judging me at all. He only wanted to help me and teach me new ideas.

"You cannot be her teacher. She must have an outside teacher who will teach her and make her excited about music. Your responsibility is to notice the positive parts of her music and to comment on them. Do you understand why? Because we spend a vast amount of our time and energies to point out mistakes. Our emphasis on mistakes is disastrous. When we pay constant attention to mistakes, we discourage our children. You being her teacher and watching her for her mistakes can only be discouraging to her. She will hate music if you continue this pattern. *Probably* she already does." His accent was much heavier on some words than on others, and "probably" was one of those words. He rolled his tongue when he said it. "You must get out of it and allow another teacher to excite her about music. Meanwhile, you look for her strengths. This will give her an opportunity to enjoy her music if she wants to do so. Do you understand?" He wiped his brow with his handkerchief, waiting for my reply.

"Yes!" My head moved up and down as if in slow motion. "Yes," I said again as his words went through my head a second time. I understood quite well that Maria would hate music if we continued like this. After all, that was how it was for me when I was growing up. I know that even though I myself am an excellent pianist, there was much more bitterness than joy in my musical history. And this was exactly what I was passing on to my daughter— the same negative pattern.

I took a deep breath as I looked at Dreikurs and said, "Okay, I understand now what I am doing. Unless I learn another way, I will pass on to Maria many of the same negative feelings and negative ideas that my mother passed on to me. I learned it from my mother!"

He watched me and listened closely, smiling. "Absolutely," his voice bellowed through the large room.

"I can do it differently? It is possible?"

He waited to see if I was finished. I was. It was beginning to sink in. My eyes looked deep into his. I was feeling more and more relief.

"Now, let us go through the routine of a typical day, starting in the morning. How does the morning go? Who gets up first in the household? Do you have difficulty in getting any of the children up? Tell me exactly how it goes."

"I don't have to get them up in the morning because they wake up about 5 a.m. and start fighting immediately. This wakes me up. It would be a miracle for our days to start without fighting. Then I get up, already angry and in a bad mood, and start getting all their stuff together for them while fixing breakfast, combing hair, stuff like that."

"Do they have their own alarm clocks?"

"No." The question startled me. It sounded crazy, and yet I knew this man was very serious and wasn't making jokes. Maybe it wasn't such a crazy idea, just one that I had never thought of.

"Get each of them their own alarm clock for their room. Show them the time they must leave for school and what time you will be serving breakfast. Let the rest be up to them." He continued, "Then what happens?"

"While I'm making breakfast, their lunches have to be packed too, so I do those things. I also referee fights and scream a lot." I laughed nervously.

"Do they help you with any of the chores?"

"Not too much," I sighed.

"Show them how to make their lunches, then get yourself out of the kitchen and let them do it. Share this responsibility with them. Parents and teachers cannot *teach* responsibility. We can only *share* it. Shut your mouth! Get out of the kitchen after fixing their breakfast! Give them a chance. See what they can do. Your kitchen will not be perfect, but allow them to do it. Tell me, what else?"

I couldn't think of anything else I would love more than to get out of the kitchen. I hated our ugly kitchen and I hated cleaning up mess after mess. But could I actually get out and let them do it all by themselves? I didn't know for sure.

"Then they all start running around like crazy, looking for their things for school. They continue fussing and fuming at each other while no one can find anything. And the boys are also trying to get all of Maria's things for her."

"Maria is the princess in this family with all the boys at her service?"

"Well, I never thought of it that way."

"Is it true?"

"Yes, now that you mention it, I guess it is true. Yes, everyone does wait on Maria," I said, mulling this over.

"Then what happens?"

"Well, the four older kids finally get off to school. And after I clean everything up, Christopher and I are off to the community center where I work as a volunteer a few days each week."

"And when do you see the other children again?"

"After school."

"What happens then?"

"They come in like gangbusters and throw their stuff around everywhere. I'm usually right behind them picking it up and yelling at them to do it themselves. They have snacks, do homework, fight, and all that kind of stuff until it's time for dinner. Then we have dinner. Sometimes they fight through dinner—measuring who got the most, spilling things, teasing, and crying. Most of the time the fights just don't end. I feel like I'm going crazy with the constant battles."

"What about going to bed. How does that go?"

"Well, I read to them almost every night before they go to bed. Very rarely is there a fight when it's time for our stories." A smile crossed my face and I remembered what a miracle it was that I read to my children. "Bedtime goes about the best, I guess. I'm totally exhausted by that time so it feels good to just sit on the floor and read to them without having to move a muscle." I laughed and he smiled back at me. His face moved closer to mine again.

"Do you spank the children?"

Oh my God...now I was going to have to tell him I spank them. I hated telling him this part. I hated spanking them but what else was there to do if I didn't spank? I reminded myself that I was here for help. I had to tell him, although it seemed like he knew the answers before I said them anyway. This man was really smart. He knew stuff.

"Sometimes," I said slowly, as if waiting to be reprimanded. He smiled gently and somehow I knew he understood.

"Do you think that spanking helps?" His voice was soft and respectful. He tilted his head slightly sideways as he kept his eyes fixed upon me; his glasses were halfway down his nose. He waited for me to answer.

"Probably it only helps me," I laughed at myself. The audience laughed loudly and Dr. Dreikurs had a twinkle in his eye. He responded quickly.

"Yes, I don't doubt that. Are they good after you spank them?" he asked.

"Yes! But they aren't good for too long."

"But tell me. Do you know why are they not good before you spank them and why are they good afterwards?"

I knew he had the answer for this question even before he asked it. But I couldn't answer it. I didn't have the slightest idea why it happened this way.

"I don't know," I said softly, my eyes searching him for the answer.

He turned to the audience again. "How many of you heard the story about the woman and the girl playing in the street?"

He paused, without waiting for an answer, before continuing. He used his hands as he talked.

"It was a quiet street," he began, "A woman was walking down the street and saw a little girl playing on the sidewalk. Three stories up a window opened and the mother called out, 'Mary, come up. Lunch is ready.' Nothing happened. And after a while the mother called again, 'Mary, come up. Lunch is ready.' And again nothing happened. By this time the woman wondered what was going on. 'Is your name Mary?' she asked. 'Yes, Ma'am,' the little girl answered. 'Was that your mother?' 'Yes Ma'am.' 'Well, why didn't you go up?' 'Oh, Mother hasn't yelled yet!'" the little girl answered.

The audience laughed and he turned back to me. I was laughing, too.

"Your children get your goat. They know they have you where they want you. They don't mind you until you yell or spank them. You can learn to deal with these children without resorting to open conflict, yelling, or spanking. Understand? I tell you this story to explain to you why the spanking apparently hasn't trained the children. Do you understand?"

"Yes." I understood many things that I had never thought of in my entire life up until 45 minutes ago. I hoped I wouldn't forget one word.

"And, yes, in America, parents are no match for their children. The mother becomes a slave and the children run the household. Do you think that we will mind if you are a slave to them?"

"Yes, you would mind and from what I am learning tonight, it seems that many of the things I am doing are not good for my children."

He leaned back for a second in his chair, looking out again to the audience. He used his hands, almost like a conductor of an orchestra, as he spoke. His voice grew louder.

"So we cannot blame the parents but we must educate them. It is not good for them—when you spoil the children and deprive them of their proper function. What we see here is part of the tragedy that is characteristic of our time. Like millions of others, this loving, sincere, and good mother could ruin her children with her efforts to do the right thing. The desire of mothers to be so good will be doing much damage to all of our next generation. In part, our so-called experts are at fault." His voice did not blame, but understood. "They tell parents to give their children more love. Is there a mother anywhere who gives her children more love than this mother?" He pointed to me. "I am in the unfortunate position to make you a bit uncomfortable by showing you the things that you are doing wrong. But I cannot blame you. You are doing the very best you can. It is the very concern for the welfare of the children that leads you astray. But still I have to make you aware of what you are doing."

"I understand," I answered. And I did.

"And your husband, where is he?"

"I'm...getting a...divorce." I still had a little difficulty saying the word.

"And you are afraid of him, no?"

"Yeah..." How did he know that already?

"You see, you're frightened. You are afraid of your children, you are afraid of your husband, and you are afraid of your mother. Am I correct?"

"Yes." I knew he could see inside of my head, and felt comfort knowing that.

"Regardless of your age, you are just a frightened little girl, afraid of everything. Am I correct?"

Yes, I was afraid of everything. I was afraid that all the names my mother had called me were true. I was afraid of my husband and what he would try to do to me and the kids. I was afraid of how stupid I was with all those kids I had to raise. I was afraid of playing the piano in front of my mother. I was afraid of being disowned by everyone related to me. I was afraid of not having any money and not knowing how to do anything to make money. I was afraid of going to downtown Chicago. I was afraid my mother would find out I smoked. When she came to visit, I was afraid of her making fun of me and embarrassing me in front of my friends. l was afraid of her making everyone call me Mary Cecile and of her snickering at me because I was such a baby. My mind raced with an endless list of fears.

"Yes." I looked down to avoid his eyes. He went right on with his business.

"I want to see the children now for a few minutes and then I will teach you how to handle these situations in which you now find yourself. You should be familiar with the procedure since you have been here before. I will interview the children after you have left the stage."

"Okay."

I stood and hesitated for a moment, not sure of which way I should exit. Someone behind the curtain motioned to me. I walked off the stage. The playroom director brought the children out to the stage. I smiled at them as they walked by me. I wondered what they would say to Dr. Dreikurs. Would they be mad at me for doing this? What would he ask them?

I was not supposed to hear what they were saying out there. That's the way it was done at these demonstrations. The mother and father usually weren't supposed to hear the children the same as the children didn't hear the mother or father. I wasn't out of earshot yet and could hear the audience "Ooooohing" and "Ahhhhhhing." How could they not? Those kids were cute. And they were darn wonderful kids. I'd be the first to tell you about them. But this wasn't about wonderful or not wonderful. This was about training them. I peeked through a hole in the curtain.

Dreikurs spoke right away, interrupting my thoughts.

"Hello...hello. Will you come in? What is your name?" He motioned them to come join him in the chairs.

"Maria."

"And?"

"And this is Joey..." Maria began introducing her brothers.

"And you are..."

"John."

"John, and you are..."

"Anthony. "

"And you are?"

"He's Christopher," Maria answered for him.

"How do you do? I'm Dr. Dreikurs. Do you know why all these people are here?"

"Not really." I recognized Anthony's $6^1/_2$-year-old voice from where I was standing behind the curtains. He spoke up loudly and the audience liked it. There were a couple of chuckles. Dreikurs continued.

"All these people are parents and teachers who want to find out what to do with children. So without you, I could not teach them."

If the children responded, I didn't hear them. He started again.

"Do you have an idea why your mother came?"

"Because." It was Anthony's voice again. The audience laughed, so I knew he was probably entertaining them already with his face. He did that well.

"Because of what?"

"Because of us," Maria answered immediately.

"For you. You are quite right. But why for you? Do you have any idea?"

"Because we fight?" Maria questioned.

"You are quite right. Do you know why you fight all the time?"

Dreikurs paused and waited for an answer from them.

Silence.

"Do you mind if I tell you?" He had no time to waste.

They all nodded. Anthony answered, "Okay, tell us." The audience said "oooh" and "aaah" again and I knew he would continue to entertain and make them laugh.

"Could it be because you want to keep Mother after you and busy with you?"

None of the children responded verbally, but I could now see their faces through the hole in the curtain and they lit up with recognition.

"Would you like to talk with me? I would like to help you. What else is there that Mother does not like?"

"Probably fighting the most and maybe us not putting our things away," Anthony smiled as he continued to be the spokesman for the group.

"Do you know what I am going to tell Mother?" They shook their heads and waited for his answer.

"I am going to teach Mother to become a match for you. Whenever you fight she is going to go into the bathroom with a radio so she cannot hear you and she won't come out until the fighting is over," he paused, "What do you think about that?"

"It doesn't sound like such a good idea," Joey mumbled.

"Oh, and why not?" Dreikurs had a serious face.

"Because it's her job to stop us. She has to stop us," Maria joined in.

Faith took my arm and motioned for me to follow her off the stage. I went with her behind the curtain and out into the hallway. She stepped into the next room, waited for me, and then closed the door.

"They won't be with him long, Mary. I'll be back to get you shortly." Then she disappeared through the door.

I sat down; my mind was racing. It was such good stuff he was saying. What else would the kids say? Would Anthony continue being the clown? The kids were probably all being comedians out there now. So what, I thought. What other people think doesn't matter right now.

The door opened and Faith was back already. It was quick—maybe five minutes?

"Dr. Dreikurs wants to talk to you again now," Faith said as she guided me gently back on stage and I wondered, what would he say to me now? The murmuring audience quieted immediately as I again walked across that huge stage.

Dr. Dreikurs took my hand and we both sat down. No matter what, I knew I was safe with him. He understood me. He understood my difficulties.

"You have a wonderful group of children," his eyes comforted me. "I had a good talk with them. At this moment, they are all against you, but you can win them over to your side. They can all be on your side. First of all, you must learn how to use the bathroom properly."

Both the audience and I roared with laughter.

"Use the bathroom properly?" I asked still laughing.

"Exactly!" He continued on. "You will need one of those little radios. How do they call it here in America...?"

He turned to the audience, looking for help and someone yelled, "Transistors?"

"Yes, a transistor. You need a transistor radio, some bubble bath, and magazines in the bathroom. You must tell the children that you are no longer going to stop the fights between them. From now on, when they fight, it will be their business and you are going to be in the bathroom. Once inside, lock the door, turn your radio up loud so you do not hear them, and stay in the bathroom until the fight is over. No words, no sermons, no talking of any kind, just go to the bathroom and stay there until the coast is clear. Do you understand?"

I felt my eyes grow wider. Did I understand him correctly?

"But what if they hurt each other?"

"They will not hurt each other. It is difficult for parents to understand that children fight for their parents' attention. When you leave the battlefield, they will stop fighting. Right now, you are making it worse by trying to stop it with preaching and sermons. What you try to prevent, you are only making worse by your actions. Now, what do you think of that?

"That sounds great," I giggled as I said it.

"Sounds great yes, but will you do it?" He wanted a commitment now.

"Yes, I will do it." My insides were jumping. It sounded wild, but made sense at the same time. He had more to tell me.

"The fighting will increase and intensify. It will get worse before it gets better. Do you understand why?" he watched me. "The children will not believe you and they will test it out."

"Oh."

"If you have anything valuable that you do not want broken, you should put it away. But other than that, you must go to the bathroom at the first sign of trouble. If the fighting gets really bad and goes on and on, then you draw yourself a bubble bath and relax in the bathtub. What do you think?"

"Sounds like a great idea to me," I said laughing hard. My thoughts were going a million miles a minute. If everything he said was indeed the right way to train children, I had been doing everything wrong. But I remembered him saying that it was not my fault and that I should not feel guilty about it. Inside I was jumping with excitement.

"Good! Now about the clothes and other belongings that you pick up after them each day. You need to have a meeting with these children and tell them what you are going to do. You will need to have a meeting every week. Every home in America should have a family meeting every week to decide how the family is going to run and how to work out difficulties. If we can teach mothers to become democratic leaders in the home, then we will have democratic leaders in our classroom and our communities in the future. Having meetings each week inside our homes will help us begin this task of training our children."

I listened intensely. It was all so new and unlike anything I had ever heard in my life. Bathrooms, bubble baths, and democracy—all in one night. I wanted to stand up and cheer. With each new idea, I felt as if he was lifting a heavy rock from my shoulders.

"So, you will tell the children that from now on, after everyone has gone to bed at night, you will go around the house and pick up all the things that are left out around on the floor. When you pick them up, you put them in a locked room. What do you call it here in America?" he looked for help again from the audience.

"A closet?" a faceless voice yelled.

"Closet! You will put them in a locked closet and they will get them back at the end of the week and not before."

"Take everything that is left around?!" My eyes almost popped out of my head. Was I hearing him correctly?

"Everything." He did not mince words.

"But they will have nothing left," I protested. "They won't have coats to wear to school! This is Chicago and it's the middle of November! It's cold outside! Take their winter coats in the middle of the winter?!" I was shocked at this. Never had I heard anything so far out. Or was it? I was sure my face said I couldn't believe what I was hearing, yet...maybe it made sense...

"In the winter it works much faster than in the summer!"

Roars of laughter came from the audience. I knew he meant business. I had never met such a confident human being. I knew he was serious and that I had heard him correctly. I couldn't imagine doing what he said, but I wanted to hear more.

"And their school books?" I couldn't wait to hear his response.

"Yes, if school books are left around you will treat them as any other object. You will take whatever has not been put away properly and put it into the locked closet and they will not get it back until the end of the week."

I was astonished at his words and could only stare at him.

"Should I tell them that I am going to do this?"

"Yes, of course you tell them and in a very friendly way!! You must remember that *all* training must be done with a friendly attitude!! There can be no *anger*, for then it will be a *punishment!* You need to *train your children!!* Your children have *trained you* to do everything for them and they are learning nothing about how to be responsible for themselves or for each other. You are taking it all away from them. They do not know how to care about each other because you, as a good mother, think you should make everything right for them, stop their fights, and watch their every movement. 'Good' mothers think they should do all these things you are doing for your children, but you have taken all responsibility away from them!! The desire to be 'good' mothers makes them the worst mothers. These 'good' mothers are America's tragedy. Do you understand what I am saying?"

His words echoed throughout the hall. Every human being within the range of his voice—myself included—sat motionless. This man knew what he was teaching. I wondered how many people in this hall tonight realized this. At that moment, I knew things would never be the same for me and for my children. My whole world had changed tonight! And not only had my whole world changed, but everything I had ever been taught or learned about raising children was being challenged.

"Yes," I answered with conviction. "I understand what you are saying." I knew my search for another way to raise children was over. Dreikurs' ideas were based on common sense; that was evident to me.

"I am not just saying this just to you, but to every mother here. And when I speak of mothers, I mean mothers of both sexes. Parents, wanting to be so good and do everything for their children, are teaching our youngsters that they need not be responsible for anything! They don't have to be! Do you want to raise a group of children that grows up only knowing how to use other people?"

He already knew my answer and smiled, waiting to hear my answer.

"No," I answered, shaking my head.

"I didn't think so. And so you must do what I am telling you in order to win your children over to your side and to train them in responsibility! You must get my book and find yourself a study group in the area in which you live. If there is not one in your area, then you start one of your own!"

"Me?" Surely, there was some mistake. He didn't mean me. Maybe it was his difficulty with the language.

"Yes, of course I mean you! Gather the mothers in your neighborhood and get them together. Tell them that you must study with each other and help each other. You can do it!!"

I stared at him in disbelief.

"About bedtime. You have a wonderful time reading to them. They also enjoy this very much and have told me so. Continue this ritual with the children, but no longer tell them what to do before the reading starts. In other words, stop the talking. Tell them once, at your meeting, about what is necessary to get ready for bed and how story time will start after they have brushed their teeth, taken their baths, and all those things, and not before. But bedtime goes well for you, so continue reading to them and have a good time together. Other things will start to go well, too, once you begin training these children.

"About the kitchen. It is simple! You cannot cook in a messy kitchen. If the kitchen is not clean, you do not cook. No mention of 'you did not take out the garbage,' or 'you did not wash the dishes,' or, 'you didn't do this,' or, 'you didn't do that.' No words about anything. You just cannot cook. No lectures, no sermons. In other words, stop the talking! And if you'd like, on the nights you can't cook, you can go out for dinner by yourself or with a friend. What do you think of that?" he smiled, knowing and obviously enjoying the fact that he had reached me.

"Well, that sounds like a wonderful idea..."

"*Ah, yes, a wonderful idea, but will you do it?*" He wanted more than words from me. He again wanted total commitment and he wanted it now. I noticed little beads of perspiration under his glasses and on his forehead. He pulled a handkerchief from his pocket and wiped his face.

"Yes. Yes, I will do it." I giggled, but I meant my words. It felt right inside me!

"*Good.* What I tell you to do is not easy," he paused. "It will be difficult for you, but you can do it."

"I will do it!" I said it again, more to myself this time than to him.

"Mornings. The children can make their own lunches for school. You do not need to make all those lunches. Let them do it. They will love doing it. You no longer need to be a maid for these children, making them helpless and crippled. A mother who constantly reminds and does things for a child unnecessarily not only takes a child's responsibility away from him, but also becomes dependent on him for her feelings of importance as a mother." His eyes stared into mine. "Do you understand what I am saying?"

"Yes," I wanted to ask him to repeat that, but he had more to add.

"And keep your mouth shut. You're talking too much. All mothers talk too much. Our children become mother-deaf, not listening because they have been beaten up by all those words. If mothers only talked when the children were willing to listen, we could eliminate ninety percent of all parental talk. Children do not listen to mothers and teachers because they are constantly beating them up with words: preaching, sermons, and lectures. Words are futile most of the time."

I already knew I was sitting with a genius. For this man to understand all he did about families was absolutely unbelievable to me. If only I could remember every word.

"And you must not give up! What I tell you to do will be most difficult, but you can do it! And remember, it will get much worse before it gets better! Do you know why?"

"No." I felt like my head was filled to capacity.

"Your children will be losing you as their maid and will not give you up easily. They will pull out all the...how do you say it in this country...? ammunition? They will pull out all the ammunition to draw you in again. So it is important to remember what I am telling you about it getting worse before it gets better. If it gets worse, that will be your signal to know that what you are doing is effective. If it does not get worse, then you are not doing what I have taught you tonight. It is the same as ringing the fire bell. If someone rings the fire bell and no fireman comes, what do they have to do? Ring it louder, of course, so the firemen will come to put out the fire! It is the same with the children. They are a strong group. They are all working against you, but you can win them over to your side if you do the things I have told you tonight. So you must begin now to train these children. Do you understand?"

"Yes," I could feel the courage swelling inside me. I didn't want this feeling to end.

"Do you have any questions?"

"At the moment, I have none. You've said so much I hope I can remember half of it." My shoulders felt a hundred times lighter than when I first sat down just a little over an hour before.

"Did you learn anything here tonight?" he asked, putting his face directly in front of mine again.

"Yes, I've learned more than I ever thought possible. I feel like rocks have been lifted from my shoulders. I have never felt so relieved in my whole life. Thank you, Dr. Dreikurs!"

We stood and again he took my hand into his.

"You're welcome. I appreciate you coming to help me with this demonstration. I would not be able to teach all these parents here tonight if you had not come to help me. You have shown much courage. Now you may take your children and leave so I may answer questions for the audience. Good night."

"Good night."

We looked at each other and I could see in his eyes that he knew he had lit a fire deep inside of me. He stretched his arms quickly and sat back down in his chair. The audience burst into thunderous applause as I walked off the stage quietly, floating.

I picked up my children from the playroom, and walked through the auditorium to the exit in the back. People were thanking me, but I was in a daze. What I had just learned was incredible. Almost unbelievable, yet very believable! I wanted to savor that feeling, that moment, forever. This man knew about families, about human beings. It all made sense to me.

I realized anything could be accomplished with these children. There didn't have to be hate within families, it could be different. My search had ended.

You have a group of children who are against you but they can all be for you played over and over in my head as I made my way through the crowd. I was in charge of their guidance and how they turned out. It wasn't in the genes. I had doubted that "in the genes" theory ever since I was a little kid. My mother talked about it often in reference to Tommy and Kathryn.

"You cannot be concerned about what others will think of you if you want to train your children properly," he was saying to someone in the audience.

I knew I could climb the highest mountain if I wanted to. Nobody could take away this hope inside of me. Hope, that was the secret. Hope, courage, common sense, and understanding! He said so himself.

Parents had learned from me, he said. He had even thanked me. How exciting! I could see in their eyes and felt in their handshakes that they had learned from me. All I had to do was put those ideas into actions. No big deal! I had no doubts inside me that night.

I remembered my other family: my mother, my brothers, and my sister. Maybe now I could really help them, too.

We reached our car and soon were off for home. I asked the kids if they liked Dr. Dreikurs, and got one "no," three "he was okay I guess," and one "yes." I had loved the whole night: the session, Dr. Dreikurs, and Roslyn, whose idea it was in the first place, and who had stuck with me, absolutely refusing to give up on me. The courage swelling inside me was unlike anything I'd ever felt in my life.

Next thing I knew, we pulled up in front of our house. I couldn't even remember driving home; time had a whole different meaning that night. I told the kids that even though it was late, I wanted to meet with them for a few minutes because I had a couple of important things that I wanted to tell them before going to bed. We would skip the story, but would make up for it tomorrow evening if they wanted to. A little reluctantly, the kids gathered around the kitchen table.

Joey and John exchanged a couple of shoves, and Anthony let out one of his blood-curdling screams. I pulled up a chair to the end of the table and patiently rested my chin in my hands as I waited for them to stop. I felt like I could probably wait forever. Maria took over, telling the boys to "stop it" so that whatever it was that Mommy had to say she could say. A minute later, they were silent and I began.

"What I want to tell you tonight is about this fighting thing," I began, looking at them, "I have decided that I am no longer going to stop you from fighting, as Dr. Dreikurs already told you at the demonstration. If you want to fight, that's going to be your business. I am no longer going to try and stop you," I said it again and paused, looking slowly around the table and allowing my eyes to meet theirs, one by one. "In fact, when you start to fight, I am going to go to the bathroom and take a little radio that I'm going to buy tomorrow. And I will not come out until the fighting is over," I said softly.

"What do you mean you're not going to stop our fights?" Maria jumped in right away, her voice high-pitched and her eyes on the verge of tears. "It's your responsibility to stop us! You have to! You are the mother and..."

"What I mean, Maria," I looked directly into those big brown eyes of hers as I spoke, "is exactly that, sweetheart. I am not going to do it anymore. I-am-not-going-to-stop-your-fights. From now on, like I said, I am going to go to the bathroom when you fight and I won't come out until you are finished." I was the picture of calmness, speaking slowly and clearly.

"You can't do that! You have to stop our fights!" Maria's voice dripped with drama. But I was totally sure of myself and it showed in every word I said.

"No, I don't really have to and I've decided that I'm not going to anymore," I said. "It is your responsibility now and no longer mine." I sat in my chair, feeling like the queen of all queens. Nothing or no one could ruffle my feathers.

Maria arched her back and threw her shoulders back before she spoke again. She sure was a cute kid, I thought. She had dainty little hands that moved gracefully when she spoke. She definitely had my nose, but somehow it looked smaller on her. "You can't do that! You have to stop us from fighting! It's your responsibility to do that!" She grabbed a napkin and wiped away her tears. "You have to stop us! We won't have any friends anymore! All our friends will hate us! We won't be like a family anymore!" Maria sounded like a well-seasoned orator at almost 10 years of age. "We will all be like the leaves on the trees falling to the ground," her arms rose and her fingers moved, making a trickling motion of leaves falling to the ground. "We'll-all-be-separated; we-won't-be-together," she looked at her brothers as she spoke, clearly pronouncing every word exactly as I had just done. She stopped to wipe her tears again from her red face. Her speech was broken with agony and her hands were moving as fast as her mouth. I listened patiently. Why, I wondered, was Maria being so dramatic?

"You can't do that, Mommy, you just can't and you know it. It just wouldn't be RIGHT!" On the last word, Maria let out a deep sigh and it looked as if she would rise from the chair as she put her palms on the table. She rested her case while she glared at me through her tears.

It was not just a command, but it had the tone of a moral command. Maria knew what was "right," and she was going to make sure that I knew also. I wanted to laugh, but didn't. I was wishing I had a movie camera. The Academy Awards could have be given out right here in our own kitchen this very night.

The ideas just kept making more sense to me. The children felt my courage and my determination. I wasn't sure how kids knew things, but somehow kids have that talent—somewhere inside them. I knew it wasn't a coincidence that every time I picked up the phone to make a quiet phone call the kids all appeared noisily out of nowhere.

Flash bulbs started going off inside my head! FLASH: I was going to get out. I was going to leave the battlefield. FLASH: They wouldn't have control over me any longer. It wasn't going to settle well with them. FLASH: I didn't have to stop their fights. FLASH: I have been making it worse. I wondered, can I do this? FLASH: You bet your life!

I leaned forward and put my elbows on the table.

"You can say whatever you want to say," the words came out very slowly as the children glared at me. "I'm not going to stop your fights anymore. It's that simple. Whatever you want to do with it is up to you. You can cry all you want. If you want to fight, fight. If you don't want to fight, don't. It's your choice whether you want to get along or not. I'm not involved anymore." I leaned back and crossed my legs. I was getting wordy again and needed to shut my mouth. Dreikurs' instructions were playing in my head again: *No lectures. No sermons. Stop the talking.*

"But, just so you know," my voice was very soft now, "From now on, when you fight, I'm going to the bathroom. I will only come out when the fight is over." I hoped I had said it for the last time. I took a deep breath and exhaled slowly. Silent, disgusted faces filled the room.

"Oh, there's one more thing I forgot," I raised my index finger and moved to the edge of my chair again, "From now on, I am no longer going to nag you to hang up your coats or put away your boots, scarves, hats, gloves, books, toys, and all the things I nag you to put away each day. I am not going to ask you to put them away anymore either."

Every face showed doubt and every voice snickered.

My voice was gentle. "From now on, after everyone goes to bed at night, I will make a trip through the house and pick up whatever has been left around. I will then put these things away," I paused, "I will put them in a locked closet where they will remain for one week. At the end of the week, you may have your things back if you want them. This is the way I will handle all belongings left around in the general part of the house from now on. It will eliminate all the nagging from me and we will have more time for fun things," I smiled at them confidently.

"Okay, sure, Mommy," Joey spoke for all the kids as they sat on the edge of their chairs, waiting to make fast tracks out of there and go to their bedrooms. They weren't sure how seriously to take what I was saying. Later, in the privacy of their bedrooms, they would probably say, "She is getting weird, *really* weird."

"So, that's all I have to say, except I think we need to have meetings like this once a week, don't you?" I asked matter-of-factly, making more of a statement than a question.

"Sure, okay, if you want to," they all agreed, shaking their heads while not having the slightest interest in anything I was saying at this point.

I watched the sad faces around this table and could feel the strong vibes. I loved the I-am-in-charge-of-me-feeling I had. I pushed my chair back, got up from the table, and walked through the house with feelings that I'd never felt before. I would no longer be their maid, and obviously they were upset over my newly found ideas from Dreikurs. I felt on top of the world.

"Come on now; I'll tuck you in."

They followed me upstairs.

6

It was very early. The sky was just beginning to show light. But it was definitely not too early for the first fight of the day. Upon waking, I was already anxious for them to be off to school, but a glance at the clock told me that this wouldn't happen for another three hours. I was excited about what I had learned last night and chuckled inside when I heard Dreikurs' voice in my head saying, *you must learn to use the bathroom properly*. I needed a few essentials—most importantly the radio. Bubble bath, magazines, and his book were also important, but the radio was vital. The radio might just be able to save my sanity, I thought. Roslyn told me we could purchase the book next week when we got together at the Child Guidance Center, but until I bought the radio, there was not much I could do about the fighting. The training could not be accomplished without it.

Before going to bed I had wondered if the kids would still fight in the morning, after everything I said, but guesswork was no longer necessary. They were fighting big time and screaming continually.

"Who took my folder!?"

"Did anyone see my pencil case?"

"Where is my library book?"

I walked around nervously, picking things up after fixing breakfast. I didn't tell them to stop fighting, but the minutes seemed like hours until it was time for them to leave. In fact, those three hours seemed like days. Finally, the school bus blew its horn. To me, it felt like the longest morning in history. On and on it went. One last trip up the stairs and through the bedrooms. A few more tears. Kisses. The front door slammed and they were off.

Christopher and I were alone at last. It was my turn now. I was excited, thinking about a new life with my children. I couldn't wait to start. I kept giggling to myself.

There was no hesitation inside me that morning. I hated borrowing money but I would do it to get the radio. I called my friend Leslie to see if she'd be home and if I could stop by with Christopher. There were several people who were really good to my children and me, and Leslie was one of them.

"I need to borrow some money," I told her, after we'd said hello and hugged.

"How much?" she asked without hesitation.

"Twenty-five dollars," I said.

"Okay, don't worry, no problem." Leslie smiled warmly. Then, she went to her bedroom to get the money. She came out and handed it to me.

I thanked her, promised to call her later, and left. It was that quick. Ordinarily, I would have stayed and talked with Leslie, but not today. Today I had a one-track mind! Go to that little store down by the el station and get that radio. *How do you call it here in America?* Dreikurs had asked. "

Transistor radio!" Someone yelled from the audience. I smiled hearing his voice in my head. Christopher slipped his hand inside mine as we walked down the stairs toward the car. He stopped in front of a fire hydrant and stared as if he had never seen one before.

"What is this, Mommy?" he asked, pointing to this object that was exactly the same height as he was.

The older kids had taught him so much in his short life that a question like this momentarily took me by surprise. His brothers had toilet trained him without me, but he didn't know what a fire hydrant was? After a few minutes talking about fire hydrants, I made a mental note to tell Christopher "stuff." Then I laughed, remembering how kids had a way of relaxing us at the right times if only we would let them.

I hoped that ending the fights in our home would be as easy as it was for Joey, John, and Anthony to teach Christopher how to use the toilet. I thought it was funny how uninvolved I had been when my own mother had always been so involved in my visits to the bathroom.

I was a junior in high school before she stopped making me lay down on that cold bathroom floor every week to give me an enema. It was that way for as long as I could remember. Never allowed to flush the toilet until she "checked" it for a bowel movement. The ritual of lying there with my pants off always made me feel so embarrassed, worthless, degraded. If I cried, it was: "You cry and I'll leave it in longer, you cry baby." I always wanted to scream. Sometimes I thought I was going crazy.

The sales person was helpful. I purchased my radio and we left the store. I held it tightly in one hand and gave my other hand to Christopher. The radio was black, about three inches high, two inches across, and in a little black case dotted with tiny little holes. I'd never had my own radio before and I felt rich. If it had cost a million dollars, I couldn't have liked it more. Twelve dollars could buy a couple huge bags of groceries, but somehow I knew that this little radio was symbolic of maintaining my sanity. I couldn't put a price tag on that! Luckily, I had enough money left over to purchase Dreikurs' book, *Children: the Challenge*, the next time I went to the Center.

My task was completed and Christopher and I headed home for lunch. I started gearing up for the afternoon. Christopher took a nap while I cleaned up before the other kids came storming in from school. After a while, I could hear Christopher's footsteps upstairs.

"Are those little fairies I hear running around up there?" I yelled up from the first floor hallway.

"It's me, Mommy, not fairies," he yelled down, "I'm going potty." I loved it when he responded like that. He had total faith in everything I said.

"Okay, honey, come on down when you're finished."

The older kids were going to be home any minute and I could feel it in my stomach. I squeezed the tiny radio in my hand. What would they do today? Would they fight? Would I really go to the bathroom?

As these thoughts were going through my head, the school bus pulled up in front of the house. I could feel my insides pulling. I didn't know if I was tense or excited or what—maybe courage, anxiety, and hope were all mixed together. Perhaps I was also a tiny bit scared, but not too much. I knew I didn't have to be scared. Dr. Dreikurs told me so last night and I believed him.

"STOP IT!" Anthony screamed at the top of his lungs as the front door flew open, slamming back against the wall. I needed to put something behind that door to prevent it from knocking a hole in the wall; every day it knocked off a little more plaster.

"YOU STOP IT!" Joey yelled back. Book bags landed loudly on the floor.

"YOU STARTED IT," Anthony was going down on his knees, already in tears.

"I DID NOT. YOU DID!" Joey was going to win.

"Quit hitting me! MOMMY, JOEY'S HITTING ME AGAIN!" Anthony was at his loudest pitch. I knew he was looking for help from me.

This was where I, as a good mother, usually stepped in and did the usual routine—punishing the bad guy, comforting the good guy, giving a little sermon about loving each other, and dishing out punishments if their screams were loud enough. Good mothers did everything for their children if possible. Good mothers followed their kids around all day pointing out their mistakes, telling them to say thank you, and hoping for their children to be perfect so that they, as a mother, looked good.

I knew I had never allowed one child in this family to work out anything without me. I was always in the middle. I was guilty of doing everything for my children. But then again, Dreikurs had said not to feel guilty because I just hadn't known any better. I knew I'd been ignorant, but I wanted to erase some of that ignorance.

The fight moved into the kitchen—right next to me. There hadn't even been enough time to say hello before I realized I had to put some actions behind my words. I quickly picked up my radio from the kitchen counter, tripped over something in the front hall, and almost fell as I started up the stairs. I didn't turn around, but I felt their eyes glaring at me.

In our little house, there were fourteen stairs to the second floor. From the top of the stairs, I took two more steps to the left and into the bathroom, where

I locked the door. That's what he said to do: *Go to the bathroom... Lock the door... Turn the radio on loudly and stay in there until the fight is over.* "Okay, I'm ready," I said out loud to myself.

In less than thirty seconds, it sounded as if hundreds of kids were right outside the door. They began to pound on the door louder than anything I ever heard before. I knew it couldn't be more than five kids because I only had five kids, but it sounded like an army. Maybe I would have to turn the radio up louder—a lot louder.

The banging was something fierce and the narrow strip of woodwork around the door buckled in and out. I thought that maybe the doorframe would cave in. The radio was as loud as it could go, and still the screaming was unbelievable! There was absolutely no way I would ever be able to describe this scene to anyone. It all seemed so farfetched. Was I actually locked inside my bathroom, in my own home, with a little radio blasting at top volume, "using the bathroom properly?" I would laugh for the rest of my life when I remembered Dreikurs' voice saying that phrase.

But doubts crept into my head, too. Doubts were common to me. No matter what I did, I was always great at doubting myself. What if their father phoned the kids tonight to talk to them? He called almost every night now since I told him I wanted a divorce. He had talked to them more in the last two months than he did in their whole lives. Before, he showed no interest in being their father, but it was a different story now. At least he kept saying it was different.

He always was great with words. I can remember the romantic love letters from years past. How I used to read them over and over while lying in my bed, alone in the still of the night. Folding them up and re-opening them time after time. His words had always made me feel so good inside. No one in this world loved anyone as much as he loved me. Without me, he said he would die! I used to believe it was true.

A particularly loud bang brought me back again and I realized I was still in the bathroom with the radio blaring. Would this go on all night? My head was starting to ache. What would happen if Anthony told his father that Joey was beating him up and that Mommy was locked in the bathroom with the radio blaring? Maybe he'd say I was an unfit mother or something and want to take the kids away from me. No, he wouldn't do that—he wouldn't want them. He couldn't even remember their birthdays. But then again, could I be sure he wouldn't try it? People did awful things to each other when they got divorced. Hadn't I told him over and over that I didn't have enough money for food for the children? And didn't he always respond with a nasty sneer on his face, saying that it was my problem?

The pounding on the door started to ease up slightly as the crying became louder. I switched stations on the radio to catch Nat King Cole in the middle of "Unforgettable." I loved his music and his voice soothed me for a moment—even at top volume.

I knew people were talking about me in our parish church. They were talking about how bad I looked, about my pending divorce, and about how I might be involved with Father Pat. And if anyone could've seen me at that moment, they would probably have said I was crazy. People were quick to judge; I'd certainly learned that first hand.

But this act of "using the bathroom properly" made so much sense. After all, weren't parents everywhere punishing their children when they fought? Weren't parents everywhere giving their children lectures each day about how brothers and sisters should love each other? Weren't parents everywhere doing the exact same things for generation after generation, with the same ineffective results—just as I myself had been doing? Spankings, rewards, punishments, lectures, grounding, belittling. Had that stuff ever worked, at least in a positive sense? Not from what I could understand about families. Certainly not in the family I came from.

I watched as the little doorframe continued to move in and out with the pounding. I couldn't imagine any sadder family than mine—my own parents and siblings. They were by far the saddest group of people I had ever seen.

My mother, who always saw me as a piece of property that needed to be controlled and beaten, is still probably the unhappiest person I have ever known.

BOOM! BOOM! BOOM! It was like the beating of a drum.

"Now! Now! Open it now! Now! Now! Now, now, open it now, now!" They were in unison, and *loud*—like a football cheer. Then they stopped, briefly.

"Mommy! Mommy! Mommy, open this door! Please, please, do it now! Joey's hitting me!" It was Anthony.

"John is biting me!" That was Joey's voice.

"Mommy, open this door up now...please?" It was Maria now.

I was not going to answer, and although the music was still at its loudest, there was no radio in the world that was loud enough to totally drown out this noise. I turned on the shower and then flushed the toilet. This helped a little bit, but the screaming and pounding continued. I had no idea how long it had been going on. Two minutes? Two hours? I had lost track of time and wasn't giggling anymore. I was tired.

Weren't they going to give up soon? Maybe I really was going crazy. I felt like I was watching a movie of someone else being locked in a bathroom. I turned down the volume. It sounded like some of the kids had gone downstairs. Only a couple of whiny voices remained. I lowered the radio another notch.

"Mommy, are you ever gonna come out? Are you gonna stay in there all night?" John was guarding the door. Maybe they were taking turns guarding me.

I can clearly picture you, Daddy, standing there on the edge of the garden, leaning on your hoe. Your t-shirt is all soaked in sweat and your pants are barely hanging on your hips—if one could say you even had hips. You're talking to that old guy Emmet, who stopped by every spring, talking about how you took care of the different vegetables and how they grew. How you were sure it wasn't your imagination that the ones you liked seemed to grow more than the ones you didn't like. How you fertilized the tomatoes and how gorgeous they were. How it was a law of nature, you said: what we cultivate grows. It's that simple, you told him. I remember old Emmet laughing and calling you "Ole Conway" as he slapped you on the back. At this moment I could see how it worked the same way with children—if we fed their negative behavior, it would grow. And if we fed the positive behavior, that would grow, too.

That day is easy to remember because it was one of the few times I ever heard you talk to anyone else, and Lord knows we never did any talking to each other. I could probably count on one hand the things I heard you say in my whole life. Mother said you talked to your old cronies when you went downtown on Saturday afternoon, but for me there were all those years of silence. All those years you were completely mute. She would say, "He's been pouting for three years now," or "six years," or however many years it had been at the time. I didn't understand; all I knew was that until I was about seven years old, you and mother fought over breakfast, dinner, and supper. You didn't have a job and there was no money, so you were home all the time with these loud, knockdown, drag-out fights every day. Then, all of a sudden, boom: you didn't talk anymore, Daddy. Mother had only bad things to say about you and I knew I hated you. But I didn't know any better, Daddy. If Mother said that someone was bad, I believed her. Inside, I wondered about lots of stuff but would never in a million years say it out loud. And when I'd come in after school, you'd disappear, as Mother would scream after you: "Tell her what you really want! Tell her." It was a long time before I knew what she meant by that.

I always thought you hated me too, until the day I got married. And then, after mass, I saw you standing on the church steps with tears rolling down your cheeks. I was shocked to see you crying and it took me a few moments to realize you were crying for me. You could have knocked me over with a feather when I saw that, Daddy. I felt awkward and my insides were a wreck walking down the aisle holding your arm. Well, you know, we never got physically close to each other in the same room, and I don't think I ever knew what a hug was.

It seemed like the next thing I knew, I had a bunch of babies, and it was the day of your funeral. I knew I'd never see your face again after they closed that coffin. You looked really good in that gray suit, Daddy. You definitely were a handsome man. They say I have your nose. I guess I do. Everyone had a chance to talk to you, but by the time I got to St. Louis, you were already in a coma. Your silence didn't really bother me, though; it wasn't something new. Joe had been his usual self, doing me the favor of breaking away from his important meetings to come to your funeral. I was very happy that I fooled you the times we visited and you never knew how he really was towards the kids and me, but then again you were pretty sharp so maybe you did know.

I still think about your beautiful garden. Lots of people said it was the greatest garden in the whole town. You'd always get mad at me when I messed up your lettuce bed. I promise, I won't mess it up ever again, Daddy. The more I thought about the simple life you had, the more I realized how wise you were. I could picture your face and that helped because I knew those next few weeks were going to be really hard. But I did have a new hope inside of me. I wished I could tell you all about it. You would have been proud, Daddy. You'd have been proud because I decided I was going to make it different for these grandkids of yours. So far, this first day had been really wild. But for some reason, I knew you wouldn't have made fun of me about all of this. Maybe you would've been able to understand the whole thing better than I did.

It became quiet outside the bathroom door, so I turned the radio off. Then I took a deep breath, unlocked the door, and walked out. I stood in the hallway and took another deep breath. Maybe three seconds later, before I could exhale, John was out of his bedroom and had slipped his hand inside of mine.

In three more seconds Anthony wanted to hold my hand, too. The same hand, of course! John and Anthony pushed, screamed, and shoved, starting another fight. Some people had instant oatmeal; my children had instant fights, I thought as I turned around and quickly stepped back into the bathroom.

Anthony was holding my hand so tightly that I had to force myself free of his grip as he screamed. I didn't want to slam any fingers in the door. Calmly, I first lifted John, and then Anthony, into the hallway and quickly closed the door. It was a matter-of-fact movement. I did what needed to be done. My mind was clear again.

Another riot broke out in the hallway. Quickly, I turned on my little black box. Much louder this time. Their feet took their positions against the door.

"Can you hear us, Mommy?" yelled John.

"She can hear us! Don't you doubt it!" screamed Maria.

"Mommy, Mommy! You just don't care. She doesn't care about us!" John again.

"Mommy! Mommmmyyyy! PLEASE COME OUT OF THERE!" Anthony once again lived up to his status of being the loudest.

Even with the music at top volume, I could still hear them right outside the door. I drew water in the tub for a bath.

"Oh, noooooooo! She's going to take a bath." It was John's voice. I could see him in my mind's eye, down on his knees and elbows, slamming his little fists on the floor.

They didn't know I could hear them over the blaring radio. The pounding continued. They knew a lot, but not everything, I thought to myself. More pounding. I remained silent inside the bathroom, supposedly relaxing, when actually I wanted to go out there and spank them hard—very hard. The pounding didn't miss a beat. Maybe the bath would help, I thought as my clothes fell to the floor and I stepped into the tub. POUNDING. I had no bubbles, but the running water helped. Perhaps, if it had been a bigger bathroom—POUNDING—this one was getting smaller by the minute. It was about five by six feet, including the bathtub. POUNDING. Pukey shades of greens and browns. POUNDING. A tiny window that no one could actually see out of, without standing on the edge of the bathtub. POUNDING. But probably the most beautiful bathroom in the world would not have made a difference now. POUNDING. I laughed again.

"Training. I'm doing training. I'm training my children," I was talking to myself out loud now. "It's a little harder than I had imagined, but then again who could have imagined this? Can they hear me talking to myself? It will be dinnertime soon. I wonder how long the batteries in my new radio will last? What would Mother say if she could see me now?

"Dreikurs said it would get worse before it got better. And he said it would not be easy. That's an understatement." The pounding continued. "Either I am full of courage or totally crazy. But nothing else has worked so far. They're testing me but I meant what I said, I am not coming out."

The pounding weakened. I moved my legs around in the tub to make splashing noises and turned down the radio. Things were quiet in the hall again. The pounding stopped. Completely. I've probably seen the worst of it, I thought. I wondered how long I had been in the bathroom this round. Time was not relevant to me now though, it was the training that mattered.

I stepped from the tub, dried myself with a damp towel, and combed my hair back from my face. Not one curl, at least not in this lifetime. Always straight and sticking out, just like Mother always said. "That girl's hair has been sticking out like that since the day she was born, never could do anything with it no matter how hard I tried." I wiped up the water from the floor, dressed myself, and opened the door. I could hear them downstairs in the den. Calmly, I took a deep breath before I went downstairs. There were other things to do besides sitting in the bathroom; I wanted to get dinner started, for one.

Maria, Joey, and John were on the floor doing their homework. Anthony was throwing little blocks on top their books. Christopher sat there watching. I was not in the kitchen for more than two minutes when Anthony started screaming.

"Stop it. Stop it, Joey! I'm telling Mommy!" I was sure that everyone on the block heard that one.

Before I could close the refrigerator door, it got louder.

"Stop it or she'll go into the bathroom again!" Maria shouted.

Maria came into the kitchen to ask me a homework question while John began teasing Christopher. John loved to tease and he was good at it. The kid always had a twinkle in his eye and as my daddy would say, he was a "pistol." Blond and cute, he was as quick as anybody and kept people laughing and screaming at the same time. He always had something else up his sleeve. He definitely lived up to being the middle child, with a keen sense of what was fair, always calling me on it. I loved when I finally learned to say, *"life is not fair, life is not unfair, life is life."* This helped very much with the measuring stick that develops between kids, and I didn't fall for the remark anymore from any of them.

Joey continued beating up on Anthony. Just that quick it went from screaming to fighting. I knew I had to disappear again. I headed for the stairs, realizing I had already waited too long.

"We'll stop!" they all yelled at the same time. I kept going.

"We'll stop Mommy!" Their voices were desperate, but I didn't miss a step.

"Don't gooooooooo, don't gooooooooo, MOMMY!" John made another plea.

My head was aching something awful, and I wasn't sure if it was from the loud music, the fighting, or from being hungry and tired. This had certainly been a full day's work. I locked the door behind me, turned on the radio, and once again waited. Again the screaming and yelling moved right outside the bathroom door. I put the bathmat on the floor and sat down. I wished that I had a book. I wished this were over. I changed stations. Music. Voices. Singing. News. All stations at full volume. I waited. The intensity outside the door started to die down. I wanted to get out of that bathroom. I turned the radio down two more notches. It really sounded quiet. This fight did not last as long.

Again, I went downstairs, but within less than two minutes I was back in the bathroom. Up. Down. Up. Down. Up. Down. Three more times. Every pore in my body oozed courage and determination. For the seventh or eighth time since they arrived home from school, I quietly emerged from the bathroom and went back downstairs. It looked like a couple kids had grabbed a sandwich. I walked past them, into the kitchen.

"Did you guys eat? Christopher, did you eat?" I wasn't sure exactly what I felt—other than determination.

"Yeah, I gave him a sandwich, Mommy," Maria answered proudly. I was amazed at how much Maria sounded like me, and I hated the way I sounded much of the time.

"Thanks, Maria. You guys want to read a story tonight?" I asked as if nothing was different.

How unique and difficult it was for me not to end their fighting with a punishment. It was harder still not to give them a lecture. Maybe I should have told them, just one more time, about loving each other. No! That's the way I always had done it. No anger, no lectures, I said to myself. This would have made the training a punishment. I didn't want to fall back into that again. Please keep your mouth shut, I said over and over in my head.

"Yeah! Could we have a story?" Anthony smiled from ear to ear as he answered my question. Didn't he have the greatest smile in the world?

I told them I would wait in Joey and Anthony's bedroom tonight and, as soon as everyone was ready for bed, I would begin the story. I waited patiently. They teased and were pretty loud in the bathroom, but I didn't get involved. They disagreed about which story they wanted tonight, but I remained quiet while they fussed.

I wondered how long I would have to sit and wait for them tonight. Would I know when it was "bathroom time" again? Finally, they agreed upon the story. It was the only time that day when I was encouraged by the results of my silence. I took another deep breath. I had taken a lot of those in the last twenty-four hours.

"Okay, you guys, I'm starting now. 'Once upon a time, Little Brown Bear...The End...that's it, you guys," my head fell back on the pillow.

"Ohhhhh..." The kids stretched out on the floor. The yawns were contagious.

"Everybody's tired. Come on now and I'll rub your backs and tuck you in."

I stood up and stretched. It had been a long, long day. Longer than any I could remember.

"Will you rub mine, Mommy?" Anthony wanted to be first and ran for his bed.

"Sure," I said softly. I loved the quiet when I rubbed their backs. Even though it was only a few minutes, it felt good. Anthony's back rub lasted about three minutes, but it seemed like an hour to me. I gave his little butt a love tap—the signal that I was finished, pulled up his covers to his ears where he always wanted them, and kissed him goodnight. One down and four to go. I was so very tired.

"Good night, Anthony, I love you," I said, standing up, readying myself to rub Joey's back on the top bunk.

"Did you see this big scratch I have on my arm, Mommy?" Anthony raised his body up and instantly untucked the covers.

"Want me to rub your back, Joey?" I ignored Anthony's attempt at tattling on one of his brothers.

"Yeah!" Joey moved to the edge of his bed.

I reached under the covers, looking for his back with my hand. Their top bunk was high, making it difficult for me to reach the person on the top. But that was the way I had asked my Daddy to build it, so an adult could sit on the bottom bunk and not bump their head on the top bunk—as was the case with store-bought bunk beds. "Yep," Daddy would say, "I put 280 screws in that bunk bed for those wild grandkids from Chicago." He loved calling them his wild grandkids from the big city, and then he'd laugh! "They won't be able to shake this one loose for a while." That bed was a wonderful idea, except when it came to giving back rubs on the top bunk.

"Aren't you going to say anything about my arm?" Anthony asked.

"How does that feel, honey?" I said to Joey.

"Umm yeah, great, thanks, Mommy. Mmmm, right over here," he said pointing to his left shoulder blade.

Anthony didn't ask me about his arm again. I was pleased that I didn't respond to the tattling. I took a few steps down the hall to the next bedroom to finish the ritual. Two down, three to go. Tonight, as if for the first time, I realized how much they were the same and yet how unique and different each child was. Each was beautiful in his or her own way. It was much easier for me to see this revelation at bedtime when I was grateful the day was over and knew I would soon have a few moments alone.

I was too tired to pick up the mess that was all over the house and put everything in a locked closet like I said I was going to do. I'd have to wait on that part of the training. The bathroom thing itself was exhausting. But Dreikurs had said it would get worse before it got better. I thought I'd probably seen the worst of it, and I needed to relax. Gnawing in the back of my head was the thought of their father, and I hoped that if and when he called, the children wouldn't say anything about all this to him. I knew I shouldn't be afraid of him, but I was, at least some of the time. This training could easily have been misunderstood by anyone who didn't know what I had learned at the demonstration. I flopped down on my bed and was asleep before I could get completely under the covers.

"How could I not think you were getting killed? It's six o'clock in the morning and you were right outside of my bedroom door, three feet from my eardrums, screaming at the top of your lungs! It sounded like you were being murdered!" I was in tears as I screamed at all the kids in the hallway.

"Mommy, he was hitting me *hard*," Anthony leaned against my bedroom door, sobbing as he spoke.

"I'm really sorry that happened, Anthony, but I'm sure you and Joey can work it out." I knew I was saying the right words, but I heard the doubt in my voice. It was my attitude that they would hear anyway, not my words.

I grabbed the bathroom doorknob as a stuffed dog went sailing past my head. I couldn't believe it was starting so soon. But then, I guess, it wasn't that unusual; it had been the same every morning for Lord only knows how many years. I knew that I was not supposed to say any words and only use actions, but after yesterday I really thought it would be better. Instead, it was starting as early as it always did, and maybe it was my imagination but it seemed louder. I was so sick of it. I turned the radio on when I got inside the bathroom, but the fight was right outside the door and the music couldn't drown out all of the screaming and crying.

"Mommy, Mommy, can I come in? I have to go to the toilet. Can I come in, please?" It seemed like John was always there first to start the begging.

"See what you did? You made her go in there again!" Maria yelled at John.

"Shut up, Maria! I did not!" John burst out, "It's Joey's fault! He hit me!"

"You're a big baby, Johnny!" Joey snarled back. He hated it when John tattled to Maria.

I turned up the volume. They were pounding again. What a way to wake up. I chuckled one minute and was mad the next. It was so early. This was day two, and I told myself that I could not and would not give up. I was not going to let them think they could get me out of here. I would stay in the bathroom until it was over. I was determined.

They were screaming that they would wet their pants soon. Interesting, I thought, since they could go downstairs where there was another toilet.

"You make me sick!" someone yelled at me from the other side of the door. Sounded like John. That was okay. No matter what they said or called me, one thing remained clear in my mind: I was not coming out.

I had to get them off to school, but there was still plenty of time. I wondered what was going to happen. This was all new to me, too, but I felt that courage swell inside me again. I'd just have to rely on that feeling.

It grew quiet again, so I came out. It was amazing how quickly it could get quiet. There were still a lot of fights, but maybe they were over quicker now. It was 7:30. Lunches had to be made. I went back downstairs.

"Please turn off the TV." I felt a little nervous on the inside. Could they notice it? But then again, what didn't they notice? They watched me like a hawk and I believed they had x-ray vision into my thoughts.

"Want some oatmeal this morning?" I tried to sound relaxed, but wasn't sure I accomplished that. I put the water in the pot and turned on the stove.

"Yeah, thanks, Mommy!" Maria and John both answered eagerly, running into the kitchen.

"Please get your bowls and spoons, okay?" I stood facing the stove so they didn't see my expression. I held my breath and felt very nervous. I hoped it wouldn't show.

"I'll get them." John pulled a chair from the table and started to climb up.

"Here let me do it," Joey was immediately there behind him, pulling on the chair.

"Stop pulling the chair, will ya, Joey?" John screamed as he swung his arm, trying to hit Joey.

"Was I pushing you, Johnny?" Jocy was taunting him now. He ducked his head to avoid the arm coming at him.

"You guys better quit or she'll go to the bathroom," Maria was nervous and tried desperately to get things straightened out.

It quickly became a full-fledged fight. I turned off the stove—better to have raw cereal than an unattended flame on the stove. I realized that I had probably waited too long again. I quickly left the kitchen, took three steps through the den, and started up the stairs.

"No, don't go, Mommy, we'll stop!" they yelled, running right behind me.

I hesitated for one brief moment and someone grabbed my leg.

"Please don't go, Mommy, we're sorry," it was Anthony's voice.

I turned around and saw that they all were standing at the bottom of the stairs staring up at me, their eyes begging for mercy.

"Let go of my leg!" I yelled hysterically.

I wanted to stay calm, but it was impossible. Anthony continued to hold on. His arms were wrapped tightly around my leg. As I slowly pulled myself up the stairs I kept yelling for him to let go but his little body dragged behind me. It would probably have been funny to watch, but at the time I was frantic to get away. And Anthony just held on as if his life depended upon it. I remembered Dreikurs saying, *your children will be losing you as their maid and they will not give up easily.* It was true that they were losing me. But when would they realize that **I** wasn't giving up either?

When I got halfway up the stairs, I plucked Anthony loose from my leg. I wondered if my being hysterical had ruined the training. Oh well, the important thing was that it all made more and more sense to me now. They were losing me as their maid. And I no longer had to be under their power. Safely inside with the door locked and the radio blaring, I waited as they kicked, pounded, and let out blood-curdling screams.

"Mommy, the cereal tastes funny and we can't eat it!" Maria led the pack.

"What about our lunches?" Joey followed suit.

"We have to go to school. Don't you know we have to go to school?!" Maria screamed demandingly.

"She doesn't care. She can hear us, but *she doesn't care.*" That was John's regular line now.

"You don't know if she can hear us! Maybe she can't!" Joey was protecting me. He definitely protected me more and more since Joe left.

"Yes, she can, she can hear us," John sounded so sure of himself, but he also said anything to disagree with Joey.

I remained quiet. As I was basking in the "I'm-in-charge-of-me" feeling, I realized that their control over me was gone. However, I did hope they would stop soon so I could come out and help get them off to school. There was no reason not to have this all worked out and over with! The day before I had gone to the bathroom every time the fighting started. The radio said it was eight o'clock as Paul Harvey started his broadcast. The bus would be here at 8:25—there was still time. But the banging on the door sounded like hammers, and there was no indication of it ever stopping.

Dreikurs said to *relax* in the bathroom. Relaxation must come with practice. At this point I could not relax. I was confident that I had started a process that would make the whole world different for all of us. I talked and screamed a little bit this morning, but not as much as usual. I did want to see them off to school, though. I had never sent them off to school without kissing them goodbye. Even if I was upset or angry, I always kissed them when they left. But with the minutes ticking away, I wondered if I'd be able to. Somehow, Maria knew I was not coming out, and informed the boys:

"Now you've done it boys. She's not coming out," spoken like a true second-in-command.

My heart ached for those good-bye kisses, but they were not going to happen. I knew I had to give up all my lectures and kisses and remain silent inside the bathroom. Only my quiet withdrawal would allow these kids to learn the consequences of their actions. A few final screams surged up from the first floor before I heard the door slam, then they were on their way to the bus without me. I had outlasted them. This whole time I may have been outwardly silent, but I had never talked to myself so much in all my life!

It was not what a "good mother" would do—retreat into the bathroom, refuse to settle the fights, leave breakfast unprepared, and send them to school without a kiss. But it was better this way. *Be proud*, my inner voice coaxed me. *Be proud that you are training your children. Remember how he said that they were a group against you and how they could be a group for you. Remember how good it felt with Dr. Dreikurs the other night. Don't let your mixed emotions rule you. You know what to do; things will get easier and better if you stick to it.* Inner voices could be magical.

After school, it seemed as if I was back in the bathroom even before the kids got off the school bus. The fighting started before the front door slammed shut, but I was more than ready for it—I had gathered my strength during the day. I really didn't want to go to the bathroom again, but I knew I had to. Still, I was encouraged because I noticed a change in their behavior. They were no longer fighting about things between themselves, but rather about whose fault it was that I went to the bathroom.

"You made her go in there!" John said, almost crying.

"I did not! It was Anthony's fault!" Joey yelled as something large hit the door.

I sure was getting my money's worth from this radio. While turning the dial, I thought about how I should probably pick out a station that the neighbors might enjoy. The radio's volume was at its highest and there was no doubt in my mind that the people in the apartment building next door could hear it. I chose some elevator music, hoping it will be the least annoying as it echoed between the buildings. I had to chuckle when I thought how crazy this whole situation would look to someone else.

It will get worse before it gets better. That statement was beginning to get on my nerves. Especially since, so far, it was the truth. Besides that, tomorrow was Saturday. The kids would be at home all day long. I knew I'd be on one side of the bathroom door—the kids on the other. I could feel it coming.

With the coast clear once again, I headed out into the hallway. They had not done too much damage. There were a couple pictures off the wall. Those cheap frames from the dime store were falling apart anyway. I picked up the pieces. I noticed a few nicks in the bathroom door. Before, these marks might have bothered me. But not anymore. I leaned back against the wall and slid down to the floor as I stared at the wall covered with pictures of their smiling faces. All those snapshots I had taken, capturing their inner spirit. These pictures filled the entire wall, like a star-filled sky in the summer. This was my favorite spot in the whole house. I would have traded a million marks on the doors for what I felt at that moment. The whole world looked different. I felt drained, but deep inside I knew I had the world in my hands. I had knowledge. And I knew what to do with it. Carefully, I pushed the picture frames back together with my thumbs and hung them back on the wall.

Saturday was the big day for TV. It was my third day of training and again

I awoke to the sound of screaming and fighting—thunder and lighting right inside my home. My first few hours were spent going in and out of the bathroom. My trips to the bathroom now numbered nearly a million, or that's how it felt, anyway. I had probably set some sort of record, I laughed to myself. With the lid down, I sat on the toilet and listened. Now the only thing I could hear was the TV. I knew they were down there with their faces plastered to the screen. It was 11 a.m. Humming the last song I heard before turning off the radio, I again left the bathroom. I pulled on my gray sweatshirt, swearing (as I did each day) that if I didn't get rid of it soon, I'd throw up. But new clothes were not a part of my near future and the gray sweatshirt couldn't be tossed yet. I headed downstairs.

I was tired, but it was not the same level of exhaustion I'd felt before learning to stop my incessant lecturing. I was in charge now, wasn't I? I took a deep breath and walked quietly into the den.

"Time to turn off the TV, you guys." My voice was soft but matter-of-fact.

Total silence. Not one body moved. I curled my hair around my ear, trying to act casual.

"Hey guys, it's time to turn the TV off." I wanted my voice to sound calm and firm. I shifted feet, still messing with my hair. They did not answer, acting as if they did not hear me. Then, after a long silence came, "do we have to, Mommy?"

"Yes, it's time." My voice was definitely not as calm as I wanted it to be, and I knew it. And if I knew it, didn't they know it too? My thoughts were interrupted by another question.

"Can't we just see the rest of this?" Maria, Joey, John, and Anthony all asked in unison. Christopher listened silently and watched. He was taking it all in.

"How much longer is it?" I asked, hesitating.

"Just until 11:30. Fifteen more minutes. Please, Mommy?" John and Maria were begging. Those two always stuck together.

"Okay. But that's it then," my voice sounded shaky.

John must have sensed the doubt in my voice and began shouting about how all his friends got to watch TV, while he, along with his sister and brothers, didn't get to do anything. "You think you are the boss of everything. We can't ever do nothing around here," he shouted at me as he glared and stomped his feet. He was waving his arms, his face red with frustration.

I was not going to answer his charges and get into a shouting match with him but I hated it when I heard those words: "the boss of everything." This was not the first time John had called me that. He had to know I hated it. He always challenged me. He kept walking a fine line, saying stuff that the others were afraid to say. At least I think they were afraid to say stuff like that to me. I ran my fingers through my hair again, hoping I still appeared casual. I had to wait a minute to make sure I wouldn't sound angry. I hoped the right words would come out.

"Well, that will surely change when we start having our meetings every week, sweetheart." I was sincere, although I did want to slap him for screaming at me the way he did. Sometimes I wondered if they got away with murder like my mother and sister always said my kids did. Things would be easier after we started our weekly meetings, I assured myself. After all, it had been less than a week since I'd started all this training. And, I thought, it would probably take at least a month or two to get things in order and running smoothly. Democracy took time. True democracy I meant, not just the word that everyone throws around casually. Learning how to be respectful to children without them taking over and walking all over me. "Learning how to be the leader while not being the boss. Now that was a challenge," I said out loud. Being kind and at the same time being firm. I'd have to learn about mutual respect that Roslyn had talked about with me. It sounded easy but I knew it wasn't. John would keep me practicing that part, that's for sure.

I rubbed my nose to cover my smile as I turned around and walked into the kitchen. Of course, I was sure they had me all figured out, anyway. Maybe that's what Dreikurs meant when he said he wanted to train me to be a "match" for them. It was obvious that they were much quicker than I was. Dreikurs was a genius.

I rolled my sleeves up and started washing the dishes. Fifteen minutes passed unnoticed. It was time to shut off the TV. I was beginning to dread the rest of this day. I hated to be a clock-watcher and policeman, but I knew I had to back up my words by following through with firm actions. I wished this moment were over; the novelty had worn off.

You have a whole group against you...You can win them over to your side...It will get worse before it gets better. Over and over I heard his words in my head. It gave me strength as I struggled to hang onto the courage I had felt two nights before. How could something that sounded so simple and made so much common sense be so difficult?

"Please turn the TV off now," I said, wiping my wet hands on the dishtowel. I was standing in the wide doorway, physically between the kitchen and the den but mentally I was standing between peace and war.

"Cut it out!" Anthony screamed as he jumped up in front of the TV.

"You started it!" Joey screamed back. He, too, jumped to his feet but lost his balance and fell onto Maria.

"Gimme that, you bully! It's mine!" John screamed louder than usual as he backed into the corner, trying to give himself more protection from his older brother.

"It's not yours! Give it to me," Joey raised his shoulders and made his little hands into fists. He was going to win again.

It was routine now. One, the kids started to fight. Two, I went into the bathroom immediately and locked the door. Three, I turned on the radio, loudly. No hesitation. No longer waiting briefly to see if it was really going to be a fight. It always was. This was no fairy tale. This was real. My kids fought over everything. And I learned that the fighting was for my attention and not really for the toy or disagreement. It made sense to me now.

I had lots of work to do after I got this training down. But I could do it and by gosh I was gonna do it. This was what I had to do to break the cycle of abuse. There was no other way. It wouldn't be easy but it was what I've said I wanted to do all my life. Now I had the tools to do it. What could be better than that? Nothing that I could imagine. This had been my life dream, to do it differently and effectively better. This thought made me excited on this inside like nothing else I had experienced. I would not raise *normal children who are not adjusted* as Dreikurs said that night.

I put the dishtowel on the kitchen cabinet, turned the water off, took another deep breath, and started towards the stairs. Inside my head, I said over and over: "I'm training my children. I must do this to train my children." It kept me going. I was sick and tired of going to the bathroom after these three days, which had felt like years. Days, hours, minutes—they all ran together.

The kids were pushing and screaming as John continued to yell, "You're making her go to the bathroom!"

Maria was crying. Anthony and Joey were hitting and calling each other names. Little Christopher just watched. In less than a minute, I was in the bathroom. Lucky for me, it could be reached quickly from anywhere in our small house. There was this slow bam, bam, bam at the door, but wait...it was not as loud or powerful as it had been, was it? And it stopped quickly—almost as quickly as it started. A fist hammered once and then that stopped, too. Someone threw something once. I climbed onto the rim of the tub to get a look out the tiny bathroom window and saw someone going into the building next door. I wondered what they thought when they heard the radio blaring. I looked around some more. It was a warm, sunny day. The children were never inside sunny days, but today I was doing training and knew that none of us would be seeing much of the outdoors.

Maybe the worst was over. There was a change, but I wasn't confident enough yet to say it was over. Besides, I thought the same thing yesterday. There wasn't much I was sure of, although I knew I was no longer involved when the children fought. And I knew I had cut my lectures to a minimum. My sermons were at an all-time low. Except for a couple times when I fell back into my mini-sermon sessions, I left when the fights began. They were still fighting as loudly as before, but the fights were over in seconds, literally. By the time I would get to the top of the stairs, there were a few "Shhhhhhhhs!" and then silence. My actions were powerful. They fought and I was gone. I was gone and the fighting stopped. It sounded so simple, even if it wasn't, and it made so much sense. All these years I had done exactly what my mother had done with me—I talked, preached, threatened, bribed, and punished. I never liked doing all that, but I didn't know anything else to do. I began to wonder, though, was this the answer? I was wishing I had someone to talk to—someone over the age of eleven.

After opening the door a tiny crack, I listened. They must have gone down to the basement because I couldn't hear a sound. I went and flopped across my bed for a minute, exhausted but still able to laugh a little. Then, before letting go completely, I heard noises again. Yep, they were coming up from the basement. It sounded like a whole army.

A parade, I thought. They had pots and pans for instruments. Yelling and screaming, they stomped up the stairs to the first floor. They paraded through the hall and started up the stairs to the second floor, where I was. It was time to retreat again and I got up off the bed; it wasn't over. I locked the bathroom door just in time. John and Anthony were crying. I turned on the radio.

"Mommy, come out and see our parade!"

"Oh, don't bother. *She doesn't care.*"

That phrase used to cut into me like a knife, but now I understood it. The fighting wouldn't last long. That much I knew. And it didn't. It stopped almost as quickly as it started. I was free! I was no longer a slave! I wanted to shout out the window and let everyone know about the wonderful discovery I had made. After all those years of all that fighting! Over! It was late Saturday afternoon and I was still alive. It was quiet downstairs. They were talking so softly that I could barely hear them. I stretched out again on my bed and giggled like a little kid.

I must have fallen asleep because when I opened my eyes, it was dark. I went downstairs to find the children were still quiet. The TV was on but very quietly. They had set the table, pulled out the napkins, fixed drinks, made bologna sandwiches, put out carrot sticks, and dished up some jello. It felt different—like some kind of breakthrough—but I swore to myself that if anyone made one peep or lifted one finger and started a fight, I would leave and not come back down for the rest of the night. They knew and I knew. And they knew that I knew.

I believed the worst was over. Three days of "using the bathroom properly." Three days of training. Three days of *hell*. Three days of tears, laughter, craziness, and courage. I loved my radio but really didn't want to spend the rest of my life in the bathroom listening to it. And now I knew I didn't have to.

I sat with the kids on the floor in the den and we ate the makeshift dinner they had prepared. There were no pushes or shoves. No one picked on anyone else. No little feet "slipped" or "accidently" kicked another foot. No one complained that someone else got more than they did. No one took anyone else's place. As I sat there with my children even the air felt peaceful. My children had stopped fighting. Was this a miracle? Would it last? I didn't know the answers to those questions, but I now had my feelings of hope and courage. I had learned why my children were fighting, and more importantly, how to end it. I had learned what I heard my daddy say: "It's a law of nature, what we feed grows." I had learned that *when I changed my reaction, my children changed their behavior.* I was the center of it all. And while they are young, I was the one responsible for how they behaved. I was the one who had to do the training. "It's me, it's me, it's me," I kept saying over and over, talking to myself. The kids glanced at me for a moment and then looked back at the TV. Obviously it was taking me some time for this all to sink in. "It's me!!!!" I said again out loud!

The next morning, I awoke to silence. I felt like calling the newspaper! There was actual peace in our home! I just wanted to share this with somebody!

Morning passed quickly. Downstairs some of the kids had breakfast and some didn't, but there was no fighting. I just waited for something to break or someone to scream. It didn't happen. I was elated.

"Let's get ready for church," I said, wiping the kitchen cabinet.

What a wonderful feeling. The last three days had left me feeling more dazed and more excited than anything I had ever experienced. I was in charge of me and it felt great. If the strength and courage I felt could be bottled, I could make a fortune.

After lots of donuts and visits with friends at church, we arrived back home. I was ready to relax, but soon realized that was a silly thought. As I went into the kitchen, John began teasing someone. I didn't see who was involved, nor did I need to. I turned around and started towards the stairs. I was halfway through the den when Maria began to plead.

"Don't go, don't go, please, Mommy, don't go!"

I didn't bat an eyelash as I walked up the stairs, slowly this time. I was only going through the motions. There were no screams. In fact, it was so quiet you could've heard a pin drop. It was over. I went into the bathroom, closed the door, and turned on the radio. There was no fighting outside the bathroom door. I went to the bathroom on principle that time. I passed the test. Who would have believed this?

Sunday was our designated family meeting day. I was ready. There were other bridges to cross. I sat down on the living room floor with all the kids. The whole idea of us having a family meeting at a regularly scheduled time was foreign to all of us. I didn't know how it was supposed to go. There was nothing to compare it to since we'd never had one before.

"Okay you guys," I started, "I'm going to do this locked closet thing that I told you about last week but didn't get to."

They stared at me in silence.

"From now on, after you have gone to bed for the night, I will walk through the house and pick up whatever is lying around and doesn't belong there." I stopped and looked at everyone, waiting for a response.

Silence.

I folded my legs under me and continued, "So I won't be nagging you to pick up your things and put them away anymore, okay?"

"Okay," they mumbled. They continued to stare at me blankly.

"So, no matter what the belongings are, if they are left out in the general areas of the house on the first floor, they will be put into the locked closet. You will not get them back until the end of the week." I stopped for a second time, waiting for their response.

"Gollllll...." John finally said as he shifted his position on the floor.

"Gollllll what, John? What do you want to say?" My whole body leaned forward as if to pull more words out of him.

"Never mind," he leaned back and did not look at me.

"No, tell me," I pleaded.

"Naw, never mind," he said, looking at Anthony.

"Well, okay then. Does everyone understand what I've said? I won't be preaching anymore or punishing either. I'm just going to do my job and pick up stuff if it's left around." I looked at each of them.

"We understand, Mom. How many times are you going to say it?" Maria said. She was irritated.

"Okay, I won't say it anymore." I guess I expected more of a response. I hoped that they believed me. No one else had anything else to say so that ended our meeting.

After stories and back rubs that night, I went downstairs for my quiet evening and sanity-saving time. Tonight I would start the second step of my training program. I took a big green garbage bag from under the sink and started through the house. I filled it completely. It almost seemed as if there were more things around than ever before. I jammed the bag into my closet and locked the door. I couldn't begin to imagine what would happen in the morning.

The sun was shining and it was unusually quiet that next morning. The calm before the storm? I was nervous. I had no idea what to expect, not that I could ever know what to expect with five little children on any given day. I was in the kitchen making hot cereal when I heard them.

"Maria, did you see my folder?" John questioned.

"Joey, did you see my reader?" It was Maria's voice.

"Anthony, did you take my sweater?" Joey asked, perplexed.

"I can't find my coat!" Anthony cried.

"Where are my gym shoes? I left them right here!" John sounded like he was getting nervous.

"Where's my coat?" Joey's voice was angry now.

"Christopher, run up to my room and see if my book bag is there, please," Anthony again.

"Do you think she...?" John whispered so I couldn't hear.

Then, out of the uncharacteristic quietness came a loud question.

"Mommy! Did you happen to see my folder?!"

My heart jumped and my stomach tightened as I calmly answered, "Well, yes, as a matter of fact I did see a folder, John. Someone's folder."

"Well, do you know where it is, Mommy?" he demanded.

"I put it away, John," I said softly.

"Well, can I have it, please?" He was staring at me now. His eyes were angry and his hands were on his hips. I knew I needed a full tank of courage to finish this conversation. I needed firmness without anger. This was going to be hard, but I felt I could do it and I answered him calmly.

"Yes, John. You may have it back at the end of the week."

"OOOOOOOOOH NOOOOOOOOOOO! I need it today! NOW! For SCHOOL!" he shouted. "What about my gym shoes? I HAVE to have them."

"I'm sorry," I turned my back and looked out the window over the kitchen sink.

He grumbled and groaned and stomped out of the room screaming, "She took it! She took my folder! Can't find your book, Maria? SHE took it. Can't find your shoes, Anthony? SHE took 'em. 'Put 'em away,' she says. Ask her! See what she says! Can't find your pencils, Joey? SHE took 'em. 'Can't have them back till the end of the week,' she says. SHE put them in the locked closet. Think it's funny? Well, I'll be taking your stuff that's lying around, too, *Bossy!*" he screamed from the next room. "You think you're the boss of everything around here!"

He ranted and raved, upstairs and back down again. I had to be careful not to laugh out loud—this scene was priceless.

"WELL I'M TAKING YOUR STUFF TOO! JUST YOU WAIT! You think you can do anything around here!" John was not finished. He went into the bathroom and slammed the door.

I immediately started justifying my actions in my head: *You guys can't say I didn't warn you. I've been preaching for years...talking until I was blue in the face...everyday of my life I have picked up your things...bitching and complaining...silent and angry...but no matter what I've said...all the words have been useless.*

John came out of the bathroom as everyone else started towards the front door. It was 8:25 and the bus was waiting.

"Mommy, pleeeeeeeeeeease can I have my folder for school? I have to have it. Just this once, pleeeeeeease...? I'll never leave it out again! Pleeeeeeeease, Mommy?" I didn't answer and just stood silent, looking at the floor.

Maria waited patiently for John to finish.

"Mommy, I know I forgot last night and left my book out, but I will never do it again. None of us will ever do it again, I promise, because now we know. So please, may I have my book back now instead of at the end of the week? I need it for class. My teacher said I'm supposed to read out loud today. Me and the boys talked it over and decided that we will never do this again. We know we should put our things away without you having to tell us to. Please, Mommy, can I have it?" They all stood staring at me in silence, searching my face.

"Uh, I don't think so, Maria." My voice was sincere and strong.

"Ooooooooooh-kay! I'm leaving...come on you guys..." Maria screamed as she stomped dramatically towards the door.

Not this time, Maria, not this time. My head was clear. They began to yell at each other and I then knew it was time for me to leave. Part of me wanted to give their stuff back. I wanted to give them one more try. I wondered if I should. Maybe they had already learned. Would I really leave their things locked in the closet until the end of the week? If the kids thought this was hard on them, what about me? They probably thought I was a witch. But no, I couldn't give in now. I needed to give this a chance. I needed to test this and see if actions really did speak louder than words. I had to follow through and go to the bathroom even though I wanted to give them one more chance. I started up stairs.

"Oh nooooooooo," John said, "Now she's going to the bathroooooooooooooooom."

"Now look what has happened!" Maria cried.

It was time to turn the radio on and "use the bathroom properly."

I could hear crying and fussing in the front hallway. I held my breath, knowing that many of their clothes were missing also. Besides that, I had locked up several pairs of shoes, too. They wouldn't die without my being involved; I discovered that last week. But for sure they would now be going to school looking like little orphans without a mother. What would their teachers think of me when these kids arrived at school today? Many people in the parish were already talking about my divorce. I cringed. If I wanted to train my children though, I could not allow their opinions to influence me. I couldn't be concerned about what other people thought of me. The kids were crying as they frantically ran around helping each other find things to wear. I knew it was very cold outside—around 20 degrees. I listened from the upstairs hallway. They mumbled under their breath but they didn't fight. Instead, they were helping each other.

The bus driver blew the horn for the second time. Maria directed everyone out the door. I ran to my bedroom window to peek out. I stared in disbelief. Anthony had on Maria's old red boots and was wearing two old sweaters from

Nana that had been in some drawer for years. It was the "layered look" long before its time! Nana would've been happy to see someone finally wearing something she knitted for them. He looked as wide as he was tall and could hardly bend. Joey had white socks on his hands for gloves and a large brown corduroy shirt that had been left behind from their grandfather's last visit. John had put on that old gold coat with the fake fur around the hood that was given to Maria by her little friend. I knew he had to be fuming inside but at least he was warm. Maria had on her old navy blue Easter cape and another bulky "Nana sweater" underneath. The scarf around her neck looked like an old silk pillowslip from the dress-up box. I couldn't help laughing, though at the same time I was cringing. She was wearing my old winter boots; she must have found those in the basement. Joey was the only one with shoes of his own. No one was wearing a hat. The bus disappeared down the street with no kisses, no good-byes. I could just imagine the conversations at school.

"Where is your book, Maria?"

"I don't have it, ma'am. My mom took it last night and said I can't have it back till the end of the week."

No…surely they wouldn't say that, would they? I didn't think they would but didn't have any guarantee. Who would believe them anyway? Their mom took their books? Besides, I didn't *take* their books. They left them where they didn't belong; I just put them away. Our house was small but there were places for everything.

When they came home from school that afternoon, I felt confident that they would put all their things away and the "closet" training would be over. Leaving their things out last night was just their way of testing me to see if I really meant it. I passed this test too and was glad for it to be over. Ten days before, I couldn't have imagined successfully raising my children or keeping my sanity. I was ready for them to still be angry with me, but they came in and never said one word about what had happened that morning. Later, I heard John whispering:

"You better put that away now, Maria, or Mom will take it."

She whispered back, "I will, I will, don't nag me."

"Time for dinner," I yelled from the kitchen.

"Oh yeah! Hamburgers," Joey smacked his lips.

"And French fries, too?" John asked hopefully as he slid into a chair.

"Well, not tonight, but we have French fries sometimes, John," I said, defending my dinner.

"Not much," he said filling his plate.

I silently chuckled about what had happened this morning, knowing I had to be very careful. I didn't want them ever to think I was laughing at them. It just felt so wonderful to finally be in charge of my life. After dinner, the kids went upstairs.

"Let me know when you're all ready for bed and I'll come up for our story," I yelled.

"We're ready now, Mom," Joey yelled right back down to me.

When I went upstairs, I had to hop over all the things that had been left on the floor. I was confident that the kids would run downstairs as soon as the story was over to put their things away. After their story I kissed them goodnight, gave back rubs, and then went into my bedroom. Sure enough, I heard them run downstairs. Great, I thought, the second day of the locked closet and already they had learned. Thank goodness it wouldn't be like the bathroom scene. I was so happy that I had bit my tongue all evening and did not give any warning. But later after they were in bed I went downstairs and my mouth fell open in surprise. Their things were still everywhere. What could I do except get another garbage bag and get to work.

Into the bag went another pair of tennis shoes, two more books, a uniform tie, some markers, a truck, some blocks, a box of raisins, a scarf, a book bag, a comb, a doll, a library card, and some empty candy wrappers.

All evening I had wanted to say the very words John had whispered to Maria. "Don't forget to put your things away." I could hear the singsong, nagging, mommy voice in my head. It was extremely difficult not to remind the kids just that one last time.

I picked up every item off on the floor, from the living room to the kitchen. I wished I could just disappear for a couple of days, but this was just another test. The kids were testing me. I took the bag upstairs and locked it in the closet.

The outfits the next day were just as creative as the day before. Heavy sweaters for coats, boots for shoes, socks for gloves, a man's tie for Joey's uniform tie. Anthony, with dirt smeared across his face, chuckled at John because he was wearing Eva's old gold coat again. There wasn't much complaining that morning, but lots of amazed looks and a little lecturing.

"I told you guys to put your things away last night, didn't I?" John reminded everyone.

"Anthony, put something on your hands. We're going to be late if you boys don't hurry up. Where is my book bag?" Maria took over.

"I'll get your book bag, Maria." All her brothers worshiped the ground Maria walked on.

I overheard Joey whisper that he was going to ask me again, but Maria told him not to bother. My ears would probably be burning again today, but there was nothing I could do about it. The closet was jammed packed with all I had picked up during the week. I would be just as glad as the children when I emptied my closet at the end of the week.

I wondered what Anthony's teacher would say if she saw he had no shoes, only lots of socks inside his boots. I hoped no one from school would question me about how the kids looked because I didn't want to even attempt an explanation. There was too much other stuff on my mind. This training had been so intense that most all my energy and thoughts were spent figuring out how to back up my words with actions. At least it took my mind off the pain of divorce and my fear of continuing on alone.

On Saturday morning, ten days had passed since I learned to "use the bathroom properly" and seven days had passed since I began "the locked closet." I took the two large bags out of my closet and dumped them in the middle of the floor in the den. My five children dived into the pile and recovered the things they had lost during the week. They acted as if it were Christmas morning! The fear that I had held inside all my life was starting to dissolve. Although I knew I probably couldn't explain it rationally, I knew that unbelievable things had begun to happen inside my home, my children, and myself. Was I to become a mother *and* a woman who could think? Without having gone to college, without seeing a psychiatrist (well, yeah, Dreikurs was a psychiatrist), without a social worker, and without the approval of anyone, I had learned something I could do right inside of my home. I had always thought I was stupid. And here I was, a single woman with five little children, unafraid of trying new ideas—ideas that were not as easy as they sounded, but that were totally common sense. The excitement I felt was amazing. And above all else, I had hope! Lots of hope!!

7

Six weeks had passed since I started my training. I poured myself a Coke and lit a cigarette as I walked into the living room. The kitchen was such a mess that afternoon, I couldn't stay in there any longer than it took to pour the drink—at least not without wanting to slap a few kids very hard for letting it get so dirty. They were upstairs, supposedly having quiet time. It wasn't quiet at all, though, and I was already angry. I put down my glass on the coffee table, took the stairs two at a time, and arrived at the bedroom door in seconds. I pushed it open so hard that it crashed back against the wall, knocking plaster loose.

"Didn't I tell you that this was quiet time?!" I screamed. Was I angry about the kitchen or because "quiet time" was not quiet? I wasn't sure and I didn't care. I wasn't in any mood to let them get away with anything.

"It wasn't my fault, Mommy, it was..."

"Don't you dare blame someone else," I interrupted, feeling myself shaking already. "I'm sick and tired of you kids doing that. 'It was his fault; it was her fault; it wasn't my fault; I didn't do it.' I'm so sick of hearing it that I could puke. Blame, blame, blame! You all make me sick. Now shut up and get in your beds or I'll spank your butts good." I bent to pick up a toy and threw it into the toy box with a loud crash. I was already in tears.

The kids didn't make another peep. They got under those covers so fast their movements were blurred. I hated the sound of my own voice screaming and carrying on like that. Why had I screamed all this stuff again?

It was so easy to slip back into the old ways. The last couple of days had been filled with tiny fights, and I had let them go by without disappearing to the bathroom. I needed to make mental notes to myself again. I needed to write on the palm of my hands like I did the first couple of weeks.

Somehow I had to remember to notice the good deeds, and to thank the kids for any job or act of kindness that I noticed, I told myself. And if I didn't see something positive right away, then I needed to look for something. *Encouragement, not praise.* Don't glare at them, because even if my words say something different, they can feel my anger. I had to stop thinking about Anthony as the "cry baby." *Stop pointing out mistakes.* That was a difficult concept to understand, even though it made sense. Our whole lives are spent pointing out mistakes, especially the mistakes of our children. Can't build on weakness, only on strength. *Encourage. Encourage. Encourage. Focus on the deed, not the doer,* I talked to myself as I walked to my bedroom.

I had practically memorized the encouragement part, but it was so easy to forget. I must bite my tongue and stop the negative words, no matter how hard it was. Start each morning as a new day, just like the kids did. Don't carry stuff overnight. "If you could remember only one idea that Dreikurs taught, encouragement is the most important one," I heard someone say at the Child Guidance Center. Yes, that had to be true. I took a minute to gather my thoughts and wished I had brought my Coke upstairs with me.

I went back downstairs, picked up my glass, and took a big gulp. I had been doing so well for these few weeks with the bathroom thing. In fact, all their fighting had completely stopped for several weeks. Sure, the kitchen was a pigsty, but the fighting had ended. So why were they doing it again? What was I doing wrong? How did I get almost right back to where I was before I met Dreikurs? Well, not really that bad, but things had certainly slipped again.

I needed to talk to Roslyn. I went to the phone and dialed her number, hoping she was home. I let the phone ring several times, but no one answered. Picking up my Coke again, I walked into the living room and sipped it slowly. Okay, I needed to learn more stuff. That was clear. Things were feeling lousy again. My thoughts flip flopped. Maybe I wasn't going to be able to do this training after all.

After finishing my cigarette, I lit another and stared out the dirty windows. I wasn't sure how anyone ever had clean windows in Chicago, unless they had a maid or something. The only maid I had ever known was myself. I took a deep breath. I knew it wasn't as bad as those three days with the radio blaring in the bathroom, but the children were definitely fighting again. And I was definitely feeding that behavior by giving a little sermon and screaming here and there. I paced back and forth, puffing on my cigarette like a steam engine. I stopped at the phone and dialed Roslyn again. This time she answered.

"Roslyn, I don't know what's happened. The kids are fighting again and I'm getting mad and giving sermons. I don't know where I've gone wrong, but it's horrible. I just want to slap them all again," I stopped for a response.

She told me she was on her way out. "I'm going to the store, and then I have to pick up the boys from playschool," she said, "I'll stop by tomorrow and we'll talk."

The next afternoon when the doorbell rang I threw my arms around Roslyn, while her boys Robert and Richard raced to join the other kids in the yard.

"I don't know what's happened," I blurted out. "Why are they suddenly fighting so much again?"

As I waited for some much-needed words of wisdom, Rosalyn started out by saying, "My kids love coming here more than anywhere else. Did you know that?" she smiled at me as we sat down. "It's different here and the kids feel it. Well adults do, too, but kids are more perceptive than we are, you know." She continued, "Anyway, about the kids, it's a test. They're testing you to see if they can get away with it again. To see how far they can get. You need a 'refresher course.' As I've said before, we need to go to the Center on a regular basis."

She paused before adding, "If you start going to the bathroom again, the fighting will stop as quickly as it started."

I knew she was right.

"It won't take three days like in the beginning. I doubt if it will take more than one trip to the bathroom," Roslyn looked at me. "And have some fun. Have you guys done anything fun as a group this week? I know you read stories every night, but what about physical fun like playing something outside?"

She had a point, it had been a while since we'd gone to the beach or played at the park. It was harder in the winter.

"With the divorce and all, I know that you're upset, but you have to think of other things, too."

Things had been so intense. I didn't feel like Roslyn understood—even a little bit—what it was like in my world right now. She had a husband who supported her both emotionally and financially, and I didn't feel like getting involved in a conversation with her about divorce. I talked with Roslyn about learning and children, but not much else.

"Well, Roslyn," I said, scratching my head, "When I told the children about the locked closet, they did test me the first week to see if I would do what I said I would. When I followed my words up with actions, they learned very quickly to put their things away when they came home from school and before going to bed. In less than a week, it was routine.

"But, if I missed a night of picking things up, the next thing I knew, their things were everywhere again. It was the same way with the bathroom. If they had a fight—not counting the first three days in the beginning—and I didn't go to the bathroom right away, the fighting intensified. But if I kept my word and left immediately, the fights stopped quickly." I lit another cigarette and looked at Roslyn. I had been smoking lots of cigarettes lately and was hating myself for it.

Roslyn chimed in, "Well, I have heard Dreikurs talk about how children try things again and again, just to see if the rules still hold. You know these kids are smarter than we are; that's why Dreikurs is always saying he wants to teach parents to become a match for their children." She pulled her hair back, putting her barrette in place, as she waited for me to say something.

"I think I'm beginning to understand this stuff better. Hopefully, anyway." I laughed, and inside my head, the thoughts were racing. *So that's the way it works, they try things out again every so often and if I give it attention, the behavior grows. My attention is the fertilizer. If I don't give the behavior any attention, it will stop.* Maybe it was that simple. But then I remembered again it was silly to think that any part of this training was going to be simple.

Roslyn broke the silence. "What else is happening? What else are you doing?"

"Well, we're having a terrible time with the kitchen," I answered, shaking my head.

"How terrible is terrible?"

"Pretty terrible, I think. They sign up every week at our meetings to do jobs, but half the time they don't do them. The kitchen usually looks like a bomb has just hit it. That is, until I clean it up after they've gone to bed at night." I half laughed, half cried. "Snacks after school means a sink full of dirty dishes and glasses with milk scum. And by the time I'm through with the dishes, I've got peanut butter covering the bottom of my socks. Then there's greasy frying pans and dirty pots on the stove." My words were gaining momentum. "There's garbage piled halfway up to the ceiling with old homework papers, newspapers, cereal boxes, apple cores, milk cartons, and gooey half-cooked oatmeal, all overflowing like a water fountain. And that's only half of it."

"And how are you feeling while all this is going on?" Roslyn's lips held back a smile.

"I'm boiling mad! I want to kill them all," my voice grew louder and I felt tears welling up in my eyes. I tried to hold them back because I always felt like such a baby when I cried. But if Roslyn noticed, she didn't say anything.

"But what do you do in a time of conflict? Have you read the chapters on natural and logical consequences in *Children: the Challenge* yet?" Roslyn inquired as if she were giving me a test.

"Yes, I have," I said, becoming silent for a minute, "I've got to withdraw, I guess. Drop my end of the rope in the tug-of-war. Run away from home?" I laughed at myself as I spoke. I knew the answers in theory at least, even if I didn't act upon them.

"Running away from home isn't the answer," Roslyn chuckled and went on. "What's the most important lesson in those two chapters? Can we do any training when we're angry? Can we ever win in a fight with a child?" she was serious now.

"No, of course not. No training can be done in time of conflict," this was a lesson I'd already learned so well. "If I'm angry, it's a fight. I forget that all the time, about the anger part. Then I think I'm training them when all I'm really doing is fighting with them—with or without words. Telling them I'm the boss and trying to punish them." I paused, "But can't I be the boss just a little bit?" I laughed, "just kidding!"

Roslyn looked at me and smiled. "I understand how you feel, and I'm sure every other mother in the world understands! But that's the part we're learning. We can't be the boss. We have to lead with kindness and firmness, and it's combining those two that's really difficult."

That really was the truth, and I kept listening.

"Many people can be kind without being firm and many people can be firm without being kind but combining the two is difficult and rare. I've heard Dreikurs talk about that and it's true. So read that chapter next, okay? On kindness and firmness. Then we can talk about it."

"I'm reading the whole book. Well, trying to, anyway. All of it sounds so easy, but it's so hard."

"Don't get discouraged, Mary Cecile, this all takes time. Besides, look at how much you've already done. It's so easy to forget the positive parts because we've all been trained to notice mistakes."

I nodded; I knew she was right, and it made me feel a little bit better.

"But just as we're learning to notice the positive things about our children, we also have to learn how to notice the positive about ourselves. This is not easy for us, but we can learn it.

She stood up and grabbed her purse. "I'm sorry we can't talk longer, but we'll talk again later, okay?" she said as she opened the door and stepped out onto the porch. I followed her.

"Thanks, Roslyn. Thanks a lot." I put one arm around her, giving her a half hug, when the phone started to ring.

"You're welcome. I'll be asking you for the same help soon, I'm sure!" Roslyn motioned to Robert and Richard that it was time to go, "Let's go to the demonstration at the Center tomorrow afternoon," she called as I went back inside to answer the phone.

"Okay," I called back.

"Hello?" It was my sister Kathryn again.

"Mary Cecile, are you still getting a divorce?"

"Yeah."

"Oh, Mary Cecile what is wrong with you? What has happened to you? You are just a sick soul. You are going to go to hell and burn and you don't even care! I feel so sorry for those poor children. They have a heathen for a mother. I wish I could take those poor children away from you. Thank God Daddy is dead and doesn't have to see this. You are killing my mother...do you hear me? You'll kill her before this is over! Do you hear me missy?! You're a sick sinner and I'm ashamed to even refer to you as my sister! God will punish you. Mark my words! You'll burn in hell for this!"

Click.

Each time I put the phone back on the hook, my sister called right back to curse some more. Kathryn never gave up. The phone rang again and again. I answered it again and listened in silence.

"You are going to go to hell....you know that, don't you? The devil has you now. How disgusting you are to get a divorce from that wonderful man. Shame on you to do that to your mother and those poor little children! Those poor children, I feel so sorry for them, you nasty fool. You are going to kill your mother and when you do, don't you ever dare come to her funeral, you hear me? Shame, shame, shame on you!"

My stomach was in knots and had been for as long as I could remember. I listened until Kathryn finished and hung up on me again. I knew if I let her hang up on me that maybe she wouldn't call me back that day. Sometimes that worked and sometimes not. This was one of those days when the calls kept coming. But each time I got a call from Kathryn or Mother, it just reinforced my determination to continue with this training. Their constant tirades reminded me of the part of my life I wished I could forget.

Bedtime didn't come a minute too soon that night. After our story, backrubs were short. I went downstairs and flopped down on the couch. I wanted to practice my guitar for a while but I was too tired. My eyelids closed and, before I knew it, it was two o'clock in the morning. I rubbed my cold arms, pulled myself up, and went upstairs into bed. Tomorrow would be a better day because I was going to spend the afternoon working at St. Mark's Community Center. I always felt better when I could get out of the house to help others. And I loved spending time talking with Father Pat. We made a great team working together there. Everyone who came to St. Mark's liked my ideas and that really made me feel good. We only had two visitors that day so Father Pat and I had the time to pour our hearts and problems out to each other.

"I'll come by tomorrow if that's okay and spend time with the kids," he said. "They seem to like that."

"Actually they love it when you come and play with them. It always makes things better for a few days."

When we had our family meetings, I always visualized that perfect harmony in our family would follow because all the ideas sounded so good and made so much sense when we talked them over. The previous Sunday's meeting was a perfect example. After discussing a Sunday outing which we all happily agreed upon, we talked about the jobs around the house.

"Anthony, do you want to take out the garbage this week?" Maria asked, after I listed the jobs that needed to be done.

"I did that last week," Anthony answered with a big sigh as he looked at the floor.

"Well, what do you want to sign up for then?" Maria was getting irritated. She sounded exactly like me.

"Okay, I'll do it again." Anthony wasn't going to be to concerned about the whole thing.

The meeting continued and the kids signed up for everything that needed to be done like they always did. Signing up was the easy part. The real problems began later in the week, when someone would complain about jobs that hadn't been done.

"Alright, who wants to wash the dishes and who wants to dry and put away?" Maria was now running the meeting.

"Me and you can do it, if you want to," John answered, looking at Maria.

"Okay, me and you, John. Now what about cleaning the bathroom? Who will do that?" Maria stayed in charge.

"Isn't it your turn to do the bathroom, Anthony?"

"Mind your own business, Joey, and stop telling me what my jobs are, okay!" Anthony was irritated and made sure he spoke loudly enough for everyone in the Midwestern United States to hear.

"Well, somebody's got to tell you," Joey yelled just as loudly.

"Do I tell you what to do, Joey?" Anthony screamed, getting closer to Joey. "Why do you think you're the boss all the time?" Joey quickly grabbed Anthony's t-shirt as Anthony started pulling away. "Stop it, Joey! Mom, Joey ripped my shirt! Thanks a lot, Joey! Did you hear me, Mom?"

"I heard you, Anthony. In fact, probably everybody on the block heard you." I fell right into the argument. "Why can't you guys just do your jobs? I don't understand all these fights. Everyone agreed about which jobs they would do. Why does this have to happen all the time? I get so sick of this CRAP!"

"That's just what I was telling them upstairs, Mommy. Just exactly what I was saying," Maria answered as the second mother. I didn't like where this was going so I stormed out and went upstairs. Things just intensified downstairs. I knew I should have gone to the bathroom earlier but I couldn't pass up the temptation to straighten everything out and get everyone in line. So I went back downstairs. The words came out like bullets.

"Clean it up! Put that away! Come in this kitchen and get this awful garbage out of here! Who's supposed to do the dishes? Who's supposed to clean the table? Get in here and get these jobs done now!"

I walked into the hall, turned around and started again.

"You act just like a big bunch of babies when you get like this! I am so sick of this stuff I could puke! This kitchen is never clean! Crumbs, garbage, jelly, honey, there's always something all over the cabinets or the floor! Clean this up and then get ready for bed! I've had it with this crap! Day after day and week after week!"

Finally I shut up and went upstairs. When I got to my room, I could already hear them beginning to clean up. I felt terrible and good at the same time. I was tired of them ruling me. At least, it felt like they were ruling me again. Either I was the boss or they were the bosses. Would I ever get it right?

I turned on the radio and searched for a station with a quiet song as I picked up the phone to call St. Mark's. If Father Pat was there, I could cry to him for a while. He listened well. But he wasn't in the rectory.

Two weeks had passed since I blew up about the kitchen and I thought that if I could just get this kitchen thing straightened out once and for all, I'd feel great. At the next family meeting, I decided to give detailed instructions on how each job was to be done. I outlined my definition of clean, thinking that would probably help. Number one, all the dishes were to be done, *completely*. All the garbage needed to be taken out, *every day*. Everything on the top of the cabinets, except the toaster, napkin holder, and salt and pepper needed to be put away. The floor was to be swept. The sink needed to be scrubbed with cleanser. What was so difficult about those rules? Nothing, I thought. What was wrong with making it perfect sometimes? Maria made a separate list of all the things that needed to be done in the kitchen. Then, everyone signed up for the jobs in the kitchen separately from jobs in the rest of the house. The kitchen was a special room and it had to be kept separate, I told them.

All jobs were done on Sunday after that meeting, but by Tuesday things quickly fell apart again. I walked into the kitchen and my shoe stuck to the floor. I lifted it up and found a big glob of peanut butter on the bottom of it. I was instantly angry, although I tried to pretend I wasn't.

"Sorry, but I can't cook in a dirty kitchen." I said as I turned to exit. I was so angry I thought my insides would burst. I sure hoped it didn't show. A fight exploded in full force and I dashed for the stairs. They knew—how could I ever dream that they wouldn't know how angry I was?

Anthony started it off. "I told you we'd get in trouble if you didn't do your job! But no, you had to read your comic book first. Now we're going to get it and it's your fault!"

"Oh, shut up, you weenie, or I'll knock your block off!" Joey angrily answered his brother.

"Mommy, Joey's calling me a weenie! He's using bad words again." John started for the hallway to follow me upstairs. He ducked as a baseball mitt flew through the air at him.

"Leave him alone, Joey," John yelled.

"Shut up, you stupid jerk!" Maria screamed. She was standing in front of Christopher like a protector of the young. She glared at Joey but obviously didn't want to get hit with any flying objects. "You're going to break Mommy's lamp, you stupid idiot. Stop it!"

"Who's going to make me, Maria? You and what army?" Joey loved acting out the tough guy role.

"Will you guys cut it out before she gets really mad?" Maria commanded.

I was back downstairs in a flash. "Oh shut up, all of you! You make me sick! Clean up your mess and don't you dare use this kitchen! If I see any one of you using this kitchen tonight, I'll stuff whatever you're eating so far down your throat that you'll wish you had never seen food. Do you hear me? By God, I mean it!"

I had tears in my eyes. "And when you're finished, we need to have another meeting. No, on second thought, let's wait until Sunday. I don't feel like talking to you now anyway. I can't stand the sight of any of you at the moment. You all make me sick!"

I started back up the stairs again, convinced that soon they would be threadbare from all the trips I made up and down. I felt bad; I always did after I screamed and yelled like that. This was not the way it was supposed to be. I flopped down on my bed. Downstairs it was quiet again. I knew they were following my orders and cleaning up. By now my eyelids were heavy from crying. I gathered myself together, got up, and went back downstairs to look in my wallet. I paused for a minute and then pulled out a ten-dollar bill.

"Here's ten dollars. Maybe you guys would like to go to McDonald's or something," I walked into the kitchen, avoiding eye contact. I felt bad about neglecting their dinner.

"Uh, sure Mom, thanks," Maria answered. She fumbled as she stuffed the ten dollars into her pocket.

"You mean we can go to McDonald's to eat, right?" John asked with amazement on his face.

"Yes, as soon as you all finish cleaning up this kitchen, you can go to McDonald's for dinner," I knew this all sounded silly. The only consequence they suffered from not having cleaned the kitchen was getting to go to McDonald's.

"Thanks, Mommy." They were holding back their smiles.

I went back upstairs into my bedroom and looked at myself in the mirror .

"You're nuts!" I said to my reflection, "Totally nuts!" But tomorrow was another day. A chance to start over again.

Later, when I told Roslyn the story about the kitchen and McDonald's, Roslyn laughed her head off.

"You sure are a *good* mother, Mary Cecile," she teased.

My weekly phone call to my lawyer was the same as all the earlier ones.

"I'm sorry Mrs. Carlotti, but we were unable to reach your husband's lawyer this week. These things take time. Our hands are tied about getting you more money for the children." I had those words memorized after hearing them for several months. I hung up the phone.

Another week, another Sunday, and another meeting brought more long faces. It wasn't that we didn't skip the meetings sometimes, because we did. Though they were more regular now than they had been in the beginning. One by one everyone silently walked into the living room. I was sitting on the couch and already on the verge of tears.

"So what do we want to talk about first?" I was looking down at the rug. I swore to myself that I wouldn't start off complaining.

"What do you want to talk about, Mommy?" Joey asked, pretending as if everyone didn't know.

"What do I ever talk about besides the kitchen?"

Everyone looked at each other. Silence.

I continued, "I really don't know what to do anymore. Obviously I can't make you clean up the kitchen. I try, but it doesn't work. I yell and scream and forbid you to use it, and then I give you money to go to McDonald's." I was trying to hold back my tears.

"But, Mom, that's okay, we didn't mind." Anthony was half-teasing. Everyone laughed at his remark—even me. I wiped my nose and started again.

"I don't even know why we have these meetings anymore. All I do is complain while you guys sign up for jobs, say you'll do them, and then don't. I'm so sick of all of this. Sometimes I wish we didn't have a kitchen. You know, Grandmother is always telling me what a mess I am with you kids. Maybe I am. Maybe she's right. I just don't know anymore. I don't have any answers. And with this divorce thing going on...it's just really hard. That's all I've got to say. It's just really hard." I wanted to go on and on with a few more thousand words, but I stopped myself. "What are we going to do for fun this week, if anything?" I attempted to change the subject.

"Mommy, we'll do our jobs this week. I promise." Anthony looked at me.

"Yes, we will. Anthony's right, Mommy. We will. Things are going to change around here, you'll see," Maria said, "Don't cry."

They all assured me again that things would change. And I always believed them.

"Mommy, I know that we didn't do our jobs well this week. I know I've slacked off." Anthony sounded so sincere and with that angel face, who wouldn't believe him?

"Oh sure, you say you've slacked *this* week," John challenged his brother. "You never do your jobs at all. I usually end up doing them for you."

"Yes, I know you did this week, John. You're so perfect." Anthony answered hoping to knock his brother off of his high horse.

"Are you guys going to start fighting now?" I couldn't keep my mouth shut. Keeping my mouth shut might prove to be the hardest part of all this training.

"God, can't we ever say anything? We're not fighting." John said in a superior tone.

Sometimes our meetings were awful. They were a place where no one wanted to be, and yet no one would ever miss them. Besides, if someone wasn't there, they'd be signed up for jobs that no one else wanted. The phone rang again, prematurely ending our meeting.

"Mary Cecile, did you hang up on your sister yesterday?"

"Hi Mother."

"I asked you a question, young lady. Did you hang up on your sister?

"Well I..."

"What has happened to you to act this way towards your own flesh and blood? You'll put me in my grave sooner than you think. My time is getting short, Mary Cecile. And you know your sister's not well, but she's right about church. You need to get yourself a good check-up by a good doctor and get yourself to confession and get yourself straightened out. The devil's got hold of you good. I don't know what it will take to get you back on track. Are you still determined to get that divorce?"

"Yes, Mother I..."

"Then you need to pull yourself together ...pack up those children and come down here to Perryville to live out your life like a respectable mother." Click.

Roslyn and I attended the bi-monthly sessions at the Child Guidance Center together now. It always proved to be helpful. It was the place where we had met Dreikurs, and later where we met Meg. She had studied under Dreikurs, and it showed. Meg had become the regular counselor. Roslyn and I found her to be an encouraging and wonderful teacher. Soon I signed up once again to be the demonstration family—I really needed some help about this kitchen thing.

After eight long weeks of waiting, I finally got my turn to go back under the bright lights of that stage in front of the audience for a conversation with Meg.

"We have family meetings almost regularly, but it seems like I am the only one that ever talks," I started. "The kids promise every week that they will do their chores. Sometimes they follow through, but lots of times they don't. And when they don't, it usually involves the kitchen. The kitchen has forever been a battleground, it seems. I'm always complaining about it."

"The children's behavior will change or will reoccur depending on how you deal with it. Exactly what is happening in the kitchen?" Meg asked.

"I get angry when they clean it only halfway," I started. "Last week I stopped going to the store! I didn't buy any more peanut butter! I locked up the food that was left and pretended it was all gone. They knew I was angry. I pretended we just ran out of food, but I'm sure they knew it was a punishment, even though I tried to disguise it as a consequence."

"How did you feel when you were doing this?" Meg asked.

"Angry! I thought to myself, 'I'll show you whose the boss around here,'" I answered truthfully. "Last month, when they started to descend upon the kitchen, I stopped them in their tracks. 'Sorry, the kitchen is closed' I said.

'Too dirty to eat in it today and I haven't gone shopping anyway.' They left quietly without saying much of anything. They just accepted it. Then, after I thought about what I had said to them, I felt so bad that after they cleaned the kitchen I gave them ten dollars and told them to go to McDonald's. Tell me, does that make sense? I forbid them to use the kitchen and then give them money to go to McDonald's?" I laughed. Meg smiled at me.

"Making sense is not the issue here. The problem is in your thinking you can be the boss rather than training your children to cooperate," Meg spoke softly and leaned closer to me, "But we both know you cannot win in a fight with your children. So what must you do now?" Meg waited for me to answer. "Can you train them when you are angry?"

The audience leaned forward in anticipation of my answer. It was so quiet that you could almost hear the cigarette smoke come out of people's mouths. I looked out to the audience to see if someone might help me with the answer. A lady in a blue coat that I had seen before at the Center before was waving her hand in the back. Meg was not going to call upon her, I could tell. The woman in the back lowered her hand down and grumbled under her breath loudly enough that everyone heard her. Laughter came from the next room where all the kids were in childcare. I leaned back in my chair and clasped my hands on top of my head as I responded to Meg's question. "I must not get into a fight, that's for sure. Drop my end of the rope, I guess, and not get angry." I sounded as if I had done this training my whole life and was now telling others how to do it. I knew the answers, but knowing and doing were two different things.

"Yes, not get angry, but what else? What else can you do?" Meg didn't let me off easy.

"I'm supposed to go about my business and not say a word. When anyone asks me about dinner, I very casually say, 'I can't cook in a dirty kitchen,' and leave it at that. I can even go out to dinner with a friend if I want to, but I am not to act in anger." I paused. "Well, I do say the correct words, but I'm so angry when it happens."

"And why do you think you are so angry?" Meg smiled.

"Probably because I want to be the boss," I laughed because I began feeling embarrassed. "Isn't that it?" I couldn't help laughing at myself again because once I'd said it out loud; I saw the humor in it all. "I'm embarrassed," I said, "I feel so silly."

Meg turned to the audience. "Is there anyone here who has done the exact same thing that we hear Mary telling us tonight? Has anyone here tonight made these same mistakes with their children? If you have, please raise your hands." Meg shifted her body and looked into the audience.

There was an overwhelming show of hands. It looked like almost every person raised their hand and smiled. "See, everyone here understands exactly what you are doing because they have all done it themselves. Everyone here knows how you feel. Am I correct?" Meg turned again to the audience.

"Yes." The audience responded loudly.

Then Meg moved her body around so she could look straight at me.

"Can you be the boss with children?" she asked. "Is this possible today?"

"No, I can't be the boss. No parent can anymore, but it seems like I just keep trying. You would think I had learned by now. But I still get so frustrated I can't even tell you." I felt myself wanting to cry, but I bit my lip and held back the tears.

"When you want to train the children how to use the kitchen and clean up afterwards, you have to be in a training frame of mind. You must also be willing to let the kitchen become a mess for as long as it takes. Remember that you are training your children. In order for logical consequences to work and be effective, there can be no anger. When you are willing to allow everything to fall apart without concern or anger, then the training will begin. It would not take too long—probably less than a week. It is your attitude on the inside that is most important. I believe you already know this."

"Yes, I do know it." I felt a tremendous relief at being able to say it out loud to people who understood—people who were making the exact same mistakes as I was.

"I'm sure you do. But what you are learning is very difficult, as you have already discovered. I believe that once you concentrate on this one area, you will train your children about the kitchen the same way you trained them about the fighting. Weren't you ready to lose your mind from all their fighting? Isn't that what you told Dr. Dreikurs the night he worked with you?"

"Yes, it is." I smiled, remembering that wonderful night.

"You have done so well. You have won your children over in some very important areas already. They no longer fight, isn't that right?" Meg's voice showed strength and respect.

"Very seldom." I shook my head in amazement, remembering how the children used to wake me each morning with horrible fights. It was amazing how much the children's behavior had changed because I had changed my behavior.

"And if they do fight, do you know what to do?" Meg wanted me to give myself some credit.

"Yes, I do."

"And it didn't take you very long to train your children about fighting. Be pleased with your successes and stop being so hard on yourself with your mistakes. You have a wonderful group of children. When you are ready to train them in the kitchen, you will do so. It will happen when you decide that you no longer want to be the boss and when you no longer act in anger."

"I know you're right. I'll go home and start again." I felt great relief hope, and was ready to start over again.

"I'm sure you will." Meg smiled at me with confidence. "And continue to come to the Center. Listening to the other parents can be as helpful to you as you and I talking this way with each other." Meg stood and held my hand in hers.

"Yes, two weeks ago when I listened to the mother on stage, I could have sworn it was me. Her problems were the same as mine. Even her mistakes were the same as mine."

"Exactly! That's the idea. Keep coming."

I left, feeling relieved and inspired. Just being able to talk out loud to someone about everything made me feel better.

I talked to the kids about the kitchen and together we decided to work on our conflicts. I was calm and had no anger. The next week, everything went pretty smoothly. I believed that, at last, the kitchen problems were on their way to being resolved. I also realized that I needed to talk about this training with other people, other parents, to keep myself on track. Talking with Roslyn every once in a while was just not enough.

8

I went after all the mothers in the neighborhood with a vengeance, telling each and every one of them about Dreikurs' book and some of the things I had learned. I invited them to meet each week at my house so that we could all study together.

About six mothers came that first night. After everyone helped themselves to something to drink, we sat in my living room, talking and sharing our experiences, frustrations, and concerns. There was no way I wasn't going to tell them about my discoveries. Besides, it was exactly what Dreikurs himself had told me to do on that famous night— *Gather the mothers in your neighborhood and get them together. Tell them that you must study with each other and help each other. You can do it!*

I was excited because they were interested in what I had to say and wanted to hear more. We even planned to meet again next week, after everyone had a chance to buy Dreikurs' book.

After it was over, I was still sitting in the living room, so wrapped up in my thoughts that I didn't even notice Joey standing next to me until he began to speak.

"Are they going to go to the bathroom if their kids fight?" Joey asked as he pushed his glasses back up on his nose. It seemed he was forever doing that. I knew he hated that patch on his eye.

"Maybe," I answered. Daddy always had said, "Those Carlotti kids sure didn't miss a trick." He had been right on the mark.

"I'll bet they don't do it to their kids. I'll bet Edith won't go to the bathroom." It was John yelling from the den. "We never do things like the other kids do in their houses. We always have to be weird."

I hadn't known that John and Joey, or anyone else, had been listening to our meeting. I decided not to answer to what sounded like a challenge.

After that first successful evening, I was pleased with the outcome of my efforts because soon there were some moms who began to come regularly. They questioned me constantly. Sometimes it felt like they thought I was the expert when actually I was in the same boat with them. Edith, however, a mother with two children the same ages as two of my own, started ringing the doorbell each and every weekday morning with a crisis.

The routine was always the same. Edith rushed in, a package of cigarettes in hand and a long lit one hanging out of her mouth. The ashes hit her chest before they tumbled onto the floor. Not that she had a big chest—it was just the angle of the cigarette as it hung there on that moist spot on her bottom lip.

"You've got to help me with this one," she said as she flopped down dramatically on the kitchen chair, letting her arms dangle limp from her sides as if she had no control over them. "I don't know what I'm going to do now," she took a deep drag on her cigarette.

"I'll get coffee," I was being nice as usual, but begrudging it inside.

"It's the fighting," she said as she took another deep drag on her cigarette. It seemed like the whole cigarette would turn into ashes. "I just can't take it anymore. Honestly, Mary, I just can't. I'm getting too old for this stuff," she laughed about the reference to her age.

I didn't even respond to that remark because somehow I knew, we both knew, that she could and would take it forever, if need be. I believed that she actually preferred complaining to learning something new. She needed someone to gripe to whereas I needed someone to talk through ideas. Someone over the age of ten. It definitely helped when I could talk. And even though I still had Roslyn, I felt like the more I talked about it out loud with someone else, the easier it would be to make it all work. And hopefully it would continue to make a difference in our lives. Plus, talking a little every day was even better than just once a week with the study group.

Then Edith began to tell me that I was able to do things differently because I didn't have a husband. I bristled. We discussed the pros and cons of it being easier without a husband. Neither of us could convince the other to change her mind. I just continued to refill my coffee cup.

"Got to quit smoking," we both mouthed the words at the same time. The overflowing ashtray that I had already cleaned four times that morning filled more than my nose and the air around me with disgust. I hated the habit.

"Edith, if we want to train our children we cannot be concerned about what others think of us. That includes husbands." I was astounded at how profound the words sounded coming out of my mouth. I realized I was always telling the other mothers what I myself needed to learn most. It was new for me to say exactly what I was thinking to someone else, rather than keep it inside.

"I still think it would be easier without a husband," Edith said it again. I refused to respond a second time.

I leaned back in my chair and stretched. "Everyone is coming to study together tonight. I hope you'll come."

"I'll try to make it if it's okay with William," Edith answered as the coffee missed her mouth and she pulled at her dress to dab it. "Got to go," she said, slamming her cup down on the table and dashing for the front door. "Thanks for the coffee and the good advice."

"I don't give advice," I laughed as I followed Edith to the door.

She waved good-bye as she bolted across the yard, only stopping to pick up her lost cigarettes that had fallen from her narrow pocket. Narrow pockets and narrow minds, I thought to myself as I closed the door. Then I told myself to stop judging people like Mother always did.

Our living room took on the character of a smoke-filled pool hall about ten minutes after all the mothers arrived, but I loved every minute of it. I loved having people come over to our house for any reason at all. That never happened when I was growing up. Mother and Daddy never had company. Never.

Everyone knew to go into the kitchen to get her own coffee, tea, or another clean ashtray. The six-foot-long coffee table looked like a day-old battlefield with all the ashes spilling over in a few short minutes. Copies of *Children: the Challenge* were everywhere. Edith always started the conversation with a very dramatic opening statement and tonight was no exception. "I've had it for sure this time." The smoke circled her head slowly as she spoke and everyone else leaned back in their chairs knowing this could take a while. The discussion was endless and no matter what suggestion or idea someone came up with, Edith had an excuse. "Oh no, William would kill me if I did that," was one of her favorites. It felt like a griping session now and looking at the faces and the rolling of eyes, I knew it was time to move on.

"Are these kids returnable?" I blurted out.

Laughter filled the room and broke the mood. I was relieved. "If not, we better study instead of griping so much." I couldn't believe those words came out of my mouth either and stared down at the floor. But at the same moment everyone agreed that they did not want this to be a griping session either. We decided upon reading chapters three, eleven, and twenty-six for next week. We weren't reading the book straight through but instead picked out a variety of chapters each week. It was something I had picked up from the Child Guidance Center. Dreikurs' book could be useful in whatever order you felt comfortable with.

I really didn't have a clue about how to keep these mothers on track, but I knew I always learned something each week. The support of everyone was invaluable. Knowing that everyone had the same difficulties and problems with their kids formed an unbelievable bond.

We heard little footsteps upstairs from time to time. One mother reported that a couple of kids had been sitting on the stairs the whole evening, listening. John and Anthony she thought, but wasn't sure. The children had been as quiet as mice the entire time. That seemed to prove something, at least that they weren't fighting.

I was excited by the fact that all the mothers agreed to continue meeting weekly. They promised faithfully to read the material so that they could move past the gripes and into learning and understanding. I knew I definitely wanted to learn more. I couldn't get enough.

"But have your kids really stopped fighting, Mary?" The question was full of doubt and I could only stare at Edith.

"Yes, they have really stopped fighting. Why wouldn't I tell you the truth? Do you think I could lie about that anyway? You're here almost everyday, what do you think?" I didn't care if the irritation showed in my voice. I put my book down and stood up.

"I know. I just want my kids to stop, too." Edith said as she sighed with her feel-sorry-for-me tone. No one paid her any attention and the meeting ended quietly.

Later that night the doorbell rang. When I went to answer it, both Father Pat and my soon-to-be-ex-husband Joe were standing on the front porch under the light. I hadn't been expecting either one of them, and wondered what on earth they were doing there together. Joe was smoking and glaring. He grabbed the handle, jerked that door open, and stormed past me and into the den.

He started searching frantically through our bookcase. Books fell all over the floor, banging as they landed. I had no idea what he was looking for or whether he even found it, but finally he stormed past me again, shouting as he stepped onto the porch, "Don't you think I know what's going on here?"

We stood there staring at him until it dawned on me that he thought Father Pat and I were having an affair. I didn't say a word, I was too much in shock. There was nothing I could say that would have made any difference anyway.

A couple days later, I found out from Frank Wulk—the man Joe was staying with—that Joe had a gun stored in that bookcase, and that later Frank had walked in on Joe pointing the gun at his own head. Frank said he caught him "just in time." I wasn't sure I actually believed the whole story, though. I had witnessed Joe being pretty dramatic at times when he was angry.

It was true that I had been talking with Father Pat almost every day. He came over many afternoons and spent time with the kids and me. He was a good friend. I knew this began to cause a great amount of gossip among the parishioners at church, but decided not to allow that to alter my friendship with him. He always listened to me and supported my decisions. I knew he loved the kids and thought they were very special, too. He was one person I could really count on.

I also listened to him talk about his unhappiness with his life and his church. He told me things he had never told anyone, he said. I made no judgments about him and I could make him laugh, something that seemed rare in his life.

We were good at being able to help each other, I thought. This made me very happy, and it made Father Pat happy, too. One day he said to me, "I wish you were single and I wasn't a priest." I wanted to tell him I wished the same thing, but could only think of my Daddy's words: "Wish in one hand, honey, and spit in the other, and see which gets full first."

9

Some days, the kids just played and played and played, and I never heard a complaint out of anyone. The good days were so good that it seemed impossible that there were days when I couldn't stand any of them—like the days when I thought the world would end over a dirty kitchen. I was a bitchy perfectionist about the kitchen and that was the only way to explain it.

Today had been one of those good days. It was a beautiful summer day and I wished the kids were playing outside, but they had some really good game going on down in the basement and I wasn't going to complain. I never disturbed them when they got into a good game. It was so peaceful. Many a time I sat at the top of the stairs and listened to them as they played and laughed, without them ever knowing. How wonderful they all were when their creativity was unleashed: it was limitless. And those great laughs.

But when they played house, I would still cringe when I heard Maria being the mommy. I didn't like what she had learned from me; I hoped I was changing. Hearing Maria use my tone of voice and my words pushed me on to learn more like nothing else.

I began to feel it in my gut that perhaps today they were just a little too quiet. I listened from the kitchen. Yes, they had been too quiet for too long a time. I should check. I dried my hands on the dishtowel and walked to the door leading down to the basement and listened. I listened closely but couldn't make out the muffled words. Then came a loud "Shhhh!" Again and again. "Shhhhhhh!" and then stomping. Stomping of little feet. More "Shhhhhhhhhhhh!" Something was going on. I flew down the basement stairs, my heart beating fast.

"Mommy's coming," John whispered loudly.

"You stupid idiot! See what you've done?" Anthony's voice sounded full of fear.

"Somebody better tell Mommy." John was definitely scared.

"Boy, you guys are going to get it now," a panicked Maria whispered.

"Shut up and keep stomping," Joey was trying to sound tough, but his voice quivered.

I shouted nervously as I reached the bottom steps. "What's going on down here?" my voice cracked, and suddenly I saw smoke. Little ghost white faces stared at me from all sides. I screamed hysterically.

"What in the hell do you think you're doing? Trying to burn us all up?" The evidence was there —the book of matches and the smoldering spot where had managed to stomp out the fire. "Do you want to burn this place down? Do you want us all to die?" My words came out like bullets from a machine gun.

Joey looked up at me, the tears streaming down his face from under those thick Coke-bottle glasses. His eye patch was dirty and wet.

"Answer me!" I screamed. "Somebody answer me! What happened here? Tell me now!"

"It wasn't our fault!" they all cried at once. They began telling on each other, blaming everything mostly on Joey, and trying to prove their innocence.

"Every day we read stories about children playing with matches and burning themselves up. Why would you do this? This is crazy! We could have all been burnt up! Is that what you wanted to happen? What's wrong with you? You're acting so stupid. We could've all been burnt up! We could've all been burnt up!"

I couldn't stop the words, the tears, the fear. The kids stood in silence and didn't move a muscle. I knew I should've called someone for help but I just stooped there in the middle of the floor and threw the toys in the box.

"Oh my God, oh my God, where have I gone wrong?" I screamed it over and over and they remained like statues. My head was spinning and I felt like I was going to be sick. I didn't know where else to turn, so I ran upstairs to the phone and called the Child Guidance Center. My heart was in my throat. I belched up half of my stomach. My body was shaking.

Dialing took forever. Ringing took longer. *Oh please*, I prayed, *let someone be there! Please!* I recognized Mrs. Greenberg's voice and she knew exactly who I was from the Center. I skipped the formal greetings and immediately described what had happened in the basement, shrieking hysterically. Mrs. Greenberg interrupted me and asked if anyone had been hurt. The question startled me.

"No, no one was hurt," I said catching my breath.

She continued calmly, "You need to teach these children about the dangers of matches and how to use them properly. Have you ever given them lessons in how to strike matches safely?" Mrs. Greenberg questioned me.

She stopped me in my tracks, and I began to breathe again. "No, I haven't," I answered, "I have never even thought about it."

She then proceeded to give me explicit instructions on how to teach the kids this process.

"Most importantly, you must do this when you are in a teaching mood and feeling no anger towards the children. Then, teaching can take place. That has to be the first rule, no anger, no 'I'll show you who's boss around here' attitude. Do you understand?" Mrs. Greenberg asked.

"Yes," I answered.

"And remember, it doesn't matter which kid was actually doing the striking of the matches. You must 'put them all in the same boat,' as Dreikurs would say. They must be treated as a group and that means no singling out of the 'good guys' and the 'bad guys.' Remember, while training your children you want to always work to overcome the existing competition and its bad effects on children by putting them all in the same boat. Does that make sense to you?" She paused as my mind kept racing.

"I think so. It's like what Dreikurs said in his book, that if we treat them as a group then they will learn to take care of each other, rather than trying to get the 'bad guy' in trouble and be the 'good guy.' Now, if only I could do that," I said doubtfully.

"You can do it if you decide to train your children about the dangers of matches. Do you remember when you 'used the bathroom properly?' You were using the same concept. No one was singled out as the instigator of the fight. Everyone had to deal with the exact same consequences. And now the question is not *if* you can do it but rather *when* you decide to do it. Do you understand?"

"Yes."

"Anything else I can help you with?" Mrs. Greenberg asked.

"Not at this time, except maybe..." I hesitated, "could I say it back to you so I'm sure I understand what you said?"

"Of course," Mrs. Greenberg seemed flattered.

"Okay, so I get a big dish full of matches, sit them down at the kitchen table, have them strike matches over and over until I am sure they know how to do it properly. I show them how to close the cover before striking. I need to stay in the same room or close by while they do this; it will probably take them a while. I have them strike matches until the whole dish full is gone even if their fingers are tired and they complain and want to quit. This can only be done when I have a friendly attitude. This must not be a punishment, but a lesson. It is for everyone's life that they learn how to strike matches properly," I said each sentence slowly as I kept mental notes.

"Yes, you have it. Now you must carry it out," Mrs. Greenberg spoke firmly to me, "and stop getting hysterical in a time of crisis. This only teaches your kids to get hysterical in a time of crisis. Understand?"

"Yes, I understand it now, thank you very much." I quietly hung up the receiver. Of course Mrs. Greenberg's words made sense when I backed away from the situation and calmed down.

I took a few deep breaths, stood up, walked through the den to the stairs, and called for the children to come into the kitchen. I felt their presence as they watched me shyly from the next room. They were fearful of getting to close to me, with good reason, it turns out. I had thought I was calm, but when I heard my voice it was full of fury and fear. "Who do they think they are?" I kept mumbling under my breath. I wanted to spank them real hard.

Someone was asking, "Are you talking to us, Mommy?"

"No, I was talking to myself," I growled back. "I'm going for a walk.

Clean this kitchen while I'm gone."

They're lucky I'm not spanking them right now, I thought as I started down the street, leaving the screen door to bang in the wind.

My insides twisted as I rounded the block for the third time. Was it the third or thirtieth time? I'd lost track. I walked to the drug store to buy some matches, and finally walked down to the lake, saving the best for last. Lake Michigan, the place that had saved my sanity since I arrived in the city. Water, sand, beaches, trees, sunrises, sunsets. Waves making wonderful sounds. The lake always took my breath away.

I arrived home one hour later, this time feeling truly calm. The lake had once again relaxed me. Lake Michigan was my tranquilizer.

I entered through the back door of the kitchen, walked into the den, and greeted the kids. I relished the calmness I felt at that moment, especially after such a frightening experience earlier in the afternoon.

"Thanks for cleaning up the kitchen, you guys," I said, hanging up my coat.

"Well, they didn't help. Me and John had to do it all ourselves." Maria stood in the doorway, not even batting those long lashes as she stared at me. Her glasses were thick like Joey's and those lashes almost hung out from under them. Her long thick brown hair was pulled up from both sides of her face to the top of her head with one huge barrette. A clasp big enough to hold all of her hair was a rare find. John stood like a soldier by his sister's side. They were determined that I knew who deserved the credit for cleaning up the kitchen. I looked at Maria and gritted my teeth in order to not laugh out loud.

Was Maria really as pretty as she looked to me, or was that mother's pride taking over? Maria and John stood side by side, quietly demanding individual praise of their work. John had deferred to Maria's lead, as did all her brothers. They waited in silence.

"Thanks for cleaning the kitchen, guys," I repeated sincerely, ignoring the tattling and refusing to pit the "good" guys who did work against the "bad" guys who didn't.

"Is that all you're going to say?" Maria demanded to know.

"What else do you want me to say?" I asked innocently.

They refused to answer and both pairs of feet stomped out of the kitchen.

"It's just like when she puts those notes on the refrigerator about money missing from her wallet. We get blamed for everything even though we didn't do it," Maria was talking loudly from the next room now, for my benefit.

"It's not fair, it's just not fair and she knows it," John spoke loudly too.

I would thank them individually at some other time but right now it was most important to thank the kids as a group. I had to "put them all in the same boat" for the matches thing too, even though I was pretty sure I knew who the guilty parties were. I poured myself a Coke and sat down at the kitchen table. I then called all the kids in to join me. They came quickly, their faces full of apprehension and fear as they gathered around. I looked at each face and began speaking slowly.

"I want to talk with all of you about something really important," I began. "I have to be sure that you all know how to strike matches properly. I have to know this so I can feel more at ease—if that's possible—with the fact that you play with matches. I don't want you to play with matches, but if you insist on doing it, then at least I will know that you are able to strike them properly." My voice was calm and I felt confident inside. "Before coming home, I went by the drugstore and picked up some matches. Please sit down at the table with me so I can teach you how to strike matches properly."

My announcement was received with great surprise and happiness. Every face silently marveled: This is our punishment? What's the trick? Our friends won't believe this one. She's gone off again.

As my first-born son, Joey took the more serious role, as he tended to do quite often. He moved close to me and, to make sure he had understood, asked, "You're going to teach us to use matches and you want us to strike them now?"

"Yes, that's correct," I said as I emptied the bag from the drug store into a large mixing bowl. There were about one hundred matchbooks in that bowl and I hoped it would be enough to get my point across.

"This is the way you do it— after closing the cover," and I demonstrated the technique. Then I motioned for them to try it. With excitement and enthusiasm, they all started striking. I stood up, gave Anthony my chair, and stepped back. I busied myself at the sink, staying close but uninvolved. I wondered how this would all turn out. They talked and joked and struck matches.

Twenty minutes passed and they were convinced that they had learned their lesson. The enthusiasm had passed and it was quiet around the table.

"Can we quit now and go outside, Mommy?" Joey asked.

"Yeah, Mommy, we know how to do it now, real good. Can we stop?" John was right in there with Joey on this one. Maria and Anthony asked too. Christopher sat silently. Christopher couldn't strike the matches but was getting a lesson along with the rest.

"Oh, no, not yet," I said warmly. "You still have lots of matches to do." I looked at them lovingly.

"How much longer?" Joey asked.

"Well, I don't know how long it will take you, but you need to finish all the matches here in the bowl."

"You mean ALL these matches?" Joey's voice went up an octave.

"Yep! All those matches." I turned, walked three steps into the den, and turned on the TV. I was calm and it felt good. I knew this was going to be a good lesson because I wasn't angry but instead I was determined. The kids were very quiet again. There was not much talking or laughing.

Time passed and I was questioned once more. "Can we stop now, Mommy?" It was Joey.

I walked into the kitchen and saw that they had indeed struck a lot more matches, but the bowl was not yet empty.

"No, Joey, not yet. You still have lots of matches to strike. I have to be sure that you all can do it properly," I remained kind but firm.

But the kids insisted the lesson had gone long enough as they each assured me most definitely that they understood the dynamics and results of striking matches. I listened to their arguments.

"Mom, we know how to do it now. Can't we stop? We've done this almost two hours. We know how. Besides, our fingers hurt real bad, if you even care," Maria was definitely irritated.

It was difficult, but I stood my ground.

"I'm sorry if you're tired, but I still do not feel confident about your abilities to strike matches properly and safely. Until I feel confident in your ability, you may not quit. This is an important lesson. In fact, literally speaking, it's a matter of life and death." Playing with fire must be dealt with in that manner, I thought. I went back to the TV.

It took another hour before I honestly felt confident and consented to quitting time. And although the kids were bordering on extreme anger, there was something between us—a new feeling. Perhaps it was the foundation in love and respect that had been developing over the last couple of months. They promised never to strike matches again without an adult present.

"I am hoping, too, that you will never again play with matches but, if you insist on doing it, at least I feel like I have taught you how to do it properly." I kept going, "I can't follow you around every minute like a policeman. At this point, I have to trust that you'll never do it again." I gave each one of them a kiss and sent them out to play. They were happy because they were finally able to leave that table. I was happy because I was beginning to actually feel smart.

10

Being the only provider for a family of six was a heavy responsibility that sometimes distracted me from my training with the children. My stomach would hurt so bad sometimes that I convinced myself I must be dying and that my small children would be left to the fate of my relatives.

Summer was coming to an end and all I could think about was where I would get the money for the children to go to school in the fall. St. Mark's was a good school, an expensive school, and with us being Catholic there had never been any question about where the children would receive their education. But now there was no money in our lives, other than the $60 per week from Joe. It had become quite evident in the several months since he moved out of the house that he would no longer help with the food situation, either. No more sharing the handouts he received from Nanu. This was my punishment for wanting the divorce.

I took a quick sip of my Coke and dialed up St. Mark's. I wanted to get the call over with early so I didn't have to think about it all day. I was going to give it my best shot, my last shot.

"May I speak with the Monsignor please?" my voice was shaky.

"Just one moment please," a woman's voice responded.

I waited on hold long enough to smoke another cigarette. Finally he answered the phone.

"Hello, this is Monsignor. How may I help you?"

"Monsignor, this is Mary Carlotti. How are you?"

"I'm fine," his voice was sharp like a razor edge. Then silence. Evidently he had no intention of asking me how I was.

I gulped and tried to regain my composure despite the tears that were already burning my eyes.

"Monsignor, I'm calling to ask about the children going to St. Mark's School in the fall."

All I could hear was his slow breathing.

"The only thing is...I won't have the money to pay the tuition, so I'm wondering if the kids can go there anyway...without me paying the tuition...or what could I do...and that's why I'm calling," I mumbled. I wanted to say the correct words into the tremendous silence screaming at me from the other end, but I couldn't think of anything to say.

"Well, Mary," his voice was angry, "I really don't think money is the problem. The children would be more than welcome in our school if money were the issue, but there is a rumor that you want to marry Father Pat, and therefore, you may not send your children here anymore." He paused before saying, "Your children are not welcome here at St. Mark's. It would be best for you to send them somewhere else."

Now it was my turn for silence. I couldn't get any words out of my mouth.

"Your children are no longer welcome here," he said again. He cleared his throat and waited.

I rested my elbows on the cabinet and realized that all the kids were standing there in the kitchen with me. I had no idea when they entered the room. I couldn't hold the tears back any longer. I waited for him to ask me if the rumor was true or not. He didn't ask. His voice was judgmental and sharp. His voice told me that I was a sinner.

"Well, that's all I wanted to know," I said crying. I thought he would at least give me the benefit of the doubt, but his voice dripped with disgust and he had no intention of doing that.

"Okay then, thanks anyway," I choked out the words. I wanted to scream at him, "Did you tell this to Father Pat, you judgmental god person?"

The receiver clicked on the other end without a good-bye.

I stood and held the phone in my hand for a minute. It was true what I had learned; one's tone of voice said everything. Words were secondary. His tone of voice had said that I was dirt. I hung up the receiver on the wall and buried my face in my hands, sobbing. The kids surrounded me silently.

Finally Maria asked softly, "What is it, Mommy? What happened?"

They stood and waited patiently. I couldn't answer. I could only continue to cry.

"Please Mommy, tell us, whatever it is," Maria asked again sadly.

I really didn't want to tell them. I didn't want them to worry. I wanted to protect them from things like this but they knew it was something terrible. I had to tell them, it would be worse not to.

"I was talking with the Monsignor to see if you could go there to school in the fall and he said," I choked, "He said...he said no, you couldn't go there. He said you guys couldn't. He said my kids can't go there because of the rumor. He said there was a rumor that I was going to marry Father Pat. He never even asked me if it was true. He was so judgmental and sarcastic. He even sneered when he said it," I sobbed. "Where will you go? What will we do? How can this happen? This makes me so mad. How can he do that to my kids?"

"That's okay Mommy, we can go to Kilmer like the other kids around here do. Don't worry; we'd like to go there. Are you really going to marry Father Pat, Mommy?" Anthony asked.

"I don't know. He has spent time with us but that doesn't mean we're getting married. He's trying to be supportive of us, and I love him for that. He likes feeling like he's part of our family. That's what he's told me. Anyway I would talk to you guys about something serious like that."

"We love him too, Mommy," Joey said.

"You do?"

"Yeah Mommy, we really do! Don't we boys?" Maria turned to her brothers, excited.

"Yeah, we do Mommy. It's okay, you can marry him if you want too, we won't mind."

"Yeah and I think it would be great to go to Kilmer. Can we really go there?" John asked with excitement in his voice.

"Yeah, I'd like to go there too," Anthony followed his brother.

"Yeah and we could come home for lunch."

"And we could walk! No more school bus! Yeeaah!" Joey was in heaven.

"Yeah and you could marry Father Pat, that would be great."

"Would we call him Father Pat, Mommy?"

I felt overwhelmed. I really didn't want to talk about marrying Father Pat. That's not where my mind was but I loved the way the kids were talking about it so openly and so innocently.

They knelt around me as I sat on that kitchen floor. They were holding my hands, kissing my face, and trying to get on my lap. They were excited about their new school as well as the fact that I loved Father Pat. I listened to them and dried my tears. Never had I felt so loved and supported. The powerful force that I felt from this group of kids at this moment was incredible. No human force would ever be stronger.

"Are you divorced yet, Mommy?" John slipped his hand inside mine. How did they always seem to know exactly what was on my mind?

"We sign the papers tomorrow. That's all that's left to do. Everything is worked out." I could hear the tears returning in my voice and John heard it also.

"Will we still go out with Dad on Saturdays?" he wanted to know the facts now. He held my hand tighter.

"Yes, of course you will. That is if you want to go and he wants to take you," I said. I was trying to get it all straight in my own mind.

"What about Father Pat, Mommy?" Joey asked. I knew they had more questions.

"Well, I love him very much as a wonderful friend. He has helped us a tremendous amount." I stopped to look at each one of them. "I don't know how it'll all turn out. I do love him. I'm not sure what that means, but I know if we ever decide to marry, you will be the first to know," I pulled them closer to me so I could get my arms around all of them and whispered, "I would never do anything like that without first asking you what you think of the idea. We will make all our decisions together."

I also knew that Father Pat was too frightened to even say the word "marriage." We agreed we didn't believe all the things we had learned during our Catholic upbringing. We agreed that we didn't care what other people thought, but I knew he still did. We agreed he should talk with his parents about what he was thinking about everything, his church, leaving it, hanging out with a divorced woman and her five kids. We agreed that I should talk with Dan and Diane Huber, my best friends who truly looked out for my best interests.

Father Pat and I didn't agree about money. We didn't agree about a platonic relationship. There were hang-ups we didn't talk about so I was excited my friends were coming to Chicago next week and we would be able to talk. I could say anything I wanted to them and it would be okay.

The kids smiled at me and I could tell they felt relieved. The closeness, the bond between us, was a hundred times stronger. I didn't know at the time what a powerful statement I had just made. *We will make all our decisions together.* It had just slipped out of my mouth as if I had planned it yet I was surprised that I had even thought of it. Were my children too young for me to be able to say things like that to them? Not really. I was learning that kids knew much more than we ever gave them credit for. This was the best age that kids could be. I was sure of it.

I told the kids to grab their towels because we were going to spend the rest of the day at the beach. I quickly made ten peanut butter and jelly sandwiches and threw them in a bag. Fifteen minutes later, we were lying on our towels in the sand. This was heaven for me and as I watched the kids build their first sandcastle of the day.

The whole parish found out that the Monsignor said my children were not allowed to attend the school and the church's board of directors took it upon themselves to challenge his ruling. They put up a good fight for me and the kids. We were finally told that my kids could, indeed, attend the Catholic school. But something had already changed inside of me and for the first time in my life I spoke out loud about all the hypocrisies of the church that I had witnessed since I was a kid. I thanked the parish for their support but refused to send my children back to St. Mark's. I no longer had any desire to ever walk into a Catholic church again. But I knew in my heart of hearts that I was just rebelling and that this would pass someday and I would want to go back. After all, the Catholic Church had always been a part of my life.

I talked with Dan Huber and was shocked at his feelings and thoughts.

"Don't think of marrying him, Mary Cecile. Don't marry him."

"Why not? What if I love him? And he loves me?"

"Love him all you want. Live with him if you want, but don't marry him."

"I thought you liked him?"

"I do like him. He's a friend of ours, but I still don't want you to marry him," he said in a strong deep voice. "Do whatever you have to, but DON'T MARRY HIM, Mary Cecile."

He would never tell me why he was so against it. He was just against it. He would sort of giggle nervously but he obviously didn't want to say negative things about Father Pat. They rarely said negative things about people. That's just the way they were.

He paused a moment before continuing, "Would I lead you wrong? No. We love you and those kids very much too. I know it's hard right now in your situation, but I've never felt so strongly about anything in my life. Don't marry him."

"Can't you say more? Can't you give me reasons? I can make him laugh. I can make him happy. I'm so sure of it."

"It's just not a good or wise thing for you to do. I know about the love thing. I know you think you love him and this could be a good thing for all of you. I know what you're thinking even if you haven't told me, but I don't want you to marry him. I am looking out for you, Mary Cecile. And this is my advice to you."

He looked at me long and hard and then gave me a big hug before leaving.

I was so upset that I was at a loss for words. Dan Huber was a wise man with more common sense then any of my friends. I'd never seen him so adamant about anything in his life so I had to listen to him, even though I was thinking that perhaps he just didn't understand.

Inside I was shaken.

11

I was almost always the last one to arrive in the living room. I knew that sometimes the kids liked the meetings and sometimes they hated them. I felt the same way, but no one ever wanted to be left out in case they missed something.

"Anybody have anything to say at this meeting?" Joey took over as chairperson. It was amazing to me how quickly we fell into the routine. Just a couple of months of meetings and already the kids were rotating leadership.

"I cleaned up the kitchen by myself most of this week," John was looking for sympathy and recognition as the "good" guy.

I remained silent but made a mental note to thank him when we were alone. Putting them "all in the same boat" was necessary in order for them to learn to take care of each other, to be responsible for each other, and to not look for a reward for contributing to the group. The idea was to teach cooperation rather than promote competition, but a thank you later in private was also necessary.

"And I don't think it's fair," he continued, trying to get a response.

More silence.

"I really appreciate everyone's help." I answered.

"You just don't care!" John looked me directly in the eye.

I really had nothing more to say about the subject at this time and decided to sit silently and wait for the meeting to continue. It was hard but I was learning to keep my mouth shut sometimes.

"Anyone else have anything to say?" Joey began again.

"Yes, I do," Maria said, "I don't like the way our bedtime has been set up. I wonder if we could change it. I just don't think it's fair that we all have to be in bed at 8:30." Maria liked to use the word "fair."

I not only hated the word, but also refused to fall for it.

"Fair? Fair, Maria?" I challenged her and was ready to lecture. My tone of voice always gave me away.

"Okay, Mom, please don't say it. We've heard it a thousand times. 'Life is not fair, life is not unfair, life is life.' I don't really mean 'fair' okay?" Maria was irritated and not afraid to show it.

"Okay, let's talk about it, all of us," I backed off and invited their ideas.

"Well, I just think we could stay up a little later," Joey knew my invitation was real.

"How much later, Joey?" I asked.

"Five hours? Just kidding," Joey laughed and winked at me.

Their mouths were silent, but all their eyes were searching each other now, darting back and forth, wondering who would speak up first. I got the sense that they had discussed this among themselves in private. I waited for someone to speak up, and was pleased with myself because I was keeping my mouth shut. That still was one of the hardest things for me to do—keeping my mouth shut.

"How about if we go to bed when we're tired?" Anthony made it sound so simple.

Anthony always came up with good ideas. Sometimes it was obvious that the older kids, Maria, Joey, and John got a little jealous of his ideas and remarks. But they didn't criticize or laugh at him this time. They waited for my answer.

"How would we work that, Anthony?" I invited him to feel free to say exactly what he was thinking. Anthony loved it when anyone responded to his ideas and didn't treat him like a little kid. I knew how it felt to be the little kid in a family where no one ever listened.

"Just like I said, Mommy. Everyone would have to figure out when they needed to go to bed. Figure out just how much sleep they needed. Like, I've figured out that I have to get to bed early. I've figured out that I obviously need more sleep than Maria, for example."

Maria arched her back, waiting for him to finish, and then before anyone else could say a word she piped in, "I think we should set a certain time, you guys."

"Why, Maria?" I wondered what her reasoning was.

"So we'd know for sure when we're supposed to be in bed," Maria answered impatiently, as if everyone should have already known the answer.

"Well, I think we should pick our own bedtime. I think that would be better than Mommy always telling us what time to be in bed," Joey spoke matter of factly.

"I agree, I think you should pick your own bedtimes. I'm very much in favor of the idea," I said confidently.

They stared at me in disbelief.

John immediately got angry, "I don't think it's funny, Mom. I know you're not going to let us pick our own bedtime and I, for one, don't appreciate your joking around about this."

I was surprised at John's disapproval. "I am totally serious, John. I'm sorry if you think I'm joking around because I'm not," I paused and looked at each one of them, and then turned back to John, "I think it's a marvelous idea!"

"Really Mom? This isn't a trick?" Joey didn't totally believe it either.

"No Joey, this is no trick. I don't know when I've tricked you with something like this. Perhaps you better enlighten me about my tricks," I was a little insulted, yet remained calm.

"Well, maybe not exactly tricks, but you have to admit that we do things differently than other people since you met that Dreikurs," Maria said, coming to the defense of her brothers.

"Okay Mom, what if we picked three o'clock in the morning? Are you going to allow us to stay up until three o'clock in the morning?" Joey challenged me.

I was on the spot now and knew they were going to test me on this. I answered softly, "I really don't think you're going to pick three o'clock in the morning, do you?" As the words came out of my mouth I realized that my question might be interpreted as a challenge to them. I didn't mean it that way and held my breath, waiting to see what they would say next.

"Well, maybe not three in the morning, but what about one in the morning?

What if we pick one o'clock in the morning, hmmm?" Joey leaned closer to me as he spoke. In fact, the whole circle had gotten smaller. They all quietly looked at me.

"Well actually, I don't think you will pick one o'clock in the morning either," I laughed and shrugged my shoulders. "Maybe you will but I don't think so," I remained the picture of confidence but now felt they were going to pick a late hour for their bedtime. I felt it coming. They were going to test and see how far they could go with me.

"Well that's where you're wrong Mom, because I'd love to have my bedtime be at one o'clock," Maria said, "Then I could read for as long as I wanted to."

"Yeah, well, I'd like it too," John agreed immediately with his sister. They stuck together like glue those two, just like Joey and Anthony.

"I'd like it too," Joey said and then bent over to whisper into Christopher's ear.

"Me too," Christopher said as Joey pushed him with his elbow.

"Hey, it would be great for me," Anthony chimed in, " I wouldn't mind a couple more hours. Like everyone says, our bedtime is really too early and to pick it ourselves would be the greatest. My friends won't believe this," he said smiling and obviously overcome with joy.

"So you want to stay up until one o'clock?" I asked. I could hear my voice was a pitch higher. "You want to stay up until one o'clock?" I repeated the question, stalling for time while I searched for what to say next. "Well okay, if that's what you all really want to do...." my voice trailed off.

"Of course that's what we want to do. We'd love it and you know we would," Maria was speaking for everyone.

I shifted nervously in my position on the floor.

"I just don't think you'll be able to stay up till one o'clock, that's all. I think it's too late on school nights. You'd never be able to get up the next day. I just don't think it's a good idea," I said seriously.

"That's what I thought. I thought you'd change your mind. I knew you weren't serious. I knew you wouldn't really let us choose," Joey jumped on me immediately.

"No, no that's not what I'm saying. I said you could pick your own bedtime and I meant it. Stop making it sound like I'm a witch, Joey, I'm not. If you guys want to stay up until one o'clock, I'll go along with your decision. After all, we can live with any rule until next week's meeting." I paused, "But what about if you fall asleep before one o'clock? What shall we do then?" I remained sincere.

"It won't be a problem, Mom, we'll stay awake," Joey said with determination.

"Okay, but just suppose you do fall asleep before one o'clock? Can I wake you up to make sure you keep your part of the bargain?" I held my breath while holding in a smile, hoping they would agree with my idea.

"Don't worry about that part, it won't happen," Maria said confidently.

"I'm not worried, Maria. I just want to know the rules," I answered her right back, firmly insisting upon an answer.

"We can do it Mommy," Christopher chirped in with excitement in his eyes.

I just looked at them all and smiled. I loved looking at them. I always wondered if they were really so beautiful or did I just think so because they were my children? No, they really were beautiful, I decided as usual.

"I guess we'll just have to show you that we can do it. But I'm telling you, Mom, it won't be a problem for me to stay up that late. I don't know about everybody else, but for me, it will be great," Joey was jubilant.

Everyone was tired of discussing this issue, including me but I wanted an agreement.

"What if you fall asleep before one o'clock?" I insisted on an answer.

"Mom, I am not going to fall asleep. But let's just say if I do, you can wake mc up. How's that?" Joey was never more confident about anything in his life.

"The same with me," John said.

"Me too," Maria said.

"Fine by me," Anthony agreed.

"Me too," Christopher followed suit.

I was surprised at Anthony's response because he had just expressed the fact that he knew he needed a lot of sleep. It was pretty funny, but I had no intentions of laughing because at that point they would think I was laughing *at* them,. They had never been so serious or so sure about anything in their life. They wouldn't mind proving me wrong either. I was sure of that. I knew my job now was to stand by the decision and allow the consequences to occur. The new bedtime was to start that night. The subject was finally closed.

"Anything else to talk about at this meeting?" Joey was tired. "Christopher? What is it? You don't have to raise your hand."

"Joey, when you die, can I have your trophies?" Christopher asked seriously.

"Christopher, God, *I'm not old*. Tell him, Mom. God, I can't believe you said that." Joey was extremely upset.

"He doesn't know, honey. To him, you're probably old," I couldn't keep from cracking up with laughter along with everyone except Joey.

"Anything else for this meeting?" Joey wanted this long meeting to end.

"Not really," Anthony answered for everyone.

That very night at 10:30, every one of the kids was out like a light. I wondered how long I should let them sleep before I woke them as per the agreement. I wanted to finish the dress I was making for Maria, but if I was going to follow through with this lesson, the dress would have to wait. I was very tired but sleep would have to wait, too. I couldn't help chuckling as I looked at them all stretched out on the living room floor, books held loosely as they slept. It was a funny picture and I grabbed the camera to record it before waking them up. This was going to be a wild night, I could feel it in my bones.

After taking a couple pictures, I knew I couldn't put it off any longer. I had to follow through.

"Wake up! Wake up! C'mon you guys, it's only quarter to eleven and you're asleep," I stepped between their bodies, shaking each of them.

Maria growled, "Mom, I am not asleep. I was resting my eyes for a minute, but I'm not asleep."

I continued shaking them, "Anthony, Joey, c'mon wake up! You're all asleep. C'mon now, open up those pretty eyes."

"Funny, Mom," Joey held his head up and, as if it were on a puppet string and someone let go, it fell back to the floor.

I sat down on the couch. I hadn't intended for it to be funny. This was the deal we had agreed upon. I called them again in a soft yet firm voice, telling them to wake up. No one stirred. I repeated my request. It was time to get up; it was not one o'clock. They had a couple hours to go. I struggled to make my voice kind and firm. I wanted to laugh so badly, but realized that if I did it would come across as an "I told you so" attitude. I hadn't gone this far to blow it now.

"Well, I didn't mean it to be funny. I'm just following through with the deal," I said in my kindest voice.

"Okay, Mom, enough!" Joey yelled.

I watched as their arms pushed the top part of their bodies up slowly. They were angry and they were going to let me know just how angry they were. I again told them that it was eleven o'clock and they had wanted to stay up until one o'clock. Every hand was busily rubbing sleepy eyes. I watched them and felt frozen inside. It was the same feeling I felt when I first learned how to use the bathroom properly. I hated it when they got mad at me, but the training had to be done and I knew it wasn't going to be easy. It made me the bad guy. I swallowed hard. How could I always feel so afraid that they would tell someone the things I did yet at the same time feel so confident in my training? I didn't know the answer to that question.

I insisted the kids all sit up for a little while rather than read lying down. They grumbled under their breath but they sat up and read their books for a while. Slowly they began to lie down again and their eyes closed two by two. My insides twinged as I woke them once again. I didn't like this part, but had to do it. I felt sorry for myself and would be glad when this was over.

The next morning the kids were obviously very tired and didn't talk much. When they got home from school that afternoon, Joey asked me if it was going to be the same as the night before. I played dumb and only grunted an, "Uh huh." Judging by the scowl on his face, he was not pleased, but he said nothing. It appeared peaceful as evening changed to night, but I wondered how the night would end. My stomach was tight but I acted as if nothing unusual was going on. I sat at my sewing machine, sewing and waiting. The kids were talking quietly in the living room. I wondered how long it would be before they would be asleep. I checked my watch. It was 9:20.

At 9:40, it was totally silent. I walked into the living room and looked at my children. They looked like angels. Couldn't I just let them sleep? No, I knew I couldn't.

I shook each and every one of them to wake them up, just like the night before. It was part of the deal—if they fell asleep, which the kids had insisted wouldn't happen, I was supposed to wake them up.

"Wake up, John. Come on, Joey, wake up now. Maria, wake up. You're asleep already."

"Cut it out," Joey yelled as he swung an arm to shoo me away.

"Get up then, honey," I was cool. "Come on Johnny, it's not one o'clock yet, better wake up."

"Dang, stop it," John yelled angrily as he sat up.

"It's what we agreed to do," I thought my voice sounded more scared than confident.

"We're awake now, Mom. Okay?" Maria was definitely angry.

My stomach lurched and I went into the bathroom so I could talk to myself. Was I doing the right thing by waking them up when they were so tired? Yes, that was the deal that I would wake them up if they fell asleep. This was only the second night. Why did it already seem like a month? Would this turn out like I hoped? Would they learn how to pick a bedtime that was right for the sleep they needed? I laughed quietly. In the midst all my worrying, this was still kind of funny. Thank God I still had my sense of humor. I certainly wouldn't make it through without one.

On the morning of the third day, the kids all asked if we could have an emergency meeting that afternoon. Their angry faces were terribly unpleasant that morning and a little scary. I was relieved and hoped that a meeting would end our midnight madness. Ordinarily, decisions made at meetings would remain intact until the next week's meeting. An emergency meeting was rare and should remain rare, but I wasn't getting enough sleep either, and if there was ever an occasion for an emergency meeting, this was it.

They found me in the kitchen when they got home from school.

"Is this really an emergency, you guys?" I didn't want to consent too quickly to this meeting or appear too easy.

"Yes, Mom, it is and you know it. Don't be funny," Maria rolled her eyes as she spoke, obviously in a bad mood. Her books fell loudly on the table as she placed her hands on her hips.

"I'm not trying to be funny, Maria. What's the emergency?" I held back any trace of a smile and folded my arms across my chest. I waited patiently for the silence to pass. I knew already that this lesson had been effective.

"Everyone feels like they are dying because of you waking us up all night long, and you know it. You know we're all tired and it's not our fault. Stop acting like you don't know it," Joey's voice was loud and tense as he reached for a box of crackers, almost knocking Christopher over in the process.

I switched the weight of my body from one leg to the other and continued to lean back against the cabinet. My arms remained folded and I could feel my confidence.

"Fault? It's *my* fault because you're tired, Joey? Come on you guys, get real." I would not accept responsibility for what they had set up themselves, nor was I willing to allow them to lay a guilt trip on me. The kids refused to let me off the hook that easily.

"You know what we mean, Mom. You know what we're talking about. I hate it when you act like this." Maria got a glass of water from the faucet as she spoke. She didn't look at me.

"Okay, if everyone agrees that we should have an emergency meeting, then let's do it," I said, remaining cool.

"Mom, everyone else agrees if you do. We're all ready," John, with the twinkle back in his eyes, wanted it made clear who was on whose side. This was definitely them against me.

They hurried into the living room and sat down and I followed.

"One o'clock is too late to stay up," Maria began.

Joey supported his sister immediately. "Yes, it's too late," he said as he stretched out on the floor.

"I agree," John said, lying down also.

Maria cleared her throat, preparing to speak for everyone.

"We've decided it would be a good idea if we went to bed when we are tired. Because we are all different and need different amounts of sleep, we think it would be a good idea if each of us was responsible for our own bedtime. Anthony, for example, gets tired long before I do, so when he is tired, he can just go to bed. I like to stay up and read. John likes to mess around. You know, we're all just different. You were right about us not being able to stay up till one o'clock, but we just really thought we could. Maybe we could start quiet time at 8:30. Is that too late, Mom?"

"No, I think that could work out. We can try it for a week and see how it goes. We can always change it at next week's meeting if we want to," I left their options open. I was relaxed.

Maria continued. "If we want to read our stories together like we do, we can do it before 8:30. That's what we've decided. What do you say?"

"I think it's great, you guys. I think your decisions are very wise. When you set your mind to something you guys always come up with good stuff. What? What is it, Anthony?" I paused waiting for him to speak.

"I'm tired. Can we end this meeting soon?" Anthony's eyes were already half closed.

"Yes, let's end it. I'm going to bed soon too, honey. We're probably all tired," I smiled.

"No, kidding," Joey laughed but looked at me with a face that hadn't totally forgiven me for the last two days of minimal sleep.

Christopher, though he rarely said anything at the meetings, ended this meeting with a line destined to end many of our meetings and become a family joke, "When you're tired, go to bed."

That evening was extremely quiet. Every time the kids came up with a concrete and common sense solution. I marveled at their brilliance and faulted myself for every doubt I ever had about them and their ability to solve problems. These kids were something else. They were genius. They figured this out because I gave them the chance to figure it out. I shut my mouth at the right time. I remembered to get an agreement from them that it was okay to wake them up if they fell asleep before the designated one o'clock bedtime. Was it just my kids, like people said, or were all kids this smart? It had to be all kids, I decided as my eyelids became too heavy to fight any longer. I had to believe all kids were smart when the parents were given the tools to understand behavior and the encouragement to guide and lead their children, as I had received from Dreikurs.

12

Things were going really well again. I was still getting used to the idea that I wasn't going to get things perfect but that this was an ongoing process. It was difficult for me to accept that I wouldn't get it perfect. Wasn't I supposed to get it perfect?

I was going nuts with hearing the word "Mommy" a thousand times a day. Or at least it seemed like a thousand times. I had to think of something to give me some relief. "I've got it," I said out loud to myself as I walked down the stairs.

"I've decided to change my name for today," I announced at breakfast. I smiled and noted the kids' dumbfounded reactions. "Starting right now, I will not answer to the name Mommy for a while. Until further notice, you can call me 'Apple.' The name Mommy is making me crazy. Do you understand?" I waited a moment for their response.

No one said anything. Maria stood up and began pulling up her sock.

"'Apple?' You want us to call you 'Apple?'" Maria rolled her eyes and started to laugh. All the boys started to laugh, too, and finally I joined in. It did sound funny but I meant it. I had had it with the Mommy word. *Let them laugh*, I thought.

"We're supposed to call you 'Apple?' Right Mom. Come on Anthony, let's go play," Joey sounded as casual as if he were talking about the weather. He jumped off the porch steps as the back screen door slammed. "Come on, John," he yelled, "Let's go."

That was all I said. They just laughed. They weren't necessarily laughing at me, but probably at the thought that their mother had gone off the deep end once again. With the kids all in the backyard, I sat down for a Coke and a cigarette break. "Apple," I whispered to myself; I liked the sound of it. When they called out for Mommy I was silent, and then they remembered to say Apple. We laughed often about it, but my name remained Apple.

The following Monday, the sun went down on what felt like an extremely long afternoon. The kids had been crabby since they came home from school. Some days were just like that. For about fifteen minutes, I laid on the couch listening to them. Although they were whispering, they were loud enough that I could hear them clearly, of course. I was pissed. They were whispering "bad" words. That always got my goat immediately and they knew it.

Then it struck me, why not go along with them? I jumped up from the couch and went into the kitchen to start dinner. The kids were right around the corner in the den.

Shit. Damn. Fuck. Asshole. They'd been using them all. I was glad that I had abandoned punishing them for bad words long ago—something I had witnessed many times as a child. My brother had his mouth washed out with soap more times than I wanted to remember, but it had never changed anything. I suddenly felt so smart because I knew that these "bad" words were just for my attention, like their fighting had been. And I was in the mood to go along with them, or "spit in their soup," as Dreikurs would have said.

I went into the kitchen, opened up the cabinets, and said in a loud, friendly voice, "Where the fuck is that pot? I can never find a goddamn thing in this shitty kitchen. Motherfucker! I wonder what asshole put that fucking pot away? Where's the fucking spoon? Where's the goddamn shitty lid for this motherfucking pot? This cabinet is such a motherfucking mess. The whole kitchen is such a fucking mess. What asshole took that lid? Oh shit, shit, shit, fuck, shit!"

I exploded! Inside I was laughing so hard that I thought my sides would split. There was no anger in my voice. I stood in that kitchen repeating every swear word I had ever heard over and over as I struggled to hold in my laughter. I could feel their eyes piercing me from around the corner. My eyes were watering, but I continued to hold in the laughter. *I'm not angry at you guys*, I thought to myself. *I'm training you! I'm getting as smart as you guys now! I'm getting as smart as you!* I paused and then started all over again.

The house had never been so quiet. I heard them shut the windows. For the next ten minutes, which seemed more like ten hours, I continued my charade in the kitchen. I never looked them in the eye, but kept right on cooking dinner. Then I told them dinner was ready and sat down with them as if nothing had ever happened. The kids were silent. They kept their gaze downward as they gathered food onto their plates. Dinner was eaten in unprecedented silence. I watched unconcerned as they exchanged looks with each other.

The rest of the evening also remained unusually quiet. We had our stories, and soon everyone was tucked into bed. I was so proud of myself I could have burst. I wondered what would happen after this episode? Only time would tell.

It worked! It was a shocker. I shocked them instead of them shocking me. Yeah, I was becoming a match for them. Again I felt so smart inside. One thing for sure, kids do not want their mom saying dirty words. They don't want that coming out of their mother's mouth. Between Apple and me cursing a blue streak, it was quite a week.

13

Several months later, the phone awoke me early one morning.

"Mary Cecile?" *Oh my God*, I thought. It was Kathryn.

"Yeah?"

"Aunt Cecily died and she's left her estate to her nieces and nephews. It's a lot of money, Mary Cecile. At Christmastime, we'll all be getting a big check. We won't get all the money at once, though. Okay, I have to go. Goodbye."

I had no idea what that meant, "a lot of money," and that was all she said. She didn't curse at me or give me a lecture. There was a first time for everything, I thought. What was a lot of money? Since I never had any money in my life, any amount would probably fit the description. I'd have to wait and see. In the meantime, I told Pat the news.

Two weeks later, I received a letter from the Morgan Trust Company in New York. It said that I would be receiving several thousand dollars. I couldn't believe it. I wanted to think over how I was going to tell the kids without them getting the wrong impression. At that moment I decided that I would make a wonderful rich person. I promised the heavens above that it would not change me. It felt great!

The one unfortunate consequence, however, was that Mother started calling again. This confirmed my belief that I'd held since I was a young kid. Money can do strange things to people.

"Mary Cecile, are you still planning on marrying that priest?"

She never said "hello" or asked how I was. I was shocked to hear her voice with that first call in many months. She hadn't spoken to me since I'd told her I loved Pat and she'd given me all that grief about it.

"Maybe," I answered.

"Well, you know about the money from Aunt Cecily, right?"

"Yes, Kathryn called and told me."

"Well, let me just tell you something, young lady, even though you think you know it all. First of all, put it in your name alone. Don't get that priest mixed up in it. Do you hear me?"

"Yes, Mother."

"Now you know why she did it the way she did it, don't you?"

"Did what, Mother?"

"The money. The reason that my sister, your namesake Aunt Cecily, did it that way was to make it easier on me. She knew it would be too big a burden for me to handle all that money, so instead of giving it directly to Aunt Eleanor, or me, she gave it to the children. But she did it that way so that you would take care of it and give it back to me. You understand that, don't you? How she knew it would be too big a burden on me?"

"I'll give you whatever you want Mother. If you want all the money, I'll give it to you. Whatever you want, you know that." And I meant it. If that would make her happy, I would've been glad to do it. She never had anything. Both my mother and daddy were very poor, to say the least. I certainly understood that.

"Oh now you're sounding like the old Mary Cecile again." Her tone was back to ridiculing, but I could ignore that. "Listen to me now and don't put that money in both of your names. I know you're so in love now but listen to me and don't do it. Okay, Mary Cecile?"

"Okay, Mother."

"Now I wouldn't want you to give it all to me. I'm sure you could use some of it or put it in an account where no one knows about it. And if your sister and your brothers do what they are supposed to do, if each of them does their share, then it will be okay. But who knows if Tommy will do the right thing. He may drink all his up. That boy needs help bad. But I have to go now. Bye."

I knew Tommy hadn't talked to Mother for years and had no intention of having anything to do with her. He never went back much after that drunken scene when I was a little kid. I understood why he didn't.

"Do you think something's wrong with me?" Pat stopped the car and turned to me. I had never seen him get so upset before and never heard him shout with such anger.

"No," I said softly, though I was instantly afraid. As much as I liked to tell myself that I had gotten rid of most of my fears, I knew that it wasn't true.

It had been a few months since Pat and I had decided to try and make our relationship work as a couple. In a sense, we had both just gotten a divorce— Pat from the priesthood and I from Joe. The out standing joke was that Pat left the big church and now we were his little church.

The truth, however, was that we were going nowhere fast. Pat kept saying how much he loved the kids and me, and I knew the kids loved him as much as I did. He hung around us all the time, but his fear of what people would say seemed to be much stronger than our love. And who did we really have to talk to now? We needed to see someone and get an outside opinion. Roslyn suggested that Pat and I go see the counselor that she and Robert had been seeing to get a little help. I felt strongly about this. If we didn't go, our relationship would continue to stand still, so Pat reluctantly agreed.

Jason was great. He was down to earth and Pat and I both believed he was full of common sense. It was exciting to find someone with common sense answers about the difficulties in our relationship. After seeing the counselor a few times, it became clear that Pat had to stand up to his parents, his world, and to make a decision about our future together. I wanted to go ahead and get married. Did he feel the same?

The words from my friend Dan Huber replayed over and over in my head, so I called him to tell him that despite everything he'd said I wanted to marry Pat. His position hadn't changed, "Live with him, Mary Cecile but don't marry him." Obviously I wasn't going to heed his advice since I loved Pat and wanted to marry him. Living with him was not enough for me, and for Pat that was not an option. He considered that to be a sin; he even thought we'd be excommunicated from the church. His ideas about sex were narrow to say the least.

He definitely gave off different about us marrying after I told him about the money from Aunt Cecily. He liked the idea of the money. I could tell it made a difference. That made me a little nervous. Maybe Mother was right, but I decided to ignore my feelings about it. I did wonder if he would have wanted to marry if it weren't for the money. Well it's understandable, I told myself. After all I did have five little kids. I didn't feel like going into it any further.

Maybe it was just my imagination. I wanted to talk to Dan about the money part but was too afraid. He had already shared his feelings about the whole idea of us marrying and he was very strong in his beliefs. I just decided to keep it inside. After all, Pat loved the kids and me. I could make him laugh, and I totally believed the kids and I could make him happy. Love would fix everything.

First, I told the kids, and then a couple friends. Our good friends said it was not the time for either of us to consider marriage. I loved my friends but decided that friends could be wrong. Pat's parents condemned his decision of marrying a divorcee with five children. If he insisted upon leaving the church, he could do much better, they said. It wasn't all pleasant and rosy, but we knew it wouldn't be. My kids' opinions were the only ones that mattered to me. They were happy for me, for us.

But when the kids and I finally met his parents in person, they accepted us and treated us with respect and love. My family, on the other hand, stopped calling altogether. They wanted nothing more to do with me. Honestly, I felt relieved

I made the kids new outfits. Pat got a new suit. I got a new skirt. We had a simple wedding on the coldest of January days. And then we were both officially excommunicated from the church.

Things were different, of course, now that we had a new member in our family. The kids called him Pat with ease and they played together. His parents often expressed that they'd never met such wonderful kids before. "Grandma" and "Grandpa" were not the only ones who had told me that these kids were different. I knew why the kids were so wonderful, but never said much about it because I didn't think I could explain it all. Whenever someone asked me about this directly, I would just say that I had learned a lot of things about raising kids, things that anyone could learn. If I could learn, I would say to them, anyone could. And I meant that with my whole heart. Unfortunately, most of the time people didn't understand. They thought my kids were different because they believed I was either a wonderful person or very lucky, or it was because I had a girl first. Because I had a girl first was the most popular belief.

It had been six years since I was pregnant with Christopher, so each and every one of us looked forward to this birth. Much teasing went on between the kids. Maria threatened, with a laugh, that if it was not a girl she would run away from home. Anthony volunteered to help her pack. "I was just kidding," he assured her later. Joey, John, Anthony, and Christopher all voted for a boy.

I felt confident that at least I knew a few things about having babies and nursing them now. I had actually doubted whether I would get pregnant again since I'd had an ovary removed after Christopher was born, but obviously getting pregnant was not one of the difficulties in my life, I laughed to myself.

I thought our marriage was almost perfect. The children loved Pat. We had a new baby on the way, and I believed I was becoming totally democratic with these kids. Everything seemed as pretty as a picture. Almost unbelievable, I thought.

The baby girl was now five months old and I had never before experienced feelings like these. It never occurred to me that having this baby was going to be any different than when I had the other five babies, so these feelings of unhappiness came as quite a shock.

Everything was different. I had finally gotten all the children into school full-time and a new baby meant starting the whole process over again. Never in my wildest dreams could I have imagined that having another baby would be anything but thoroughly enjoyable.

The depression became unbearable. Someone told me that maybe it was the after-holiday blues. But I didn't agree. It was more than that. Besides, it was October, so what holiday were they referring to? Getting myself out of bed every day was a major task. Breast infections came one after another and my whole body ached with pain. It seemed like her crying never ceased, but in reality it was probably just that I wasn't used to having a baby around anymore. Nursing her was no longer a joy. In fact, I didn't like it.

And how did it happen that I now had six babies instead of one? What happened to all the training I had done all those months with the other children? The kids were fighting like crazy while I lay in bed, depressed and crying continually. Would I ever have dry eyes again? Would I ever get out of my bed again?

I didn't go to the bathroom when they fought; I was too tired. I felt weird, crazy, and was afraid to say any of it out loud. Every time I would lie down to nurse the baby, all of a sudden there would be six babies instead of one. They were crawling all over me, literally. Everything I had worked so hard to accomplish was gone.

Inside, I was scared. The fighting and the dirty house were back full force, worse than before. Wasn't I the one who had said, just a short time ago, that I was sure there would be no problem with the kids when I had this baby? Was I dreaming or what? I really believed there wouldn't be any problems. Sometimes I can't believe how stupid I was.

When I would walk into the kitchen and see a knife on the cabinet, the thoughts inside my head were very disturbing. *If they knew what was inside of me, they would have never left a knife lying around*, I thought. *What if I picked up the knife and killed the baby?* I was terrified of these horrible thoughts but too afraid to tell anyone. I thought that I was surely going "mental." The tears streamed down my face. I knew I was in a deep depression with no idea how to snap out of it.

From my bed I could only scream at the kids. They would walk into my bedroom, listen to my sermons, say they would stop, walk out, and just start fighting all over again. I couldn't stand the sight of any of them. I thought constantly about running away, just disappearing. But where could I go? Where could I possibly go?

I had truly lost grip of the whole situation. The kids now owned me, as tyrants do. They were in charge. I knew it and they knew it, too. I was beginning to hate them and resent anything I had to do for them. I had to get away for a couple days to clear my mind. It was going to be a difficult task to accomplish with a baby to breast-feed. But I was losing it and decided to swallow my pride and dial Pat's mom's number. After the third ring, Grandma answered.

"Hello?"

"Grandma, I'm wondering if you and Grandpa could possibly help me out and come over and stay with the kids for a couple of days?" I didn't even ask how she was.

"What's wrong, Mary?"

"Oh nothing! We just need to get away for a couple of days," My voice was high-pitched and I was already sweating under my arms. I hoped she couldn't hear the desperation in my voice. "Pat says it's okay with him. We'd just stay downtown a night or two. We just need to get away a little bit, that's all. Nothing big," I hoped the request sounded like an everyday occurrence.

"Well sure, Mary, we'll help you. We could probably come over sometime this weekend or early next week," Grandma answered. "How does that sound?"

There was a long silence before I laughed nervously and a little loudly.

"Well, actually I was wondering if you could come over before the weekend," I knew that my voice was no longer hiding my desperation.

"Like when, Mary?" Grandma asked, taken aback.

"How about tomorrow?" I whispered.

There was silence again on the other end. I felt my stomach tighten as I waited for Grandma to respond.

"Tomorrow?" Grandma asked. She sounded shocked.

"Tomorrow, Grandma," I said as the tears started to flow. "I just can't wait any longer than that." My stomach started to jerk as I tried to hold back the sobs.

"Well okay...let me check with Grandpa and I'll call you back," Grandma answered in a kind voice. "What about the baby? Are you still nursing her?"

"Yes!"

"What will we do with her? The doll-baby is still so little," Grandma said nervously.

"I'll have to come home in the middle of the day and nurse her, sometime while the other kids are in school. I just can't stand the sight of the kids right now. I have to get away," I finally let the tears flow freely.

"I'll talk to Grandpa and call you back, Mary dear."

"Thanks Grandma," I said softly and hung up the phone.

The next morning, after Grandma and Grandpa settled in and received all their instructions, Pat came home from work and we took the elevated train downtown and checked into a hotel. In the middle of the day when I could no longer stand the pain as my breasts filled tight with milk, I took the el train home, nursed the baby, then headed right back downtown. For those two days, I really didn't do much. I slept quite a bit. Pat and I got to be on our own and we savored the peace and quiet. Without those six kids crawling all over me, I was able to pull myself together and clear my head. Two days of peace and quiet made me a new woman.

When Pat and I returned home the next morning, I thanked Grandma and Grandpa for saving me in a time of desperation. Even though they looked confused, they didn't question me. No questions, no judgment, only help. They had come when I desperately needed them. That was not something I had ever experienced from my family in Perryville. Gratitude swelled inside me.

When the kids arrived home from school that afternoon, I called them to my side for a meeting. They sat quietly on the rug and hardly moved a muscle as I spoke. It seemed they knew something different was in the air.

"Okay you guys, I've had it," I said, glaring at them. My voice was still a little angry. "I've called you all together for this special meeting to get a few things straight. You've all reverted back to being babies and it has been making me crazy. It's understandable, I guess. That can happen when a mom brings a new baby home, but somehow I never thought it would happen to me. I sometimes forget that I am human.

"This will probably be a lecture, but right now I don't care. It's hard enough having one baby, but now I've got six of them. You've worn me down and completely drained me, but being away a couple of days has restored my sanity. Your days of acting like babies are over," I was gaining back the strength in my voice now. "I am putting Anno on the bottle and you all can take turns feeding her," I paused. "I have had enough of the shit that's been going on around here. There will be no more bossing me around! And no more acting like babies. It's not as if I haven't been giving you every ounce of my attention.

"I am going to go to the bathroom when you fight. Things left on the floor will be picked up and put away until the end of the week. And I'm not cooking dinner every night!" That was a statement. My voice was strong now. "Where is it written that I have to cook every night? I hate cooking! You can do it as well as me. Who made the rule that moms have to do all the cooking? I'm not going to do it all the time anymore. I'm quitting as the maid around here!"

No one moved. They just sat there and stared at me. This felt great—my insides relaxed and a great weight was being lifted from my shoulders. Perhaps I was teaching myself.

"And I'm not listening to homework complaints anymore, either! You did your homework fine before Anno was born, but since her arrival, you've become helpless. I need someone to watch Anno when you get home from school so I can get out of here for an hour or so before dinnertime. I'm sick and tired of being the maid around here! Maid service is over." I stopped there. I didn't want to keep repeating myself.

I waited a moment to let my words settle in. Then I took a deep breath and continued.

"Joey and Anthony, I know it's crowded with the baby in your room, but it's the biggest room we have right now. We're pretty damn fortunate to be able to be looking for a bigger house, but until we find it, stop complaining and make the best of our living arrangements. All you guys can help out like you did before Anno was born. I've had it with all this crap. End of meeting!"

I got up and walked into the kitchen, leaving them to consider my words. Running my fingers through my hair, I stood looking out the window. I watched a few snowflakes fall. My strength was back and I was able to get things back into perspective. I started putting the clean dishes into the cabinet. My children would no longer terrorize me. It was time for this family to get out of the slump.

It still amazed me how the kids always knew when I meant business. They sensed immediately when I was in charge of myself, when I got my courage back, and when I would no longer take their walking all over me. Dreikurs had said it many times, "Kids know." It proved to be true time after time after time.

The kids didn't hang all over me every minute. When they came home from school, I talked with them about their day for a while and then took an hour or so to go out and be by myself. When I returned, they had usually done their chores, given "Anno-Piano" (her new nickname) a bottle and changed her diaper—things that had previously been my responsibility. Things had definitely changed. I didn't know for how long, but for now things were going much, much better.

Maria was graduating from eighth grade. It was difficult for me to believe I had a child who was thirteen years old. My first teenager. It felt like life was on fast-forward—always a birthday or holiday with no regular days in between. One teenager meant that soon there would be many teenagers. That's the way it worked with kids born one right after another. Things happened in bunches, sort of like grapes.

Joey no longer wanted to be called Joey. We talked about it at our family meeting and everyone agreed to call him Joe. The other kids couldn't pass up the opportunity to tease him about being old now. It felt strange to me because now he had his father's name. At first, calling him Joe was difficult for me but I did it because I knew only too well how it felt to be called a name you didn't want to be called. I had dealt with that my entire life. When my mother came to visit, she still told my friends how to address her daughter properly. I still cringed when that happened. Here I was, in my early thirties with six of my own children and my mother still corrected—quite rudely—anyone who did not call me Mary Cecile. I had decided long ago that my kids could be called anything they wanted to be called. They had that right.

"Things are changing; he's growing up," I told Roslyn as I answered the door. "Joey wants us to call him Joe now. Can you believe he's that big already?" I rattled on as Roslyn followed me into the kitchen. "All the kids are out playing in the back yard waiting for you guys to come," I motioned to her boys, Robert and Richard. Their eyes lit up and they took off towards the back door ahead of Roslyn and me. The screen door slammed and seconds later we could hear the other kids cheer at their arrival.

"That might not be the only big change of the moment," Roslyn replied, looking coyly at me.

"What? What else is changing? Why are you looking at me that way?" I quizzed her.

"It looks like you guys might not be the only ones moving. Robert just got an offer to teach at Rice University in San Antonio!" Roslyn said. Her voice was filled with excitement.

"But we're only moving ten minutes away to Evanston. That is, if we can find a place. San Antonio is a thousand miles away. That's quite a difference,"

I said sadly.

"Yes, I know. It's really exciting and it's so many things that we've wanted but it would also be so hard to leave here. With you guys, the Center, you know, all the Dreikurs stuff that's here," she looked at me with tears in her eyes. "We just found out last night. I was going to call you but I decided to wait until I could come over and tell you in person."

"Oh wow, do you think he'll take it? I mean like, is it a good offer and stuff?" my voice sounded really nervous now.

"Yeah, it's a very good offer. Everything he's ever wanted. Everything we've both wanted. I don't know what we'll do, but he was really excited last night. In one way, I'm excited too. It would be so hard to leave you, but on the other hand it's a great opportunity for Robert. I mean, how can we pass it up?" Roslyn took a sip of her Coke, "Let's not talk about it anymore now. Let's just wait and see. Tonight when Robert comes home from work we'll talk again and weigh the pros and cons."

"Okay," I said softly, "I just can't imagine how it would be without you here. I'd miss you so bad." Tears welled up in my eyes.

"I know. Let's just wait and see, okay?" Roslyn touched my hand.

"Okay," I agreed, standing up to get more ice cubes. "Let's go out and sit on the front porch."

"The kids will want to have some Coke too, you know!" Roslyn laughed as she stood up.

"Hey, once in a while it's okay, isn't it?" I picked up my glass and a new can of Coke.

The thought of Roslyn moving weighed on my mind. Although I wanted what was best for my friend, I was scared at the thought of her moving away. I would miss going to the Center with her. And I would miss all the help she had given me throughout the time I had met Dreikurs until now. She was a wonderful friend and I didn't want there to be a great distance between us.

Pat and I had spent the whole summer looking for a house in Evanston, and as summer drew to a close it was time for Maria to register for high school. We told the real estate agent that we would be giving up our search until the following summer.

"There's one more place that just came on the market last night," he told me that next morning. "I could show it to you tonight."

"Oh, I don't know, Wayne, we've pretty much decided to stay here for another year," I told him.

"What do you have to lose looking at one more house? After all, you've done it all summer!" he teased me.

"Okay, that's true but this is it, okay?" I answered, warning him not to continue the search after this one last try.

"I promise this will be the last house I'll call you about," he said sincerely.

"Okay, how soon can we see it?" I felt excited again.

"I'll check it out and call you back," he answered confidently.

We saw the house that night and loved it instantly.

"A house is kind of like a person," I said to Roslyn on the phone. "Something strikes you immediately that you either like or dislike."

We told Wayne that we definitely wanted to buy the house. We immediately started making the necessary arrangements to complete the sale. We set our moving date for Labor Day weekend, three days before high school was to start. Maria would be able to register in a new school. All the kids would be in a good school system.

It would be a big change to leave the study group that seemed to have met in my living room for a hundred years now. I wanted all the mothers to come to Evanston to continue our studying together, but no one in the neighborhood would consider this as a possibility, even though it would only be a 15-minute drive.

I felt sad that evening as everyone shared their thoughts and dreams about their children for the last time. We laughed as Jackie recalled my bathroom scenes, the locked closet escapade, and the week my kids decided they could stay up until one in the morning! I talked a little about still wanting it to be perfect, and everyone laughed in recognition of this tendency in himself or herself.

Edith squirmed in her chair and finally said what was on her mind, "You make everything sound so easy but I still think you've got such good kids."

I lit a new cigarette as I moved to the edge of the couch. I was ready to explode inside.

"Well it's because now I have a husband, don't you think?" I retorted. "Isn't that the opposite of what you said before? Didn't you believe I could do all this stuff because I didn't have a husband?"

"Well yeah, but…" Edith stopped. She didn't know how to answer that one because she had said that to me so many times.

"I don't mean to make it sound easy," I said looking into Edith's eyes, "Do you know why? Because it is very hard. I want you to know that, Edith. For me, it's damn hard. All my life my mother's told me what a mess I am! Both physically and otherwise! She's pointed out every mistake I've ever made. Now she tells me what a mess I'm making out of my children. She tells me I only love one child. 'My baby by the priest,' as she refers to Anno. She still mimics me! She still makes fun of everything I do! She makes fun of my children. I'm used to taking it myself, but when she starts in on my kids, it makes me crazy! *And she's been my teacher of how to raise kids.* I want to change everything I've ever learned about how to raise children!

"Can't you understand that? I've never done anything harder in my life. I'm beginning to realize that nothing on this Earth will ever be harder than this job of parenting, or more rewarding either. And you keep saying that I have such good kids! Damn it, Edith, it's not 'good kids'; it's hard work! It's exhausting but wonderful! But it isn't like we get someone to practice on! Give me a break! It's just as hard for me as it is for anyone else. Maybe even harder, but who's to judge?!"

I was holding back tears. I wanted to scream, but just took a deep breath.

"I've known about Dreikurs for two years and have just gotten to the point where I sometimes naturally see the positive side, instead of the negative side. I've done everything from writing things on the palm of my hands to putting little notes up everywhere in order to remember. Tying a ribbon around my finger. It takes a concentrated effort. It is not easy. It doesn't just happen," I looked at Edith for her reaction.

She lit another cigarette and blew smoke rings silently.

Frustrated, I kept going, "Sometimes I even question myself if some of the things I say sound phony, because I don't want to be phony in any way. It only comes naturally some of the time. I want it to be there all the time. I keep asking myself if I will ever get this stuff to come out naturally? Lord knows it isn't instinct!

"Since I first met Dreikurs you have been saying week after week that it has been easier for me. It really hasn't been long since I went nuts after Anno was born, remember?" I stared right at Edith, knowing she wouldn't answer.

"I mean, that was so hard, laying around depressed for months before finally pulling it together. But when I did get it together and told the kids what I expected of them, things got straightened out and started working like a well-oiled wagon again. But I had to work hard to get there, don't you understand? It wasn't easy. I work at it every day, all day. It's not perfect at my house. It never has been and never will be but things can go better if we keep working at it.

"So for the last time, Edith, at our last meeting here tonight, I ask you: please don't look at me and say that I've got 'such good kids.' We all have good kids. We just have to learn what to do with them, how to guide them, how to encourage them, how to notice the positive parts and ignore the negative parts. How to let the negative die, like the plant we put in the dark basement and never water again. We have to learn that we are part of nature and that what we feed grows. It doesn't just happen. It's a concentrated effort, and we have to understand that we play the most important part in it. It has NOTHING, nothing to do with 'good' kids and 'bad' kids."

I paused and hoped Edith might respond now.

"Well, it does seem like it's easier for you, for some reason," Edith laughed again as she said it.

I sighed, "Edith, I think you only hear what you want to hear. You remember the parts where it goes well for my family but you never seem to remember the difficult part that we go through before reaching the good parts. You have a convenient memory! You heard me talking about how things shaped up and went well. That's all you heard! And what do you credit it all to? That I've got such 'good kids!' Give me a break, Edith, give me a break!" I stopped suddenly and it was dead quiet in the room. "I talk too much," I said softly as I reached for a cigarette. "Maybe someone else wants to say something." I lit it and inhaled. I had finally said some of the things that were on my mind. I wondered if anyone agreed with what I had said.

The meeting drew to a close. It was the end of a chapter in my life, in my family's life. I was anxious to move on to our new home and new challenges.

Marcia stood to give me a hug. "I'm happy for you and your family but another part of me wishes you weren't moving. We'll probably never see each other anymore," she said.

"I know, I'll miss you too, but we're not going to be that far away. The kids even rode up there on their bicycles the other day, and if they can get there on their bicycles, I know you can get there in a car," I answered hopefully.

"Yeah, I know, but it's not going to be like it's next door," Liz had sadness in her voice.

"Yeah, it sure isn't," Edith seconded that thought.

"Well it's hard for me, too. I'm going to miss all you guys and especially our studying together. I had no idea what I was doing when I gathered you all together. You gave me a chance to try out these ideas. You've always told me that you learn stuff from me, but I hope you all know how much I've learned from you. Everything I've told you to do is really something that I needed to learn myself. As they say, 'we teach best what we most need to learn.'" I looked at everyone and hoped they felt my sincerity. Marcia started to remove the ashtrays as the others stood up to leave. It was our last meeting and that probably wouldn't sink in until later. What was going to happen to all our children we had been talking about and learning from?

Roslyn was going to San Antonio; we were going to Evanston. We had a very difficult time the last few weeks because we knew how much we were going to miss each other. Lots of tears, joy, laughter, and love were shared as each of our families prepared for a new life in a new community. Evanston was five miles away and San Antonio was one thousand miles away. But it felt like Roslyn and I would be a million miles apart.

Still, when moving day came, I was excited beyond belief. A new husband, a new baby, a new house, a new community, a new start for all of us. The kids would be in four different schools: high school, middle school, elementary school and soon pre-school. It was going to be a wonderful life.

14

The house was huge. By anyone's standards it was beautiful. How fortunate we were! A spacious front porch with a swing. Large, attractive windows everywhere—even on the landings going up the stairs. There was a back stairway and a lovely banister on the front stairway leading up from the warm and welcoming front hall. I already visualized that banister decorated with a full garland at Christmastime. The living room with a fireplace led into the dining room. The kitchen had cute cabinets with glass doors and wainscoting inside. There were hardwood floors. At the back of the house there was a breakfast room where sunlight poured in on three sides. The second floor had four large bedrooms with another light-filled sun porch in the back. We had bathtubs equipped with old claw feet! Everywhere there was space. The third floor had two more big bedrooms and a bathroom. Sunlight streamed in from every direction. In the back yard was the biggest, grandest old maple tree, perfect for a tire swing. Towering lilac bushes completely fenced in the yard. We loved it! It wouldn't take long to turn this house into a home.

All the kids helped with Anno. My great depression of '72, as I called the time after Anno was born, had finally come to an end. Anno had literally become everyone's kid. Each of her brothers and her sister took full ownership of her. When anyone talked with them, you'd swear that they had been pregnant with her for nine months, too.

It was the first Saturday afternoon in our new house and some of the kids had gone out to look over the neighborhood. Less than a half block away from our new backyard was a huge park.

"Just perfect for softball," Joe announced when they arrived home.

"Wanna play a game sometime soon, Mom?" John asked, walking into the kitchen.

"Well sure, why not!" I answered.

"Have we unpacked all our bats yet?" Anthony asked.

"Yeah, I think they're all down in the basement. Let's go look," John yelled as he started down the basement stairs.

"What's going on in here?" Maria said rubbing her eyes. She had obviously just woken up from a little nap.

"Hey Maria, wanna go play softball?" Joe asked. He was always anxious for a softball game.

"Yeah, that sounds like fun."

Maria started putting on her gym shoes. Anthony was wiping his mitt. Joe was standing in the doorway, anxiously waiting for everyone to get ready. I was on my way out through the back yard when I heard a voice from next door.

"Hey! Where are you guys going?" It was Doug, one of the two boys who lived next door.

"We're just going to the park to play a little soft ball, wanna come with us? Go ask your Mom if you can."

"Will you wait for me?"

"Sure will."

Doug came running out of his house with his little brother Eric. They ran down the alley and stood waiting for us to join them by the back gate. I walked with all of them to the park. Five minutes later, Pat and Anno showed up. I wondered how we would divide up all these kids.

"Let's choose sides. First chooser," John yelled.

The problem was solved.

"Second chooser then," Joe chimed in, a little put off because he didn't yell first.

"I choose Mom," John said laughing, "I mean Apple. I choose Apple!"

I smiled, knowing I could hit the ball well. The kids thought it was pretty cool that I was a good hitter.

"Okay, I take Pat," Joe said immediately.

A big smile crossed Pat's face as he was chosen. He loved playing with the kids too. We all loved playing together.

"Maria."

"Anthony."

"Christopher," John said.

"Eric."

"Doug."

"Anno! Hey Anno, want to be on our side?" Joe yelled to her.

Anno looked at them and then ran as fast as her little one-year-old legs would carry her to where Joe stood.

"Okay, we get up first cause you chose first," Joe wanted to get the rules straight.

"Mom, you pitch," John yelled as he ran to first base.

I grabbed the ball. Everyone took their places.

"Ready!" I yelled to everyone.

"Let's go, Mom," Joe said as he practiced his swing.

I walked to the pitcher's mound and my heart was beating as if it were the World Series. Joe got a hit on my second pitch. He made it to second base and dramatically slid into the dirt. Anno giggled and squealed. Anthony was next and the big heavy bat weighed him down a bit. He stood with his baseball hat pulled down to his eyes, his knees bent and his little butt sticking out at an angle. He hit the ball and ran to first base. Anno was up next and did her best to lift the bat to her shoulders but no one mentioned she was smaller or less equipped to play. They took it in stride. A couple of other neighborhood kids joined the game. My team finally got a turn to bat. I hit the ball hard and made a home run.

They loved their mom being good at baseball. It was one of our favorite games together in the spring and summer and we gathered neighbor kids and played three or four times a week. Hide and go seek also kept us quite busy. We had a great neighborhood with a bunch of kids and lots of yards to play in. We played a lot and it kept us together. I loved it. So did everyone else.

The phone was ringing when we walked back into the house. I could barely say the word "hello" before she started in on me.

"Pick me up at 7:30 tomorrow morning. I want to see the house, now that you've invested your money. I hope it's better than that dump you lived in on Wayne. He'll be at work, won't he?"

"Pat, you mean? Yes, Mother, he'll be at work but..."

"Okay then pick me up! United flight # 221. Don't make me wait. Be there. I can't run up my phone bill. See you tomorrow." Click.

Instant diarrhea. It always happened that way. My body and soul were in knots. She decided she would come even though she told me repeatedly that she approved of nothing I had done or was doing.

The next day, she stormed through the house giving me orders about how it should be if I "remembered any of her training," were her words. Then she said, "It's time for you to learn how to make bread."

She made the best bread in the whole world, and I was thrilled; she was going to teach me something in the kitchen! Mother's bread had always taken blue ribbons at the fair year after year. Her bread, her jelly, her flowers. All blue ribbons. I asked her what ingredients I needed. She gave me a list and I went to the store.

"Bread takes all day," she said. "Letting it rise twice is what takes the time. But you have time now. You have a beautiful home, if you don't ruin it, and now you can make bread for the children. You have radiators to set the pans on for it to rise. They're better than forced-air heat."

I kneaded and kneaded as she watched me. I was covered with flour. The dough felt good oozing between my fingers.

She checked the consistency every few minutes. "You will get the feel of it," she said. She told me I'd be able to tell if it were too moist or too dry, enough yeast or not.

"Not too much honey or it will get too sweet, like coffee cake," she said. She sat in the breakfast room and had some coffee while the dough rose. She was happy that she was teaching this to me. I could tell. I was happy too. I'd now have at least one thing I could do in the kitchen. It would be something I had learned from my mother. *Maybe I'll even do it well,* I thought. After letting it rise the second time, Mother showed me how to fit it in the pans and then we stuck it in the oven.

"Twenty minutes at a high temperature, then twenty minutes at a lower one. That's what makes that hard crust on the outside like French bread," she said. It came out golden and the whole house smelled like bread. The kids came in from school and ran to the kitchen following their noses. They ate the warm bread with butter and honey melting on top.

"Can we have some more, Mom?" they asked.

"Yes, all you want," I answered. I wasn't going to be concerned about anyone ruining their appetite this night. Mother had taught me how to make bread. It felt wonderful. Maybe I wouldn't let her down with my bread making like I had done on my music, my children, my marriage, and the rest of my life. She left two days later and took a tiny loaf of our bread with her. I guess she liked it.

Each person in their own way had settled into their room and their jobs around the house. Sometimes reminders were necessary and sometimes they weren't. Once in a while the kids cooked easy things like hot dogs without my help, but it wasn't too often. During and after the move, I basically fell back into cooking almost every night again.

I wasn't sure how it happened, but the weeks always flew by. Sometimes we went for several weeks without having a meeting, but now it had been a couple months since we moved into the new house and we needed a regular meeting time and place. I wanted to know who was going to do what and when. We needed the routine back. On Sunday morning as everyone strolled in and out of the kitchen, munching on breakfast, I brought the subject up.

"I believe we need to have a family meeting as soon as possible and also set a regularly scheduled meeting time. We have lots of new responsibilities that need to be addressed," I paused to butter Anno's toast. "How would it be if we met on Sundays at ten o'clock or so, starting today, if that's okay with everyone. And if it isn't, then how about starting next week?" I asked loudly enough so that everyone could hear me as I lifted Anno into her high chair.

As he stirred the orange juice, Joe answered, "Yep, that sounds like a good idea!"

Maria agreed too as she emptied the last of the Cheerios into her bowl. Anno knocked over a glass of milk and started to cry, and everyone else became quiet for a moment. They had heard my question. All the kids and Pat agreed with me that today was a good day to start.

Pat always followed my lead with the children. He was in the background watching me. He was quiet and thinking, but I was in charge. He was new to the family and we loved him.

As the kids finished with their breakfast, we moved into the living room and spread out on the floor.

I was the chairperson. That's the way it always was if we missed a few meetings. I always started the meetings again and got everyone back on track. I didn't always want to be the leader but that's just the way it was. It was part of the territory. Pat was great with the kids but I was the one who held everyone together.

"Right now, I think we need to work out how we're going to do things like jobs and stuff," I always used the word stuff. The kids used it too.

"Like what! What stuff?" Joe and John asked at the same time from opposite sides of the circle.

I uncrossed my legs and leaned forward on the couch. Anthony was lying down and motioned for Anno to come rub his back. "Getting her trained early in Back Rubbing 101," he joked. I had to laugh too when I saw Anno, who had just had her first birthday, rubbing his back. I reached for a cigarette and said, "Stuff like everyone having their own night to cook. Making it a definite thing instead of just helping me some nights or doing it yourself once in a while."

"By ourselves? Cook by ourselves?" Anthony quickly raised his head straight up as he asked the question.

"Yes, Anthony, that's what I just said, doing it by yourself," I didn't move a muscle and looked him straight in the eyes. I again made a mental note to extend the deadline on my theory of when I would be done with this training. I thought maybe I just needed a few more months.

"But I don't know how to cook, Mom," Anthony was whining.

I tilted my head up as I looked at him and answered, "I don't know how to cook either, Anthony. Besides, now is a good time for you to learn." I already knew I would not take no for an answer on this cooking thing.

"Well, maybe, if you say so," Anthony shrugged his shoulders and sat up even higher. He was not pleased with this at all. And he didn't try to hide it. Cooking was definitely not his idea of fun.

As I answered him right back, my voice raised a little as well as my eyebrows.

"Well, I can't cook either. Just because I became a Mom didn't mean I knew how to cook. I don't. In fact, I hate cooking. But you guys already know that." I leaned back again and crossed my arms across my chest, "I'm not doing it anymore. Not by myself."

They felt my determination and confidence and, for a minute, there was silence. No one looked at me. They looked at each other. Those kids communicated quite well with their eyes.

Finally Joe broke the silence and he asked, rather peeved, "Can we cook whatever we want to cook?" He wanted to get the facts down straight. His loud voice showed his aggravation with the whole idea.

"Sure, Joe, why not!" I answered, wondering what he'd say next. I felt encouraged by his question but had to stay on my toes so as not to fall into a trap. These kids were quick and I knew I was still not a match for their creativity. But maybe this wouldn't be so difficult to work out with them, after all. I carried the idea farther.

"In fact, if we decide what we want to cook before going to the grocery store on Saturday, we could shop once for the entire week. That way we'd have everything in the house we need for a whole week of dinners." There was silence again and I waited patiently.

"I don't think I like this idea," Anthony sat up to make his announcement. He looked straight at me, then at everyone else in the room. His mouth turned down instead of showing his almost always radiant smile. I jumped on this one quickly.

"Well, I've been the one cooking for years and I don't like it either, Anthony! I'm just not going to do it all the time anymore. Besides, this feels like a re-run to me. We already talked about all this when Anno was about five months old, remember?" My voice remained firm and I felt proud of myself. Anno started dancing in the middle of everyone and the other kids all laughed. I felt like taking her and sitting her down but decided not to. I didn't want to get distracted by Anno. I wanted to work out a few of these serious jobs around the house. Pat got up without saying a word and quietly took her to bed.

John spoke up, his tone disgusted, "None of my friends have to do any of this stuff. They think we're weird."

The kid knew that was a good line. He had used it often with me. It always got me right in the gut. This time, however, I was able to detach myself and get past that remark without feeling guilty. At last, I was learning not to respond to it after falling for it so many times. This meeting already was feeling long but we had just started and nothing had been settled yet. Trying to be patient, I started again.

"There are eight people in this family and seven of them are old enough to cook one night a week. This means each person has to cook only one night a week." I stopped and waited for all of this to sink into their heads. "And if we want, Friday night could be a free night," I added.

I knew that my idea was going to become part of our lives. I was determined to scratch seven nights of cooking out of my life. I didn't know how it would all work out or what lay ahead. But I had learned enough from studying *Children: the Challenge* to be willing to step back and see. I loved it when I felt so confident and sure of myself, and what I wanted to do.

We talked about what they would cook. Pat called down the stairs to volunteer for Saturday nights. John ran into the kitchen and got a pad of paper. John decided he was cooking hot dogs on his night and he wanted everyone to know it.

Would I still be making bread on Monday like I had done every week since Grandmother's visit? I assured them I would. I was really liking that part, baking bread.

Were pancakes good enough for dinner?

Could they make brownies and that kind of thing?

For 20 minutes, the kids went back and forth, getting mad and then working it out. I stayed mostly quiet as they begrudgingly worked out a menu. I had taken another giant step. I'd no longer be the Cooking Queen. I would no longer be responsible for putting a hot meal on the table every night. One night was fine, but not six or seven nights a week like it had always been. It felt great and ended up being the greatest meeting we'd had in a long time. I didn't complain or cry the entire time. I had an idea and stuck with it. I felt creative and determined.

"This meeting is taking too long," Joey complained.

I agreed, "It is taking a long time, isn't it?"

"What if something happens and we can't cook on our night? What will happen then?" John asked.

"Switch with someone!" Anthony said, "Or would that be too logical?"

"What if no one wants to change nights?" Joe asked.

"Keep trying until something is worked out with someone," Maria said matter-of-factly.

"Are toasted cheese sandwiches a dinner if we make them on Mondays with Mom's homemade bread?" Chris asked.

"How about taking care of Anno after school on the same day we are to cook dinner? Since we take turns after school taking care of her anyway, why don't we make it all be the same day?" John asked, his voice excited over the idea.

"Great idea," I assured him.

"Okay, it is a deal then, on the day we sign up to cook, we will also take care of Anno and kill two birds with one stone," Anthony chuckled.

"Who's going to do the shopping for dinner?" Maria asked.

"I don't mind doing it on Saturday," Pat said coming back into the room after putting Anno to bed. "I'll take care of Anno half of the day on Saturday too."

"If we forget to take something out of the freezer in the morning before going to school, would you take it out for us?" Joe asked looking at me.

"Not a good idea," I said, knowing they would not like my refusal. "I'd rather not be in charge of taking the meat out of the freezer for you."

"You already know that Mom's not going to do that," Anthony said, his tone of voice confident as if they were being ridiculously stupid.

"What would that hurt, her taking it out of the freezer?" Joe wanted to know.

I didn't answer. I had already stated my position.

"Well since we HAVE to cook now, one night a week is a good way to handle it," Anthony said still teasing, but also kind of serious.

I reminded them again, "No one *has* to cook any night. No one *has* to do anything, remember!"

"Oh no! Let's don't even mention that stuff again, Mom," Maria said dramatically.

"What stuff, Maria?" I bristled, not liking the insinuation.

"You know what stuff, Mom. When everyone just does whatever they want. And then we all end up in a big fight because everything is such a pigsty. There's total chaos and it's awful! That always turns out to be a big mess when we do it that way."

"Okay, Maria, I understand, but I also am not going to be the big boss around here and say that everyone has to cook on their night. If we are going to take turns cooking, that's great, but I'm not going to be the bad guy, the one who watches everyone else's movements to see if they are following through with their responsibilities. I really don't want that job anymore. I realize that it's quite easy for me to fall back into that role and tell everyone what to do. Hey, I'm learning just like you and I have a long way..."

"Okay, Mom, okay, I get the point," Maria said, cutting me off from what had the potential to be one of my mini-lectures.

"Can we end the meeting now? I have other things to do," John spoke for everyone.

"Does anyone have anything else to say?" I hoped the answer would be no.

"Just one little thing, I was wondering if you guys would start calling me Tony instead of Anthony?" he asked with a serious look on his face.

"Oh no, changing your name too, Anthony? Got a girlfriend, lover boy?" Joe teased him.

"No, I don't have a girlfriend already, Joe!" Anthony mimicked his brother's voice. "I'd just like to be called Tony from now on. Would that be okay with you, Mom?"

"Sure honey, of course it's okay. It's your name. I love both names, Anthony and Tony. When I was in high school, there was a Father Tony that I really loved. Actually, I named you after him..."

I began thinking about when I first met Father Tony. He had set up retreats for all the girls and we got to talk about everything. He always said we could talk to him about anything we wanted to—even sex and boys. Mother had told me a few months before what people had to "go through"(is the way she described it) to have a baby. And when I had asked her what the word "pregnant" meant, she got furious and wanted to know where I had learned that word. She told me to stay away from the girl who "talked like that." So I asked Father Tony about it. He said it wasn't a bad word, but only one to describe a woman who was going to have a baby. I thought from then on if I had a question, I would ask Father Tony. He never laughed or got angry with me. I had almost begun to believe that old phrase that people say about high school being "the best time of your life." That is, until Mother got involved.

"Mary Cecile, please set the table. Supper's just about ready." Her request was more of a demand.

"Yes, Mother. Umm, did I tell you that Father Tony is having another retreat for the girls in my class next week?"

"No."

"Well, he is and I was wondering if you would let me go."

"What exactly does he talk about with all the young girls?"

"Last time he talked about boys and about what happens when a girl gets her period."

She slammed down the pot on the stove.

"I thought this might happen," she yelled. "He has no business being with young girls. He has no business talking about those things. I'm against the whole thing. You may not go on another retreat with that man. Don't you ever dare talk to him again, young lady. Do you hear me?"

"Wait, Mother! He said good things, not bad things! Let me explain..."

"No! Not another word!"

Oh no, I thought. Oh my God, no. Please don't say that...please. Mother, don't take this away...it's all I've got. You can't. But you can. You always do. He's understanding...real...genuine... kind. There are not many people like him in the world. If only I could say these words out loud to you.

"I forbid you to talk to him again."

"Mother..."

"I don't want to hear another word. And don't you dare sass back at me, young lady. If I ever find out that you've talked to him again, I'll beat you so bloody that you'll finally know what a real spanking is. How disgusting to have some priest talking to all those young girls. I'm going out to that school and believe me, you'll wish you never heard the name Father Tony. That priest does not belong in a high school with young girls. I'm going to look into this and see if he can be removed. Besides, Mary Cecile, you should be able to

ask me about anything."

"But..."

"Silence. It's a closed chapter."

Please, dear God, let her change her mind. I prayed to God that she would change her mind. But she wouldn't. I knew she wouldn't. She never changed her mind. I was forbidden to see or talk to Father Tony ever again. I then decided that high school was definitely not going to be the best time of my life. It was a closed chapter, she said. There were so many closed chapters in that house.

"Thanks, Apple," Tony said, putting his hand on my shoulder and bringing my focus back to the meeting.

The teasing had stopped and everyone agreed to call him Tony.

"Anyone else have anything to say?" I was sure we were finished now.

"I do," Christopher said laid back and relaxed.

"What is it, Christopher?" I asked with a tired voice.

"When you're tired, go to bed." He used his hands to express simplicity.

"Okay, thanks, Christopher. End of meeting," I sighed with relief.

It was the only thing Christopher said at our meetings thus far, and he was usually struggling to stay awake when he said it.

I returned to the Child Guidance Center by myself. It felt strange not having Roslyn with me and I missed her tremendously. The demonstration family that night was working on bedtime. I was amazed again at how much I learned. Everyone really did make the same mistakes. Even though getting the kids into bed had never been a problem for me, I could still see glimpses of myself in that mother. We both wanted to do everything perfectly. I realized more than ever that night that the struggle to be perfect was a huge part of a lot of people's lives.

"We're all walking around trying to prevent mistakes rather than learn from them," I told Pat upon arriving home that night, "Seems to me that everything is based on the idea that in order for kids to learn, we have to point out their mistakes. We do it at home and then that's the way it is in school. Every mistake is pointed out with the red pencil. No encouragement on all the things done well. Comparing each child with the other siblings. My daddy's words keep coming back to me. *What we feed, grows; it's a law of nature.* No wonder kids are so angry by the time they get to be teenagers."

The rest of the week was interesting, to put it mildly. Dinners were a riot. That was the only way I could think to describe it when I dared to tell anyone what was going on inside our house. That was happening less and less now though because most people usually looked at me like I was nuts when I tried to describe the way our family ran itself.

Monday night was Joe's night to cook. His dinner included burnt toasted cheese sandwiches on my own homemade bread and a side dish of corn. He probably figured he couldn't go wrong if he used the homemade bread, and he was correct. It was really the best bread ever. A clean tablecloth fresh out of the dryer hung down almost touching the floor on one side, and barely covering the table on the other. He received compliments on the nice tablecloth and great sandwiches. No one mentioned the burnt part. I noticed that there were only forks, no spoons, and one community knife. By the time we started eating, the toasted bread was cold and the cheese was hard. There was nothing to drink until almost the end of the meal when Joe jumped up and got everyone their choice of water or milk. Not a soul mentioned these obvious facts. The meal was filled with laughter. John told a funny story about one of his friends. Dinner ended with a "Thanks for cooking, Joe," from everyone. Nothing negative was said. It was amazing.

Tuesday night, we had pancakes and orange juice. The pancakes were a little moist and soggy in the middle but, once again, no one said a word about it. Tony was complimented on the golden color of the pancakes. We were out of milk so everyone drank water. The kitchen had as much pancake dough on the stove and floor as we had in our stomachs. Maybe more. John said it was a pretty neat idea having pancakes for dinner since everyone loved them and time didn't allow pancakes to be a choice for breakfast. Maria complimented Tony on how huge his pancakes were. His smile extended from one ear to the other. I thanked him for the good dinner and bit my tongue to refrain from pointing out any mistakes. The syrup was all gone before everyone got some. Tony immediately replaced it with honey. Joe, who was first upset at not getting syrup, was amazed how good honey tasted on pancakes. He complimented Tony on his discovery.

I had told the kids many times that honey was as good as syrup, but no one ever paid any attention. Now after John suggested it, honey was great. Who knew how that all worked, I wondered to myself. I was concerned about not having any vegetables, but told myself not to mention it. Tony had put clean placemats on the table but the crumbs from their snacks after school had not been cleaned off. I wanted to wipe the table free of crumbs and stickiness but refrained. Again, we had lots of laughs during dinner. I wondered if there was more laughter than usual. Maybe.

Wednesday night's dinner consisted of hot dogs and potato chips. No one knew where John had found the flowers, but he was complimented on his arrangement. A smile grew across his face when he was thanked. I knew the flowers came from a neighbor's yard down the street, but how could I say anything about it? I, myself, was guilty several times of picking flowers in someone else's yard. His brothers and sisters had only good things to say. The hot dogs pretty much squashed the hot dog buns and John had called everyone at least ten minutes too late, allowing sogginess to set in. Maybe it was the rainy day humidity that caused the potato chips to be soft. He made red Jello for dessert. Joe and Maria said they loved it. I thanked him for planning ahead and making Jello.

This was the third night of a kid being in charge of dinner and not once, so far, had any of them said a negative word. I watched their faces when they spoke. They were completely sincere with their compliments. The words just flowed out of them. They made no notice of things that were missing, things that were soggy, things that weren't cooked well, or that the menu consisted of starch and more starch. Kids are amazing, real and sincere, I thought lying in bed that night.

Thursday night, Maria made hamburgers and French fries. It was the first day that someone had remembered to take meat out of the freezer early enough to use the same night. There were clean placemats were under each plate and the flowers from yesterday were still on the table. The hamburgers were very well done and the french fries had obviously been in the oven too long, yet Maria only received compliments.

"Thanks, you guys," Maria said, beaming. She was pleased with herself and it showed.

"Hello?"

"I'm so excited about everything," I told Roslyn over the phone, "I want to tell everyone I meet, but who'd listen to me? "

"What are you talking about? What's happened?"

"The kids have started cooking. It's been a riot. I'm so excited and so relieved. It's the same kind of relief I felt the day I learned that I was no longer going to be involved in their fighting," I explained to Roslyn.

"They've been cooking? Like actual dinners? You're serious, aren't you? God, what did they make?"

"Lots of toasted cheese sandwiches, hot dogs, pancakes—basically lots of starch," I laughed.

"Anything else?"

"Let's see...oh yeah, jello! They made jello, too!" I said still laughing. "And I only talked about the positive parts and didn't say anything about the negatives all week. Can you believe it?"

"Of course I can believe it. You've always said lots of encouraging things," Roslyn assured me. "You just don't see it yourself."

"Well, I don't know if I always have, but the kids notice the positive things and I guess they're learning it from me. Boy, that's hard for me to believe," I said.

"Of course they're learning it from you. You've always been so hard on yourself," Roslyn was comforting me.

"Whatever. It all seems like a miracle." I said, sighing.

"Sure, Dreikurs always talked about that."

"About what?" I asked.

"He said we're all so discouraged that any time something good happens with our kids we think it's a miracle."

"Yeah, I remember now. Well that's true. I was taught everything was hereditary and 'in the genes.' All that stuff is ingrained into us as the only possible reason why kids act the way they do. We've all had that same training. Now, I want to go around and shout out to the world. I want everyone to know that if we build on the positive, even if we have to force ourselves, our kids will learn it from us. If we point out the negative, the kids will learn to point out the negative too. It's true that what we feed will grow."

"How well I know. I'm sure feeding on the negative these days."

"Oh I'm sorry Roslyn, I didn't even ask how things were going with you in San Antonio. What's going on with you guys?"

"Well, actually it's been really hard. I feel like I'm losing everything I learned from Dreikurs. But we're going to see this guy next week. Sort of like therapy. I think that will help."

"I'm sure it will help for you to have someone to talk with but I thought you would start a study group with some other mothers out there. We both know that helps tremendously," I reminded her.

"I'm sure it would, but I need some help right now. Hopefully I'll start a study group soon, but until then, I'll have this. Would it be okay if I called you back tomorrow night? Robert and I were on our way out."

"Oh I'm sorry, why didn't you tell me?"

"It's okay. I had time to talk for a few minutes. I'll call you back tomorrow."

"Okay kid, bye."

"Bye. Love to the guys. Talk to you tomorrow."

"You too."

Lying in bed that night, I thought about Roslyn and how discouraged she sounded and how encouraged I myself felt with the wonderful things that had been happening around the dinner table. I wanted Roslyn to have that wonderful feeling too.

Friday night, we had pancakes with orange juice again. Christopher made a side dish of toast to complete our week of "starch, starch, and more starch." He was complimented on his choice of placemats and his orange juice with ice cubes was a great hit, too. No one had ever put ice cubes in orange juice before so Christopher was considered quite innovative.

I thought for sure that someone would complain about having pancakes again since we had them just three days before. But no one complained. In fact, John, Tony and Joe joined Christopher in the kitchen and helped him out. Tony proudly told his brother that he was now an expert on making pancakes. Christopher loved the help. John washed the table clean before setting the table that night. John liked things clean and in order, which is why I was amazed he didn't say anything the other night when the table was so sticky and full of crumbs.

I thanked Christopher, telling him how good the pancakes tasted and then thanked everyone again for cooking the entire week. I was in awe of what had happened these last five days, how they all found something positive to say every night at the dinner table. The kids sincerely saw and pointed out something positive in everything that revolved around these dinners. Maybe it was the snowball effect, I thought.

I took my turn cooking as did Pat. True to form, only positive things were said about our dinners. Although my meatloaf was pretty dry and almost a whole bottle of ketchup was used that night to moisten it, no one mentioned the crispness. But then again, the kids had never complained about my cooking before, no matter how bad I thought it had been. Actually they really didn't know any better.

A month went by and even though we planned a menu each week at our meeting, what was planned was seldom served. More often than not, the kids still forgot to take the meat out of the freezer and then had to remedy the situation with something quick—like toasted cheese sandwiches. I wondered how long the forgetfulness would last, but didn't mention it. Sometimes the meals were so bad I thought they had to be doing it on purpose, sort of to prove that they couldn't cook in hopes of getting out of the job. But criticism never surfaced and the fun and laughter increased. No one ever noticed that the table wasn't perfect. I started to notice it less too. It was no longer at the top of my list. I made a conscious effort to change my perspective on it and was thrilled I could do it sometimes. The children were good teachers.

Each week, when they came home from school and took their turn taking care of Anno and then cooking dinner, there was a sense of pride in their eyes. They were still fussing once in a while because "none of their friends had to do that kind of stuff," but at each dinner meal, they were complimented and they ate it up. And each week, the meals improved. Not huge improvement, but there was definite improvement. The toasted cheese sandwiches were almost burnt-free after three weeks. The small black part could be scraped off easily now without half the sandwich ending up in the garbage. I was excited and relieved that I was no longer totally responsible for cooking all our meals. I kept my mouth shut except to compliment, and that felt so good inside. I was doing what Dreikurs recommended: sharing the responsibility rather than trying to teach it.

Nevertheless, three months later we were definitely back to the part where meetings were not much fun. Sometimes I hated the meetings as much as anyone else but I never said that out loud. It was the yo-yo effect. Up and down we went. Skipping them didn't help; things got worse if we didn't have meetings on a regular basis. I wondered if we would ever get it. Would I ever get it? Would democracy ever come? I tried different things to make the meeting a little bit more exciting. Sometimes we would do something fun together—like play a softball game in the park—before we had the meeting.

Then the good feelings from playing together carried over naturally to our meetings of course. But lately I was feeling worn down again. I was picking up things that were left around, asking people to put away clean clothes, and asking someone to clean the kitchen. Today at the meeting, I brought that stuff up again.

"Maybe if it's still warm this weekend we can play softball again. You guys want to?" I wanted to start out on a positive note, but John wanted to talk about something else first.

"I'd like to say that I think our meals are a little dull and usually leave something to be desired. Paul's mom makes all sorts of good meals," he looked straight at me when he said that. I remained patient although his statement irritated me.

"John, maybe we need to do more than just talk about planning our menus. Everyone said they thought it was a good idea, but we haven't done it so far."

"Yeah, that's a good idea, Mom, but I'm talking about really good stuff to eat. The stuff that Paul's mom makes, well, we just don't know how to make that kind of stuff," John was insistent.

The toasted cheese sandwiches were getting old. Cooking was not my favorite thing and they all knew it. But I did feel encouraged because I made such wicked good bread. Everyone loved that, including all the neighbors who looked forward to getting their loaf of bread each week. My recipe had indeed grown bigger. Yet I really couldn't foresee learning how to cook a bunch of new things. Silence reigned for what seemed like hours until Tony took the initiative.

"Okay, I'm cooking hot dogs this week," he said with great enthusiasm. Hot dogs were one of his favorite meals. Besides, they were easy to fix.

"Tony, you got to fix them last week. That's not fair," Joe protested. He wasn't too fond of this cooking idea either, but usually didn't say too much. "Besides, I'm getting pretty sick of hot dogs."

John had it organized. "I'll put up a list of things we eat and everybody can choose what they want. Then we won't have to spend three hours at a meeting trying to figure it out. I have other things I want to do today."

"So do I, John," I said.

"We know that, Mom!" Their voices rang out in unison, showing their irritation. The kids looked at each other and talked with their eyes.

"What else?" Maria said finally.

"We've been in this house several months and had enough time to get settled and find a place for all our belongings." I started. "A big house has many advantages, one of which is that there is plenty of room and a place for everything. Still, I'm tripping over people's belongings from the front to the back door. Starting tonight, I will pick up all the things that are in the general area of the house, mainly on the first floor and put them away."

"Oh no, not that again, Mom, please! Don't you think we're getting a little old for that?" Joe said, frowning something furious. Everyone else groaned.

"Well for sure *I'm* getting a little old for it," I laughed. "Just put your stuff away please and stop acting like we have maid service around here. We don't."

"Okay, Mom, we will," Maria answered for all. Everyone wanted this meeting over. No one looked at me.

"Okay, anyone else have anything they want to say? Christopher?"

"When you're tired, go to bed," Christopher said as he sat straight up.

"Christopher, is that all you're EVER going to say?" Maria was up on her knees now, ready to head out.

"What's wrong with it, Maria?" Christopher looked shocked.

"Nothing, Christopher. I'll go to bed when I'm tired," she leaned back on her heels as she spoke.

The meeting ended.

I was glad I brought up what was bothering me the most, even if the kids didn't like it. I felt confident that at least now everyone would put their things away before going to bed. They just needed a reminder. It was not as if they hadn't done the locked closet before. A reminder would be sufficient.

After the meeting, Pat and I talked about his job at Insurance Co. He didn't like it much but decided to stay a little while longer and give it a chance. I knew he needed a job where he was helping people more directly.

"People loved you at St. Mark's, Pat. You need to be in a helping profession and you don't have to be a priest to help people."

He insisted he wanted to give the Insurance Co. more of a chance since he had only been with them for a few months.

"A few months or a few years won't make a difference," I told him. He was not in the right place. It was obvious to me but not him. That's the way it is many times, though.

All was quiet when I started walking through the house later that night. I expected to find the floor clear of any stuff and be able to go straight to bed. I stopped in the hallway and stared. My mouth fell open. Right there, in the middle of the floor, was Maria's algebra book. At least, I thought it was Maria's. Yes, it had to be. No one else had an algebra book. And there were Joe's gym shoes. Tony's jacket and stocking hat. Someone's belt. A notebook. A set of keys. More and more stuff.

I started mumbling to myself, "Damn, you guys, quit testing me with this stuff! This is so hard and we already know how it goes. You leave it out. I put it away. You get mad. I get nervous. You say I'm a witch. I agree with you. You stomp out. I go in the bathroom. You question me after school. I don't answer. You stay in your room. I stay in my room. You talk about it close enough so that I can hear. I pretend I don't hear you. You scream at me, 'You think it's so funny, living like this! I wish we were a normal family.' I scream back, 'We are more normal than you know!' You don't eat breakfast. I don't eat lunch. You yell. I scream. You slam the door. I breathe a sigh of relief."

I'm thinking, "Why don't you just put your stuff away? It would be so much easier. Why do we have to have these tests? It's true that the tests are farther and farther apart, but why do you have to test me at all? Can't you remember the rules or do you have to show me you can break them? Why can't it run smoothly all the time? Is it just me wanting it perfect again?

You're older now and share so many responsibilities. Why do you have to issue more tests?"

Sometimes I get so tired of these tests that I don't even want to be the mom. Who can I tell that to? No one that I know of, not even Pat. He's great and I love him with all my heart but sometimes I get tired of trying to make him happy. And sometimes when his mom asks me every time we get together, "Is Pat happy? Do you think he's happy?" I want to scream out, "No he's not happy, but I'm doing all I know how to do to make him happy." He married me when I had five children and he loved that part. We joked about it being his little church. I can't really expect him to know about children because he's not had any experience in that part of life and it's a big thing. But I strongly believe he has every right to be happy.

Everyone always told me how lucky I was that a guy married me when I had five kids. But honestly sometimes I wanted to say, "Well he got himself a pretty good deal. Maybe he was the lucky one to get these five wonderful kids and me." I know I'd never say anything like that because they'd think I was being conceited when I don't mean it that way at all. But I say it to myself sometimes. These are damn wonderful kids, and with the training they're getting who knows what all they'll do when they get out in the world. I mean, I have given every ounce of me to train them. I can say that at this age they are funny, kind, and crazy kids with a marvelous sense of humor.

Yet sometimes I get tired of training them and want to quit. Where are all those people who say how "lucky" I am to have such good kids? Where are they now when I'd like to say, "Damn, this is hard and today I want to give up." Well, I've certainly had that feeling before, and it will go away again. This is what it takes to break the cycle of abuse. No one ever said it was going to be easy.

There are positive things, though, and sometimes I forget to acknowledge them. The children play with each other and help each other. They take care of one another—not just Anno that one day a week. They guide each other and help with homework. They watch out for each other daily. They yell and fuss, but the next moment they are helping again. Sure, they may take each other's stuff, "borrow," they say, but they make amends and give it back. They are such a strong group and everyone who meets them feels it.

They really are special and different, and it's not because I'm a better mom. I'm not. It's because I am learning stuff that anyone can learn. I'm no smarter than anyone else, that's for sure. And every day I see how it's not in the genes but rather *what you feed grows*. It's "What you do with what you got," as Uncle Remus says.

I keep wondering how will this all turn out. How will *they* turn out? Is the proof in the pudding, like I say to those who make fun of me? During the good days the good is so good and I definitely think the sky is the limit. The power of building on strengths is mind-boggling, and right now I do believe this is the best age that kids can be! The feeling makes me higher than a kite.

15

I was more determined than ever that our home would be warm, wonderful and inviting at Christmastime for my children and any friends or family. My childhood Christmases were the most tense and horrible time of the year. Our bitter gatherings usually ended with loud, emotional fights around the table, doors slamming, suitcases packed in a hurry, and fast departures. Ever since I was a little kid I had dreamt about having a Christmas party, and living in our new home made it possible.

Our family meeting that week was a huge success. Without realizing it, we were laying the groundwork for a tradition that everyone would come to love and cherish. The planning of the party set a warm and cooperative tone in our meeting.

"A show for the guests?" Joe asked when I brought my idea up at the meeting. I could tell that he liked the sound of my suggestion but was a little shy about how it would work. "What kind of show?"

"I don't know, sing or something. Make up something like you guys always do when you play with your friends, you know," I said.

They were natural hams, forever after me to watch something they had made up and were acting out. So it wasn't a matter of *if* they could do it. It was more a matter of *would* they? This was a new idea and I knew I needed to be silent while they thought it over and discussed it among themselves. I listened and waited.

"Me and Tony could do a puppet show!" Christopher announced excitedly. He was not the least bit hesitant.

"Yeah, that's a good idea. What else?" I paused and waited for them to think.

"We could do a bunch of skits, and make hors d'oeuvres and things. Would you let us do that?" Maria asked.

"Let you?" I laughed. "You know I can't do that kitchen stuff. If you want to do it, that would work out great," I said, pleased I had refrained from making more suggestions.

"Sure, Mom, we'd love to help!"

And they did. The kids decided the whole menu. There would be a cracker and cheese plate, carrot sticks, celery sticks, and peanuts. When anyone called to say they were coming to the party and asked if they could bring anything, the answer was always "yes."

The night of the party, the table was filled twice over with cakes, cookies, cheeses, vegetables, hot dishes, and desserts brought by all the guests. The kids started out with a dance routine. Then they sang and acted silly. After they got their first laugh, they were on their way to being the complete hams they loved to be. It was hilarious. Joe sang "A Boy Named Sue" while I played the guitar. He stared at me with that innocent face and those big brown eyes twinkling and as the words "I grew up fast, I grew up mean" came out of his mouth, we all had to cover our mouths to hold in the laughter. Everyone loved it. In fact "the show" turned out to be the highlight of the evening. The kids were as proud as Pat and I. They felt just as responsible for everyone having a good time as I did. Friends told me I was "blessed" with good kids. This wasn't anything new for me to hear, but it always felt good, no matter how many times I had heard it before. Of course I knew I wasn't lucky; I knew it was because of the ideas I had learned from Dreikurs, from studying his book *Children: The Challenge* and from going to the family demonstrations at the Center.

"We had a really great time, Mary. Thanks for inviting us. Your kids are absolutely wonderful. My kids would never do anything like what your kids did tonight," Julie said as she put on her coat.

"Oh, you'd be surprised what your kids would do. They're natural born actors you know, all of them," I said.

"Yeah, but your kids are different," she said pulling on her gloves, "they're just different than other kids."

"Thanks, Julie, I've had a lot of help," I responded humbly.

"Help! What do you mean?" her eyes questioned.

"Well, I've done a lot of studying, and I go to this Center where I learn stuff."

"Really?"

"Absolutely! I'd have been on the mental farm a long time ago without my study group in my old neighborhood. Now I survive by going to the family demonstrations at the Center."

"Study group?" she closed the door and came back inside.

"Yeah, it's a bunch of mothers getting together and studying about other ways to raise children. It's wonderful! We use Dreikurs' book as we study and help each other, encouraging each other. You know, stuff like that," I shifted feet as I talked.

"Wow, that sounds great. Are you doing it now?"

"No, but hopefully I'll get a group going soon. Would you be interested in coming when I get one started?"

"I would," Trish said, listening in on the conversation. Three more couples gathered in the hallway by now.

"Yes, most definitely," Julie exclaimed. "This must be what Patricia was telling me about the other day. Patricia! Hey Patricia!" she yelled across the crowd. "Mary was just telling me about some study group. Is that what you were talking about the other day?"

"Yeah, hold on a minute, I want to get my cheese dish," Patricia said as she looked over the table of food.

"Mary, sign me up. I'll come if you get this going. How soon do you think it will be?" Julie asked anxiously.

"Hopefully soon," I said gently. "I need it so much myself."

"Well thanks a lot, Mary. I loved the party," she looked for Ron in the crowd as she talked. "Come on honey, let's go. It was great. The kids are great. Best party we've ever been to."

"Thanks Julie, glad you could come," I said closing the door.

It felt so good to hear the compliments about my kids from people. It gave me courage to go on. It gave me confidence that I was not only doing something effective, but that it showed. Lots of people were saying that now—that my kids were different and wonderful. Although I still had difficulty explaining any concept of exactly what I was doing, obviously it was "working" and I was elated. It was going to be different for my kids. After that night, our parties became twice a year affairs, with the kids' entertainment becoming the most desired and loved element of the party.

My mother arrived for a visit a couple days before our Christmas party. Even though I was "living in sin" because I married a former priest, she couldn't stay away forever. It had been a couple of years since she had last visited us in Chicago for Christmas. Would this visit turn out to be as devastating as her visits always were?

Sure enough, Mother made fun of me. She made fun of my husband, my children, my friends, the way I was raising my kids, and my psychology. "You and your psychology" she'd yell every chance she'd get. The list never ended.

When she visited, I had to talk to myself regularly. I reminded myself to be patient, understanding, and whatever else it took to avoid feeling beaten down and vulnerable to her attacks.

Inside, I screamed at her, *"Why do you have to condemn so much? Why do I have to hold my breath when I am in your presence? Why do you want to own my thoughts? Why must I be strangled in order for you to be happy? Why didn't anyone ever come into our house? In all those years, no one ever came. That's a pretty perfect record, don't you think? Do you know why?"*

I had given up the hope of Mother ever saying something kind about me, but I still hoped for her to say something kind about my children. I knew Mother enjoyed the party even though she criticized everyone. Her visit strongly reinforced my vow to raise my kids differently than I had been raised. After all, isn't it "like mother like daughter" or "the apple doesn't fall far from the tree?" Her visit was my refresher course. It left me devastated, as her visits always did. And I realized those feelings might never go away.

"It blows my mind," I said to Meg the next time I was at the Center. "I have no idea why things happened the way they do when my mother comes to visit. Although the kids are very responsible and have learned to do many things differently already, there are also many days when things are absolutely miserable and fall apart.

It was our turn to be the demonstration family again. While the kids were in the playroom, I was back on stage in front of the audience pouring out my heart to Meg. "Things work well for a few days, then, suddenly I'm screaming at them again for the messy kitchen or something else that's out of place. But when Mother comes to visit, every little thing gets unbelievably perfect. I can't for the life of me figure out what happens or why it happens." My hands moved as fast as my mouth as I explained in detail.

"Not once did the kids forget to clean up the kitchen or wash the dishes. John swept the floor, took out the garbage, and straightened up. Anthony folded the clothes. Joe and Maria started dinner. Anthony played with Anno. Maria asked Grandmother if she wanted a cup of coffee. Anthony asked her if she wanted to play Scrabble. Joe massaged her feet. Christopher asked her if she wanted him to brush her hair. John brought her the paper. There was well-organized movement everywhere." I took a deep breath. "It was as if someone wrote a script to a play and no one wanted to miss a line. Life on the big screen. It was absolutely mind-boggling!"

Meg seemed to sense that I wasn't finished and remained silent.

"I understand how kids know when and where parents are most vulnerable—at church, in front of company, in the grocery store, any place really where we want to look our best in front of others. But this was right inside our own home. And it wasn't just for one day but it was every day during my mother's visit," I leaned back in my chair and sighed.

Meg then began in a soft voice, "Your kids could have totally devastated you in front of your mother, but instead they provided you with an almost perfect home life for the two weeks their grandmother visited. The most important part of the total dynamics is for you to know that you have won your kids over. Instead of embarrassing you in front of your mother, the kids have gone out of their way to protect you against her wrath by behaving in a manner almost unheard of in today's family," she stopped and looked at me in silence, patiently scanning my face.

After a long pause, I said slowly, "You mean, I'm doing it? In spite of the millions of mistakes that I've made, I'm doing it? Changing it? Is that what you're saying?" I could feel the tears burning in my eyes as I looked down at my hands.

"Yes, you've gained a tremendous amount of respect from your children. You've come such a long way since you first met Dreikurs. You don't give yourself enough credit for doing a great job. You still put yourself down quite a bit."

I looked up at Meg.

"And," she continued, "You still want to get it all perfect." She smiled as I allowed her words to soak in. Then she proceeded to enumerate my strengths as everyone listened. She asked the parents in the audience how many of them felt the same way I did. There were an abundance of hands.

When we finished the session, I gathered the children and walked to the car. It was true; I did want to get it all perfect. Damn, would that ever go away? I had a lot to think about on the drive home from the Center that day. Later, I called Roslyn to tell her about the session.

"We were the demonstration family at the Center again," I told her.

"How did it go?" Roslyn asked anxiously.

"It was great. I understand now why the kids act like they're perfect when my mother comes."

"They probably don't want her to attack you, right?"

"More or less, that's how Meg explained it. Anyway, how's it going with you? I miss you so much."

"I miss you too and I can't tell you how much I miss the Center. Just listening to you talk I realize how much I've slipped right back into my old ways. It's terrible. Today I was comparing the kids again, getting in on their fights, and falling for their tattling. I mean, I've done it all in the last 24 hours. It's so hard without the study group. You don't know how lucky you are to be able to go to that Center, Mary Cecile," she said.

"I know, but I also need to start another study group. It's easy for me to slip back too. Have you thought about starting a group, Roslyn?"

"Well, not really. We're not settled yet. Maybe after we get settled."

"Are you sure that's the reason, Roslyn? Or are you just afraid like me?"

Roslyn laughed her wonderful laugh, "Probably a little bit of both, but I've got to run. We can talk about it again another time."

"Okay, but I seriously think you need to start one, my friend," I pleaded with her.

"Well, we'll see," Roslyn said, but I could hear the doubt in her voice.

16

Since we moved in on Labor Day weekend, this would be the first summer in our new home. Pat and I decided we would take a family vacation - our first ever vacation, because vacations were for rich people. Poor people didn't do that kind of thing. I decided to tell the kids about the money from Aunt Cecily so they would understand what was going on. Until we moved we had lived in a tiny house and never had a dime for anything. Now we had a big house in Evanston and were planning a vacation. Stuff like that didn't just happen. I wanted them to know that part.

Everyone was excited beyond words. Since Maria was the oldest and was going to be the first one to leave home, it was agreed that we would go to Colorado because it was her dream to see the Rocky Mountains. It was okay with all the kids and Pat for me to invite their grandmother to go along with us. I hoped that Mother would enjoy herself and be too busy having a good time to be on my case all the time.

We drove to Colorado and stayed for a week at a wonderful ranch in the mountains. It was incredibly beautiful. We were up where the tops of the mountains could touch the blue sky. The air was clean, the water was pure, and we could drink out of the stream. Actually everything was more peaceful than any of us could have ever imagined. We rode horses, went on hikes, ate the greatest meals in our whole lives, and laughed with new friends. We had to carry pillows with us everywhere in case we wanted to sit down, because none of us were used to riding horses all day long.

One of my dreams had come true. I had always dreamt of a vacation with my children and a husband. Grandmother enjoyed herself too, and her criticizing was at an all-time low. After the week on the ranch, we dropped her off at the airport in Denver and headed for home.

While crossing through Nebraska, Anno started screaming and threatened the safety of our eardrums, as well as ruining our chance at a peaceful ending to our wonderful vacation.

"We've got to pull over," I whispered softly to Pat.

"Here? Out here in the middle of nowhere?"

"Well, I'm not sure we can plan where or when Anno will start screaming," I half laughed when I said it, but I was serious.

"Just pull off here?" Pat still didn't like the idea.

"Hey, all I know is she's screaming and it's making me crazy. The way I've done it before is when one of them started acting up while I was driving, I just pulled over at my earliest convenience and sat in silence until they stopped."

"But you weren't ever in a hurry to get home with a thousand miles left to go either. You probably did it on the way to the grocery store, didn't you?" Pat suggested, clearly irritated as he steadily drove along.

In the back seat, John and Maria tried to get Anno to shut up. The more they tried, the louder she screamed.

"Well honestly, Pat, I really don't remember ever having the opportune time to train kids. In fact, I don't ever remember jumping up and down with glee about 'using the bathroom properly,' the locked closet, or any of the rest of it. But when I got in the car and they acted up, I would pull over. If I didn't, I would've got into a wreck. For me, it was that simple. If you want to keep driving with her screaming like that, go ahead."

I had to remind myself how much I loved him because there were definitely times when his attitude showed that some things were only the 'mother's job' and he wanted no part in them, even though he pretended he was part of everything.

"I'm really not in the mood to stop. I thought we wanted to make it to Iowa tonight," Pat was still irritated and unwilling.

"Hey, don't pull over then," I said looking out the window.

Five minutes passed, but it seemed like hours. Anno kept screaming. It was horrible. Pat finally pulled over.

"Oh no, not this," Joey moaned from the back, "Anno, shut up! Mom, are we going to stay here until she stops crying?"

I got out of the car, gave Joe a you-know-what-we're-doing look, and slowly started walking away. Pat followed. Anno screamed. The vivid red sun was going down between the mountains. The rays felt warm on my face. I walked a few steps further.

"What are we going to do, Mom?" Maria called as she followed me.

"We're going to stay pulled over until Anno stops screaming, Maria. Please ask the guys not to say anything else to her. Let's just ignore her screaming. I think it will stop soon."

"Okay Mom," Maria said, turning around to repeat to the boys what I had said.

Anno sat strapped in her car seat, still screaming.

"I think she'll stop soon," I said to Pat.

"Maybe so." He watched the cars go by.

She did stop, but it took forty-five minutes. A tired and disgusted group climbed back inside and took off without a word. At last there was rest for our eardrums.

We reached Iowa later than planned but still found a decent place to stay for the night. Pat carried Anno inside. She had finally fallen asleep about a hundred miles back. We had done it. We had lived out my dream vacation.

17

Summer drew to a close and the kids and I were enjoying one of our last days on the beach. The mother who had spoken to me a couple of times at the water's edge was there again today. She approached me slowly as she lit a cigarette.

"Hi, how are you?"

"Good, Helen, and you?" I said holding up my hand to shade my eyes from the sun.

"Could we talk a minute?" she asked.

"Sure."

"Well, I've been reading the book you suggested and I think it's the greatest. I'm wondering if you've thought anymore about starting that study group? I've talked with a few mothers I know with small children and told them what you did in your old neighborhood," she took a deep drag on her cigarette.

"I apologize for having put it off for so long. I told you I would do it and that's all the farther it's gotten. I've promised others, too, and still haven't followed through," I said, drawing lines in the sand with my toes. "If you call me later we could find a time to get together and work out the details."

"Really! You'd consider it?" Helen asked, thrilled.

"Yes, no more putting it off!" I exclaimed. "I need it as much as anyone. We could definitely learn from each other and help each other."

"Oh thank you, thank you very much. I love Dreikurs' book," she reached out to hug me.

"Yep, I love it too. Like I told you the last time, I've met him and he was fabulous!" I smiled as I remembered Dreikurs.

"I'll call you later, thanks again," Helen said rushing off.

"You're welcome, thank you too," I was so happy. I'd have to call Roslyn and tell her. She'd be proud.

Helen called me the next day and we worked out all the details of starting a group in our neighborhood. We decided to meet in Helen's home every Tuesday morning at 9:30 sharp for two hours. Helen would have coffee for all of us. We told all the mothers to get a copy of the book, *Children: The Challenge*. I checked with the bookstore to see if copies were available. "It isn't a problem," the man at the bookstore told me, "It's a steady seller so we always have copies on hand." Helen had nine mothers signed up to come for sure and two more who were hoping to change their schedules in order to attend. I couldn't wait for Tuesday to arrive, and that night I read several chapters in my book to refresh myself.

I woke the next day to a million thoughts racing through my head. I decided that I wanted to get a part-time job. I'd been reading the ads in the local newspaper without telling anyone, and saw an opening at the local paint store. I could help pay the bills and get a discount on paint and supplies to fix up our home. The kids would always be my greatest responsibility, but I was excited about the thought of having a job where I'd get my own paycheck. Although I had done thousands of hours of volunteering, this would be quite a step for me—leaving home for a job.

These feelings and new thoughts about having a job—other than being a mother and wife—seemed like a lot. More and more I realized the tremendous impact a mother has on her children, yet I never really thought I was capable of doing anything outside my home, other than volunteering. The whole concept of getting a job was overwhelming to me. I'd never had much time to think about these things because there were lots of kids and each one always wanted a little part of me, a little time alone with me, as did my husband. They would seek me out when I was alone. I still hadn't learned how to get a few minutes alone for myself.

Thoughts of getting a job and starting the study group made me a little nervous. The children were growing and getting older so quickly. It seemed like the months flew by with only a few pauses for birthdays. I was constantly ripping those months off the calendar.... Still, Anno would need a baby sitter if

I got a job.

"You're not the boss of me, Tony!" Anno screamed at him and broke my thoughts. It seemed like she screamed that statement at someone every day. Yes, Anno had said that since she started talking, and it seemed like she started saying it as soon as she came out of the womb, almost three years ago now. She would have no part of anyone telling her what she had to do because they "said so" or because they were older, but she would listen to anyone who spoke respectfully to her. It was clear that the "I'm the boss because I'm bigger and older" kind of thinking would never work in this family.

Although I was upstairs in my bedroom and Tony and Anno were down in the kitchen, it sounded as if Anno were right outside my door. That kid had a strong voice. Tony was patient with her. I stood in the hallway and listened.

"I never said I was the boss of you. Do you want to help me make dinner?" he answered her back, paying no attention to her screaming and treating her as if she were his best friend.

"Okay," she said in a softer voice.

It was an amazing experience to see and hear Tony work with that kid. I had listened to him walk her through making hamburgers, brownies, and a few other things on his night to cook. Although the kitchen looked like a bomb had exploded by the time they were finished, I knew it was worth it. When I got downstairs, I saw Tony sitting on the kitchen cabinet with a book in one hand, reading like always, and looking up now and then to direct Anno with the next step.

"Now get two eggs from the fridge and crack them on top of the meat," he said to her.

"Okay," Anno said, running to the fridge. Holding one egg in each hand, she ran back to the cabinet, put the eggs on it, and pushed over the dishtowel to keep them from rolling off onto the floor. She climbed back up on the stool.

"Now, crack them right into the bowl," Tony said looking up again.

"Like this?" she was excited as she cracked the first one.

"Exactly," he looked over again.

"Now the next one?" she asked.

"Yep, do that one too."

"Now what?" she said dropping the shell and wiping her hands on her t-shirt.

"Now you've gotten to the greatest part. Put in your hands and mix it all together. Just start squishing it like this," he said as he reached over with one hand and squeezed eggs, breadcrumbs, and meat through his fingers.

"Let me do it! Let me do it!" she screamed with delight.

He let her squeeze it while he read.

"Okay, that's good, now we are going to make the actual hamburgers. Get a real big handful. The first thing we're going to do is make it into a big ball," he said as he grabbed a handful himself, still holding his book in his other hand.

"Like this, Tony?" she asked.

"You're doing a great job, Anno, now put it on the counter and see if you can make it flat like a pancake."

I listened and watched, amazed, from the hallway right outside of the kitchen.

"Now what do we do next, Anno?"

"I don't know, what?"

"Sure, you know. What happens next?"

"Fry it?"

"Yep, you've got it."

"Can I do it by myself?"

"Of course, I'll help only if you want me to," he answered.

"I can do it myself," she said, trying to turn on the stove.

He jumped down from his spot on the cabinet and sat on the stool next to the stove, helping her without her even knowing he was guiding her.

Whatever the question was, he guided her to the answer. When they were finished, it was obvious that Anno thought she had done it all by herself.

The next morning was Sunday. And even though I knew someone was waiting outside the bathroom door for me, I took my time. Sure enough, when I opened the door, Maria was there in the hall, leaning against the wall.

"Are we going to have a meeting today, Mom?" she asked me immediately.

I walked by her. I always got irritated when any one of the kids asked me that question now. I didn't hide the irritation in my voice.

"It's Sunday, isn't it?" I snapped at her. "Aren't we supposed to have one at ten o'clock on Sundays? Isn't that the time we all agreed on? Or shall we just have one when I say it's time? I'm tired of being the boss. At ten o'clock, I was in the living room and no one was there. So I came up here." I turned and walked into my bedroom, combing my hair.

"Everyone is downstairs waiting for you now," Maria said lingering, knowing not to say anymore.

I put down my comb and looked at myself in the mirror. How could I stall for time so I could get my thoughts together and say what was on my mind in a positive way? Last week, I had gotten really upset and cried at the meeting. I didn't want to do it again this week. The kids were doing great things by taking care of Anno and cooking dinner, but what about the rest of the household jobs? Was I supposed to remind them about those things? I didn't want to fall back into that again. How could I present it though? I walked slowly down the stairs and into the living room. Everyone was obviously waiting for me but no one said a word. I sat down on the couch as they watched. Was there anything about me they didn't watch? Probably not.

Maria was chairperson today and started the meeting. "Does anyone have anything to say?"

Immediately John spoke up, "I do. None of my friends cook at their houses, not that I mind or anything. In fact, it's been kind of fun these last few weeks."

I answered quickly, defensively, "Well, I thought we already knew that none of your friends cook, probably no one's friends cook at their houses.

What else is new?" It was a statement more than a question. "I took out the meat almost every day this week for whoever was cooking, even though I swore several weeks ago that I would never do that. Anyway, from now on, if you're going to cook, please take out what you want to use that night. Okay?" I was irritated with myself because I knew I was starting to lecture again.

"Okay. If it's a big deal, Mom," Joe said, plainly feeling my vulnerability and zeroing in on it. "Don't take the meat out, for crying out loud."

"It's not a big deal, Joe. It's just part of the responsibility that belongs to you all and I've been butting in. I don't want to do that anymore." I was still irritated, not at them, but at myself and all the words I sometimes used without following through.

"Anyone else?" Maria asked quickly, hoping someone would change the subject. "John?"

"Yeah. Well, this is a different subject, but I think it's pretty messy around here sometimes."

"Yes, it is, John, but we're still getting settled into our new home," I answered right away and then kicked myself because I never seemed to wait for anyone else to answer. Did I always have to have all the answers? Couldn't I keep my mouth closed at these meetings? Obviously not. No wonder they hate these meetings most of the time.

"Are we going to get any rugs?" Tony was nervous and tried to change the subject.

"Yes, I hope so. But that all takes time and money, you guys," I snapped as cigarette smoke circled my head. "It seems to me like we're doing pretty good, for Christ's sake." Suddenly I was on the verge of tears and Tony knew it.

"Yeah, I know, Mom. I was just wondering," he moved over and squeezed my hand, "I just wasn't sure, okay? I know we're doing really good. In fact, I think we're doing great. I wasn't complaining, Mom."

I knew he understood and that I had jumped on him too quickly. I smiled at him and touched his face. "Let's move on," I said calmly.

"Yeah, please! I did one of your jobs this week, Tony. I took out the garbage again several times," John complained. He wanted me to know that he had done Tony's job. He looked around the room to see what kind of response he would get. Everyone remained quiet except Tony.

"Yeah, sure, John," Tony answered. He was angry at how John presented his case.

"I did," John wouldn't let it die. He didn't want it to end there. But no one else in the room was going to get involved.

"Thanks, but you didn't have to. Nobody asked you to do it," Tony answered, turning up his nose.

"You're welcome," John answered with a smile on his face. He obviously felt he had won whatever was going on between the two of them. And he wasn't finished either. He looked at me this time as he spoke, "And I'd like to know why Maria gets her own room. Just because she's a girl?"

This was obviously John's morning to challenge everything. I wondered if there was anything this kid wasn't going to question.

"It's not just because she's a girl, but because Maria and Anno are so far apart in age that for them to be in the same room would be pretty difficult. Not that it couldn't be done, or hasn't been done. It's just that in our family, this seems to work out best."

I wanted to change the subject and brought up the idea of my getting a part-time job at the paint store.

"The only problem is that I will have to work on Saturdays. Everyone has to work on Saturday because that's their busiest day," I was asking for their approval. I was unsure about working on Saturdays while everyone else was at home. I had always been available for them every waking moment of their lives so this was definitely new territory for me. Pat spoke up saying he would continue to take Saturday as his day to take care of Anno and cook.

"It's okay for you to work on Saturday, Mom," Joe said.

"Yeah, it's okay Apple," everyone chimed in.

I smiled, relieved.

Tony asked for the meeting to be over and Christopher added his trademark ending to our meetings.

"When you're tired, go to bed."

"Okay, Christopher, thanks."

End of meeting.

It happened often now—John challenging me. I knew that Tony always felt that tension, and would come up with something to try and keep the peace. Joe agreed with John lots of times, but he kept quiet rather than get involved. The competition between those two was probably the strongest. Maria thought I was perfect and never questioned anything I said. Christopher sat and looked lovingly at all of us as he listened. Lots of times Anno played quietly by herself but was always sitting in the middle of all of us.

Our meetings were much better than they used to be but I still felt like a bossy mother and often wondered if I'd ever get over that. Would my fear of being controlling like my mother ever leave me? I didn't know the answer.

18

It was the fifth week of our study group meetings in Helen's kitchen.

Jenny asked, "Why couldn't you have taken the meat out of the freezer since you were home? What would that have hurt? It seems to me that it would have been a lot better for the whole family."

"Yeah, you said you had been eating toasted cheese sandwiches, pancakes, and for a real treat, jello. What kind of meals are those?" Alice's face was full of skepticism.

I wasn't exactly sure how to deal with all of their questions. Our study group tended to consist of my explaining why I did certain things with my kids. That was hard for me because I felt like we never really got to the lessons in *Children: The Challenge.* But at least Jenny's question related to the lesson of natural and logical consequences. I decided to attempt to explain this lesson.

"Well, first question first," I said, realizing that these mothers were already upset. "If I took the meat out of the freezer, why would they ever have to remember to do it themselves?"

Rose answered, "But they would remember it eventually. At least, that's what I hope for my kids."

The other mothers sipped their coffee without saying a word.

"So you're saying that if I repeat it over and over enough times they'll remember?" I asked the group.

"I'm not sure," Jenny laughed, "but it sounds to me like you had horrible meals. I couldn't imagine eating those meals. I mean, how healthy are they? Maybe I've missed something," she sighed.

I leaned forward and put my arms on the table. Softly and slowly I explained, "It's that part about teaching responsibility, Jenny. Contrary to what we think, we cannot *teach* responsibility, we can only *share* it. If I took the meat out of the freezer, no one else would ever share in the responsibility of taking it out."

"But were your meals as horrible as they sounded?"

"Do you mean were they starchy meals with side dishes of starch and more starch?" I laughed.

"Yeah," Jenny looked at me, finally laughing herself.

"Well, yes, starch would definitely describe what was on our plates. But I honestly can't say that I thought the dinners themselves were so horrible because there was much more involved besides our taste buds and nutrition. First of all, I was learning how to let go and keep my mouth shut. Secondly, I was learning that lecturing doesn't teach, but that consequences teach. It was funny and it was encouraging. To hear them each find something wonderful to say was such an eye opener for me. And thirdly, our meals now are pretty darn good. They are balanced most of the time: meat, vegetable, salad, like that. So we've learned a lot as I've learned to keep my mouth shut lots of the time, and to encourage more and more."

"But you already talk like that too, don't you?" Jenny asked. "I mean, you're encouraging. Helen's already sung your praises about how you have fun with your kids on the beach."

"I'm sure I do encourage them sometimes but to see them naturally encourage each other is the exciting part. I've had to learn to encourage; actually, I'm still learning it. But it just flows out of their mouths. I heard John telling Maria how much he liked something she was playing on the piano the other day. It was the greatest thing just to listen to him. I'm just not used to hearing brothers and sisters talk to each other that way," I smiled as I kept going. "It was the same thing at the table. The contents of the meal became secondary. What was on the table was not really the issue."

"I know what you're saying. It's that part about encouragement that we talked about a couple of weeks ago, right?" Winnie asked.

I nodded my head.

Winnie continued, "Yeah, I tried that with the dishes last week. For some strange reason, they always want to do the dishes. Eric usually wants to more than Jesse, but last week for the first time I let Eric do it, and instead of getting on him about the soap suds getting everywhere, I just thanked him." She paused. "I could tell he liked that because he then wanted to take all the glasses out of the cabinet and wash them too," Winnie smiled as she recalled the incident.

"Yeah, that's exactly what I'm talking about. We need to let them feel the positive results of their actions instead of criticizing the parts that aren't perfect," I looked around at all the faces. They were beginning to understand; I could tell.

"Are we going to talk about that other chapter today?" Alice wanted to move on.

"Yes, we are," I agreed. "We'll come back to this over and over again I'm sure. Remember, this is still only the beginning."

"Not exactly, this is our fifth meeting. We're halfway through our ten weeks already," Alice corrected me. She sounded worried.

"Well then, let's move on to the next chapter now," I suggested. "Remember, we can still continue to learn even after the ten weeks." I wanted to plant the idea that parenting lessons need to go on and on. I myself wasn't sure how long, but I was already into my second year and still learning.

Sue announced that she had done everything wrong and made a million mistakes since last week's meeting. I reminded everyone how easy it was to "slip back" because we are surrounded by a world full of people who think that *talk* will *teach* and *negatives* will *nurture*. I smiled at myself when I said things like that. I knew it helped the group but it also helped me.

"Who was to report on Chapter 30 today?" I asked, eager to move on.

"That's mine," Alice spoke up.

"I can't wait to see how these kids turn out, Mary, " Helen chimed in. "In a couple of years, you are going to have a lot of teenagers in your home. Doesn't that worry you?" She had to have an answer before we moved on.

"Sometimes, but not too much. Do you think it should?"

"Well, most people believe that teenagers rebel. Surely you've thought about that."

"Of course I've thought about it, but I don't believe that my kids will rebel. They won't have to. It's not normal for teenagers to rebel, even though we've been browbeaten to believe that it is. It's only because we do not know how to treat them properly or train them when they are young. I believe that by the time they are teenagers, they have already been pushed down by abuse for many years. Parents do this unknowingly and out of ignorance, of course, but it's still abuse. I honestly don't think my kids will rebel, but I guess I'll have to wait and see."

"Have you told them not to abuse drugs and alcohol?" Helen insisted on continuing this tangent.

I wanted to do our lesson but knew I had to answer the question. "No, not really," I said.

"Are you going to?"

"No," I answered confidently.

"Why not?" Helen looked confused.

"I'll continue to build on their strong suits and to focus my energies on encouragement, rather than on lecturing about drugs or things that they already know about. There is not enough time in the day to do both. I'd rather continue to build on the foundation of courage and strength inside of them. They will say no to drugs because of their inner strength. The strength that comes from feeling good about themselves and not because of any lecturing or moralizing from me or the outside world."

"You really believe that, don't you?" Helen asked.

"With my whole being. These are the people that I love most in the world. I am giving them the best that I can and I feel confident about the results. If I do not feel confident about what I want to teach them, how in the world could they ever have confidence in themselves? I think it would be impossible."

"I hope I can have all your dreams," Helen lit a cigarette.

"It's more than dreams, Helen. It's our only hope for the future: to end the unknown abuse that is an everyday occurrence in our homes." My voice sounded tired now. I wanted them to question me but just not during our lesson time. But perhaps this was more important than today's lesson.

Helen's voice was full of kindness when she responded, "I believe you, Mary, and I think I understand what you are saying -- maybe not all of it but most of it, and I like it. You are the first person I've ever met who makes sense in what they say about children and families. And not only that, but it appears that you are actually doing inside your own home what you are teaching to others. I'll have to admit though, it really is different than anything I've ever experienced."

That night, Pat and I talked again about his job. He still didn't like it but I wasn't surprised any longer. He was just going through the motions and not willing to deal with it. Nevertheless, he once again encouraged me to continue with school. "It's your turn to go to school now, hon." I loved it when he said that, even though it scared the life out of me. Later, as I crawled into bed, I tried to actually picture myself in college. I fell asleep before I could see it clearly in my mind.

The next morning I could not find the sun in the sky. It looked as if it was going to be a dreary day. We had gone for three weeks again without a meeting. Everyone was feeling it. I found most of the kids hanging out between the refrigerator and the living room. I came out of the bathroom with thoughts about how to handle the situation.

"Shall we have a softball game and then have our meeting since it looks like it might rain later?" I asked. I knew if it rained we wouldn't get outside. Besides, when we played together there was a world of difference in everyone's attitude and we had much better meetings.

"Can we? Before our meeting?"

"Sure, why not! Let's do it," I was already grabbing my gym shoes.

Our game was great and I felt brilliant about remembering to do something fun for us.

"How shall we start this meeting? Does anyone have anything to say?" An line that was commonplace now. I was tired from softball and so was everyone else, but there wasn't any silence today.

"I do, Mom," Joe responded immediately, "I think we need these meetings every week, even though there's lots of bitching at them. It's worse to go without them."

"I agree with you," Maria leaned towards Joe.

"Me too," John's voice was loud and emphatic.

Joe leaned forward on the rug and everyone knew he had more to say.

"It seems like our meetings consist of Mom starting to cry and then our saying we're going to do our jobs the following week. Sometimes we do, sometimes we don't, and I don't know how to change that part or how anyone else feels, but I'm sure sick of listening to the same things every week. Or every third week, or second week, or whenever we have these meetings."

"Couldn't we make a list of what needs to be done and put it on the refrigerator?" John made it sound simple.

"Yes, let's do it!" Maria commanded. Everyone was agreeable.

"We can sign up after we finish the meeting. Is that okay with everyone?" Joe spoke assertively.

"Sounds great to me," John got up on his knees.

"What else?"

"Well, I would like to know, Mom and Pat, if we could get another phone line. My friends say they can never get through when they try to call me. And all my friends have at least two phone lines."

"Have you thought about limiting your phone conversations so one person doesn't stay on the phone too long?" I asked all of them.

"Well, yeah, but I still think we really need two lines. We have a lot of people in this house and one phone just doesn't seem to be enough." John presented his case again, "Everyone of my friends has at least two phones."

"Well, John, who is going to pay for this extra phone line?" I asked.

"I thought that you and Pat would pay for it. Us kids sure don't have that kind of money."

"I don't have that kind of money either, sweetheart. If you want another phone line it's okay with me, but you and your brothers and sisters will have to pay for it."

"Oh God, we always have to be different. My friends already think we're strange. None of my friends go home and cook. Or make their lunches. Or take the bus to school. Or take care of their sister. We always have to be different...can't even get another phone line...can't do anything around here...that's for sure..."

He rambled on for a while and everyone just listened. No one commented. Time passed.

Maria sat up straight, the way she did when she was leading the meeting, and broke the silence by asking, "Anyone else have something to say?"

"Yes," I answered then paused, "I wanted to tell you guys how much it means to me and how much I appreciate you helping me with Anno. I don't know if you know it or not, but I was so depressed and scared after she was born. I didn't know what was wrong with me. I was through the 'having babies' part, but I didn't know it. To say I'm glad that we have Anno is an understatement, because she's the greatest thing that's ever happened to us, but there were times I thought I'd surely lose my mind. Your helping me, the way you all have done, has saved my life. I couldn't have done it without you."

"We know that, Mom. You've said all that before," Maria reassured me as everyone else nodded their heads. I took another deep breath.

"I don't know if I've ever said it formally though, so I wanted to say it today. You know, I don't want to thank all my friends for things and forget to thank you guys. You know what I mean?"

"Oh, you're welcome, Mom. We love having the kid, too. It gives us a chance to practice on somebody like you've practiced on us," Joe laughed.

"Let's end this meeting so we can make our lists. That is, unless anyone else has something to bitch about—ha ha—just kidding!" Maria laughed as she tried to end it. It had been a long one again.

I had one more thing I wanted to mention.

"Getting places!" I started, "I want you guys to be able to join any activities at school or the YMCA or wherever, but please don't count on me taking you there or picking you up. You will have to be able to get there by yourself. I don't want you home after dark so you'll have to fix your schedule. I encourage you to join activities while at the same time being responsible for your transportation. I won't be running a taxi service anymore."

"Mom! All the other parents drive their kids places and they..."

"I'm not the other Moms, Joe, and never will be," I cut him off. "We've talked about this part many times."

"Oooooh, Mom," he sighed dramatically and threw his baseball cap down on the floor.

"Oooooh, Joe," I said, imitating him.

"Never? You won't ever pick us up somewhere?" Joe sounded desperate.

"You know there are exceptions, but I'm speaking of the general rule."

"Okay...I guess."

"What else?" Maria was getting frustrated, "Yes, Christopher?"

"When you're tired, go to bed."

"Christopher, do you think you'll be saying that forever?"

And that's how it started. First, there were the job sign-up lists on the refrigerator. Then came the other notes. Many revolved around food and possessions. "Who took my Cubs t-shirt?" "Who ate all the ice cream?" "Who ate the last of the cookies?" The questions were posted in seriousness as if someone would answer them. It worked wonderfully in many ways. "Can someone switch cooking nights with me?" "Can I use your bike tomorrow, Joe? I have to be at school early and I've got a flat."

Then came the thank you notes:

"Thanks for bringing in my mitt before it rained, Joe."

"I loved the picture you made me, Anno."

The appreciation notes:

"Thanks for picking me up after band practice, Apple, I know it's not your favorite thing to do."

"Thanks for letting me take that loaf of homemade bread to my teacher. She loved it."

"Thanks for getting pizza last night, Pat."

The loving notes:

"I love you too, Tony, you farthead."

The funny notes:

"Return my new socks or you're dead, Joe."

The mad notes:

"I really don't appreciate you taking most of my loose-leaf paper, John."

The sad notes:

"My chemistry teacher has cancer, Mom, and we're all going after school to get him a present so I'll be late. Love, Maria."

The questioning notes:

"Why can't I go, Mom? You said last time we would talk about it."

The threatening notes:

"Tony, pretend you're me on the phone again and you're a dead man!"

The more notes I wrote, the more notes they wrote. Everyone loved getting notes and like other good things, it continuously regenerated itself. There was just something wonderful about someone saying wonderful things to you in writing. You could save it, and read it over and over. You could read it at another time when you were alone. It was like getting a wonderful letter in the mail. It was difficult to describe how great a letter could be. Who doesn't like getting something wonderful in the mail? In our case, it was on the refrigerator, but the feelings were the same. The notes were marvelous and a source of great vibes between all of us! They were inspiring, clever, funny, encouraging, challenging, uplifting, refreshing, and most of the time, full of wisdom!

19

I was convinced that whenever I found a rare minute in the evening to sit down and listen to the quiet, a bell went off inside each kid's head that shouted a different version of a familiar phrase: "It's totally quiet, do you know where your Apple is?" And before two minutes passed, you could find one of them practically sitting on my lap.

I turned my head and, sure enough, there stood Joe quietly with a pair of pants in his hands.

"Yes, Joe?" I questioned his presence.

"Could you make these pants shorter for me?" he stepped in front of me, his voice soft and deep.

"Yes, I could," I paused and smiled at him, "but so could you."

He pleaded ignorance and innocence as he sat down on the floor beside me. "I don't know how to use the sewing machine, Mom—I mean Apple."

We both knew what was going to come next and Joe smiled coyly at me. He hoped against hope that he could get by just this once with his "I don't know how" statement. For me, not falling for the "I don't know how" line was one of the greatest discoveries I had learned thus far.

With a big, sincere smile, I looked at him and said, "I know you don't know how to use the machine, Joe. But now would be a good time to learn."

It felt so good whenever I said that line; it was so real. I could teach him how to use the sewing machine and he would be able to do it himself from then on. It was a small step in teaching him something new and yet a giant step along the road of life as he learned to take more responsibility for himself.

"Oooh Mom," he groaned, "you always say that."

"Oooh Joe" I groaned back, smiling brightly at him, "isn't it true though?"

"Could you show me right now?" he sounded a little irritated, but figured if he had to learn, he might as well get started.

"Of course. I would be glad to. Let's go upstairs and get out the machine." I got out of my chair and looked longingly where I had wanted to sit for a while. But if it hadn't been Joe, it would've been someone else. It worked that way with lots of kids around. I didn't mind most of the time, especially when it involved a lesson. Sure, maybe it wasn't as important as his math or science class at school, but it was a little part of life and it made me feel good inside. I knew that the chances were good that Joe might teach one of his brothers how to use the sewing machine later on. The kids did that kind of thing now with each other when they learned something new.

The way they encouraged each other made my heart swell. They were much better at it than I had ever been. I still had to keep little notes around to remind myself how to be encouraging. For them, it was second nature. At times it was exciting and at other times it was frightening to see how they imitated everything I said and did. When I stepped back and listened, I could see how they learned from my actions and repeated my words.

I took the sewing machine out and put it on the table. I handed the cord to Joe and he plugged it into the wall. There was already dark thread in the machine, but the bobbin was empty.

"There's no thread on the bobbin, so let's start with that," I motioned for Joe to come closer as I talked him through the directions of how to thread the bobbin.

"It seems easy enough," Joe said as he watched.

"Here's how you connect the threads, honey. You need both threads to come out this same hole, right here," I pointed to the hole with my finger. "Turn the wheel like this, then make sure the thread comes out here," I turned the wheel as I demonstrated.

"Okay," Joe had his nose close to the needle.

"Don't ever put your finger here by the needle," I said, pointing, "I don't want you to sew your finger. It can happen very easily. Believe me, many an expert seamstress has gotten a finger sewn. I don't want that happening to you," my tone was serious.

"All right," Joe said, "Just don't tell me a story about somebody who sewed their finger, okay?"

We both laughed because sometimes I went off, rambling about something or another. I put the pants in line for the needle and let the foot down on the machine by the place we had marked. It was silent now except for the hum of the machine. I sewed and Joe watched.

"So, Mom?" Joe broke the silence with a different tone of voice.

I wondered what he was going to ask this time. He had a habit of starting serious conversations with me when we were alone.

"So, Joe?" I answered him with the same tone of voice. I stopped the machine for a minute and we raised our eyebrows at each other. Slowly, I placed my hand back on the wheel to start again as I waited for him to say what was on his mind. That kid came up with some good ones, but didn't they all? I knew only too well that nothing was ever going to be dull in this family.

"I've been wondering, Mom," he said after more silence, "Do you ever think about going back to school, like Pat said so much?"

Oh Lord, I thought, I hope he doesn't start getting on me about this school thing like Pat has. I continued sewing, slowing the machine down to a soft purr as I answered him.

"Well, I don't know why I'd go, Joe. I'm just not the college kind of person," I opened my eyes big as I looked at him, hoping to make him laugh. It was a fact of life, I thought. I was not a school person and Joe should know that by now. I was a little irritated that he would even ask but I knew he meant it well. I hoped I would set him straight once and for all.

"Yeah, but you want us to go to college, don't you?" his voice, though kind, challenged me to explain why there were different standards for them and me.

I looked at those big brown eyes as those long lashes swept his face. He's so gorgeous, I thought. Then, feeling like there was no reason to discuss a silly comparison, I said, "Yes! I think it would be great if all of you went to college. But it is really up to you if you want to go. Now watch me cut the thread back here behind the needle and I'll show you how to finish up your pants. You turn the machine off here, like this."

I watched his hands follow through with my direction. I was pleased with our lesson. He'd know how to sew by himself the next time. I smiled as I walked back into the living room. But he was right behind me, and that meant he wasn't finished. He had me alone, and who knew how much he had on his mind. The whole house was so quiet with everyone completing big homework projects. I sat down on the couch and Joe sat down right beside me.

"Mom, I wanted to ask you something else," he frowned like he always did when he was serious. "How come you don't care about our grades in school but we still get good grades? I don't mean you don't *care*. I know you care, but you don't say much about the grades we get. Larry's mom is always after him to get good grades and he doesn't do well at all. And he's really smart. You treat it so differently than other moms," Joe tugged at his sleeve as he spoke. He looked up at me as he continued, "I mean, Larry is smart. He could get all A's without any problem, but he doesn't."

I was surprised at his question. It was obvious he had been thinking about this for some time. I somehow figured that all the kids knew why they were different, how their family was different, and how differently they were being raised. They certainly made a point of talking about being different when they got irritated or angry. But if Joe could ask a question like that, with the most serious look on his face, then he must really not know. I wondered what in the world the rest of the kids thought. I tucked my legs up on the couch as I turned to face him. How could I explain it without sounding as if I was superior to other parents? How could I make sure I didn't sound as if I was bragging? How could I explain it period?

"I've learned some new ideas, some new ways of looking at life, Joe. Things that anyone could learn. It's not because I'm smarter or anything like that. I probably put in the same amount of energy towards raising my kids as other parents do, although sometimes I feel like I work harder because what I'm doing is the total opposite of what everyone else does. Well, maybe I shouldn't say that I'm doing the opposite of other parents, but rather that I am learning to encourage you guys instead of rewarding or punishing you. That alone takes strong concentration, believe me. Most parents praise when you are 'good' and punish when you are 'bad.' Encouragement, however, makes no judgment on the person. Encouragement focuses on the deed rather than the person. Dreikurs said that we need to separate the deed from the doer. When I say I am encouraging you guys, I mean that I am trying to focus on your strong points instead of pointing out all of your mistakes. Well, most of the time anyway. You know, it's a myth that in order to learn, we have to point out mistakes, but it's hard to learn that stuff and switch it around. Instead of 'you do it because I say so,' I've tried 'we do it because it's necessary.' You know, stuff like that. I paused and could hear Mother's voice in my head again.

"Can't you be the top of your class this year?" She was so upset with me, but that was really nothing new.

"I can't do that, Mother. I'm just not that smart."

"I can't believe that none of my four children have been the top student of their class. I guess I just didn't think you would let me down like the rest of them, Mary Cecile."

"I'm sorry, Mother. I am just not as smart as Pauline."

"I don't believe that. You could have tried harder. None of my children tried hard enough to make me proud."

What a joke. Me, the top of the class? I couldn't even read out loud in class because I didn't know all the words. If Mother had known that I could never have even passed a test without cheating off of Pauline, she would've died.

"Mother? I was wondering if we could talk about me getting a bra this year." I knew I probably shouldn't have brought that up seeing that she was already in a bad mood. But I really wanted a bra. I felt really stupid wearing these cheap undershirts while everyone else had a bra.

"A bra? You don't need a bra, Mary Cecile."

"But everyone in high school has one, Mother, and these undershirts—"

"Okay, young lady, show me what you need a bra for. Take off your shirt and we'll see if you need a bra like you so desperately say you do."

It was so humiliating. I knew I didn't really need a bra, but did she have to stand there, stare me up and down, and then LAUGH?

"Young lady, I see no reason for you to get a bra. We'll talk about this when you might have a NEED for one."

That was it. No more discussions. It was bad enough that time. I knew if I brought it up again, it would mean punishment. I knew I wouldn't even touch the long underwear issue again. I thought it looked dumb, but Mother said it provided warmth and also protected me from boys who would try to look up my skirt. She probably would have killed me if she knew I always rolled them up when I got to school. I had decided I would rather have a big lump at the top of my legs than be seen with those faded pink long johns covering my legs.

I looked at Joe and realized he was waiting for me to continue.

"I want you guys to learn because you find it exciting, not so that you will bring home a grade that is better than someone else's, or because you're going to get a reward, like money, for it. Does that make any sense?"

"Well, yeah Mom, I guess that makes sense. But I still don't understand why we continue to get good grades even though you're not paying us for them."

"Well, I've explained it as best as I can. At least for right now."

"I still don't think I understand it," he said, slowly standing stood up.

"Well Joe, let me just tell you this. Your training inside our home will carry over to the rest of your life. I would hope that you are learning in school because you want to learn rather than because with a good grade, you'll be better than someone else. I hope you're learning to do jobs around the house because they need to be done rather than doing them for whatever is in it for yourself. This is what I hope I am teaching you. Have you noticed that at all?"

"Yeah, sure I've noticed Mom, but that doesn't mean I understand it. When we talk like this it really helps. All my friends think we're weird because we cook, wash clothes, take care of Anno, and stuff like that. I don't tell anyone anymore about what we do around here—like John," the sadness Joe felt showed in his voice.

"That's okay, honey," I said softly, "You don't have to tell anyone if you don't want to." I moved over close to him and gave him a hug.

"Yeah, but I really wish all parents could learn what you've learned, you know?" I could tell by the drop in his voice that he felt this deeply. He was like that about the things that I did. He wanted the world to know. Tears filled his eyes. He looked straight ahead and wiped them away. Then there was silence.

Finally I spoke, "Yeah, I do know, Joe. Families today are in great pain. Good ideas are still being kept secret, that's for sure. But if I can learn this stuff, anyone can. We both know that."

"Yep, I know. I love you, Mom," he reached over and took my hand in his and squeezed it.

"I know you do, Joe," I squeezed his hand back, "I love you too. I especially love the way you always find time to be alone with me. I know you've always felt responsible for me since your father left," I didn't know why I said that. It just came out of my mouth without my thinking about it.

"Is that wrong?" his eyebrows rose as he questioned me.

"No honey, of course it isn't wrong. It's not a right or wrong. But I don't want you to worry about me so much," I hugged him again.

"I don't," he said as he buried his head in my shoulder.

"You'll always be my man, Joe. You know that, don't you?" I kept my arms around him. I couldn't see his face but could feel his breathing and his heartbeat. Something else was still on his mind. I didn't know what it was. I waited.

"Yeah, I know. I really hate going down there to South Carolina to see Dad and always being his favorite child. How come he treats me different than everybody else? I'm not any better than any of the guys, so why do I get special treatment? I hate it...it feels so lousy." It all came out in one long breath.

Oh, so that's on his mind too, I thought. The tears were back in his eyes. This kid was so sensitive. He always tried to figure out why things were the way they were in life. I wasn't sure how to answer him.

"Yes, but you are very wise and know how to handle it," I said displaying total confidence in him. Then I quickly added, "Actually, it doesn't feel good to anyone to be the most favorite kid or the least favorite kid. When someone puts you 'up' or puts you 'down,' it feels equally painful. The 'good' guy doesn't feel any better than the 'bad' guy. But your father doesn't know any better, Joe. He doesn't mean any harm. It's just ignorance." I knew I couldn't talk positively about their dad. It was time to stop talking. I had answered him—even if it was a short answer. Besides, I was exhausted and we had covered enough heavy subjects for one night. "Anyway, I need to be alone a little bit now, Joe. But we'll talk again. Remember what I told you."

"What, which part? You told me a lot," he laughed.

"No one can ever take your place in my heart. You have your own special place and no one can ever take that," I sat back down on the couch and Joe stretched his arms to the ceiling, "Just in case you've ever wondered. Please don't ever doubt your place in my heart, okay?"

"Okay Mom," he smiled again, "I won't."

"Now give me a kiss and get out of here," I shooed him away like a fly.

"Thanks Mom," he said.

"You're welcome." I knew he was okay now. "And Joe?"

He had already hopped up half the stairs so he stopped and turned around again.

"Yeah?"

"You're the greatest!" I loved telling them all that.

Joe stood there for a second and just smiled that gorgeous smile.

"And you know what else I love about you?" I wasn't through with him yet.

"What?"

"Your wonderful, wonderful sense of humor," I winked at him.

He beamed as he continued up the stairs, two at a time.

20

Under the windowsill in the room that served as both a pantry and a walkway between the kitchen and the breakfast room, there was a little shelf everyone used to make their sandwiches for lunch. Anno pulled out the small white stool, climbed on top of it, and made her own sandwich with all the other kids. I had to giggle when I watched her; it was a marvelous sight to see a three-year-old kid making her lunch all by herself. No one in the family treated Anno like a baby and she sure didn't act like one either. I often thought it was like the chicken and the egg situation. Did Anno not act like a baby because no one treated her like one? Or did they not treat her like one because she did not act like one? I believed it was because no one treated her like a baby.

"All my friends' mothers make their kids' lunches," John said that morning.

Before he finished his sentence, Tony added, "All my friends' mothers wake their kids up for school in the morning."

Then they looked at each other and laughed wildly as they kissed me good-bye. They loved to razz me with that stuff: what "good" mothers did for their kids. Sometimes I knew they half meant it. Life inside our home was an experience that anyone outside the family could not imagine or believe, unless they were close friends who visited often. It had gotten to the point where I barely shared my stories with others for fear of sounding like I was bragging. Nothing could be accomplished by bragging—other than frightening people away. Besides, bragging wasn't my style. Although my experiences of studying with other parents were limited, I had already learned about the tremendous difficulties parents experienced and the pain they suffered behind closed doors in the privacy of their homes. And could I ever forget the devastating family I grew up in?

Later that afternoon, I sat for a moment and soaked up the sunshine that poured through the windows of our breakfast room. It was my favorite room because three of the walls were full of windows. Basically, there were only two pieces of furniture in that room. The most prominent was the huge, long harvest table that Daddy gave me. It was perfect because the whole family could fit around it and eat together with plenty of room. As I sat there though, I looked toward the smaller table we kept in the corner. I loved having something that could accommodate smaller children when they came to visit. All my kids had now pretty much outgrown that table. That's why it was so odd that lately John had been sitting there alone during dinner. It was a little strange. It made me wonder if something was wrong. But then I reprimanded myself about always wanting everything perfect.

"Mom?" Maria was already sitting down next to me before I noticed she was there, "I was wondering if I could have a date Friday night with a guy from school."

"And who is the lucky guy?" I could feel my stomach tightening as I tried to act casual.

"His name is Grant. I sit next to him at band practice," I could tell Maria was feeling a little shy talking about it. She was looking down at her feet. "We were going to go to the movies," she took a deep breath, "I mean, if it's okay with you and Pat."

And instantly I heard my Mother's voice...

"What do you mean he asked you to go to the movies?" She immediately started throwing pots and pans in the sink so they sounded like bombs exploding. *"He's part of that filthy family from Edgemont Boulevard...and they have babies running around everywhere in dirty diapers with the filth from their front porch...no one looks after those babies! They're all filthy dirty...the scum of the earth...and you want to go to the movies with him...you'll just end up like the rest of them...that's what you want to get mixed up with...that filthy family with the dirty mouths...everyone knows how they talk...you'll be the laughing stock of town just like the rest of that filthy*

family...no I say no...you can't go out with him...not unless that's the way you want to end up...dirty babies and dirty diapers everywhere."

Her screaming tirades always shook my soul.

I took a deep breath myself and felt my stomach jerk again, "Well yeah, I guess it's okay, provided we work out the details. Like, what time I should expect you home and that kind of stuff."

Maria was fourteen now and wanted to date. I was hoping I would pass this test. Sometimes the common knowledge of how horrible teenagers were seeped inside me. The teenage years were starting—Maria was just the first. I was determined to beat the odds against teenage rebellion, but I didn't dare say that out loud to anyone. Inside me that challenge burned like a fever. I waited for what felt like a million years and finally Maria answered, looking straight into my eyes.

"Would eleven o'clock be okay? In case we wanted to stop for something after the movie?" Maria was at the toaster now, buttering a piece of toast. Her voice sounded as casual as if she was asking to go to the library.

My voice was a little high pitched as I answered, "Eleven o'clock sounds good to me. Does Grant drive a car or how will you be getting there?"

Maria brought her toast back to the table and sat down, "He just got his license, and his parents are going to let him have the car. Even though it's not far, we were going to drive..." she hesitated, "if that's okay."

"Well, it sounds like it will be okay. We can talk about it again before Friday and agree on the details."

"Sure Mom, that's great. Thanks a lot," Maria smacked her lips against my cheek.

"You're welcome, sweetheart," I said as she started to leave. "Did you tell your brothers yet about your date?"

"No, not yet. You know what they'll do," she stopped for a moment and sighed deeply.

"Without you, who would they have to tease, Maria?" I asked.

Maria rolled her eyes and then disappeared around the bend in the hallway. I turned on the stove. Time for another cup of tea and a little thinking by myself. I looked into the glass door on the oven and started messing with my hair. I felt it had gone well with Maria. The nervousness in my stomach was gone.

Maria went on her date and was home by eleven o'clock. When she told her friends at school how it had worked between us, not one of them believed her. As their discussion continued about parents and rules, Maria told her friends that she and her brothers got allowances every week but it had nothing to do with grades, punishments, or whether or not they did their jobs around the house. They were learning how to budget their money. It was like a share in the family income, Maria said using my exact words. Her friends didn't really believe her though. Basically, she said they laughed and said her mother must be crazy.

"I feel sad that none of them have what we have," Maria said to me, "They just talk about how they hate their parents and compare the kind of trouble they get into."

"I know, sweetheart," I felt that way too. "But you had fun on your date!" I reminded Maria and her face lit up. I felt sad about the things she told me about her friends. I wasn't surprised, but definitely sad. But at least Maria and I had passed the first "test" of teenage dating and I felt encouraged.

We decided at our next meeting that we would go back to the ranch again the following summer. That night, we went to Pat's parent's house for dinner and invited them to go along too. They thanked us graciously but declined the invitation. Actually, I felt relieved because Mother was coming again and Pat's parents had such positive attitudes about everything that the thought of Mother being with them scared me. Her presence could always instantly create such a negative atmosphere. I guess I felt ashamed that my mother was so negative. After dinner, Grandma Dalton and I did the dishes together in the kitchen.

"Do you think Pat is happy?" Grandma whispered to me. When she asked me this question I always felt nervous.

"Oh yes, he's happy," I said after a long pause, trying to dismiss any doubt she might have had. I didn't know what else to say. My mind raced. I knew that Pat was not happy about himself or his job, but I knew I could still make him laugh. And at least he'd started talking about his unhappiness. I knew that I loved him with my whole heart and that the kids did as well. They had totally accepted him when we got married. That alone was a major event. I knew we didn't have the problems that most people had re-marrying when kids were involved. But Grandma Dalton's question unnerved me because she could see his unhappiness. She knew and I knew and we both felt bad about it. I hoped that someday it would be different for him.

21

The nervousness in my stomach made loud gurgling noises as I talked on the phone. I slid off the tall stool and walked to the window to look outside as I listened in silence to my friend on the other end. John paced back and forth impatiently as he waited for me to finish my conversation. It was rare now that any one of the kids attempted to interrupt me on the phone. That was one of the first things I had learned at the Center. "Kids don't hang around and keep bugging you for long if they see they aren't getting through," Meg had said. And even if someone did distract me, I didn't let it show. I would silently look out the window without even batting an eyelash. Today, though, I was no longer able to concentrate with John pacing behind me. I had to end my conversation with a polite, "I'll call you back later." He barely waited for me to hang the receiver back on the wall.

"Why can't I go, Mom?" he frowned with displeasure as he stood close to my face.

"Because I said so," I turned around to catch my breath. This kid sometimes threw me for a loop with his constant challenges.

"But that's not a good enough reason. You've even said so yourself before," John looked at me in the eye as he presented his case.

"I know, John. I know it's not a good enough reason," I openly acknowledged his accuracy. I always wanted to be honest with the kids. "I'm not even saying I'm right. I just don't want you to go. Right now, all I have to go on is my gut feeling," I stopped and looked out the window for a minute. Then I continued, "It's not easy being the mom. And I know I make lots of mistakes. But the only reason I can give you at this moment is that I am the mom and I do not want you to go." My voice wavered back and forth between firmness and doubt. "I think we need to talk about this at another time when neither of us is upset."

"I guess so," he said angrily, "but it makes me really mad when you say 'no' like that." He was not going to let me off the hook without telling me exactly what he thought.

It was becoming a meeting of the minds and I wanted to be what I so often told other mothers to be: kind and firm. It was so hard to be both at the same time, I knew only too well.

"I understand," I said, "but it's very seldom, almost never, that I say 'no' this way. Isn't that true?"

He paced the floor, waving his arms as his face began to flush. He ignored my question.

"This is really important to me. All of my friends are going," his voice was tight. I thought he was going to storm out of the room.

I turned and faced him. In my most sincere voice, I answered, "Yes, I really do understand, John. I promise you," I stood still with my eyes upon him, hoping that he would accept my decision and not scream at me and say he was going anyway. I hoped I had built a bond with this thirteen-year-old that was strong enough that he would not do that.

He turned away and was halfway out the door before coming back in and saying, "Okay, but I don't like it," he slammed the door.

"I understand that, too," I said mostly to myself. I heard him climbing the stairs. He was angry, but he accepted it. I had not weakened this time, even though it was easy for me to do with this kid. Probably more so than with the others. John kept me on my toes more than I wanted.

"What was that all about, hon?" Pat had come in on the tail end of our conversation.

He put his package down on the kitchen counter.

"John wanted to go out tonight with Steven and Michael and I said no. I'm just feeling a little uncomfortable about those two. I don't know why. I can't put my finger on it, but I just feel uneasy about them," I said, searching for the right words.

"Oh?" Pat probed further, "Why?"

"I'm not sure. All I have to go on at the moment is my gut feeling. We can talk about it later," I wanted to think about it some more. I couldn't explain my feelings, so I brushed it off as my wanting everything inside our family to be perfect.

It continued to bother me, though, because many times at dinner, John continued to sit at the little table in the corner. He usually ate fast and then excused himself before anyone else. On the surface, everything in this family looked wonderful. It *was* wonderful. But underneath, something nagged at my insides and worried me. One morning, I stood on the porch and called John back, "It's a rule that you kiss me goodbye," I said. I was trying to make a joke out of it. But we both knew I was serious. My gut feeling remained one of uneasiness.

It was Saturday morning and I was the last one to get up. Gone were the days when Saturday mornings meant the twisting knots in my stomach from the fighting that began at five o'clock. Saturday mornings were now one of the greatest times inside our home. We had finally gotten it down, I thought. I grabbed a damp towel as I got out of the shower. I still never took a dry, clean towel for myself when I showered. That was probably a throwback from the years when I was the only person who ever did the laundry. But even though the kids knew how to do the wash, I still never took a fresh towel. As I slipped my white t-shirt over my head and pulled on my jeans, I could hear music from the first floor. By the time I brushed my hair and got downstairs, everyone was already engaged into their chores. Saturday, formally a day of dread, had literally turned into a day of good feelings and fun.

"Here, Anno, put all this on the kitchen cabinet and throw that stuff in the garbage," John directed her.

Christopher had moved the vacuum cleaner out to the middle of the living room floor but had been sidetracked, stopping at the kitchen table to finish eating his toast. "Hi, Mom," he called as I walked into the kitchen.

"Good morning, Christopher," I greeted him with a kiss on the cheek.

Tony was folding clothes and the stacks were quite high. It didn't take long for lots of clothes to pile up during the week and if someone forgot to put them away, the piles grew to the ceiling. How could there be so many clothes when it seemed like no one ever had anything to wear? At least that's what they all said. Joe was cleaning the downstairs bathroom but decided to stop to grab another glass of orange juice. He hated doing the bathroom and didn't mind sharing that bit of information with everyone—even though he never got any sympathy.

John teased him, "How long do you think you can drag out that job, Joe?"

Joe didn't answer. He just grumbled something under his breath that made Tony, who was within earshot, laugh.

"I'll help you, Joe. I'll do anything but floors," Maria said, pausing at the bathroom. Maria would do anything for anybody if they would wash the kitchen floor for her when it was her turn.

"Anno, come back! Did you get lost? Hurry up, Peanut," John called to her. He was in a hurry to get his jobs finished. He had to be at the YMCA at eleven o'clock to meet his friends. He wasted no time by getting Anno's help to pick up, clean the bathroom, vacuum the stairs, and whatever else he had on his list. A new rule had been voted on at their meeting two weeks ago that said no one could leave on Saturday morning until all the jobs were finished. I wondered how long that rule would last because some people were finished with their jobs long before others.

There was no doubt that John got everyone moving on Saturday morning. Some kids went faster because of his direction and some went slower. The dynamics were always exciting to see as each of them vied back and forth, sometimes stepping on toes, sometimes teasing to the point of tears, and sometimes gliding through beautifully.

"I'll change the music," Maria yelled from the dining room. Everyone groaned as she put on *The Sound of Music*. Her brothers loved to tease her.

"Did anyone have anything else they needed from the store?" Pat asked as he picked up the grocery list from the edge of the counter. No one answered him and he took off for the store.

"Dang! Who threw these wet clothes in here? Looks like some of Joe's handy work," Tony wanted Joe to hear him as he grunted in the laundry room.

"No, Tony. Why do I get blamed for everything?" Joe was pissed but kept cleaning.

I finished my own jobs before sitting down for a cup of tea. I was the leader of the band. I played the role well now and made sure I found plenty of positive points that I could comment on. I wasn't sure what the kids thought and of course I couldn't ask, "Hey guys, am I being encouraging to you?" But I felt I was doing pretty good with the encouragement stuff. I didn't have to write it on my hands to remind myself anymore.

"Christopher, the phone's for you," Joe yelled from the kitchen.

Christopher loved getting phone calls and ran to pick it up. "No, I can't go until I finish my jobs," he said quickly into the phone. Then over his shoulder he yelled, "Mom, can Greg come over while I'm finishing up my jobs?"

"It's fine with me Christopher, so long as everything gets finished." This wasn't my rule; we had all agreed at the meeting that all jobs had to be finished before anyone could leave.

"Want to come over, Greg?" he asked into the phone.

He did indeed. He was there within sixty seconds flat!

As Greg sat down by the kitchen table to watch, Christopher said gently, "Come on, Greg, you can't sit down. You can help me vacuum."

"Really?" Greg sounded surprised. "I've never done it before. Are you sure it's okay?" he asked quietly. "We have a maid that does all our cleaning for us."

From then on, Greg became a regular visitor on Saturday mornings. He "got to vacuum." At least, that's the way he described it to his other friends.

Answering the phone was a full-time job. It was always ringing. This time it was for Tony.

"Yep, I'll be ready as soon as I finish my jobs around here," he spoke into the phone, "About forty-five minutes should do it," he said after listening to the other end. "Okay see ya then," he hung up the receiver.

Tony was a man of few words on the phone, that's for sure. Joe got the next call, followed by two for John. John never mentioned anything about jobs or chores. He only discussed the time he would meet with his friends. Maria repeated the same ritual, only the time and place of meeting was mentioned. The whole house buzzed and if an outsider entered with no clue as to what was happening, it would probably be mistaken as (and sometimes was) chaos. But if they took the time to look just a tiny bit closer, they could see that something very different was happening inside our household. And that it felt good to be there. Each time someone visited our home for the first time, they commented on it.

When Saturdays went as well as this one was going, I felt reassured that I had "won them over," as Dreikurs said. Forgotten were the times when I made them do the kitchen floor over and over until they got it right. "Today I want it perfect," I had said to them a few times. I hoped I'd never rule again with an iron hand, but facing the reality that I was still human, I realized that I'd probably make that mistake again. Even though it was not the end of the world when that happened, it was still much easier for me to tell that to other parents than to believe it myself.

It was nine o'clock now and I was in no hurry since I didn't have to be at work for a while yet. My job at the paint store on Saturdays was going well. I enjoyed the work outside the house and Pat and the kids adapted well to my absence. Life seemed to be going at a slower pace than normal today, I thought as I bit into a piece of toast. The ring of the phone startled me. The man at the other end identified himself as Officer Brown, the youth officer from Haven Middle School.

"Do you have a few minutes to talk?" he asked politely.

I told him I did. He sounded so warm and sincere, I felt like I knew him and instantly liked him.

"Yes, I have three sons at your school this year," I told him.

"Have you heard anything about the recent break-ins that have been happening in your neighborhood?" he asked softly.

"Really? No, I haven't heard a thing about it," I was surprised but not alarmed by his question. I had no reason to be. We talked a few more minutes. "I will be glad to call you if I hear anything," I said cheerfully and I thanked him for calling. Then I went upstairs and didn't give the call another thought.

That afternoon, Officer Brown called back, saying he wanted to ask some questions about my son. This seemed a little strange.

"Which son?" I wondered out loud.

"The one in seventh grade," he told me, "The one named John."

I paced back and forth from the kitchen to the breakfast room as I listened to him talk. I grabbed the sponge and started wiping the cabinets and counter top as I started to answer his questions. I definitely was a wiper. Whenever I had something troublesome on my mind, everyone knew I could probably be found in the kitchen wiping one thing or another. I put down the sponge and grabbed a cigarette. Cigarettes and wiping the cabinets. I felt my stomach grab me and I quietly belched. Another familiar sign of nervousness.

"Does he wear glasses?" he asked.

"Yes, he wears glasses," I answered. "All my kids wear glasses," I laughed nervously, "They all inherited my weak eyes."

"Does he have a greenish-colored coat?" He just kept asking questions.

"Yes, it is sort of greenish," I answered. I wondered what difference it made what color John's coat was. Why so many questions? I knew that John was not involved in any trouble. The officer was just doing his job; that was all. And like he said earlier, he was questioning all the parents in the area. I had no reason to worry.

"Where was he last night?" he didn't let up.

Now I had to say something in John's defense. After all, how was Officer Brown to know that it wasn't my son they were looking for? How was he to know that my children were "different" and they wouldn't be getting into any trouble? I was as sure of that as I was of my own name, but he wasn't to know that. My cigarette was a butt already. I lit another one. The counter top shined like new.

"He went out for a little bit, but don't you worry, my son isn't the one you're looking for," I said with more nervous laughter. I kept wiping the counter top, "I don't mean to sound high and mighty, but my son wouldn't be doing any of the things that have been happening in the neighborhood. He just wouldn't. I'd bet my life on it. I'm one hundred percent sure of that," I finally got the words out that I had been wanting to say. I could understand his concern, but wanted to make myself clear.

Then I began to question myself. Could he be doing something like that, breaking into houses? Absolutely not, no way. If I could ever be sure about one thing in life, this was it. Thank goodness for my training and the things I had been continuing to learn.

"These are just routine questions, Mrs. Dalton, thank you for your time," he broke the silence.

"Please call me Mary. You're most welcome, sir, and thanks again for informing me and caring so much about the kids."

I hung up the phone and wiped the cabinets one last time then I lit another cigarette and looked silently out the window for a moment before the babysitter rang the doorbell. Anno came down the stairs when she heard the bell. Perfect timing, I thought. I kissed Anno goodbye and headed off to work.

On Monday morning, Officer Brown called back. He sounded as warm as ever but I wondered what in the world he wanted this time. He had already asked so many questions. There was nothing left to ask. He quickly spelled out his reason for calling again.

"I would like to ask your son a few questions and was wondering if that would be okay with you," he asked kindly.

"No, I don't mind, I guess," I hesitated a little then quickly added, "When did you want to do it?"

"I'm heading over to Haven School in about a half hour and was thinking I'd get him out of class this morning and talk to him, if that was okay with you?"

"Sure, that would be fine." I was upset at this point. "But I think I'd like to be there when you question him. Could you give me a few minutes and let me call my husband?" I needed time to think and wanted to ask Pat his opinion of the whole thing. Why did the officer want to take John out of class to question him? What was the big rush? Why couldn't he do it tonight at our home instead of this morning at school? Now I was feeling nervous and puzzled and this came through in my voice as I spoke. But there was no reason for my voice to be shaky. I knew John hadn't done anything wrong.

"Sure," he interrupted my thoughts, "I'll call you back in a bit and you can tell me what you and your husband have decided."

I got Pat on the phone and explained the situation. He agreed that it would be a good idea for me to be there when John was questioned. After I hung up with Pat, I went into the bathroom, grabbed a hairbrush and ran it through my hair. I don't know why I bothered because my hair was always a mess. Throwing my cigarette into the toilet, I grabbed my toothbrush and gave my teeth a quick once over. The phone rang and it was Officer Brown again.

"Yes, it would be okay for you to question John, but I want to be there when you do," I confirmed my earlier request. "I'll leave right now and meet you at school."

Haven School was five minutes away by car. I parked across the street from the main entrance and climbed up the front stairs. The sign said for all visitors to report to the main office, so I followed the directions and ran into the assistant principal on the way.

"Hi, Mr. O'Brien. How are you doing?" I asked. One thing about having so many kids was that all the people at school knew who I was.

"Good! And you?" he asked.

"Okay, I think. I was hoping I could I see John even though he's in class," I said. Why was I so nervous?

"Of course," Mr. O'Brien responded. I always felt welcome when I visited that school.

Someone went to get John from his classroom while Mr. O'Brien showed me into his office to wait. I sat down on one of the three chairs that faced the big desk and looked around at the walls. There were pictures of kids everywhere. The sun was shining through the window. There was a plant on the windowsill. How long had I been waiting? I stood up. What was I going to tell John, anyway? I wondered if my being there would upset him. I walked over and looked out the window. Pretty trees. I took a piece of gum out of my purse. I chewed like a cow and knew I should never chew gum in public, but today it didn't matter. John would probably have no idea about what was going on in the neighborhood but I had to talk with him anyway. Some parents were really in for a heartache, I thought. I was thankful we didn't have that kind of trouble in our family.

I had been staring out the window and was startled by John's voice, "Hi, Mom." The floor was carpeted and I hadn't heard him coming.

I jerked around. "Hey, Johnny, how's it going?" I quickly went on without waiting for him to answer, "I came over here because there is this police officer that called me yesterday and again this morning asking me questions. He wants to come here and question you and....."

"I did it, Mom," his voice cracked.

I knew I didn't hear what I thought I did. I gawked at him.

"I did it, Mom. Me and Steven and Michael." His throat choked up and the words had difficulty coming out. His eyes filled with tears. He looked down at the floor as I just continued to stare at him.

"What?" I couldn't have heard him correctly. I opened my mouth, about to ask him to repeat himself, but he whispered on.

"I did it. I did what the police officer is asking you about, Mom," the tears were streaming down his flushed cheeks.

I stared at his wet eyes as he removed his glasses and wiped them on the bottom of his shirt that he pulled out of his pants. Putting his glasses back on, he buried his face in his hands. I took his hands gently away from his face and held them tightly inside mine as I stooped down until my eyes were at the same level as his.

"You were involved in this?" I asked astounded, the words getting caught on the lump that was forming in the back of my throat.

"Yes, Mom," he sighed, our hands locked tight in each other's grip. I felt the blood racing in my veins as tears flooded my eyes.

"You did it? You've been taking stuff? Breaking into houses?" My voice begged for him to say no. That's all I wanted, for him to say it was a mistake.

But he looked at me and his eyes didn't lie, "Yes Mom, I've done those things. I'm so sorry. I feel so bad. Me, Steven, and Michael, we've been doing all sorts of things and I'm sorry."

I knew he was sorry and I pulled him close and held him while he cried. My eyes burned with tears and my heart crashed to the bottom of my stomach, heavy with sorrow and shock. So that's what had been eating at my gut. This kid had been getting into trouble with his friends and I didn't even know it. This kid who sat at the little table, instead of with the rest of the family at the big table. This kid who always had to be first out of the house in the morning and often didn't have time to kiss me goodbye. I had gone wrong. I was the one to blame. There was no mistake here.

"The boys will have to go to the police station," Officer Brown said. I didn't even realize he was there. He said we could go later in the day, when there wouldn't be such a scene at school. He said there would be questioning and fingerprinting.

Fingerprinting! I was devastated. I felt hurt, angry, helpless, and sad. Over and over I wondered, where did I go wrong? I was the leader in this family and it was my fault. How could this be?

Maybe it was a nightmare. Maybe I'd wake up soon. Maybe he'd be like my brother Tommy who had gotten into lots of trouble with the police. Maybe it was in the genes after all. But, did I really believe that?

No, it had to be my fault. I wanted to hold him. How could he do that to me, to all of us? How could he? I wanted to hit him. What nerve! Who did he think he was? Officer Brown said I should pick him up after school and then go to the police station. He said something else but I didn't hear it and just kept walking out of the school feeling numb.

I'd have to quit the thing I loved most, having study groups with the other parents. Obviously, I had failed and everyone had a right to know. I should have figured it out but I didn't. The only thing I knew for sure was that it was all my fault.

At 3:15 I picked John up from school and we drove to the police station. Officer Brown met us there. Steven and Michael's parents had already arrived. Pat came straight from work. It was still hard for me to believe I was in the police station because my son was in trouble for breaking into houses and stealing stuff. The boys had to be fingerprinted, but first someone took down their personal history. Afterwards, the other parents motioned for Pat and me to join them where they were sitting.

"We need to get together to talk about what kind of punishment we should all give them," the dark-haired mother said.

I looked away. These kids did not need punishments. These kids felt bad enough and needed encouragement now more than ever. They weren't getting into trouble because they felt good about life, that's for sure. Kids needed encouragement most when they were down. But, if I believed so much in this encouragement stuff, how come John had gotten into so much trouble? I had been parenting differently for several years now, and my kid was in trouble just like other kids. I might as well punish my kid like everybody else was going to do.

One of the fathers handed me a note. A meeting was planned for Thursday night where all the parents could plan a punishment and stick together on it. I smiled and thanked him. We'd been there for hours by now, and I had to go home. What would the other kids say? What would I say? What would John say? I didn't know. All I knew was that I had failed. That was the bottom line. I had failed as a parent. I would have to give up my parenting classes. I was so embarrassed and hurt. What right did I have to teach someone else how to parent? Absolutely none.

"Mom, do the other guys know we've been at the police station?" John whispered as we pulled up to the house.

"They don't know what's going on, John," I said calmly.

"Did you tell them anything?" his voice kept cracking as he climbed out of the back seat. I was nervous too, and I didn't have all the answers. Maybe I didn't have any answers. "I left a note and told them Pat and I had to be with you and we could talk when we got back home."

"What are you going to tell them, Mom?" he asked softly.

"I don't think it's up to me. What do you want to tell them?" I would help him, but I wasn't going to do it for him. He got himself into this mess, damn him. Quickly, anger flared inside me again. But then just as quickly, I softened. After all, it was my fault. I was the mother in this family. Pat was wonderful but he had always followed my lead. I was the leader and director of the family.

The tears came again. "We'll have to tell them the truth," his voice trembled as he paused, "Will you do it with me?"

"Yeah, I guess I can," I was having difficulty talking, too. "Of course I can. What do you want me to say?"

"I don't know," he cried quietly.

"Let's just go inside and we'll work it out in there," I didn't know what I was feeling anymore because my emotions kept changing every couple of seconds.

It was dark outside and all the lights were on in the house. We walked across the porch to the front door, our shoes loud on the wooden floor. Once inside, it was very quiet. The other kids appeared like shadows, not running to greet us as they usually did but standing silently in the hall. Pat, John, and I hung up our coats. Then I walked slowly through the living room, dining room, and into the breakfast room. Everyone followed me in total silence. All eyes searched for an explanation. The silence was deadening. *Somebody else say something please, just this once, don't wait for me to say something.* This was one of those times when it was very hard to be the mom.

"Did anyone cook dinner?" I inquired. It was past dinnertime but it appeared that no one had eaten.

"Yes, Mom, we have dinner ready. Do you want to eat now?" Maria's voice was filled with anxiety and fear.

"I guess so," I answered passively.

Maria, Joe, Tony, Chris, and Anno carried dinner to the big table. John sat at the end, his face buried in his hands. There was complete and total silence as each person sat in a chair and then proceeded to look down. Something bad had happened, everyone knew that much. Tony and Christopher made an attempt to put food on their plates. Joe and Maria followed, but no one took a bite. Finally, Pat spoke up slowly, "We've all made mistakes from time to time in our lives and John has made one now."

What a great statement, I thought. No one could have said it any better. I smiled at Pat and it was silent again. John sat at the end of the table, sobbing softly. His face was buried in his hands. I began to cry again too.

He didn't look up but he started to confess, "I've never felt so bad in my whole life. I'm so sorry, you guys, for what I've done. I feel so lousy."

I told myself to say something and help him out. Where were my words? Say something, say something!

In a half mumble, I managed to say, "John's gotten into trouble with the police, breaking into houses and stuff. He really needs our help and support now."

Quietly, he continued to cry. I didn't know if I was crying anymore, but I could feel myself shaking.

"We love you, John," it was Maria's voice from the other end of the table. She had said the perfect words at that moment. She pushed back her chair, stood up, and went to her brother to hug him. More chairs moved away from the table, making loud noises on the floor as everyone followed suit and went to the end of the table to give John hugs and kisses. I was inside the hug, too, and it felt so wonderful.

"We'll help you, John," Joe said.

"Yeah, we'll help you, John," Christopher repeated the thought and the words.

"Yeah," Tony agreed.

We were smothering each other with arms and legs everywhere trying to be closer. Everyone was hugging now and I could feel Anno around my legs.

Maria broke the silence with a soft whisper, "I knew something was wrong, but I just didn't know what."

Cutting off the end of her sentence, Joe and Anthony said in unison, "Yeah, me too."

Maria and Joe talked more, telling him it would be okay and that we'd work it out. Between sobs, John was able to say he was feeling better already.

Joe changed the mood, saying, "Someone in the family needs a police record, John, so it might as well be you...just kidding, Apple."

My mouth fell open in shock. How could he joke around at a time as serious as this, I thought, but the rest of the room filled with laughter. I wasn't sure if I liked what he had said and narrowed my eyes, "Joe, how can you say... a joke...at a time like this..."

Joe was still laughing, "Come on, Mom, I was just kidding."

I took a deep breath, got up, and walked into the living room. I again wondered where I had gone wrong. There had been so many signals. I wanted to be alone now but Maria followed me. I spoke softly to Maria telling her exactly what I was thinking.

"I have no right to teach parenting classes anymore," I looked out the window into the dark night. Tears streamed down my face.

Maria frowned. "Oh, Mom, come on, you're reaching so many parents. I can't believe you just said that," her voice was filled with disbelief.

"Maybe so," I continued, "but I feel like a complete failure. If I can't do any better than this with my own kid then I shouldn't be teaching other parents." I didn't believe Maria could really even begin to understand the situation. I was the mother here.

But Maria refused to back down. She put her hands on her hips and shook her head, "I think you are blowing this way out of proportion, Mom. It's not all your fault. For whatever reason, this happened. Don't we have to look at it as something we're all partly contributing to? Isn't that what you teach? And haven't you told us a million times that things aren't 'faults?' Can't we turn it around? Isn't it you who has always said the glass of water can be half full as well as half empty? Obviously something is wrong, but can't we work through it? Listen to your own words."

"I do listen to my own words, Maria, but this is different," my tone of voice was superior and I refused to see any point she was trying to make. I felt I had to pull rank this time.

Maria continued her protest, "Why is this different?" she said throwing her arms into the air.

"Because I should have known, period. End of discussion, Maria, I am the mother here," I tried to raise my voice, but it just trembled more.

Maria was unrelenting, "Well, I think you better practice what you preach. You didn't want this to happen. No one wanted this to happen, but it happened and we'll work through it. We've made mistakes and we can learn from them. That is what you would tell anyone else. You always want it perfect, Mom. It's time to listen to your own words, for Christ's sake."

With that, Maria left the living room. I looked out the window, shaken. This young daughter of mine had given me "a lot of cud to chew" as my daddy would have said. It seemed every time I really felt I learned something about real life from my children, I could remember something Daddy had said a long time ago. Funny, I thought, since Daddy and I never really had a conversation together. It was strange how I missed him.

Pat and I had agreed to meet with the other parents, although I already knew I would most likely disagree with their opinions about the whole thing. One of the parents was a psychiatrist and I knew I probably didn't have enough confidence to say my beliefs out loud—that punishment was not the answer. One mom had already told me the other day in a superior tone of voice that my ideas were "very different."

"Well I'm not into punishment with my kids, because I don't believe that is the answer nor do I believe it will solve anything," I blurted it out. I couldn't believe I just said that.

As all eyes turned towards me. I took a deep breath and attempted to qualify myself. "What these kids need now is encouragement, not punishment. They're feeling down and getting lots of attention on the negative side of life. Sometimes when I think about what John has done, I am so angry that I want to kill him. But when I calm down and really think about it, I know that punishment is not the answer. When we're really down that's the precise time we need encouragement the most. Their actions tell us how they are feeling about themselves and it ain't good." I looked around at the faces staring at me, "So Pat and I are not going to punish John. Not that I wouldn't like to slap him around a bit, but I know that's not the answer.

"I strongly feel that I have much to do with John's behavior. I feel I have to look at what I'm doing at home that makes him feel so discouraged that he has gone to the negative side of life, stealing, breaking into homes, and who knows what else that I don't know about. I feel I am part of that. I don't know yet what I am doing 'wrong,' or said a better way, what I am doing that is ineffective to keeping him from staying on the positive side of things. But I am definitely part of this behavior. So I'm going to seek help from a friend of mine who is good at this stuff to see if she can help me change some of my ways, rather then put all the blame on John. I am not excusing his behavior but I take responsibility for part of it, also.

"As parents, we are quick to blame our child and come up with a punishment for them, but what about us? They didn't get this way by themselves and I believe we need to look at that. It doesn't mean we are bad parents but we are definitely ignorant parents and I believe this strongly. Maybe you guys will think I'm nuts, but that's the way it's going to be at our house," I paused and looked around the room. It wasn't what any of them wanted to hear. I wanted to tell them what I meant by the word encouragement and how it was different from praise, but I had no audience. The doctor waited for a few seconds after I finished speaking and then resumed the conversation about the punishment. It was as if I had never spoken.

I'd have to do it on my own, but I should've known that. I hated the weird looks from everyone. It was difficult to always be different, especially in a situation like this.

22

Another Christmas rolled around again, and friends insisted upon being part of our joyful celebration. By now the Christmas party was a tradition and presents were no longer top priority; we had replaced them with visits to nursing homes. I felt this was a real accomplishment.

Even though it continued to be extremely difficult and painful when she came, I always invited Grandmother for Christmas because I knew how much she liked to visit and that she was extremely lonesome after Daddy died. Of course I always had that hope that one day she would see something positive—at least when it came to the kids.

"Hi Grandmother, how was church?" Tony yelled from the living room floor as Grandmother and Maria came in the door from mass.

"I have only one grandchild that's not a heathen," Grandmother answered angrily trying to smash his cheerfulness.

"Well, that's pretty good, Grandmother. Better one than none, don't you think?" he laughed as he tried to give her a hug.

"I don't need any hugs from heathens, Anthony." She walked into the kitchen where I was, "Mary Cecile, I know you think all your children are so wonderful and can do no wrong, but there are still a few things I need to tell you."

Grandmother loved to make fun of each grandchild and always found a way to include me in the ridicule. I was concerned that she would tear down everything I had worked so hard to build. I still doubted my positive influence over her negative one, but the kids always reminded me, teasingly and lovingly, that they would never allow that to happen.

"Remember we're smart, Mom," Tony would say as he'd kiss me and laugh.

"Yeah Mom, we're smart," Maria laughed nervously, not wanting me to be upset.

And I would take a deep breath and say, "Thanks guys, I forget that so quickly when she arrives."

On our party day, everyone helped and we divided up the special chores. Pat did the grocery shopping as usual while the kids and I fixed up the house. By that evening, the place looked beautiful with all the holiday trimmings. Everyone eagerly awaited the famous kid's "show," which was wonderful for the children because they were all actors—as most kids are if given the chance.

"I'll be singing 'A boy named Sue,' with Mom playing the guitar," Joe said in his most serious voice as he put down his guitar and straightened his cowboy hat in front of the late arrivals that evening. "It's the one I'm famous for. We've been waiting for you to get here before we started," he said taking their coats and walking towards the closet. "Glad you made it. Mom said you had a hard time with a babysitter."

"Yeah, but thank goodness we have found a neighbor who was willing to fill in at the last minute so we could come," Dave smiled as he looked over the crowd in the living room.

"I'll be doing magic tricks with my friend Charles," announced Christopher, now eight, to John Quinn, who had to bend over just to bring his ears down to the height of Christopher and Charles.

"Can't wait!" Mr. Quinn enthusiastically answered. Christopher's smile beamed from ear to ear.

Before the night was over, all the kids could be found in someone's bedroom already busy planning the next time they would be on stage.

New friends who came to the party for the first time always said the same words to me, "I wish my kids were wonderful like yours are."

I always had the same response. "Your kids are as wonderful as mine. Why not come and join one of my classes?" And many times they did just that.

The kids were growing up so fast. John was already graduating from eighth grade, and had no more run-ins with the law. In fact, in less than a year he'd turned everything around. John went to talk with my friend, Maria Cameron, a professor at the Alfred Adler Institute, and she helped him to understand his recent behavior that led to the stealing and his mistaken ideas. At the same time, she helped me understand how I had been discouraging to him without realizing it.

"So, tell me about the kid? What does he do around the house? How does he get along with his brothers and sisters?" Cameron had many questions.

"He's a neat kid," I laughed, "and I mean that both in a figurative and literal sense."

"Explain," Cameron urged, her eyes watching me closely.

"He cleans the whole house, keeps things in order, puts stuff away, that kind of thing. He's done it since he was a little kid. People always thought I had a maid until they got to know the family."

"And what do you say to him about it?"

"Well, these last few months I've been trying to explain to him that we just can't keep the house as clean as he wants us to. You know, a lot of people live here. I smoke a cigarette and no more than a second after I'm finished, he cleans the ashtray," I frowned thinking about it.

"Okay, I understand what you mean to say, but what John is hearing is criticism. He hears that he can never do it good enough for you."

"But I thank him all the time, Cameron. Honest I do," my eyes were filling with tears.

"I'm sure you do but he's still hearing criticism. Think about it. He goes around the house cleaning and your comment is, 'We can't live up to your standards.' That is not encouraging, even if you mean it that way. Do you understand?" Cameron stared at me, waiting for my answer.

"I don't mean it to be negative. But when you explain it that way, I can understand that he could be hearing it that way. I hadn't even thought about how it might feel to him," I was upset already at my mistakes.

"I know you don't mean it that way, but the effect is still the same. Another thing—don't use 'but' statements. Do you know what I mean by 'but' statements?"

"I don't think so."

"'But' statements are like 'you're so pretty *but* you need to lose ten pounds.' 'I like your blouse *but* I don't think it goes with your shoes.' 'Thanks for your help, John, *but* we just can't keep it as clean as you want us to.' Whenever you use a 'but' in a statement, the person only hears what comes after the 'but.'"

"Wow, I never thought of it that way."

"Thank him for his help. Encourage him more by only seeing the positive. Look at the family constellation. You have Maria, a first-born girl, Joe, a first-born boy, Tony the wonderful clown and peacemaker, Chris the youngest boy, and Anno the youngest girl. John is the middle kid squeezed in the whole gang. He wants to be noticed for something special too. That's what you have to remember," Cameron talked softly.

"I feel so terrible. I didn't know," I began to cry.

"Of course you didn't. For Christ's sake, Dalton, give yourself a little credit. You don't have to be perfect, okay? You've made some mistakes, that's all, it's not the end of the world."

"I know, but I feel so bad. Here I am thinking I'm encouraging him when all I'm doing is criticizing him. I should have known better," I said, still crying.

"Look Dalton, listen to me, it's not the end of the world. So stop acting like it is. You are now aware of what you're doing and you can change it. That's all that's important. You're doing a great job with those kids. Stop criticizing yourself." She gave me a hug.

"Okay," I said, accepting my friend's help.

"Remember, the key is to look for his strong suits and mention them," Cameron reviewed for me.

"I will! I will! Thanks Cameron!" I was grateful beyond words.

I had seen it as the end of the world when John got into trouble. Being upset with one of your children had to be the worst pain in the world, but it turned out to be a negative situation that—when we turned it inside out— brought tremendous insight and understanding to the whole family. John had gotten our attention on the negative side, but it could be switched to the positive.

It was so easy to tell other parents what they should do, but so hard to do it yourself. So I began that day to thank him for things he did around the house. If he emptied the ashtray immediately after I put out my cigarette, it was okay. I thanked him now, rather than telling him we "just couldn't keep things that perfect." I stopped that completely. I continued to thank the other kids for their efforts, individually and as a group, and made a point to take John aside at any opportunity and thank him individually. I thought I did this before, but definitely did so now. I no longer demanded that he kiss me goodbye in the morning, but made sure I was available in the front of the house in order to catch a quick kiss if it happened. The other kids made a special effort also, and I noticed how they asked John to be part of things where as before they might not have noticed. John was smiling more and more, and the uneasiness was replaced with calmness. I knew we had overcome a huge hurdle. It still amazed me at times what true encouragement could accomplish in a short period of time.

Sometimes at night I felt overwrought, like this was more than a full-time job. But I would remind myself that six "thank you's" for me was only one for each of them. So I kept at it and felt excited when I saw the results. It wasn't "luck" and it wasn't "because I had a girl first." It was work and it was full time. This I knew now. There could be no letting up, no matter how tired I got.

He was working with young kids at the YMCA and had a new group friends. He decided he was going to go out for the high school swim team. Maria was loving playing the trombone in the band. Joe was really enjoying his printing class at school. Pat wanted to go to school and get another degree, and he often suggested that I too should go to school. "It's your turn now," he would say. But I loved my job at the paint store and didn't care about going to school like Pat did. I always felt stupid after we had conversations about it being "my turn" to go to school, but I loved him for having the confidence in me to think that I could make it.

There was a new child development program about to start at the Alfred Adler Institute that sounded interesting to me. The program was especially designed for people who didn't have a college degree. I thought maybe I would check it out. Adler was an Austrian psychiatrist who emphasized the training of parents to allow their children to exercise their own power through reason and cooperation with others. The idea of learning more about Adler and his student Rudolf Dreikurs was definitely exciting to me. But I'd only consider the program if there weren't going to be grueling tests. If there were, I'd probably end up failing them like I always did in high school. I wasn't smart about school subjects and that's just the way it was. One thing I knew for sure was that if they gave out college degrees to everyone in the world, I would be the last in line. "Some things about yourself you just know for sure," I told the kids. Even if I couldn't get a degree, I knew for sure I wanted to study this.

I decided to bite the bullet and register for the new program at the Alfred Adler Institute. Pat and the kids thought it was a wonderful idea. They cheered me on daily. Pat was especially happy that I was finally going to school. He was big on getting degrees, but I wasn't going for a degree—that would've scared me half to death. I just said it was for learning "things I want to learn," and that was the truth.

At first it was overwhelming. Not only was I going to school but I was also going downtown, finding the school by myself, and learning good stuff. Although I had lived in Chicago for many years, I had stayed close to home and had seldom ventured downtown alone.

My seminar class was held on Fridays. Despite my initial anxiety, I soon settled in and started to make friends. I worked with two wonderful women at the institute both named Maria—'Maria Maria' and Maria Cameron.

Cameron, as we called her for short, had been working with John and now I got a chance to work with her.

As the kids planned for their future, I loved to watch, listen, and learn from them. Maria wanted to work at the ranch where we had vacationed in Colorado the previous summer but was afraid to apply. I thought her fear was silly and told her so.

"But Mom, they don't hire kids under twenty-one years old. I'm only sixteen years old," Maria said in her most dramatic voice. She put her bowl of Cheerios down hard on the table, causing some milk to spill. Maria wiped it with a napkin. She was obviously irritated at my suggestion.

I continued talking with the complete confidence I always had when I talked with one of the kids. "Maria, I'm telling you, apply for the job! They really liked you and I bet you could get it." I didn't raise my eyes from the paper, thinking Maria would have a stroke after that last comment.

"Mom, get real," she said impatiently, "I'm only sixteen years old and they only hire people over twenty-one. Can't you get that in your head? It's not like it's one or two years, sixteen is a lot younger than twenty-one." She rolled her eyes. I paid no attention to her dramatic explosions.

"Maria, apply. By the way I know how old you are. They really liked you a great deal. I'll bet you could get the job. Beside, what do you have to lose by trying?" My voice was very low key.

"Okay, but I think it's pretty stupid," Maria said trying to pacify me. She finished her cereal.

I knew Maria hated it when I talked like that but when it came to any one of the kids, my confidence could not be shaken.

"You lose touch with reality," Maria started again, "when you discuss what you think we all can accomplish."

"Wouldn't you really like it?" I ignored her comment.

"Yes, I'd love it, Mom. I would love to work there, but like I said, sixteen is a lot younger than twenty-one. Can't you understand that, Mom? How many times do I have to say it?" She was angry now.

I pretended that I didn't hear a word that Maria said and continued.

"Go for it, Maria, set your mind to it and remember it was your mother who told you, okay?" I laughed a little as I spoke. She gave me another disgusted look.

After a long pause Maria looked at me again, "You're so damn confident of your kids' potential that you get cocky."

She then rinsed her dish in the sink, picked up her books, kissed me on the check and mumbled as she walked down the hall, "Okay, Mom, I will." She allowed the front screen door to slam in the wind. I smiled to myself. I loved to challenge them. I knew it made them madder than hell sometimes, but I had no intentions of ever stopping.

Some weeks, the first fifteen minutes of the study group were used for complaints, quick questions, and general tales from the past week. When I sat down, everyone was anxious to hear about Maria's job situation.

"I need to know one thing before we start, Mary," Helen begged as she lit a cigarette.

"Yes, what is it?" I asked.

"Did Maria get the job? Did she hear from the ranch?"

"She got the job!" I said. "They hired her. They changed their hiring policy and lowered the age requirement from twenty-one to sixteen. When she wrote them a letter explaining the advantages of hiring someone who was sixteen, they were very impressed. They sent her a contract, she signed it, and sent it back. It was that quick."

"Wow, that's wild. Don't you think so?" Helen's eyes got big, "Aren't you thrilled, Marydalton? Were you surprised?"

"Of course, I'm thrilled for her," I announced, "but no, I was not surprised. The owners of the ranch have been around kids for several years now. They know a good person when they see one. And I knew Maria really wanted it. She just needed to be told in no uncertain terms that she could do it. My kids have no idea how wonderful they really are and how much they have to offer." I pondered for a moment. "Maybe that's my fault for not telling them enough about all their wonderful qualities, but I...."

"Fault?" Helen interrupted me, laughing, "It's your *fault*? How can you use that word on yourself when you are constantly campaigning to eliminate that word—not to mention a few others—from the English language?"

I looked at Helen and smiled. "Thanks, you're right, it isn't a fault. Who knows, maybe they're too young to know what great stuff they have inside of them. Thanks for questioning me on stuff I do. I hope you all know that I learn from you as much as you learn from me."

Helen's pleasure showed on her face, "We learn from each other, Marydalton," she said, "Maybe it's a two-way street, as I heard someone in this group say to us more than once," Helen said as she glanced at me over the top of her cup of coffee.

"It's time now to get on with our lesson. Enough of this, okay?" I opened my book.

Jenny paid no attention. She had another question. "Aren't your other kids working too?" she asked, opening her book halfway.

"Yes," I shook my head, "Joe is working at his uncle's shoe-shop and John is working at a restaurant."

"But they aren't sixteen yet, are they?" Jenny asked.

"No they're not sixteen but you have to remember that kids are ready to work long before they are sixteen. Kids need jobs and money. The more they share the responsibility of their own lives, and this includes having their own money, the better they feel about themselves. We are not doing our kids a favor by making them wait until they are sixteen before they can get a 'real' job. Only if we learn to share the responsibilities with them—in our homes, in our schools, in their first jobs making money, in decision making—will our children be able to grow and learn to be in charge of their own lives. This is where they learn it all, first. Inside our homes. Does that make any sense?"

"Yes, of course it makes sense," they answered, their eyes glued on me.

"We've talked about this before. For example, starting when they are small it's important for us to give our children an allowance that has absolutely nothing to do with jobs or chores around the house, but rather as an instrument for them to use in order to learn the value of money and how to manage it. If they learn how much a pencil costs as a little kid in first grade, that knowledge and experience will expand and grow as they grow. But we're way off track now."

"I think this is learning too," Helen protested.

"I agree. This is a lesson too," Jenny said flatly.

"I want to hear more," Rose said in a rare comment. She was usually very quiet.

"How can John work in a restaurant without being sixteen?" Jenny wanted to get some more answers.

"His friend's father owns the restaurant. Both John and his friend are working there. Plus, John is such a hard worker. And he loves working hard. The dad told me the other day he wished his son would work half as hard as John. So I guess I'm raising hard workers.

"Don't you worry at all about Maria going off to Colorado and working with a bunch of kids you don't even know? I mean, she's only sixteen and teenagers get into lots of trouble, especially when they are away from home," Jenny asked the question as the other mothers nodded in agreement.

"Well, first of all, we know the owners of this ranch personally and they are absolutely marvelous, outstanding people. You can't help but love them. They were never able to have children of their own, and they treat the kids who work for them as if they were their own. And no, Maria is not going to get into trouble. I trust her. I honestly have no doubts about her actions away from home." Here came that familiar refrain of mine again, "Even though it has been ingrained in us that teenagers have to rebel, I don't believe that's true." I stopped talking, took another sip of coffee, and then lit a cigarette. "And do you know what else?" I asked looking around the table, "I plan on proving my theory. It will take me a few years, but I plan on proving it." I sounded determined.

"Your attitude about kids is a little unusual though, don't you think?" Jenny asked.

"Well, I guess so..." I said looking off. Yes, my family was different.

"It's more than a guess, Mary. It's a fact. You have a completely different way of looking at our kids and if you don't know that, it's time that you learned," Jenny laughed at herself telling me what to learn.

The week before Maria left for Colorado was pretty crazy. I couldn't believe she was going to be gone for three months. Everyone was excited, but it also felt kind of scary to us. We all helped her pack and then set everything by the front door for the early morning departure. After the kids went upstairs, I stretched out on the living room floor for a minute before going up to bed. Pat sat beside me on the floor.

"What is it? What's wrong?" I studied his face.

He hesitated, "I feel so lousy."

"I can tell. What's wrong?"

"All this stuff inside, I guess. I really feel lousy," he pulled at his eyebrow as he spoke. He did not look at me.

"Tell me, what is it? You look so unhappy. I want to help you."

"I am unhappy. Just hate myself, I guess."

"But Pat, you are so wonderful. I love you so much."

"I don't feel wonderful. I don't feel wonderful at all."

"But you are. You have so much inside you. Come on, let me help you."

"I just feel so lousy. I hate my job. You love what you're doing and I'm happy for you but I'm jealous too. I just feel so lousy."

I moved closer and took his hand in mine. He continued to talk and I just listened. He hated himself and his life. It made no difference what I said. I wasn't sure if I would ever make him happy. I had noticed how he would stand in the corner alone most of the night during our parties, but this wasn't new behavior for Pat. He said he didn't feel good about his life, his job, or himself. He said he didn't like being jealous of me, but that he was. At least he was honest about it. He knew I loved him like crazy and thought he was the neatest person of all, but he didn't think of himself that way and wanted me to know. We talked for four hours. I had never cried so much in my whole life. My eyes ached and burned, my heart hurt and my insides felt like they were being ripped out piece by piece. I told him again that I would support us while he looked for another job where he would be happy. For the thousandth time, I vowed that I would make him happy, and I actually felt confident that I could. The bottom line was that I would do anything for him. He knew that. We set aside a special time in the next week so we could talk again in private.

I felt uneasy after our conversation and didn't know exactly what to do with those feelings. He was already sad, so I promised myself to be extra careful about how I said things. If his mom asked me again to confirm that he was happy that he left the priesthood, I honestly couldn't say that he was. Our conversation lingered inside my head. I was going to have to try harder. That was the least I could do.

I didn't sleep at all that night. I thought about how I had finished my first year of school in the child development program and how I loved it, as well as my job at the paint store. Pat would soon find a position he felt good about. I was convinced of it; I knew he could be happy too.

Mother had a car accident and I was relieved and grateful that she was not physically hurt. Her car was totaled and she was understandably shaken up. That little gray Volkswagen had been her prized possession, but it could not be saved. I told Mother that I would come down to Perryville and help her find another little car. Even though she didn't drive much, she needed a car. This was her sanity we were talking about. She needed the freedom a car could give her. I was always elated at the opportunity to help Mother be happy about something.

I knew I had failed miserably all my life in making her happy but never gave up hope that perhaps someday I would. Sometimes I felt like I was always trying to make adults in my life happy, and without much success. Oh well, I couldn't think about that now. Pat didn't mind my helping, but didn't approve of my buying the car for her. I assured him that I would use my own money. I knew Mother's finances were slim to none and there would be no way she could get another car by herself. Pat was noticeably upset and it pissed me off. I was going to help my mother and was going to use my own money. We were using my money for mostly everything anyway, so what right did he have to say that stuff? None, I thought. This was just one of those things that I would insist upon doing and I didn't like his attitude.

23

I registered for my second year of school. Although the idea of going to school still felt a little foreign to me, I was loving every minute of it. Here I was, a student at the Alfred Adler Institute studying the principles of Adler and Dreikurs. It still amazed me at times. Pat became unusually quiet about the whole thing and stopped asking me questions about it. The kids teased me by saying they never wanted to hear the name Dreikurs again. Truth be told, they were really happy and excited that I was in school. At our family meeting, the kids reassured me that they would do any extra jobs that needed to be done around the house as long as I studied like I was supposed to do.

"Hey, isn't that my job to cheer you guys on?" I asked, astounded at their enthusiasm. "You guys make me feel like I have a fan club."

"We are your fan club, Mom," Maria laughed, "Besides, we've had more recent experience with going to school than you have. We just want to help you a little if we can. So what happened this week in your class?"

"We've done so many practical things in that class," I began. "Today we spent the day at St. John's Hospital with the children that had physical and mental difficulties. Last week we went to Lamb's farm, which is a place completely dedicated to children with physical and mental handicaps. We worked with the kids in groups, talked with them, and ended up finding more similarities than differences between them and regular kids." They all continued to watch me so I kept going, "And when we are in class, I am always totally amazed when I know an answer." I stopped and thought for a minute, "I've just begun to realize that I have learned an overwhelming amount from you characters and from my parenting classes."

"Will we have to ground you when you come home with your grades?" Tony asked, tongue in cheek. I loved it when the kids played like that.

It was report-card week for the kids. We ended our meeting and they gave me all the dates and times of their parent-teacher conferences. It meant seeing a lot of different teachers for a lot of different subjects for a lot of different kids. I usually felt overwhelmed at conference time, but I couldn't skip one and go to the other. I had to go to everyone's conference.

How could I ever have known how much the two Marias would come to mean in my family's life? With my two dear friends, I began to travel to the South Side of Chicago every week where the three of us worked in a drug abuse center. The center was in the ghetto, but it didn't seem like the ghetto to me. These people were definitely my kind of people: real, gut-feeling, honest, poor, struggling-to-survive people. I felt right at home. The three of us, along with a man named Darnell—an ex-addict who brought his first hand experience—started a new drug abuse program. I was included in the planning of the program. It felt strange that other people actually thought I had brains and ideas.

I usually drove to Oak Park by myself and from there, headed to the South Side with the two Marias. I always sat in the back seat. In this threesome, I felt like a young kid. Often, I listened in amazement as the two Marias talked about their lives. Once in a while they would talk about me and I would interrupt them and ask, "Do I have anything to say about this?" Then we'd laugh and the two Marias would just continue on with their plans for me.

"First," Maria Cameron said, "you need to be in some school somewhere offering your talents rather than selling paint at a paint store. I know St. Luke's elementary school in Hyde Park is looking for a counselor who is also currently a student. That sounds like you. And," Cameron continued, "You need to go to college."

She said it so matter-of-factly that I didn't dare respond, but I knew inside there was no way it would ever happen. Going to school at the Alfred Adler Institute was enough. My two friends in the front seat were brilliant, each in their own way, but they were over-confident about my abilities. I would never be working in a school or anywhere else as a professional. But Cameron kept insisting I had street smarts. I got goose bumps whenever they insisted I had smarts. She told me I should apply for the counselor position at St. Luke's. I agreed to go simply because it would make my friends happy. I knew it was ridiculous to even think about getting the job. I just wanted to keep Cameron off my back. Cameron didn't give up.

"I've seen your kids," she paused, "Anyone who has kids like that is brilliant."

It shocked me when she said that because it was rare for someone to notice my conscious efforts to make our life different. People either gave the credit to being "lucky" or "having a girl first."

So upon the sometimes wonderful insistence and frequently awful nagging of my two friends, I interviewed for the part-time counselor position at St. Luke's. I was offered and accepted the job. Even though Anno was only four years old, a year younger than the required age for kindergarteners, she would be allowed to attend class there on the two days that I worked. It sounded perfect. I had to plan and implement a guidance program—a first in that school. I agreed to it, knowing that the Marias would help me. I was convinced that my kids, my husband, and the Marias had more confidence in me than I deserved, but I gave my two-week notice at the paint store. Later that night, my fears revealed themselves as I cried in the kitchen.

"But Mom, you know we can take care of ourselves and the house, so what's the problem?" Joe put his arms around me as he spoke.

"I don't know. This seems so...so..." I couldn't get it out.

"So what?" Joe wanted to hear me say the words although he knew what I was thinking.

"Oh you know, Joe, this is a professional job. It's more than a job at a paint store, it's...it's... well, it's just so different," I choked the words out.

"Mom, you'll do great. The kids will love you," Joe spoke very matter-of-factly. He refused to let this be a big deal.

I didn't have to tell him I was scared. He knew that. All the kids knew it. They had had their own meetings upstairs about their "Apple" and how they had to continue to be encouraging. They had also decided that they would never permit me to stop now. I had too much going for me, they seemed to think, even if I didn't know it.

"I guess I'm just scared," my voice was tight.

"That's understandable, but you always tell us not to be afraid," Maria had come into the kitchen.

"I know, Maria, but...."

"The same holds true for you, Mom. Come on. A position in a school! It will be so great. And you can take Anno with you. What could be better than that?" Joe was still holding me as Maria spoke.

"It's just really scary," I cried and wiped my eyes with a napkin.

"We know, Mom. But that will go away," Joe said. He was the picture of confidence.

"Thanks, you guys. You're always so good to me." I sometimes felt embarrassed because they were so good to me.

"Who do you think we learned it from?" Joe asked.

"Yeah, who?" Maria echoed.

"I don't know...maybe..." my voice trailed off.

"It's no 'maybe,' Apple," they said together.

"Thanks, you guys," I whispered.

Cameron insisted I come over the rare weekend when Sonstegard, her mentor, was going to be a guest in her home. I was to meet the man who had been Dreikurs' best friend and dearest colleague and take a lesson from him.

"This," Cameron said, "will be a great experience. One for which you will be forever thankful."

I went, met Sonstegard, and got my first lesson from him that very night. He helped me form an outline of plans for my counseling program and prepared me for the following week when I would begin working at the elementary school. For some reason, I felt totally confident after spending that evening talking with Sonstegard.

"So what did you think of Sonste?" Cameron asked rather shyly that next week as we drove down to the South Side. She glanced in her rear-view mirror to see my face.

"He is an incredibly amazing teacher," my voice was full of wonder. "Now I understand why you wanted me to spend time with him. At first I was feeling a little scared because you both have talked about him so much, but he is truly everything you said he was and more," I stared out the window as I spoke. I was actually beginning to feel relaxed about starting the counselor position.

"I told you, Dalton! What all did you talk about?" I loved it when Cameron asked that question--it was so typical of her.

"We talked about how to start groups with the kids and about getting the parents involved. About not just having the 'bad' kids go see the counselor but involving all youngsters in the program. About making use of kids' ability to help one another. He told me about what is really going on in all our schools in America and how we constantly feed the negative in our youngsters because of our ignorance.

"Actually, he said that what I will be doing in this school is what I have done in my home, except that it will be on a much larger scale. We talked about every part of the school. He told me that I will need to win over the janitor as well as the principal. It was a wonderful meeting. He was extremely encouraging to me. I believe that he was the most interesting human being I have ever met in my life since Dreikurs, but don't ask me to explain why or how because I don't think I can yet," I paused and took a deep breath. I felt such confidence inside me now.

"The night I met Dreikurs," I continued, "was literally the beginning of a new life for me and my children. It was the beginning of my understanding how my good intentions as a mother were actually destructive. It was the beginning of my learning that I alone could create a different environment for my children. An environment totally different than what I experienced as a child.

"Now with meeting Sonste and spending these months working with the two of you, I am beginning to feel the same confidence toward my work in the community. I don't understand how I've had the great fortune or luck or whatever it is to have met so many outstanding people: Dreikurs, Sonste, and you two dear friends. I thank you and hope I live up to all the confidence you have in me!" I was choked up and tears filled my eyes.

Maria Maria, who was sitting in the passenger seat, reached back to take my hand. Then we all burst out laughing and hugging as Cameron tried to keep the car on the highway.

"You're welcome, Dalton. Enough mushy stuff! How is John doing? It's been a year or so since he was involved with the police, isn't it?" Cameron asked.

"Yes, and he's doing great," I beamed from ear to ear. "He's a counselor for young kids at the YMCA, on the swim team, working in a restaurant, and doing well in school," I said with pride.

We arrived at the center and Cameron pulled the car into a space.

"We've got lots of work to do, Dalton. Keep it up with those kids so you can get out into the world. Parents need you. Schools need you."

"Thanks, Cameron."

Each week when I told them about my experiences at school, the kids cheered me on so loudly that I felt like I was in the Superbowl making the winning touchdown.

One night Pat looked me straight in the eyes and said, "Mary, I want to know everything you do when you go there." His voice was excited and strong. It was the first time in a long time that I saw a sparkle in his eyes. I knew at that moment that I was doing the things that he wanted to be doing too. From then on, I sat with him each week and told him everything I'd learned. I encouraged him again to reconsider his career. I told him that I believed that he, too, belonged in the community working with people.

It was early in the morning. Mother always called early in the morning.

"Still in bed sleeping, aren't you. Those kids always did run wild while you slept. I came up and helped you with every baby. I have six grandchildren up there and never get a letter from any of them. You think you have such great children, well I've got news for you, young lady. You don't know so much as you think you do."

"Mother, those are your words. I've never said I know so much. But the children used to write to you and you'd send their letters back, circling all their mistakes in red. I mean that's pretty discouraging to get a letter back that you sent to someone with red marks all over it. Do you know what I mean Mother?"

"Don't start on me with your psychology, Mary Cecile. After all the things I did for you and for those children that's pretty poor training. Why didn't I get a birthday card, Mary Cecile? You didn't send your poor mother a birthday card. Don't come calling after I'm dead. It'll be to late then and I don't have much time left."

"I sent you a birthday card, Mother. I've never forgotten your birthday nor would I ever. If you didn't get one it's not because I never sent one, and you know that."

"I don't know anything, Mary Cecile. I have no reason to live and I might not be here tomorrow, and you'll be sorry then."

Click.

"A swim meet tonight, John?" I had obviously forgotten.

"Yeah, Mom, I told you last week," John answered as he put the orange juice back in the refrigerator.

"Okay, I'll be there. I just forgot," I shook my head wondering where my mind was today.

"You don't have to come," John said warmly, not wanting to upset me.

"I know I don't have to, John, but I want to," I answered lovingly.

"Great!" His smile reached past his ears as he left the kitchen.

Between parents' nights, conferences, fall festivals, plays, track meets, band, swimming, and baseball, it was hard to know where to draw the line with kids in three different schools. I hoped that it was a good decision to stop going to parent-teacher conferences when the kids reached high school. I decided to substitute conferences with their activities instead. The first high-school activity Maria joined was band. Her concerts were wonderful. Hopefully, I was encouraging the kids a little each day. It finally sunk into my head that the kids knew I was interested in and cared about their schoolwork even though they constantly teased me about it. Actually, they teased me about all parts of the "Dreikurs stuff."

It was late Friday afternoon when the phone rang. Although I hadn't met her yet, I had heard John and his friends talk about Ms. Smith a couple times and laugh. But when I asked him about her, John only said she had a great sense of humor, and then he would laugh to himself. Ms. Smith introduced herself and asked if I had a few minutes to talk. Her tone of voice revealed aggravation, frustration, and maybe anger. I wasn't sure. She started right in.

"I hate to have to call and tell parents this, but your son John is forever disrupting the class, telling jokes and making people laugh. He's bright, but sometimes he just doesn't do his work and it's not that he can't or doesn't understand. It is because he is too busy being the clown," she paused and I remained quiet.

Damn that kid, and Ms. Smith too. Couldn't she say something decent? I walked back and forth in the kitchen as I twirled the phone cord around my finger.

"When the teacher calls" was a lesson I had taught parents more times than I could remember. I knew what to do when a teacher called to complain about the behavior of a kid but I hadn't had the opportunity to put it into practice yet. I felt a little angry at the words I was hearing and yet I knew John surely was no angel.

After a few minutes, Ms. Smith became quiet. I did not want this teacher to feel anything other than support, but could I carry this out? Could I actually do what I believed in total sincerity? With the silence on the other end, I realized Ms. Smith was waiting for my response. What was I going to do about my wonderful but sometimes big-mouthed son? I gripped the phone tightly and cleared my throat.

"Ms. Smith," I said softly, "I am sorry that is happening in your classroom but that is between you and John. I feel certain that the two of you can work it out," my voice was calm and sincere. I did it. I put the situation back into her hands and did it respectfully. There was an awkward silence.

"But I don't think you understand..." Ms. Smith started to repeat her whole report again. I looked at my watch and listened to her talk for another four minutes. When she finished, there was silence before I answered in the most respectful voice I had.

"I thank you very much for telling me this, Ms. Smith, but I am sure that you and John can work this out," I paused. "By the way, Ms. Smith, John tells me that you have a wonderful sense of humor. He really enjoys being in class with you."

Silence reigned again for what seemed like hours.

Finally Ms. Smith said, "Thank you, good-bye," and hung up.

The conversation went well. I listened. I was respectful. I said "thank you" and meant it. Lastly, I told Ms. Smith something positive that John had said about her. He enjoyed her sense of humor. It was the truth, and it was positive and encouraging. I had no intention of taking over Ms. Smith's job or getting involved in something that was obviously between John and his teacher. I was able to put into practice the "mind your own business" idea that I believed in. I was not going to get involved in their business.

A half hour later, John came in from school.

"Oh, by the way, Mom, one of my teachers at school might be calling you today," he yelled from the closet as he hung up his coat.

"Oh really? How come, honey?" I yelled back from the kitchen.

"Oh, she says I do some stupid stuff in class."

"Well, do you do stupid stuff?" I asked.

"Yeah, but not like she says I do," John answered as he stood with the freezer door open. "What happened to all the ice cream?"

"Well, teachers do have a difficult job, John. It's pretty hard trying to teach a bunch of kids, especially high school kids and..." I wasn't finished.

"Oh, I know, Mom. Don't start with the lecture about how teachers have it so rough, okay? She's cool. We'll work it out."

"I'm sure you will," I answered, chuckling to myself.

What had started out as a small study group had evolved into many parenting classes that just kept growing. People loved our kids and it seemed that they had become major advertisements for the classes. Pat had been my co-leader in a session we started for couples but he wouldn't be able to do it for the next one. I felt bad. I believed Pat needed this to keep from feeling discouraged, but I figured there was nothing I could do if he decided not to join the class again. Personally, I knew that if I didn't have these classes to teach each week, I would've fallen back into my old ways. I, as much as the next person, needed the encouragement and stimulation the classes provided to deal with the everyday problems that occurred.

"But you've said yourself how well your family meetings go. Ours are so bad that I want to cry," a father reported as we began our class one week.

"Ah yes, they do go well. Sometimes that is," I told him, "For example, just this past Sunday I was crying again about the kitchen and the garbage like I did when we started our meetings a few years ago. I sit at those meetings sometimes and question my sanity. Here I am, teaching this stuff each week, telling you guys not to give up, telling you to keep having meetings no matter how horrible they seem and then, well, do you know what I told my kids last Sunday?" I stopped and looked around the table.

"What?" asked a loud anxious voice.

"I went on a tirade. I said, 'Why do we even have these meetings?' I asked them how many years I would have to beg for them to clean the kitchen halfway decently? Why did I have to be the policeman when someone didn't do their job? How many years were we going to trip over garbage and how high were the clothes going to get stacked before someone would put them away? I just screamed at them while they sat there quietly and stared at me. Why do I tell you this? Because we've been having family meetings for several years now and many times they go well and the kids carry their share of responsibilities—sometimes even more than their share. And many times we enjoy each other endlessly. But the point is that sometimes we do it terribly too," I paused.

"If I didn't come here and talk with you each week about not giving up, I'd have given up myself a long time ago. I tell you how it should be, but at the same time I am telling myself. Each time one of you tells a story about how you went off that week, I see myself in you. I've done the exact same thing in my own home. Believe me, I still don't want to make any mistakes. As much as I hate it, I'm still keep trying to get it perfect a lot of the time. Does that make any sense to you guys?" I looked anxiously at everyone, wanting them to understand.

"Yeah, I understand what you're saying," said Jeanne, the single mother at the end of the table, "but it seems like everything goes so well in your home. Charles tells me that when he comes to your house to play with Christopher, everything is different than it is at our home. I don't know if I could do all the things you do," she sighed and looked around the table. "Does anyone else understand what I'm talking about?"

All heads around the table nodded in agreement as Karen put it into words. "I guess we're all just pretty impressed with your kids, Mary. Even though we know that we shouldn't, we compare ourselves to you," she half-smiled as she looked at the others.

Nine o'clock couldn't have come any sooner. Class had been really good, in general. But after what Karen had said, I felt pretty uncomfortable. I knew something had to change in the way I led class. I would have to curtail, almost totally, all of the wonderful things that happened in our home. And as much as I hated the negative, I would have to talk more about my mistakes in order to teach more effectively. The positive changes that had happened and continued to happen inside our home were too overwhelming to parents in my classes. They needed to hear about all the mistakes I made.

In a relatively short time after starting my position at St. Luke's school, I had gathered many parents, teachers, and even the pastor of our parish to come to a parenting class. I invited Sonstegard—or Sonste, as he was affectionately called by everyone who knew him dearly—to come and do a workshop.

"Quite an accomplishment, Dalton," both Marias said to me that week on the way to the South Side.

"Let's see," Maria Maria said, "the principal of your school makes everyone crazy by sabotaging anything that sounds positive, but you are having Sonste—a total stranger to them—come and do a workshop for the entire community. Oh Mary-Mary, look how much is happening already. No wonder we call you Dumb-Dull-Dalton," she teased.

"Don't worry about the principal, Mary. Most principals and administrators don't know much about real education or human beings," she laughed, "and that's why they become administrators."

"Amen!" I laughed too.

Pat continued to listen to me recapture the day every evening. It had become more and more obvious that he wanted to be in the same kind of work as me. Since Sonste was staying in our home for the weekend I hoped that he might be able to draw Pat in. Although Sonste had taught around the world, he was a man with no airs. He was also a person who people loved almost immediately. Many described him as a gentle lamb. When Dreikurs was alive he would storm into a session like a lion, and Sonste would come for the follow-up session like a lamb and calm everyone down. I was sure that Pat would love him. I hoped that Sonste could help where I had not been able to. I hoped Pat would come to the workshop.

Sonste had held the audience completely enraptured. People lingered and asked questions after spending their entire Saturday at the workshop, which was supposed to end at 3:30, but was still going strong at 4:30. I realized people would stay forever, so I officially ended the session.

As we walked to the car, I said, "The workshop was so wonderful, Sonste. Everyone loved it and learned so much. I learned so much."

"Really?" Sonste seemed surprised.

"Yes!! Don't you know that?"

"No."

And as I looked at him, I knew he meant that. He really didn't know.

"Oh, Sonste, your work is so magnificent. Anyone can understand your common sense ideas. Almost everyone here expressed their immense gratitude in being able to understand you."

"Thank you, Mary." He was not one to use many words.

When we arrived home, Pat was on the front porch. I told him I was disappointed that he did not come to the workshop. He, in a superior tone of voice, expressed his concern that someone should stay with the kids, though we both knew that the kids did not need "staying with." I felt an uneasiness between us that I could not identify, but it sure made me angry. However, I did not want to try to figure it out while we had a guest in our home. The kids soon appeared and greeted us warmly. Sonste and I sat down in the living room while the kids prepared tea. Twice I invited Pat to join us, and he finally came in and sat down.

"Pat," Sonste said warmly, "this Mary of yours is doing a great job in her school." He obviously wanted Pat to be proud of his wife.

Without looking at anyone, Pat answered coldly, "I'm sure she is."

Sonste continued as I poured the tea, "Mary, you should come to do your practicum with me at the West Virginia College of Graduate Studies."

I didn't have the vaguest idea what Sonste was talking about, so with eyes wide open I asked, "What is a practicum, Sonste?"

"Well, that's the last part that you do when finishing your Master's degree, Mary."

"A Master's degree?" I was stunned. "Sonste, I've never even gone to college," my eyes narrowed as I looked at him. Obviously he's a great teacher, I thought, but he must be a little nuts if he thinks that I've been to college. People who were really smart were also a little nuts. I had heard that more than once in my life.

Sonste looked at me and was quiet for a moment. He didn't acknowledge my surprise but instead he said very matter-of-factly, "Well then, Mary, you better go."

I couldn't believe my ears. I couldn't even think of a response.

I walked into the kitchen and hoped that the conversation would continue without me. I saw this man work today and knew he was brilliant. But he had certainly misjudged me if he thought that I would want or could ever go to college. I walked around in circles, alone in the kitchen. How could he say such a serious thing so matter-of-factly? What would he say when he knew me better and found out I really wasn't smart at all?

It was time for dinner. The kids always did a little number when we had guests. They horsed around and made Sonste laugh by teasing me and telling jokes. Pat disappeared upstairs and didn't come down until dinner was long over. I was upset and angry at him for treating a guest in our home this way, but said nothing. What was causing the strain inside our home? I couldn't understand the uneasiness in my stomach about Pat.

I was in my office at school the day the principal summoned me for a long-distance call from my sister in St. Louis. The blood rushed to my head as I braced myself for the assault. It had been a couple of years now since I had heard from her.

"Hello," I said softly.

"Mary Cecile, I'm calling to tell you that Tommy died last night," Kathryn said.

"T-T-Tommy?" I stuttered. "Died? My brother, Tommy…died?"

"Yes, Tommy died last night. He had cancer. He came by here a couple weeks ago and he looked terrible. Anyway I can't talk now. Have to go and I don't know the funeral arrangements yet. Good-bye," she hung up.

I put down the receiver and stared out the window. Tommy? His life was so turbulent, but dead? My body throbbed with shock and pain.

"Something serious?" a voice inquired from across the room.

"My brother...died last night," I walked out of the office as the words came out of my mouth, vague and unreal. Someone said maybe I should call my husband. I did. Pat said, with no emotion, that he was sorry and that he'd be home after the party at work. After the party? My brother had died and he'd be home after the party?

My mind began to race. *Not my brother please...not Tommy...he was the life of my childhood and I'd never forget that...then he got old...graduated high school...left me there alone in that godforsaken place...but I could not fault him for that...no one ever wanted to go back there.*

He wrote to me once in a while after he left. I used to read his letters under my covers at night so Mother would not take them away from me. He had encouraged me to go on with my music and promised to get me out of "that place."

He wrote me a short note a couple months ago. "God I feel awful," he had written. I should have known he was ill because he never once before uttered a complaint about his life—even though he was leading a life of self-destruction. "I love you," he wrote. And then he had signed his name real big across the page like he did sometimes because he knew he had beautiful handwriting. His eyes were the most beautiful sky-blue color I had ever seen. And they always twinkled, if they were not too full of liquor.

He was my crazy and wonderful brother. Forty was too young to die and six children were too many to leave. My eyes were probably too full of tears to drive home that afternoon but I did it anyway. When I'd cry as a little kid, he always knew how to make my tears dry up and my sadness disappear. I called the kids and they waited for me at the front windows. Those kids were always there for me when I needed them

The day of the funeral it rained so hard that the mud rolled down the hills in the Perryville cemetery like hot fudge on ice cream. My mother announced that at last she had her four children together. My other brother Paul pretended I wasn't there because I "lived in sin" since I had been divorced and remarried an ex-Catholic priest. Kathryn didn't have anything to say to anyone except me. She wanted to go to the hospital for a rest she said. Her doctor would check her into the psychiatric hospital every six months or so. I left quickly after it was all over. I could feel the loss of Tommy throbbing through every vein in my body. That night, as I lay in my bed, in my brother's home and I listened to the rain and remembered my brother.

I returned to Chicago and buried myself in the luxury of my children and the challenge of my work. I learned that in a small crisis or a major tragedy, my kids were always there by my side. I was overwhelmed by the delicate care I received from them. I realized once and for all that this must indeed be the best age that kids could ever be. I wrote their ages down because I believed this was a history-making time that must not be forgotten: "Six kids: four teenagers, one ten-year-old, one four-year-old—for sure, the very best age that kids could be."

24

The National Convention of Adlerian Psychology was scheduled to be in Chicago the following summer, and Sonste called the Alfred Adler Institute to ask their assistance in finding a student to work with him at the convention.

"I have in mind," he told them, "a Mary Dalton."

I had never been to a convention. I had no idea what happened at one, but I was terribly excited when I learned about Sonste's request to have me be his student-in-training. The Alfred Adler Institute wasn't pleased with his choice. Though I had taken some master's degree courses, I had not gone to college and they didn't like that one bit. I could register again as soon as I finished my undergraduate degree but not before.

"I just don't understand this higher education and how it works," I vented to Sonste upon his arrival at the airport. But he assured me not to worry. "Hopefully," he said, "we will have a good class session at the convention."

I invited Pat to come to the convention with me to see Sonste work. I wanted him be my moral support because he understood my fear of higher education. I told him I'd love to have him there. He had missed Sonste's workshop at my school and I wanted, with a passion, for him to attend this convention. Besides, this would be something that Pat would love. I believed he should get involved in this kind of work again. Helping people had been his life and just because he left the priesthood was no reason to think he must give up his desire to help people. But Pat had no desire to attend Sonste's class at the convention and told me in no uncertain terms.

"You go to your convention and I'll stay home with the kids," he said as we stood in the kitchen putting dishes away.

I was upset but remained quiet.

"They need someone to look after them and you seem to have less time or interest to do it," he continued.

His voice echoed with bitterness and jealousy, and I felt hurt and awkward but let it pass. I believed I understood his feelings. I decided I just needed to let him know more often how much he meant to me and how much I loved him. I knew I gave the kids my all—and then some. They, along with Pat, came first in my life. There was no need to defend my record. If anyone got cheated out of time or anything else, it was me.

"Perhaps he's feeling pushed aside with your rise to the big league," Cameron told me on our way to the South Side.

"But I give him more attention than ever," I protested.

"Keep at it," Cameron told me, "He's obviously feeling left out. Plus, several people out there are constantly praising your work. You told me so yourself. It started after Sonste did that first workshop at St. Luke's. Now there's this stuff with the convention and Sonste requesting you to be his student, and it's too much too soon for him."

"But I begged him to come with me. I literally begged him, Cameron. And not only that, he's been nagging me for years to go to school, saying 'it's your turn to go to school.' Those were his exact words!" I was angry.

"I have no doubt about that, Dalton, but listen to what I tell you." As Cameron talked, she looked at me in the rearview mirror as we sped down the expressway.

"Yes, Cameron. When haven't I listened to you?" I asked dramatically.

"How are the kids? " Cameron ignored my question, "How do they feel about your new job, Sonste, and your going to school?"

"Well, they're pretty proud. They're so proud of my position at the school that they overwhelm me sometimes," I swallowed hard.

"Like how, what do they do?" Cameron wanted details. She always wanted details.

"Well, they tell me not to hesitate to ask them to do anything extra around the house or taking care of Anno, stuff like that. Actually it seems like the more active I get, the more they do around the house without me having to say anything at all. Now don't get me wrong, we still get into it over stuff like the kitchen, but that's my hang-up, not theirs. It's really been different. I don't know exactly how to explain it to you," I shrugged my shoulders as Cameron watched me in the mirror.

"They're proud of you, Dalton. You're their queen bee and they want to take care of you. It's that simple."

"Maybe. All I know is it's really something incredible," I said.

I leaned back and let the Marias in the front seat talk to each other as I caught a few words here and there. I knew they were discussing me again. Maria Maria turned around and smiled.

"Okay, what? What is it now? What are you going to say to me now?"

"Well, Mary, you have to go, you know," she reached back between the seats and took my hand.

"Go where?" I asked.

"You have to go to college."

"Yeah, right!" I was irritated. "Come on, Maria, let's get real." I knew she meant it, but at the same time it didn't feel like my two friends were listening to my feelings at all. I was sick and tired of the subject of college. I knew I could never get through it. They obviously wanted me to throw away all my beliefs and fears, which was a lot easier said than done.

"I'm serious, Mary. Don't you know what an honor has been bestowed upon you with Sonste's inviting you to study with him? He only invites the best. Although, sometimes he invites the one everyone else has given up on, the hopeless cases," she laughed warmly and squeezed my hand, "Seriously though, Mary, it is a great honor. He's taught all over the world. You already know he's a master teacher. You know because you've experienced it. You know how it was at the convention and how it was when he came to your school. Don't you believe he's a great teacher?"

"Yes, of course I do and yes, it is a great honor that he has asked me to study with him. I know all that stuff you're telling me," I paused, "but I can't go to college."

"Why not?"

"I just can't, Maria, surely you can understand that. And Sonste will discover it, too. There is just no way I could ever do that. For God's sake, don't you think I know how I am?" I said angrily.

"You mean because you think you're dumb? Yeah, right. Dumb, dull, Dalton. Oh Mary, we have to get serious. You have to go to college to get that piece of paper. Okay? It just has to be done. You have too much to offer the world to let some little thing like this stop you."

"I can't talk about this," I felt the tears swelling up in my eyes and didn't want my friends to see them.

I knew I was not college material. If they didn't want to understand the facts about me then there was nothing I could do about it. Maria Maria saw how upset I had become and stopped, at least for now. She took my hand and asked if they could talk about it some other time when I wasn't upset and feeling dumb. I agreed and she quickly changed the subject.

"What have all you guys been doing for fun lately and how is Anno?" Maria Maria's voice always got excited when she talked about my kids, and especially Anno. Anno was the only one that Maria got to spend time with alone because the older kids were always off at school or activities when she visited.

"We're into cookouts in the woods and Anno is great. Hey, they're all great," and my face beamed again like it did every time she asked about the kids. She wasn't just being polite, she really wanted to know all about them.

"Really, how do you do the cookouts? Can I come to one? Do you think they would mind? I bet Anno would let me come if I asked her. Don't you think so, Marymary?"

"Of course you can come. My God, Maria, my kids would love it. Don't you know that?"

I felt sad that my beautiful friend didn't know how beautiful she was, how wonderful she was, how encouraging she was, or how she would not be intruding but rather welcomed with open arms into my family. Why didn't we see the wonderful things in ourselves that other people saw in us?

I continued, "We take eggs, bacon, hot chocolate, a frying pan, matches, and venture out into the woods. Everyone gathers sticks for the fire—which sometimes takes a couple hours. Then we cook breakfast because by that time we are starving. After that, we play hide and seek until we all feel like we are frozen to the point of never being thawed out again. Then we jump in the car and go home. It's great and, needless to say, everyone is exhausted when we get home. Usually, Pat and I are the most tired!" I laughed.

"Oh, Marymary, that's wonderful. Do you have tents and things like that?" Maria Maria was clapping her hands now just like a little kid would do. What an artistic and beautiful friend, I thought as I looked at her.

"No, not really, there's no way I want to go that far. I've passed that stage in life, whatever stage that is," I laughed.

"Yes, I understand," Maria S. laughed with me.

"That's our wintertime sport many Sundays—going to the woods and playing hide and seek. Softball, of course, is a big hit in the summer and then the beach has always been my favorite."

"Does Anno play softball?" Maria's enthusiastic questioning never stopped.

"Yes, Anno plays right up there with all of us. The other kids treat her like someone who has always played ball. It's amazing what the kids have done with her."

"Oh Mary, that's so wonderful. Do you know how exciting your kids are? I mean," and she paused as her eyes got bigger, "Seriously, do you have any idea or are you just so used to it by now?" She looked at Cameron, "I think she just takes this all for granted and has no idea what these kids are like."

Cameron was passing a semi-truck and kept her eyes on the road, for which I was grateful. She shook her head yes as she put her blinker on in an attempt to get back into the far lane.

"Well, sometimes I probably take it for granted, Maria," I agreed with her up to a point, "but not all the time. I know they're different, but it's not like I can talk about it with anyone. Well, anyone besides you guys, I mean. But anyone could have a family like ours. That is what is so frustrating. I'm doing stuff with them that anyone could do."

"Don't you wonder what all this will mean in later years, after they leave high school? It will be so exciting to see what all they do." Maria's voice trailed off.

We had arrived on the South Side and Cameron parked the car in front of the Drug Center. Darnell was waiting for us at the door and his face showed how anxious he was for our arrival. Our typical day there was filled with an unequal balance of tragedies and successes.

25

It seemed the kids were never late for the meetings anymore and I was the one who was sometimes late. I flushed my cigarette down the toilet and said to myself for the millionth time that tonight I would quit smoking forever. This would be the last pack of cigarettes I would buy in my life. How could I ever lecture my kids about not smoking when I did it myself? There was no way I could ever say one word about the dangers of smoking.

"Am I late, you guys?" I asked as I sat down on the rug.

"No, we're just starting, Mom," Maria said.

"Good. Well, Maria, I was just thinking that it sure is hard to believe that you are a senior in high school already. Wow!" I looked around at everyone and they all nodded in agreement.

"I know. I can't believe it either," Maria sighed, revealing a little of her fear of the future. "I certainly haven't done much to prepare you for college, I guess. Time has flown by so quickly."

Tony took my hand and squeezed it as he looked at my face, "Don't start on yourself, Mom. *Come on, honey*," he always said that sentence really slow and by the time he got to the word honey, he had me smiling.

Silence lasted for a minute before I spoke again, "Three of you are in high school. Where does the time go? So much has happened so quickly. Tommy died, I started school at the Institute, met Sonste, Maria will be graduating from high school. It feels like a lot of things are always happening at once."

"Yep, I know how you feel, Mom. But what else is new?" Tony laughed, "A lot happening in this family? How unusual!"

"Oh, Tony, you know what I mean," I said, attempting to stop the teasing and be serious for a moment.

"Okay, Mom, I'll get serious," he laughed again.

I was a little irritated, but the smell of fresh bread from the kitchen distracted me. I excused myself because it was time to turn down the oven for the last twenty minutes of baking. In a few seconds, I was sitting back in my spot on the floor.

"So tell us, Mom, how did it go with Sonste?" Christopher, in a rare move, was saying something in our meeting other than his traditional "when you're tired go to bed" line. Everyone gave him a round of applause. He stood and took a bow.

"It was great, Christopher. According to the feedback I've gotten from parents and teachers, everyone loved it. I believe his great teaching talents were very much appreciated. A couple of parents have asked if we could have him back sometime. That really felt good."

"I'm glad!" Joe smiled, as did everyone else.

Then a silence took over the living room. It felt strange for some reason but I couldn't put my finger on it. Finally, Tony spoke again.

"What was Sonste saying, Mom?" Tony asked hesitantly, "I wasn't trying to eavesdrop, but when you, Pat and Sonste were in the living room, I heard him say something about you going to West Virginia College with him, or something. What was that all about?" Tony's voice sounded strained.

"Oh, he was just talking about me doing a practicum with him. That's something you do when you're just about finished with your master's degree, and a master's degree comes after you've gotten a bachelor's degree. I told him I haven't even gone to college to get a bachelor's degree. The whole thing made me laugh, if you know what I mean," I chuckled.

"There's nothing wrong with you going to college, Mom," Tony's voice was serious.

"Yeah, think about it, Mom. I agree with Tony. There's nothing wrong with you thinking about going to college," Joe had determination in his voice. He sat up straight.

I looked around the room. Maria was nodding her head in agreement. John was listening quietly. Anno was playing with her toes. Chris was watching everyone. And Pat was picking at his eyebrow, looking at the floor. He never said those words "It's your turn, hon" anymore.

"I'm serious. Think about it sometime!" Tony threw his hands in the air as he did when he felt he had a good idea but no audience listening to him.

I decided to take a stand. I was older and wiser, at least on this subject. And I wouldn't hesitate to tell him.

"Tony, I'm not going to college, okay?" My voice sounded superior, something that rarely happened, but then it came back to normal as I continued, "At my brother Tommy's funeral, I had to laugh because he had told all his fireman buddies that his sister in Chicago was a lawyer. His buddies wanted to know if I was the one who was a lawyer," I laughed. "Uncle Tommy did stuff like that sometimes—told stories and made things bigger than they were. Anyway, I thought it was funny since I haven't even been to college," I laughed again but suddenly felt self-conscious as everyone watched me in silence. After a deep breadth, I said, "Enough of this talk about college, let's get on with our meeting."

"Well, I'm just telling you what I think. And I'm not the only one that thinks it. I know that Pat has mentioned it to you a lot," Tony shrugged his shoulders as he rested his case.

"Yeah, Tony, I have mentioned it to your mom several times," Pat nodded his head very slowly with no particular emotion.

"Shall we start our meeting, you guys?" Maria asked seriously. She obviously knew I was uncomfortable with the subject.

"Oh, I thought it was already started, Maria," I said as everyone else laughed.

"It probably is, just not formally," Maria said in her let's-get-things-in-order voice.

"Anybody got anything to say?" Maria fiddled with her pencil as she looked around the room.

Tony obliged his sister in a very loud voice as if he wanted the world to hear his announcement, "Yeah, I have something to say. I think Mom should seriously think about going to college."

All the kids cheered but I was silent. I was no longer going to respond to this subject and hoped that they would drop it. I decided to bring up something that would probably be small to them but it was huge to me and I had agonized over it. My stomach was nervous.

"You guys, I have something else to talk about. I've been thinking..." I raised my gaze off of the rug.

"Oh no, every time Mom starts thinking, better look out!" Tony teased me again.

"Stop it, Tony." I tried to act mad but the kids knew I really wasn't and I burst out laughing instead.

"Just kidding, Apple."

Sometimes Tony was so irritating but how could I stay mad at him? It was impossible.

"Well, I was thinking," I looked down at the rug, "that everyone in this family but me has private things." I slowly looked up at everyone with a little hesitation. "My stuff is everyone's stuff," I paused again, "and I don't mind you using my things but I would like to have a few private things like everyone else has," I stopped and shrugged my shoulders as if I expected someone to jump on me. Everyone remained silent. I continued, "So I was thinking that I could have three things as my private property," I gulped, "My desk, my purse, and my stereo. I don't mind if you use these things," I quickly added, "but I would like you to ask me first." I looked back down at the rug again, afraid to make eye contact. How could something that seemed so small be so huge a thing for me to say? I felt stupid, yet at the same time it was very important to me.

I sat in silence and waited for someone to respond, but there was just silence. John stretched out his legs. Joe slid onto the floor from the couch. Chris rubbed his eyes for a long time. Anno started humming and Maria's eyes dashed from person to person as she waited to see if someone else would speak. Tony rocked back and forth slowly and quietly, and Pat pulled at his eyebrow and stared at the floor.

"I...guess...we could do that," Joe broke the silence.

"Sure...if that's what you want, Mom," Maria jumped in immediately, clearly relieved that someone had spoken. Then silence again and no movement.

"Am I being...unreasonable?" I asked with fear. I wondered if I should back down. Wasn't this kind of stupid after all?. But my gut told me it wasn't stupid. The silence was deadening but I waited.

"Well," Pat finally spoke up, "what if you're not here and I need the checkbook out of your purse? I guess I think...that is a little unreasonable, hon," he seemed irritated.

I was nervous and it showed, "Isn't it something that could wait until I got home, Pat?"   "Well, I just think that I should be able to get to the checkbook out of your purse," he was now taking charge of this issue.

"Then maybe I shouldn't keep it in my purse any longer, Pat. I don't know." Again, I was hesitant.

"Well, hon," he said slowly, "there are things you have either in your purse or in your desk that I need to have sometimes. I don't like the idea of having to wait until you get home from work to ask you," his anger showed although I could tell he was forcing his voice to remain cool and calm. He pulled on his eyebrow harder and faster.

I was no longer calm and with my voice high, I said, "Pat, I can't believe you're saying all this. I mean, everything I own has always been shared with everyone in this family. Everything! I don't remember ever having my own dry bath towel. Now I ask to have three private things in my life and you get in an uproar. God, I can't believe you."

"I'm not in an uproar," he stated calmly. He had me now, I was upset and he was calm. Softly, he continued, "I just think I should be able to go into your purse. That's the way it's always been and I don't see any reason to change it. Why are you so upset?" his tone sounded superior.

He smiled at everyone and continued pulling on his eyebrow. Suddenly, I hated that habit.

I was completely frustrated. It wasn't that I hated his response to my idea;

it was more than that. There was more underneath. Too many words and actions were uncomfortable, to say the least. I had to make a decision now. The kids watched, frozen in silence. Not one limb had moved in the last three minutes. Should I back down on such a small issue—which really wasn't a small issue—or should I take the chance and go for it? I decided to stand my ground. It was a first for me.

"Well Pat," I said with determination, "I don't think it is unreasonable and I don't want anyone going in my purse anymore without asking me. That's just how I feel about it," I looked him straight in the eye, waiting for him to answer.

"Well...there's not much I can say then," he pushed his lips together in a pout as he stared at me.

This whole thing really felt strange. I had thought that the kids would give me the business by bitching and complaining about my request, but I was again surprised by Pat's response. Something else was going on. I wasn't sure what it was but had an idea. I heard my voice but it sounded as if it were someone else's.

"This feels so strange. I thought the kids would get upset with me about my wanting something private, but it's you, Pat, who's upset with me. What is really bothering you?" I was still angry about the whole thing.

"Nothing," he answered, still pouting.

"I know better than that," I challenged him, "Something is bothering you. You've been upset about something for a long while now."

"No, I haven't," he glared at me.

"I walk around here constantly feeling a nervousness in my stomach. But I haven't been able to put words on why I feel that way," I said.

"I'm sorry if your stomach is nervous," he said sarcastically.

"Okay, I give up," I was in no mood to pull it out of him, "Anybody else have anything to say?" I paused, then looked at Joe, "Well, Joe, it's pretty exciting, huh, this ranch job?" My voice was upbeat. I was determined not to allow this whole meeting to end with a bad taste in everyone's mouth.

"Oh God, I'm so excited I can't even tell you!" Joe allowed his excitement and emotions to show in front of everyone. He didn't do that too often.

"And I'm happy, too, the whole third floor is mine, yippee!" John laughed ecstatically as he drummed on the floor with his fists.

"No, it's not, John. Mom said I could move up there, too," Tony challenged him loudly in front of everyone.

John didn't care; he was more excited than anyone in this family. He didn't see anything negative about his two older siblings going off to work in Colorado for the entire summer.

"We'll see about that," he laughed, "Besides, Mom isn't in charge of the third floor," he rolled back on the floor still clapping his hands with joy, "I am."

"Come on, John, quit acting like you own everything!"

"I don't own everything, just the third floor, ha ha ha!" John cracked up. "I think it's great that you guys are going to Colorado. I'll miss you but not as much as I'll love having the third floor to myself," he couldn't stop laughing.

"I'm moving up there, John!" Tony said very loudly as if he knew he had to first convince himself before he convinced his brother.

"We'll see, Tony, we'll see," John smiled.

"Well, I think things are going better around here since we started putting lists on the refrigerator. What does anyone else think? Mom?" Maria asked.

"Yes, I agree. Thanks for reminding me. Those clothes get piled high out there on the dryer though, you guys, especially lately, and then there's...well yes, it's better..."

"We'll get the clothes, Mom," Maria said.

"Thanks," I answered, "I think things are smoothing out quite a bit."

"You sure are busy, Mom. Just the little butterfly working everywhere, huh? I sure like seeing you do the things you like to do, with your new job and all," Joe winked at me, "We're proud of you, kid."

"Thanks, Joe," I felt a little embarrassed.

"Yeah, I think so, too, Mom," Maria said.

They were always encouraging me. I hoped I encouraged them at least half as much, "Thanks, Maria!"

"Yep, I second that or third it," Tony slapped his hands together, up on his knees and waiting to leave.

"I'll vote for that, too!" John said.

"Me too," Chris said.

"Thanks, you guys. You sure do encourage me," I could feel their warm vibes.

"What else?" Maria asked in a tired voice wanting the meeting to end. It had started over an hour ago. She glanced at Pat. He had not said another word. There was tension in the air.

"When you're tired, go to bed!" Christopher said to make everyone laugh.

"Oh, Christopher!" Joe and Tony yelled at him at the same time.

"Boy, we have the strangest traditions in this family," Tony said as he stood up.

26

I can remember when I thought 1977, the year my first child would graduate high school, seemed like a million years away. But before I knew it, it was that year. Maria was graduating from high school and Tony from eighth grade. I could finally understand that mother I had met in the park one day who said to me, "It will be over before you know it. They'll all be raised and gone."

Joe and Maria were going to the ranch for the summer to work. The rest of us were headed to Colorado in July. Maria was not sure if she was going to go to college immediately or exactly what she would be doing that fall. I knew it was hard for her. I wished I had known more so I could have helped her prepare for college.

At night, after everyone had gone to bed and my world was quiet, I found myself thinking, with shock and excitement, about Sonste's invitation to go to West Virginia and study with him. I also wondered if there was a slight chance that I could go to college. Week after week my two other Marias encouraged me to think about it. Although it was constantly on my mind, the thought of saying it out loud made my insides freeze with fear.

During dinner the next evening, after spending another rewarding day at the drug clinic, I was still on a high and I surprised myself by talking about Sonste and going to school. Pat lashed out at me quickly.

"We don't have the money for you to be frolicking around the country, even though you no longer have an interest in being a mother."

My mouth fell open. "My God, Pat, I can't believe you said that!" my voice cracked and I was holding back my tears.

No matter how much I tried to push it down and avoid thinking about it, I knew Pat had definitely changed from the person who was always saying "it's your turn to go to college, hon,'" which he had been saying since the very beginning. I knew he was desperately unhappy in his work and jealous of mine. I knew I must continue to be patient, but I was angry on the inside and sometimes I wanted to scream at him. I refused to believe that I couldn't make him happy, even when he became silent and unemotional when I reached out to hug or kiss him. It felt lousy. I began to doubt myself about everything when I was near him.

Two weeks went by without the mention of my going to college. That was until my Maria friends and I drove together to the Center and they began talking about ICASSI. Rudolf Dreikurs founded the International Committee for Adlerian Summer Schools and Institutes, and each summer the classes were held in a different country. This summer they were going to be held in Holland.

"Maybe Mary could go to the Summer Session with us," they said as if I weren't present.

I knew that Sonste would be teaching there. I could take his classes as well as others. But I also felt overwhelmed with so many new ideas and dreams. The idea of going to another country was totally beyond me. I wanted to talk it over with Maria and Joe, but the days before their trip to Colorado were jammed. There were two graduations and Mother was coming for another visit. I reminded myself that I could talk to John and Tony. Just because they were younger didn't mean that they didn't have good ideas or common sense. Would I dare keep thinking about going with Pat continuing with his new line that I didn't care about being a mother? I knew my kids were the greatest. They were so encouraging about all the new things I was doing. But maybe I was misleading myself? No, the kids supported me in this and I could not doubt them.

Together as a family, we planned our Colorado vacation. We scheduled it for the week before ICASSI was to begin in Holland. That sort of nixed the idea of going to the summer session, I thought, since I knew I would never miss a chance to take a vacation with the kids. In a way, I felt relieved because now when I told the Marias that I couldn't go, I would have another excuse besides money. Where would I get the money for something like that anyway?

Sure, we had some money in the bank but I rarely spent it on myself. I was not used to the idea of buying things for myself.

Later that night, after everything was quiet, I sat with my friend Helen on the front porch swing and told her the whole story. She sent a shock wave right through my body with her response to the situation.

"Hey Mary, what if I give you a 'scholarship' for your trip to Holland?" Helen spoke without any hesitation, "You've given me and my family so much with all that you've taught me. I would love to see you go."

"But, Helen, you can't do that," I gasped at her generous offer.

"Why can't I?" She laughed as she said it, "You've earned it."

I knew she was serious, in a crazy sort of way. She could do something like that. Helen had money and loved using it to help me. But for me, it was frightening. I repeated my safe argument.

"Well, I'll be in Colorado on the day I'd have to leave for Holland anyway." I was relieved to have a way out of this, but it didn't stop Helen for a minute.

"There are lots of ways to skin a cat," she said as she picked up her cigarettes and got ready to leave. "You could go to Holland from Colorado just as easily as from Chicago," and with that, she stood up and walked to the screen door before turning to say, "You think about it. I'll talk to you tomorrow." The door closed by itself as she walked across the yard without looking back.

That night as I lay in bed, in the dark, staring at the ceiling, my insides churned. Pat's breathing was the only sound I could hear. Going to Holland from Colorado was a possibility I wouldn't have thought of, but I liked the idea. Whoa, I needed to get my mind back on track. Was I a bad mother because I was beginning to consider going to school? I had always put the children, Pat, and my mother first before anyone else in this world. But through the years I heard my mother's voice constantly accusing me of sleeping my life away while the kids had to fend for themselves. "Except that child you had with that priest," she'd say so sweetly. "That child gets taken care of." I closed my eyes and wondered if sleep would ever come.

Three nights later, I was relieved to finally reach Maria on the phone in Colorado. I poured out my feelings to her. That kid always had such a level head. Maria screamed so loudly I thought I'd never hear again.

"Yes! Yes, Mom! You could do both!! And with Helen giving you a 'scholarship' it would be so perfect! You'd only have to leave here one day early. Actually, it'd only be half of a day and yes, yes, I think you should definitely go, yes! Helen is right. You've taught their family a lot. She can afford it and she wants to do it for you. Let her! It's not like you'd be taking food off their table or anything like that!" Maria didn't attempt to suppress her excitement.

"But what would I say to Pat? He's been so down and angry you know, Maria," I twisted the phone cord around my fingers as I paced back and forth through the kitchen.

"Yes, Mom, I know Pat is down but not just lately and maybe he'll get over it. If he doesn't, it's his own doing," Maria said, defending her beliefs.

"Wow, Maria, aren't you being a little hard on him?"

"I don't think so, Mom. This has been going on a long time with Pat but if you want to spend your life thinking you can change his life, good luck," she thundered.

"I can't believe you're talking this way, Maria," I gasped.

"Why not? What did I say that was so wrong?" she demanded.

"I don't know if it's a right or wrong. It's just that I've never heard you talk that way about Pat before!" I was shocked with her responses.

"Mom, you've got a lot to offer this world. We've told you that for a couple years now and we can't all be wrong. If it takes someone outside of the family to get you to realize it, then I say fine. And a cheer for your two Maria friends, at least they have the right name," she said howling with laughter.

"So you think I could do both? Come to Colorado and then go to ICASSI? That's Holland, Maria. Holland is across the ocean!" I announced excitedly.

"Great, I love tulips and so do you," Maria said nonchalantly. "Yes, that's what I think you should do. You asked; I've answered. Now I have to hang up because I'm helping the cook tonight with dinner. I'll tell Joe to call and tell you what he thinks if you want me to," Maria offered affectionately.

"Okay, Maria, thanks for everything," I whispered into the phone.

"You're welcome, Apple. I love you," she hung up.

"I love you too, Maria," I said. I held the phone in my hand for a minute before I placed it back on the receiver.

How could my daughter think I was so wonderful and have so much faith in me while my mother thought I was a total failure? Although Mother's words could still crush me immediately, I felt a shift inside. I started to believe, if only slightly, my daughter more than my mother.

Later, alone in my room, I cried and cried, happy no one was around to hear me. I was scared and excited. The thought of going to school continued to swim around in my head. I wondered if I could actually do it?

The next morning, as we drove to Altgeld Gardens on the South Side, I still had the conversation from previous night in my head. I could hear Maria's voice and see her face when I closed my eyes.

College was back at the top of the agenda of M&M in the front seat. I shocked them as I reluctantly agreed, early in the conversation, that I would apply at the university where Cameron was a professor and see if it were possible for me to attain an undergraduate degree. If I could be accepted in a non-traditional program, I would consider it, but no promises. Inside, I was almost convinced I would fail but the kids, along with my M&Ms, were absolutely ecstatic about the whole thing. They were all so sure I was on my way and I would get that degree.

Pat, however, sat quietly on the side and watched. That really pissed me off but, as usual, I was afraid to say it out loud. We had everything! We had everything one could ever imagine, in my opinion. We had beautiful, well-trained children who were normal in a world where families were full of uphcaval. We had a big beautiful house. We had money in the bank. We were going on a vacation to Colorado. Some families never got out of their neighborhood, much less had a vacation. Sure, maybe some people wouldn't think we had much money because it wasn't a million dollars, but for me it was the same as having millions. I no longer cringed inside if someone spilled a glass of milk worrying about how I was going to buy another gallon.

I knew we were rich, rich, rich. And most of the riches didn't come from the money, but from the family we had. We had the greatest kids anywhere, according to other people's descriptions of them. They were solid, normal, fun loving, crazy, smart and "full of the nick" as my daddy would say. They were fun to go home to. We had our problems, but we learned how to work through them. We learned how to speak with each other in a respectful way. We learned things that other people didn't even know had to be learned in order to get along together. We had everything. I wanted to shake Pat and slam him up against the wall. He was blinded with jealousy.

My insides felt like a volcano ready to erupt. I asked the kids that night how they would feel if I went to Europe for three weeks immediately after our week in Colorado. I told them that we would spend our vacation together as planned, but on the last day I would go to Holland rather than back to Chicago with them. They were surprised, but when they learned Sonsto would be there, they had no doubts. They knew I wanted so much to study with that man. It was not a secret, even though we didn't talk about it aloud.

"Go for it Mom," Tony said softly, "It's okay. We're happy for you."

Christopher looked down at the floor, "It's okay I guess, Mom, but we'll miss you a lot," he smiled at me but I knew he was a little upset.

"Well I don't have to go, that's for sure," I said to reassure him.

"No, no, Mom, that's not what I meant. I want you to go if it's a good thing."

"It is a good thing, Stupid," Tony teased Christopher.

"What do you think, John?" I asked him as he sat quietly listening to the others.

"Hey Mom, you have to do what you have to do," John answered simply. "If you want to go, what's the big deal?"

"Well, it's a big deal to me. I have to admit, I've never even thought about doing something like this," my eyes filled with tears as I spoke. "I'll ask Pat tonight," I said, but I was already worried.

Later that evening, with my throat feeling like it was filled with cotton, I spoke softly to Pat in the kitchen as I wiped the cabinets.

"I've been thinking about that summer session a lot. I was wondering, Pat, how would you feel if I went to it?" I cleared my throat several times in order to get the words out, "I mentioned it to Helen the other night and she said she would give me the money if I wanted to go. She called it a kind of 'scholarship.'"

He hesitated, "What about our vacation to Colorado? Now you want to cancel that, too?"

"No, never. I don't want us to cancel. Nothing could be more important to me. Come on, give me a break," I begged, "I would have to pack two suitcases, one for Colorado and one for Europe because I would have to leave from Denver on the last day of our week in Colorado. But I don't have to go," I added quickly.

Silence filled the kitchen as Pat thought, then answered rather sheepishly, "Well what can I say? I guess it's okay with me if it's okay with everyone else," the corners of his mouth pulled downward. He turned around and faced the stove again. I knew he hated the idea. I remained quiet and didn't dare show my excitement.

27

I arrived in the airport in New York and immediately boarded the huge plane for Amsterdam. I looked out the window for eight hours as other people slept. I kept trying to understand how airplanes could stay up in the air the way they do. I felt as if I were in a dream. Holland. The tulips. My M&M's. Sonste. The classes. Meeting people from seventeen different countries. New friends. The discussions. The dancing. The music. It was incredible beyond words. I really couldn't believe it was happening to me. I just kept wondering was this real or just a dream.

I returned from Europe in time to celebrate Chris and Anno's August birthdays. It was wonderful to be home with the kids and to share with them my experiences in Holland.

We were sitting quietly watching TV together when during a commercial, I spoke up, "You know, I was thinking..."

"Oh no, danger, Mom's thinking again!" Joe interrupted me.

"Oh stop. Really, you guys, I was thinking, the only times I've ever been away from you all was to have another baby. It was hard to believe that I was there, in Holland." My face was one big smile.

"Oh no, do we have to listen to this again? You guys, Apple wants to talk about Paris and meeting some man named Haile-Yesus," Tony could never resist a little teasing.

I ignored both of them and continued talking, "I had to talk to myself at night when I went to bed and tell myself that I was in Holland. I kept telling myself that I was actually going to school. And I was missing you guys so much that sometimes I felt like I was going to go crazy."

"We missed you like crazy too, Mom," Tony got serious. He knew if he didn't, I'd start crying. Things had been more tense since I had gotten back from Europe.

"Thanks, Tony," I smiled at him warmly.

"Are you worried about Pat?" Tony asked softly as he put his arms on my shoulder, letting me feel the full weight of his body.

"Tony!" I exclaimed, "I can't hold you up, silly!" He stood up straight. "Yeah, I am worried," I continued, looking away, "but he'll come around. He's just not feeling sure of himself right now," I bit my lower lip like I did when I was holding back what I really wanted to say.

"Sure, he probably will Mom, don't worry," Joe squeezed my shoulders softly.

"Yeah, I really wanted to go to West Virginia and study with Sonste, but that's probably not a good idea right now.

"It's probably better to wait, but you'd really like to go, wouldn't you, Mom?"

"He's the master, Tony. Spending six months with Sonste would be like a lifetime of learning. After being in one of his classes, it's easy to understand why they call him the master. There are a lot of people who teach Adler's and Dreikurs' principles but there are few who actually practice those principles in their own lives. Sonste really practices what he teaches. That's unusual in this world. That's what impresses me the most about him."

"Really, Mom? He's that good?"

"Yes, Tony, he's that good," I smiled broadly as I sighed, "It was unbelievably wonderful to watch him in action in Holland. He made it so exciting to learn. His classes were jammed full and had everyone talking. He is so real, so full of warmth and knowledge. It's like a ballet dancer being invited to study with Baryshnikov."

"Wow," Tony said as he glanced back at the TV.

"ICASSI was a whole new experience for me. I was amazed at how much I already knew and how much I still wanted to learn. Plus, I haven't been to many places in my life, you know. Missouri, Colorado, Chicago, and California, so to be studying in another country was unreal. A dream filled with learning and laughter.

"Everyone would get dressed up in the evening after our classes and we'd sing and dance most of the night. We shared experiences, laughter and friendships as we ate and danced. We lived together in this large complex completely surrounded by tulips. Oh, I'm sorry, is this boring?" I stopped suddenly and looked at them. They had been in the middle of a TV show.

"No Mom, not at all, go on," John said, and then half-turned back to the TV.

"The ultimate high was going to Paris with Sonste to meet this man named Haile-Yesus. Back in the 1950s, when Sonste was a professor at the University of Iowa, he was asked by the U.S. government to start the first teachers' college in Ethiopia. Haile-Yesus was a young boy there at that time, and Sonste invited him to come to the Iowa to go to college and live with him and his family. Haile-Yesus took Sonste up on his offer. The two of them are such amazing people. You can imagine how it felt to be there in *Paris* with them.

They must have thought I was nuts because I just kept saying over and over, "We're in Paris. We're really in Paris." It was overwhelming to me. I loved every second of it. It felt like I experienced a million years of learning during those three and a half weeks. I had the same feelings I felt the night I met Dreikurs almost ten years ago. I felt like I could capture the whole world. I was learning! There is a possibility I can learn things and be a little smart I thought. I finally stopped and the kids looked at me in silence and smiled, "I'm talking about it too much, I know. Sorry you guys," I said.

"Apple, no need to be sorry. We love hearing about it. We're happy you got to do it," John spoke for everyone. All their loving attention was focused on me. I was silent and, with tears in my eyes, I watched the end of the TV show with them.

September was quickly upon us and Maria started college at the University of Illinois at Chicago Circle. I was also accepted into the six-month college program with Sonste in West Virginia, which was scheduled to start in January. The kids threw me a surprise party to celebrate. It was the first party they ever threw for me. It was wonderful.

Months went by and everything inside our home changed. The war raged. It was a dreadful war. I told Pat as delicately as possible that I could love him, go to school, and raise my children at the same time. I believed it was irrational to think it had to be one or the other. He stared blankly, brooding, as the corners of his mouth pulled downward with disgust. In the beginning I waited for his approval but several months later told him if I had to get a divorce in order to continue studying, I would. I half meant it. I hoped saying that would shock him into his senses.

The kids watched it all and did not take sides—at least not openly. They listened to both of us. I had taught them well about respect and minding one's own business. He vowed that he would get me for this, prove me an unfit mother, and take the children away from me. He was going to take my children away from me? He told me to move out and get my own apartment because I no longer cared for or loved my kids and no longer wanted to be a mother. Crazy shit.

My desire to talk with him died. It was a devastating time and I couldn't believe it was happening. Whenever I would walk into a room, he became silent and waited for me to leave until he continued talking. He talked with the kids were as if I were dead. He offered vacations and material things to them. He spoke to me only to tell me that I was a failure in marriage. The blood always rushed to my head as I listened to him, and sometimes I believed him. I reverted back to silently suffering as the martyr.

He froze all the money in the bank or took it out, and he ate dinner before coming home at night.

I took the kids to a friend's home for meals, refusing to ask him for money for food.

Our Christmas party and our summer party didn't happen.

Months passed before one of the kids left a note on the refrigerator stating in big bold red letters, "I'M TIRED OF ALL THIS SHIT!!"

Family meetings had become irregular during these months. The kids now demanded a meeting.

A meeting was set and I fluctuated between giving up, going on, or suffering in silence.

Maria took me into the bathroom before the meeting, "You can't just give up. You would never let us give up a dream and I don't want you to either. Pat says we don't have the money. You say that we do and yes, I believe you over him. I believe in 'minding your own business' like you've taught us, but Mom, sometimes you carry things to the extreme. You're trying to protect him while he treats you like crap. You want to be so understanding. You're acting like a wimp. You're going to go crazy inside. Quite frankly Mom, I hate it when you act like this. I just can't see why you're allowing him to scare you and rule your life. That's just a bunch of garbage."

"Sometimes I think I want to save our marriage, but it's only because I worry about what other people will say more than anything else. You know, being divorced again."

"What other people? Who is more important than us? Who cares what other people say? Get real, Mom. Just because you want to go to school does not mean it needs to ruin a marriage. Pat is just acting like a bully and you're playing right into his hands. You know what fear does to people. I've heard you tell people over and over.

"When have we ever solved any problem in the last eight years without a family meeting? Thank God we're having one today. I really think you need to go to West Virginia because it is your turn, Mom, just like he's said for years. The fruits of your labor can be seen. Any one of us could raise Anno alone and that's because of what you have taught us. Think about that Mom, what I just said. We could raise Anno if you...well, you know, if you died.

"And going to school for six months is not the end of the world. You're acting like it is. Sure, it will be difficult, but aren't there parts of life that are difficult? That's what you tell us, isn't it? You can do both. You don't have to be our slave to be a good mother. You do not have to be owned." Her face was red from tears and anger as she continued,

"You've fallen for all his words. He has put doubt inside your soul again. Come on, Mom, listen to the words you teach other people. I'm sure the boys and Anno will agree. This meeting will be good. We've gotta do this for this family." Maria finished.

"But just between you and me, Maria, it would really be hard for me to be away that long. I nearly went crazy at ICASSI in Holland, and that was only three weeks."

"I know it will be hard for you, Mom. But I also know this is a once in a lifetime opportunity and it's something that would be extremely wonderful for you. Sonste has faith in you and for good reason. But I don't think you will know that until you go there and see what you can learn. Maybe, more importantly, what you already have learned. I wish I could go with you."

I felt an instant surge of excitement, "Well, Maria, why can't you?" my eyes got big, "You don't like school right now anyway." It was true; Maria had been unhappy at school for some time now.

"Yeah, I hate school but it would be so expensive, wouldn't it? Besides this is your time and I wouldn't want to push in on that."

"It wouldn't be so expensive and it's not pushing in, Maria. Sonste doesn't even want me to pay rent. He makes it as easy as possible for students who come to study with him. I'll only pay for the groceries I use and that's not expensive. There will be no tuition payments either because I'm not applying for credit at the university but at the Alfred Adler Institute. Money is not the real issue here anyway, Maria. Money is only an excuse for Pat to use now," I got up from the edge of bathtub where I'd been sitting and stretched my back.

"Well, what's most important is that you go. And right now we have to have a meeting," Maria said.

Before the words were totally out of her mouth, we could hear Tony's voice calling from downstairs, "Mom, Maria, come on down to the breakfast room! Everyone is waiting for you guys!"

Maria quickly ran downstairs and joined the others who were sitting around the table. I followed closely behind. Twelve eyes stared at me as I pulled out a chair and sat down. Pat looked down at the floor. The tension was thick.

I looked at my hands. They were shaking. I hoped my voice wouldn't shake. I began, "Hey you guys, obviously we need to talk about something." My voice did quiver but I went on, "Everyone knows about Sonste, right?"

"Right," the kids responded in unison.

"Yeah, we did all meet him when he stayed here last year, Mom, remember?" Tony was being funny. He was always trying to help people lighten up.

"Oh yeah, I forgot about that. Anyway, as you all already know, I would like to go to West Virginia and study with Sonste for a few months. This is a very special invitation and an honor to be asked to study with this man. The credits could also be used towards my degree. I would be living in his home, not paying rent or tuition, and I would only pay for the food that I eat, or the food that we eat if Maria decides she would like to go along.

"I would be gone from January to May. It is a long time for us to be away from each other. Right now, it seems like a million years, but in reality, five months is not so long in a lifetime. Pat says I shouldn't go because we don't have the money and because I would be stealing what money we do have away from you guys. Neither of these statements are true. I would like to hear what you guys think about the whole thing."

Silence.

"Well, I think…" Maria started slowly. Both nervousness and strength could be heard in her voice, "if you want to go to West Virginia and Sonste has invited you, and if there is not a problem with money, you should go. I don't know if there is a problem with money or not but if you say there isn't, I believe you and think you should go," she slapped her hands down on her lap to emphasize her statement. Her eyes looked deep into mine. Pat stared blankly at the floor as the veins in his neck throbbed.

"I think you should go too, Mom," Joe's voice showed nervousness too, "We all know how well you work with people. And if this is what you need to continue doing what you want to do, I say go. I mean, it would be very hard without you here but we really want you to go because this is something for you," he spoke slowly now, gaining confidence with each word. "It's exciting to us because it's exciting to you. I'm excited because you'll be helping people with their lives, doing something besides hanging wallpaper, you know, kid?" he winked at me. "I don't mean that there is anything wrong with hanging wallpaper. Don't misunderstand me. It's just like I've told you a long time ago, you have a gift to give the world and that gift is not the secret to hanging wallpaper."

"Thanks Joe," I said softly.

"I know you can do it," Joe was cool now, and he looked at his brother, "So what do you think, John?" Joe was taking over the direction of this meeting.

John swallowed hard and paused, "I think it's a good idea," he swallowed again, "Hey, you gotta do what you gotta do. I mean we'll miss you but it won't be forever. And it's not like we don't know what to do around here. We know how to run this household and we'll take good care of Peanut for sure," he looked at Anno. "She won't let us get away with much, you know with her 'you're not the boss of me' routine keeping us on our toes. But hey, we can handle it," John cleared his throat again as if from part nervousness and part relief at having stated his opinion.

There was silence and Anno squirmed as she looked at her brother.

Tony assumed the role of the lawyer and scratched his head as he began, "Well, Mom, it seems to me that this is a once in a lifetime chance for you, isn't that correct?" He looked me in the eye. Eye contact was definitely strong today.

"Yes, I believe so, Tony," I answered softly.

"And it seems like this Sonste guy is pretty special. He invites one person at a time from somewhere around the world to study with him, right? And you'll have a chance to learn things that you've wanted to learn for a long time, is that correct?" Tony quizzed me even though he knew the answers. His voice was getting higher as each question came out of his mouth.

"Yes," I heard my voice say.

"He's the guy to teach it to you and it's quite an honor that he invited you. Am I understanding it all correctly?" his voice had more strength than I had ever heard.

"Yes."

"He invites one person at a time to study with him, right?'

"Yes."

"Then, you should go," and with that he turned his head to look at his brother Chris, adding quickly without breaking the rhythm, "What do you think, Christopher?"

Christopher was silent for several moments before responding, "I guess you should go," he hesitated, "I mean, yeah, you should go," he stopped again, "I'll miss you a lot but I still want you to go. This is a special thing and it doesn't happen every day but we'd miss you a lot." He looked at me lovingly and repeated, "Yeah, we'd miss you a lot."

I was scared to breathe, but took a deep breath anyway, "I know. I'd miss you guys a lot, too. God, I don't even know if I can do this, but if Maria goes, that would help with the homesick part," my voice trailed off as Tony jumped in again.

"Yeah, that would be really neat if Maria got to go. What do you think, Maria?" Tony's voice got loud again as it did sometimes when he got excited.

Maria looked at me, "You're going. If it's okay with you guys, she's going. I don't know about me going, but I know Mom's going for sure," Maria slapped her legs again.

"Well, what about Anno, you guys, and all the housework stuff? How will we do that?" Chris sounded a little overwhelmed at the moment. He was definitely not as excited as Tony was.

"Well, I don't really see a problem," John spoke again. "We have been coming home after school and taking care of Anno as well as cooking dinner for a while now. What's the big deal? It only means that if Maria is going with

Mom, someone will have to take an extra day each week and we can take turns with that. Really, I can't see that it would be a problem to continue doing what we're doing now," John leaned back in his chair, apparently feeling very comfortable with his response.

"Right. It's not a problem," Joe's voice was strong as he quickly agreed with his brother. Usually it took a while for Joe and John to agree, but that didn't happen on this issue.

"What about you, Anno?" I thought I was calm now but my voice told me otherwise as I heard it crack. I was a wreck.

"I'll miss you, Mommy," Anno said softly.

"I know, sweetheart," I reached over and pulled her onto my lap, "I'll miss you like crazy," I hugged her as I spoke.

"It's settled then," Maria slammed both her palms on the table this time, ending the whole discussion.

Silence spread through the room for seconds that seemed like hours.

"Would anyone like to know what I think?" Pat asked, obviously angry.

"Sure Pat, what do you think?" Tony asked as he gave him the floor, "I was wondering if you were ever going to say anything."

Tony was damn brave, I thought. Nothing scared him.

Pat cleared his throat, "First of all, we do not have the money for your mother to go frolicking off around the country like this. We just do not have the money. She'll be taking money that should be for you kids to go to college," anger dripped from his voice. "Secondly, she obviously is not interested in being a mother anymore. She really doesn't care about you guys, me, or her responsibilities here. What does she ever do around here? You kids do all the work. She's only interested in herself. I am against her going and stealing money from you kids."

Silence screamed as all our hearts pounded. Everyone stared at him except me. I could see their eyes shooting daggers, disgust, and anger. No one moved a muscle. Glances dashed from person to person as quick as lighting as they sent me shots of courage. *Don't lie about my Mom, my Apple,* reflected off every face. These kids had always shown him total respect, but it seemed as if now he had gone too far.

I remained silent on the outside again but on the inside I was screaming and calling him names. I knew he was insane with jealousy, but this was not more important than my kids. Nothing in the world would ever be more important than the kids, but at the same time I was not going to live with them forever and I had something to teach the world. Sonste thought so and the kids supported me in this.

This group of kids was the most self-sufficient, caring, humorous bunch of geniuses that anyone could ever meet. That was the opinion of everyone who met them. That was not just their mother talking. With the things I had learned I had given them all the tools for life. How silly of him to try to turn the kids against me, against any mother, ever!

No words came out of my mouth but Pat could read them in my eyes. Leaving the kids for six months would be the hardest thing I would ever do in my life. I wanted to be in West Virginia to study with Sonste so badly I could taste it, yet I didn't want to leave my kids so badly that it made me hurt before even leaving.

"She's going," Maria broke the silence.

That kid was always so sure of herself when it came to her mother. She had more confidence in me than I could ever have had in myself in a million years.

"Meeting adjourned!" it was Tony's voice.

Pat sat and stared into space.

Wow, what a meeting! I needed time for this to sink in. I stood up and pushed my chair back under the table. All eyes were on me again as they followed my movement. *The kids said I should go to West Virginia.* My mind raced. *Could I really leave them?* I wasn't sure I had the courage and strength to do what I was fighting to do. It seemed as if the kids were my courage now.

We spoke in whispers about what I would take, how it would be when I was gone, and when I'd be back. I remained torn inside. I wanted desperately to go and yet felt afraid. It felt as if I were always talking about someone else when we talked about me going to West Virginia. We had private talks every evening as each kid waited their turn to find me alone. The conversations were endless and I loved them. I wondered if the kids had planned it that way in the little private meetings they held behind closed doors in someone's bedroom.

Pat continued to stay away from me, acting as if I had leprosy. Joe continued to give me little hugs and told me not to worry. He wanted everything to be perfect for me. He had strength for me and made me feel good. That kid was so intense sometimes. Although everyone was pretty intense by that time.

John said as often as needed, "You gotta do what you gotta do, Apple." When we were alone, his sensitivity overwhelmed me. He knew my worries and fears and his "Lighten up, baby," always came at the right moment and those big brown eyes were always shining full of love. It absolutely amazed me how they could all share so many of the same wonderful qualities and how they always showed them so differently...and yet the same.

Tony gave me little "don't worry" talks. It would be okay and I would learn stuff, he said. They'd take good care of Anno. Then he'd say it again, "You're gonna learn stuff."

Chris, who was 10 now, was quiet. He wanted and didn't want me to go. I understood completely because I felt the same way.

Anno didn't know how long six months was but she knew we'd miss each other even though she would have all her brothers and Pat.

Each of them touched my suitcase a dozen times and stuffed in a million little notes. Joe bought me stamps. Tony got me some stationery. John said I could have his GI Joe doll, teasing me like always. Anno and Christopher gave me several drawings. One for Sonste, one for Maria, several for me. They hugged and kissed me like never before. They pushed me out the door with one hand and held on tight with the other.

Mother's continuous letters were no longer arriving every day, but they still proved to be just as stinging. No matter how wonderful the kids were or how much time I spent with her on her visits, her condemning letters blasted me after she has returned home. Maybe it was "Boooze..." she'd say drawing out the word with sarcasm over the phone.

"Is Boooze the problem with you? Are you booozing with that priest?"

"No Mother, booze is not a problem for me. I can't get through two glasses of wine without falling asleep," I laughed as I answered.

"Don't make fun of your mother, Mary Cecile. Are you going to church? Are any of your children going to church? I know you're not. You're just raising a bunch of heathens. The mother lies in bed as the children run wild."

"Mother, you know that's not the way it is. You know..."

"Don't sass me back, Mary Cecile. I don't have much time left. You better get yourself in line before it's too late."

Click.

I wouldn't dare say anything about going to West Virginia. I reassured her that I loved her but refused to allow her words to totally destroy me as had been my pattern throughout my life. I guess my kids' encouragement and belief in me was finally sinking in. I could continue to call her from West Virginia and she would not know I was not in Chicago.

For six months starting in January 1978, Maria and I followed Sonste around the countryside, working alongside him and learning from him. His classroom consisted of schools from the elementary level to post-graduate level. Each day, except Sunday, started around five in the morning and ended around eleven at night. Maria and I learned not only what we had come to learn but an unbelievably vast amount more.

When people came to talk with Sonste about themselves, they came for a lesson, not for therapy. When they came for parenting lessons, they didn't feel at fault or to blame, but rather that they had learned something to make their home life more harmonious. That was one of the greatest lessons he taught me.

Even though every minute was literally filled with things to do, I still missed the kids like crazy. I went home for a week at Easter, leaving Maria in West Virginia. I spent the whole week down on the floor hugging and kissing the kids. Pat was quiet and distant and it made me sad but being with the kids revitalized me and made me able to go back and finish up the semester with Sonste.

"This was a wise decision, Maria," I said when she picked me up at the airport in West Virginia. "Even if Pat said I shouldn't have spent the money, I'm glad we came here. Of course everyone misses us like crazy and can't wait for us to come home."

"I know it was a good decision, too," Maria said with confidence.

Then when it came time for us to say goodbye to Sonste at the end of May, it was with a tremendous amount of mixed emotion. We were both elated about going home to the other guys while at the same time our hearts were feeling heavy because we were leaving West Virginia and all of the kindness and knowledge that we had shared there. Many of the people we met we would never see again. And Sonste had touched our souls like no other had ever done before. We were leaving a teacher who was incomparable to any other teacher we had ever met. Maria and I hoped we could do justice to the knowledge we had collected.

All the kids wished that the time we had spent apart would make things better between Pat and me. They hoped a new start could be made upon my return, but this was not to be.

Haile-Yesus came to visit the next month on his way to see Sonste. He was a quiet, gentle man and had a peacefulness about him that was a rare find in human beings. I was surprised and honored that he stopped at our home. The kids and I did our best to make him comfortable, even though we were all under a terrible strain. Haile assured us that he had a wonderful time. I felt very calm around this man. It was never necessary to look for conversation. He promised to write me when he got back to Paris. He kept his word.

For the next year, Pat and I lived as total strangers. We all continued on as best as possible in the war zone. When I had a friend over, we would sit quietly in the breakfast room and share hot tea and soft whispers. Pat turned me in to D.C.F.S. and had me investigated for being an "unfit mother." Of course he didn't get anywhere but it was hell going through the investigation. In the martyr role, my screams were mute as I struggled to make a life for the kids and myself inside this picturesque hell. We were living as if we had an incurable illness. Self-destruction was inevitable.

I received my Bachelors degree in Education on August 26th, Anno's birthday. Life continued at a painful pace but I remained their Apple and they remained my cheerleaders. When I would lay awake at night after all was quiet and the sky was dark, I felt that although we were in the midst of war, this had to be the best age that kids could ever be.

28

I had fresh new divorce papers to begin the year 1980. I had no credit, no health insurance, and no job. I knew I would not marry again until I had learned I was okay by myself. The divorce decree said that we would have to sell the house and move out within three years. The house that I had bought with my money from Aunt Cecily. I decided that divorce lawyers sucked. Lies and more lies. Cheating and more cheating. The kids and I started over new, hoping the scars would heal.

Mother had disowned me for one week after the divorce went through. But after that week, she began calling again and wanting me to "save" her from my older brother. She wanted me to get back to being my "old self."

"Mother, I can't save you from Paul. Don't you understand? You have to stand up to him if you want him to leave you alone. I can't do that for you, Mother dear."

"Well, now you're beginning to sound like my old Mary Cecile. Don't hate your brother, Mary Cecile. He can't help the way he is. Have patience with him."

"Mother, I don't hate my brother, but all my life you've been saying to have 'patience with him' like he's not responsible for his actions."

"Oh there you go with your psychology, Mary Cecile. Your life really isn't perfect, you know. It's about time you get yourself and your children back to church."

"Mother, do you know how wonderful my kids are? Do you know how many wonderful things they're doing? And how many wonderful things they have done? Why can't you ever notice anything good about them? Just once, Mother, can't you at least give them a little credit? All these years, all the fabulous things that they've done and keep doing, Mother. Can't we ever talk about that?"

"You're not well, Mary Cecile. You need to get a good checkup by a good doctor. I have to go now."

Click.

She began to say that I should move back to Perryville to take care of my children. I usually wanted to scream at her, but I would tell myself to ignore it and would tell her that I loved her. She told me that if I really loved her I wouldn't be getting another divorce, but that I would be getting an annulment. I no longer fell for the "if you really loved me" line. I would tell her sweetly that I did love her and that I always would, no matter where I lived. I knew I was probably too understanding, but she was my mother. On the other hand, I felt like I had been a mother forever and not once did she given me any credit for what I had accomplished. All I could count on was that the condemning letters and phone calls would continue. I had no reason to believe anymore that that would ever change. When she asked about the children, which didn't happen often, I would tell her about some of the wonderful things they were always doing. Usually, I was interrupted before I could complete my story. I was still a lazy mother who slept all the time and only loved my baby by the priest. That never changed.

"They don't even go to church, Mary Cecile. They're just a bunch of heathens and it's your fault because you are the mother. You just can't keep getting married and divorced. You'd better move back to Perryville and get your life straightened out or else."

"Mother, just because I don't do everything the way you think I should doesn't mean I'm being mean to you. Can't you understand that? I just have to do some things the way I feel is best. Can't you ever give me any credit, Mother?

"Credit for what? It's terrible what you've done! Getting married and divorced over and over like it's okay to do that. You are setting a bad example for your children. You are raising them like heathens. It should be a crime."

"But Mother, my kids are wonderful. They take care of each other. They care *about* each other. They are kind and they are funny. They're bright and they're leaders. Mother, they do so many things that other kids haven't been trained to do. Can't you see any of that? Sure, they have made mistakes, but that's part of life. Can't you just once see how wonderful they are, how together they are? Mother, can't you see..."

"You just can't keep getting married and divorced, Mary Cecile. You're raising a bunch of heathens and that's all there is to it."

Click.

Two graduations each year became routine. John graduated high school and Chris graduated eighth grade that following June. Our first graduations in the 1980s. I learned that there was a world of difference between when your first kid graduates high school and when your third kid graduates. John had learned a lot from watching his older brother and sister. He had already decided early in his last year of high school where he wanted to go to college. He picked Indiana University and would have to pay out-of-state tuition. I had no idea how he would do it, but I knew he would make it. I had to laugh at myself when I thought of how I had set aside money for each of my kids' college tuitions. How silly of me to think that four thousand dollars would be enough for four years of college. But it was big bucks to me at the time.

The trauma of the last three years had taken a heavy toll on each of us. We all agreed that we wanted to be together for a while and do things like laugh, hug, tease, and just "be." By now, Maria, Joe, and Tony were all working at the ranch in Colorado during the summer. So it was decided that the rest of us would go to Colorado that summer so we could all be together and those guys could keep their jobs at the same time.

John, Chris, Anno, Jenny—Joe's girlfriend and newly "adopted" member of the family—and I traveled for twenty-four hours by Greyhound to Colorado.

"Chris, quick, come sit here," John said while sitting alone in a double seat. The bus driver had pulled over for another stop and more people were getting on.

"No, John, I just moved here next to Mom. Besides, just ten minutes ago you wanted me to move away from you," Chris smiled as he whispered to his brother.

"Chris, don't you dare move from this seat," I whispered. I didn't want to share the next thousand miles with a stranger either.

"Anno, come sit with me," John's voice pleaded with her as people started down the aisle.

"Why, John? I thought you wanted to sit alone," Anno teased him without moving a muscle.

"Please Anno, just sit here until everyone finds a seat. Then you can go back next to Jenny," there was urgency in his voice now as someone picked a seat closer to him.

"Sorry, John. I like where I'm sitting," she smiled and turned to look out the window.

No more than two seconds later, a large lady sat right next to him. He shot evil looks over his shoulder to Anno before turning to look out the window. Nothing was heard from John for the next three hundred miles or so. The rest of us laughed quietly in our seats as John swore he'd "get even" later. By the time the woman got off, John had been squished down to a measly ninety pounds, or so he said. This created enough laughs to make everyone's sides ache for hours afterwards.

Never had a group of people been so happy to be together. We laughed, talked, kissed, hugged, teased, ate and slept. All the stuff that was good for the soul. Once again, everyone we met loved those kids and told me how lucky I was. I had difficulty believing that half of them would be away at college that September. It was happening so fast. I knew I was afraid of being alone.

Maria was changing colleges and needed the resident assistant job at Southern Illinois University in order to afford her full-time tuition there. I was concerned. Back home at the end of summer, Maria's own concern came out in tears.

"Maria, please don't worry, honey. You will get the R.A. job," I said putting my arms around her. As always, I was totally confident about what Maria could do.

"But, Mom, I'm not old enough," Maria got so frustrated when I had that attitude. She pushed my arms away and got a cold glass of water.

I, once again refusing to get emotional with Maria's doubts, said calmly, "You will get the job, Maria."

Then, after a long pause, I half-teased, "How come you characters don't listen to me? I know these things."

"Oh, Mom, sometimes you really just don't understand," it was rare that a stinging comment like that came from Maria.

I knew I now had to bring up one of my "don't you remember" lines.

"You were worried about the same thing when you applied for the job at the ranch. Don't you remember?" I said with just a hint of drama.

"Yes," Maria answered with her "so-what's-that-got-to-do-with-this" tone. She rolled her eyes with irritation.

I remained cool. "Didn't they lower the age requirement because of you?" I asked innocently.

"Yes Mom, they did but... but we're talking about a university now. It's different," Maria slammed her glass down in the sink. She jerked, thinking she broke it.

"No 'buts,' Maria, you need to stop worrying! You are all upset over nothing. I'm telling you. L..i..s..t..e..n to me," I pleaded dramatically with her.

"But..." Maria still didn't agree with me.

"You'll get the job, Maria. I have no doubt," I spoke with complete conviction and strength. Maria walked out into the living room.

"Okay," she sighed as she came back into the kitchen.

I knew she wanted to say more, but there was silence. A couple of minutes passed and it became clear the subject was closed for now.

"So how am I going to get John to college?" I asked, changing the subject.

"Why don't you get someone to drive him down there with you?" Maria asked.

"Maybe so," I agreed, wondering why I hadn't thought of that. "Yeah, I'll find someone to drive down there with us. It's important that he gets settled comfortably."

Maria settled into Southern Illinois University with her R.A. position. Joe settled into Colorado State University and I had just returned from getting John settled at Indiana U. in Bloomington. I arrived back home from that trip very tired but relieved that he was settled. As I started to unpack my overnight bag, my thoughts began to revolve around the divorce, the bills, and the fact that I had no credit. I stopped to put a note on my dresser to remind myself to keep my priorities straight. The kids were settled and happy and that's what was most important. Before I could get back to my unpacking, I heard Tony calling to me from the kitchen.

"Hey Mom! John's on the phone!"

"John?" I asked puzzled as I took the phone, "Hi honey, what's up?"

"Mom?" John was whispering.

"Yes?"

"I don't want to stay here," his voice was so soft, "I hate this place."

I couldn't believe my ears. "What? You hate it? What's wrong?" I thought for sure that something dreadful had happened

"I just don't like it," his voice cracked, "This is not the place for me. I want to go to Colorado and be with my brother," he paused, "or come home," he continued, "I don't know but I just don't want to be here." His voice was final.

"John, you haven't even been there for twenty-four hours yet. You're homesick, honey," I pleaded. "How about staying until the end of the week?" my voice was soft and understanding, but he would have none of it.

He continued his plea, half forcefully and half full of tears. "I don't want to stay. I want to get out of here. It's terrible!" (pause) "I can't stand it," (pause, tears) "I don't want to go to college," (more tears) "I've changed my mind," (pause) "I want to go to Colorado with Joe," (pause, sobs) "That's where I want to go," (pause) "God, this is so horrible!" he kept crying. I wanted to be able to reach through the phone and hold him.

"How would it be if we talked tomorrow? Just stay there for the night," I was hoping he would consider taking it one day at a time. "Could you do that? I'll call you later tonight and we could talk some more." I paused, "How does that sound?"

"Well, I guess so..." he didn't mean it, "but I really want to go to Colorado and be with my brother," he stated as if that had been his life plan. "I've thought about it a lot and that's what I want to do. I want to come home tomorrow, Mom," he had no doubt. "I don't want to stay here. I've thought it through and I am positive."

"You haven't even had time to unpack your suitcases. I don't think you've had enough time to think about it," I said confidently. "I don't want you to come home until you've had a couple of days there, at least. We'll talk in the morning, okay?" I remained firm.

But he was not to be persuaded, "Okay, Mom, but I know I want to come home," he cried. "I know that I want to go to Colorado and be with my brother."

My heart hurt to hear him. 'Oh, honey, don't cry so hard. We'll work this part out. Just try it for a little while. Would you please?" I knew I was begging now, but I was willing to beg if it would help get him through this first night.

He couldn't stop crying, "I...feel...so...bad...Mom...it...feels...so horrible...here...I... feel...so terrible...I miss...you guys...so bad..." his voice trailed off. I was beside myself as to what I could do. I wished I had a partner to help me, but I didn't. Again I had to do this one by myself.

So John came home the next day. Nothing I said could've persuaded him to stay. After two days at home, however, he decided to go back. By coming back home, he learned that he was ready to leave home, but he had to come back to learn that. He really did believe that he wanted to go to Colorado. He had never gone away from home before like Maria, Joe, and Tony—who had all worked on the ranch in Colorado during the summers when they were in high school. For John, this was his first time away.

With John back in Bloomington, I relaxed again in the belief that everyone was settled. That was until Jenny decided to take a semester off of college and come home because her mother was dying of cancer. After her mother's death, their house was sold immediately. And since the rest of her family had already begun their own families in their own homes, she really didn't have a place to go during school vacations and things. I invited Jenny to make her home with us and made it clear that it had nothing to do with whether or not she and Joe were dating. Jenny accepted the idea and became part of our family. The kids and I were extremely happy that we could be there to help her during this hard time.

But yet again, I could not completely relax. It seemed as if the minute one thing was settled, something else always came up. It couldn't have been more than a week later when the high school contacted me about the fact that Tony had already missed 58 days so far in his senior year. I was livid after the phone call and so I went for a long walk, hoping to quiet the anger inside me and collect my thoughts. I felt ready and was making a cup of tea the minute Tony walked in the door.

"Tony, one of your teachers called this morning," I said very calmly as he opened the refrigerator.

"Yeah?" he was taking out a pot of leftover spaghetti.

"It was quite an eye opener for me," I could hear the surprise in my voice.

Tony's back was to me as I watched him dish the spaghetti slowly from the pot onto his plate. Then he put the pot back in the refrigerator and carried his plate towards the table, "Yeah? What did she say?" he grabbed the newspaper, making no eye contact before sitting down at the table.

I knew he was dying on the inside, wondering if he had been found out. He continued looking at the paper as if he were only half interested in what I had to say.

I sat down at the table with him, relaxed and looking out the window as I spoke. "She started by telling me she felt bad because of all the bad things that had happened to us this year. I thought, of course, she was talking about the divorce and all, but she said, 'No, I mean all the deaths in your family.'"

I paused and took a sip of my tea. Then, without looking at Tony, I looked back out the window. Out of the corner of my eye, I saw that he had now stopped chewing and was staring right at me. I continued on with no emotion.

"'Deaths?' I asked her. And she said, 'Yes, deaths.'" I stopped and turned my head to look over at Tony, but he was already up getting a glass of milk from the refrigerator. His back was to me again so I couldn't see his face. He took a big gulp as he walked back to the table, keeping the glass in front of his face.

"Your teacher was calling to let me know how sorry she was that we had so many aunts and uncles die this year. Then I found out that you have been absent 58 days so far this semester and have written notes for absences signing either Pat's or my name."

There was nothing remotely resembling a smile on my face. Tony had stopped chewing in the middle of a bite. He knew the secret was out but he questioned me anyway, "Aunts?" He finally swallowed the rest of his milk.

I wanted to burst out laughing at his question but I also wanted to slap him really hard. I told myself to stay calm.

"Well okay, uncles, grandparents, or whatever. You know what I'm talking about, don't you, Tony?"

He knew he was in dangerous territory with me and that I was in no mood for messing around. He wiped his mouth on his sleeve as he picked up his plate and glass and started for the kitchen. There was no way he was going to finish his spaghetti.

"Well...you see, Mom," he said after he passed my chair, "it started out like...I mean here's the way it happened...." He talked slowly so he could put his plate in the sink and be back at the table before finishing his sentence, but as he sat back down to say more, I took over.

"No, Tony, it's like this," my voice didn't disguise my anger now. He sat staring at me, looking ready to take whatever I was about to dish out.

"Your responsibility right now is to go to school," I began, "I realize that you are bored there, but use your creativity. Do something to get *un*bored."

"I did," he mumbled, laughing under his breath.

"Who do you think you are pulling this kind of stunt? If you don't want to go to school, please quit. Get yourself a full-time job and help me with the bills." I meant it and he knew I meant it. He remained silent this time, knowing I wasn't finished, "As long as you're living in this house," it was my hands-on-the-hips tone of voice, "your responsibility is to go to school and graduate in June. Is that clear, Tony?"

"Yes, Mom, it's clear," he answered remorsefully.

"Ohhh, I'm getting out of here!" I could feel myself getting angry again.

"Oh, Mom, come on," he pleaded with me now.

"Don't 'Oh Mom' me, Tony, and get that look off your face!"

"Mom..."

"Oh just leave me alone, Tony!" I cried, "Sometimes you make me sick when you pull one of these stunts."

"I'm sorry, Mom," he felt bad now.

"Sorry's not enough, Tony," I said as I left the room, still angry. I had a right to be angry I told myself.

Between the kids, my parenting classes, and the other jobs I needed in order to make money for the bills, I felt like I worked twenty-four hours a day. We had bills piling up from everywhere and I needed to put the house up for sale soon. Life went from bills to birthdays and from high school to college. Maria, with her brothers backing her up, insisted that I had waited long enough since receiving my bachelor's degree and now needed to get my master's degree. I thought they were nuts. They just laughed and teased me by saying they were still having a hard time raising me. Money was scarce. We still had a big house and with no money for upkeep it had quickly became a burden rather than a joy. The bricks falling down inside the chimney last week reminded me of that again. I always felt stupid because I didn't know how to make money very well.

Summer meant Haile-Yesus would be coming for another visit. Although he never said in his letter when he would be arriving, it seemed like I could always feel him getting nearer. He surprised me and yet didn't. He shared some details of his work with UNICEF. Since I had seen him last, he had been to Bangkok, Singapore, Jakarta, Dacca, Bangladesh, and Bali on "the most beautiful beach in the world." And as always, we talked about his love for his people and home in Ethiopia, his going back there and my going with him "when the children were older."

"Maybe we would go back there someday and teach together," he would say as he held my hand on his heart.

What would I have to teach them, I wondered? But I would go with him one day, this I knew. It surprised me that he was not going on to West Virginia to see Sonste this trip but I didn't think too much about it. He only stayed for two days but it could have been two weeks, two years, or two lifetimes. Everything stopped and all my difficulties in life disappeared when Haile was visiting. He slipped away as quietly as he came, promising we would be together again next year. There was definitely a special place in my heart for this man. When Daddy died, I promised him in that funeral home that for the rest of my life, if I loved someone, I would tell them. That was because I never told him when he was alive. I would not make that mistake again. If I loved someone, I told them. So why did it seem like such a big deal about saying I love you to Haile-Yesus?

Tony had decided he was not going to attend college immediately after graduating high school. Instead he stayed on at the ranch, working full-time that fall, in order to help his sister and two brothers with their college tuition bills.

Any difficulties in the family were no longer just mine, but belonged to everyone. "We" had to sell the house because it was in the divorce decree. "We" had to get Apple a real job. "We" were going to have to find an apartment after selling the house. "We" had to get Apple her master's degree.

There were no more discussions about who did what jobs around the house. That part had been over for quite some time and I hadn't even noticed. We worked well together in a manner that was unknown to the outside world. There was not a "bad apple," a "bad seed," a "bad guy," a "good guy," a "pet", or a "favorite." There was room for everyone to contribute on the positive side of life. To an outside observer, it sometimes seemed that everyone inside our home did whatever they pleased. But if they took the time to look under the surface, they saw a group in action where everyone was part of the whole. We had accomplished that dream that Dreikurs told me about twelve years before when he said, "You have a whole group of kids working against you but you can win them all over to your side."

Another year passed quickly. In my current job I was working late evening and night hours at a hotel restaurant. Every afternoon, I left for work shortly after Chris and Anno arrived home from school. And every afternoon, I cried all the way to work because they spent the evenings alone without me. It was a pretty good job so I had to keep it, but when I found out I had to work on Christmas Eve, I was crushed. It had been another year when it was not financially possible for us to see each other at any time other than Christmas. All the kids would be home for the holidays and I was going to ruin Christmas Eve for everyone. I was in my bedroom crying over the whole situation when Maria called from college. I immediately poured out the whole story between my tears.

"So, Mom, what's the big deal?" Maria paused briefly, "We'll just wait until you get home and then we'll have Santa Claus," her voice was upbeat and sincere.

"Wait till I get home?" my voice was strained.

"Sure," Maria confirmed it.

"But I won't get home until two or three in the morning." I thought her idea was crazy.

"So, do you think we've never been up late before?" Maria was trying to put it in perspective for me.

"No. I mean, I know you've been up late before but..." I couldn't think of what to say.

"Then what's the big deal?" Maria asked. She knew she had just changed the whole situation around and waited for my response.

"Oh, Maria, I feel so good when you talk like that," I was relieved at such a good solution. My whole body relaxed. Maria could probably even feel it through the phone.

"So, you'll go to work and when you come home we'll have Christmas Eve, just like we always do. The only difference is that it will be a few hours later, okay?"

I half laughed and half cried, "That's a great idea. Thanks, Maria."

"You're welcome, Apple," Maria said softly.

I received a letter from Haile-Yesus two weeks before Christmas asking, "Can you zoom out here for 15 days for Xmas? Fantasy, but maybe you can. Let me know. If not, I will see you next summer. Don't know what's happened to my necktie. Please call my friend in N.Y. City if you find it there. His name is Wolde. Sweet kisses and love, Haile."

Where was he now, I wondered? Probably Bangladesh.

No, as much as I wanted to visit him it was not something I could do at that time in my life. There was still time, I told myself. Did he really like me that much? It was hard for me to imagine. He was so beautiful. I figured I was probably making more out of it than he meant. Besides, I couldn't go anyway.

That Christmas Eve, I went to work as usual. When I returned home, it was almost 1a.m. From my car window, I could see every light in the house was on. Immediately concerned that something was wrong, I dashed across the lawn, up the stairs, and in the front door as fast as my tired legs would go. Coming from the kitchen were the sounds of loud laughter, screaming, and excitement. I pushed open the swinging door and saw Tony standing on the counter-top with a broom. John was standing in the sink. Chris and Jenny were sitting on the dishwasher. Anno was kneeling on the cabinet. Joe stood on the back porch as he held the back screen door open and Maria was climbing onto a tall stool. I knew the mice had taken over our home and I had put off calling the exterminator. I just didn't realize how bad it was.

"Look out, there are two behind the stove! Maria, grab the bucket! Anno, watch-out! Mom, you'd better get up on that chair!" Tony screamed frantically at everyone.

"Here, come over here! Here's one! Look, he's pretty dead," Joe poked at a little brown fuzzy thing with the broom.

"One just ran by your feet! Get up! I'm telling you Chris, get back up on the dishwasher! Smash 'em! Here, hand me that broom!" Tony laughed more and screamed.

Joe handed Tony the broom as the screen door slammed.

"Throw water! Throw some water!" Maria was beside herself with laughter.

"No, that won't kill 'em! Chase them over here!" Joe got on top of the dishwasher next to Chris.

"I see one! I see one!" Anno clapped her hands, "Get it, John! Get it!" she screamed as she bounced up and down pointing towards the pantry.

"Stand back, Mom! We've got one cornered! Get on the other side of the stove, Joe! It has to come out one side or the other and then we'll nail it!" John was jumping from foot to foot, hoping the mouse would come out on Joe's side.

"Oh, my God, there goes another one!" Joe shouted, "We're doing pretty good huh, Mom? We're catching all the mice."

"Yeah, we can have mice soup tomorrow," John cracked himself up laughing.

"Come on you guys, let's corner that one behind the radiator! Can't have Christmas Eve yet, Mom, we've got a few more mice to get!" Tony was in absolute heaven.

I stared at them in amazement.

"How many mice are in the bucket, Tony?" Joe asked.

"Ten. We've got ten in the bucket outside," Chris answered.

"Then there are the ones we threw outside in that box. Five, I think," John said.

"Behind you! Behind you! Watch out, Anno!" Chris yelled at his sister.

"Hand me the broom, Joe," Tony begged.

"Can't. I need it. Use the mop," Joe answered.

"Can't. Broom's better," Tony grabbed the broom from his brother.

"There were lots of mice, Mom, but we've got 'em now."

The screams and excitement continued for some time. The calm came about an hour later as they put their brooms to rest and laid around on the living room floor in the wee hours of the morning, laughing softly, playing Santa Claus, opening presents, eating chocolate chip cookies, and rubbing each others' backs. Anno told all her friends it was the best Christmas we ever had. No one remembered any of the presents from that Christmas Eve. No one remembered the fact that I had worked so late. All anyone would remember was that it was our wonderful Mice Christmas. The kids always proved in one way or another what I learned long ago, "anything can be anything else."

That next summer, just like he said, Haile-Yesus came to visit. It was perfect timing. But, then again, whenever he came was the perfect time. Once again, he listened well to my trials and tribulations. And he looked great. But he always looked great. Always the same. He amazed me. He owned two suitcases, one large and one small. Everything he owned could be carried in his two suitcases. Quite an accomplishment, I thought. He had no worldly possessions and yet had all the important things of life. He spoke seven languages. Laughed deep. Teased well. Prayed well. Played well. Questioned. Loved. Cared. Worked long and hard. Helped others. Gentle. Giving. Learned. Taught. And remained humble. Everything. It was all there inside of him.

As usual with his visits, it was a warm, peaceful, loving time. I noticed that he couldn't eat very much, but let it pass. He was a tall, very thin man. I reminded myself that he had never really eaten a lot anyway. He stayed only three days and we spent half that time at the airport because the airline had lost his luggage. He talked about his country, the jungle, and going back there. Would I consider going back there with him? The question seemed more serious this time. Or was I just listening more carefully to him? I was trying to imagine him inviting me to be part of his life. "When the children get a little older," he said. I couldn't leave with the children still so young. "We'll talk again at Christmas," he said, "We'll write."

"He loves you, you stupid idiot! He comes halfway around the world to see you," my friend yelled at me when I told her about him. "For years he's been coming to see YOU! Get a clue!" I missed him when he was gone, very much. I knew I had been carrying him around in my heart since I first met him so long ago. But trying to imagine that he could love me back just sounded too good. I had difficulty imagining it was real.

We all had mixed emotions about the whole experience of selling our home. I felt tremendous relief as well as sadness. The older kids were making their own lives in other places. Our house was just was too big and too expensive for me to keep up. The walls in that home would always hold a certain feeling of peace and joy that our family had brought to it. But big houses were meant for lots of children. I felt fortunate for having it when we needed it but it was time to move on before the burdens became heavier than the memories. That afternoon, the real estate company came out and put up the "For Sale" sign. It was later that evening that the older kids started calling.

"I'll get it!" I yelled from the kitchen, "Hello," I said flatly into the phone.

"Hi, Mom," it was Joe on the other end.

"Hi, Joe, how's it going?"

"Okay, how are *you*, honey?" he asked.

"Fine, I guess," I hesitated.

"Is the sign up yet?" he asked, curiously.

"Yep," I answered, unsure of what emotion I felt.

"What does it look like?" his voice was low. I could barely hear him.

"It's just a sign, you know, a FOR SALE sign," I laughed my nervous laugh.

"Where is it?" he asked.

"Right out by the end of our sidewalk. It's on one of those poles that they stick deep in the ground. It's gray and white. It's pretty windy tonight and the sign is swinging back and forth making a squeaky noise...." my voice trailed off.

"How does it feel, Mom?" his voice was tight.

"It feels a little strange...you know. Actually, I didn't know exactly when they were going to put it up. But today when I got home from work, there it was. I've seen lots of 'For Sale' signs. But it felt funny to see one in front of our house. My stomach did a flip-flop. I guess we're moving on to the next part now, Joe...." my voice trailed off again.

Then there was silence. I knew Joe was thinking.

"It's okay, Mom, we'll get through this one," he said after a long pause.

"Oh, I know we will, sweetheart. Don't you worry now," I was sure that Joe could tell my upbeat tone was forced. "I hope it sells soon because it won't be fun keeping things in order all the time for people coming through to look at it, you know. This will probably be our last Christmas here."

"Yeah, I was going to ask you something about that, Mom," he was emphatic. "Would it be alright if some of our friends from the ranch came for the holidays and stayed for Christmas?"

"It's fine with me, honey. We have plenty of room," I insisted. He was going to bring his friends to celebrate our last Christmas in our big home. I loved the idea!

"Thanks, Mom," Joe said.

When I hung up the phone, it rang again right away.

"What color is it?...How are you feeling?...And Chris and Anno?...When did they put it up?...How big is it?...What does it look like?...Could I bring someone for Christmas, too?"

As the kids talked and questioned me one by one that whole evening and I began feeling better about the whole idea of actually moving out of that house. Even though I had no credit cards, no money, no insurance, none of the securities, and a sorry job, I knew for sure that we had lived our lives to the fullest in that home. Friends came for weekends and stayed for months. Strangers came. Relatives came. They came and stayed. They came to laugh, cry, be comforted, or give comfort. It was a home everyone loved to come to and stay at and we loved it too. And before it was over, there would be more who would soak up a few good vibes during our last Christmas there.

A severely depressed real estate market loomed overhead and our house remained unsold for a long time. Finally, early that next spring, the "For Sale" sign was covered with a big neon "SOLD" sticker. I had also started the process needed to attain my master's degree by studying through a university without walls located in Vermont. Two more milestones. But the time, pressure, and worry of those couple of years weighed heavily on me. I cried easily and often. When I was offered a partial scholarship to ICASSI, I really didn't feel up to it. Those close to me, however, thought it would be a real boost for me to go and said so. Helen, especially, promoted the session every time she stopped by.

"You know how exciting the classes are," Helen said enthusiastically. "You know how wonderful it will be to see old friends. You know how much you love taking Sonste's classes. Once you get there, you will feel better and probably not be so tired," she was still hoping to convince me into going.

"We need to have a garage sale," I protested. "We need to find an apartment that's decent for us to live in as well as being big enough for when everybody comes home for Christmas." I went on, "And it's such a big thing to move...and...I'm so...tired," I wiped the tears that had begun to roll down my cheeks.

"I'm sure that once you get there you won't feel so tired," Helen urged, "and if Maria decides to go with you, it will be wonderful for both of you."

I found myself with no response and just nodded blankly. I didn't want her to think I didn't appreciate her paying all our expenses and giving us both another scholarship. I did, but she obviously didn't understand how worn down I was.

Miraculously, we had a house sale, found an apartment, and moved in a matter of weeks. It was my first apartment and I loved it but was now completely exhausted. My gut was still telling me not to go to ICASSI, but I listened to my friends instead of my gut. A week after we moved, I went to Europe with Maria.

The classes were invigorating and many of my friendships were renewed. My exhaustion did not go away as I had hoped, though. It intensified. My body shook most of the time and although I didn't say much, Maria knew something was very wrong when she would see my hands shake. When we arrived home in Chicago three weeks later, I crawled straight into my bed. Maria had to immediately get ready to leave for an important interview in Colorado that she had planned months earlier. As I drove Maria to the airport a few days later, my worry slipped out before I could catch myself.

"See, there it goes again. My hands just began to shake again. Sometimes even my whole body starts shaking," I slapped my hand over my mouth. I was upset that I had said anything to Maria. I still wanted to be perfect in front of my kids.

"Mom, are you sure you're okay? Are you sure you don't want me to stay? I can change my interview, you know. No matter how important it is, it's not as important as you are," Maria sounded close to tears.

"Of course I'm okay. It's no big deal, honey," I answered quickly, "I'm just tired, that's all. I'll get some rest now that I'm home."

I switched lanes and looked straight ahead, hoping Maria couldn't see my tears and that I would stop crying before they ran down my cheeks. Maria watched me closely. As I pulled into the United terminal, I quickly jumped out of the car to help Maria with her luggage.

"Don't worry," I said as I hugged her good-bye. She could see my tears and how I struggled to lift her suitcase out of the car.

"Are you sure, Mom?"

"I'm sure, Maria," I said.

Maria went through the glass doors and I waved until she disappeared from sight before getting into the car. I had no idea how I got home that day because it was all a blur. I walked slowly to the beach. That's all I needed, I thought to myself, just to lie on the beach and sleep...for a few days. I heard Maria's voice as I was lying there half-crying and half-sleeping in the sand. I thought for sure that I was dreaming.

"I can't leave you like this," I heard Maria's voice crying, "The plane was ready to pull away from the gate and I started crying, 'Let me off! I have to get off! My Mom needs me!'" It was Maria. She was really there. She sat next to me in the sand crying. I was still lying on my stomach. I put my arm around Maria's legs and held them.

"Thank goodness," I said in a low voice. Finally, I sat my body up in the sand. Maria shook the sand out of the beach towel and we walked home together. I slid into my bed and stayed there for two weeks. Maria waited on me hand and foot. She even brought my meals to my bed. In the third week, the shaking stopped. Maria had been there when I really needed her.

After enough time had passed, we were able to joke about it.

"And you say *I'm* dramatic, Maria? Who could be more dramatic than you? Getting off the plane when they are ready to take off," I was teasing.

"But you were happy I did," Maria bantered.

"More than words can express. But I was talking about your drama," I said devilishly.

"Mom, I have a long way to go before I could begin to compete with you," Maria said, refusing to give an inch. She didn't wait for me to respond and walked out of my room.

I was thankful that I felt good again. In two more days, Haile came to visit.

I was glad I was not completely exhausted when he arrived. We had so much to share and talk about. It was our most wonderful time together. We knew now for sure that we would be together in the future. I felt good about what I had learned about relationships and choosing men for the wrong reasons. I was ready at last for a love relationship that was for the right reasons. I was at peace inside for the first time in a long time. He had that effect on me. We were not rushing. After two unsuccessful marriages, I felt very good about this. We loved each other and would be together as soon as possible. I had other responsibilities but wouldn't have them forever. Kids grew up fast. We could be over half a world away from each other and yet remain close. It was a rare feeling.

29

Springtime meant the popping up of all signs of life: daffodils, tulips, lilacs, and sailboats on Lake Michigan. It also brought sadness as my dearest friend Maria Maria was dying of cancer. She called any hour of the day or night when she was in terrible pain.

"What are you doing, Marymary?" she asked one night, very late.

"I was sleeping, Maria," we both laughed.

"I'm sorry, I'll call you tomorrow..."

"No, no, don't hang up, it's fine, Maria."

"Are you sure?"

"Yes, it's fine. How are you?"

"Oh, Marymary, the pain is horrible," her voice was soft.

"Please let me come to Arizona just for a couple days, Maria. I'll only visit with you for a short time," I begged.

"No, no, dear Marymary, please wait a little bit until I get better. I'm getting some new medicine tomorrow. I'm sure that it will help," Maria was talking so softly that I had difficulty hearing her.

"Please let me come, Maria," I begged her every time she called.

Maria continued to say "no" and I struggled with her request. I wanted to see my friend before she died and yet I knew I had to respect her wishes. I had never experienced such a heart-wrenching request before. Each day I prayed that my friend wouldn't die and that she would change her mind and allow me to visit. But she never did, and in a few weeks she died.

Was anyone ever ready for death? How did that part work? I believed I was too young to have so many other young people close to me die. I thought of my brother Tommy and knew I probably would never understand why some people die.

After working for three years in order to help his brothers and sister get through college, Tony decided it was his turn. He did his research, chose to go to chef school in Rhode Island, and it turned out to be a complete disaster.

"So, Mom?" Chris asked me one night as we were making dinner together, "Are you surprised about Tony deciding to move back to Colorado and go to CSU?"

"Well, no, not really, Chris," I said as I washed the lettuce.

"Why not?" Chris asked surprised. He assumed I was kidding.

"Because I knew Tony was too bright for chef school. I figured he'd get bored. It wasn't where Tony belonged," I said as I continued making the salad.

"Why didn't you tell him that before he went?" his eyes were big as he questioned me.

"We did talk about it several times. Oh, you'd better flip those hamburgers, honey."

"And did you tell him you thought he shouldn't go?" Chris asked. He was visibly upset. He held a hamburger in mid-flip as he looked at me.

"No," I answered nonchalantly.

"Why not?"

"Because he had to learn that himself. I could've talked to him about it until I was blue in the face, but he had already decided to go. So all I could do at that point was support his decision."

Chris wanted more. "Really? Why, Mom?"

"Chris, I just told you why," I answered impatiently.

"Don't you think he would've listened to you if you told him what you've just told me?" Chris urged me again.

"Yes, I think Tony listens to whatever I have to say, Chris, but I also know that it was just one of those things he had to learn for himself," I put the plates on the table as I talked. "I did share my ideas with him, but I felt it would've been disrespectful on my part not to honor his decision." I dropped a fork. "Also, I think it would've be foolish on my part to attempt to talk him out of a decision that he believed was so right." I stood and looked Chris in the eye,

"It's my responsibility to support his decisions even if I think they may be faulty. Other than that, my only responsibility is to keep my mouth shut."

"But, Mom, he used up all his money just for one semester there!" Chris shook his head, "Shouldn't you have said something one more time? Maybe he didn't really understand what you'd said." Chris still couldn't accept this idea.

I was getting irritated, "When you talk about me telling him one more time, you sound just like the parents who come to my class believing they should say everything 'one more time' as if the kid is an idiot and needs it repeated and repeated. Tony didn't need me to repeat any part of it one more time. Trust me on this one, Chris," I closed my case.

"Okay, Mom," Chris sighed, shaking his head back and forth, "I'm not sure I agree with you, but I guess you knew what you were doing." He put the hamburgers on the table.

The kids said it was only right. They said I belonged in the position of Dean of Students since the majority of our family was in college now—five of them, counting Jenny. I could continue my parent education work while I took on the position at this small college and began making a decent living. They had wanted someone with a master's degree, but since I was in the process of completing mine (and due to receive it the following April) the administration accepted my application and hired me. I was so excited. There were many areas of need at this school and it also gave me the opportunity to begin a career in academics.

It was the night before Christmas Eve and when I picked up the receiver to hear the distant click that lets you know it's a call from overseas. After another click, the operator's voice came over the line.

"I'm calling to set up a time for Mary Dalton to receive a phone call tomorrow from Haile-Yesus Abege in Ethiopia. Do you know when she will be available?"

"I am Mary Dalton. I can be here at any time to accept the call," I replied anxiously.

"Then I will set up the connection for the call to come through at 6 p.m. your time. How is that sound?" She mixed her English a little bit.

"That would be wonderful," I smiled.

"Thank you," she said and I heard the click again as she hung up. I couldn't wait to hear his voice the next day and told the kids so as to keep the line clear.

The next evening at six o'clock, if not for the clicks, I would've believed that he was right next door.

"I have tickets for you, dear Mary," he said, "I have your itinerary right here in front of me. Your flight is all booked. Ten days, dear Mary. Can you come for ten days?"

"My itinerary, Haile? What do you mean?"

"I have it all worked out. You do not have to do a thing. I have someone who will meet you in Paris and stay with you until you board your connecting flight. You will meet me in Bali and then we will have ten days together. It will be so wonderful."

"You have tickets, Haile?"

"Yes, it's all fixed, all ready for you to come, just for ten days. You can get away for ten days, No?"

"Haile, all my children are here for Christmas. They've come from Colorado, from Indiana, all over. My God, we always have Christmas together. I think I would die if I didn't have Christmas with them. I mean, to just leave... I've never done anything like that...my God Haile, why did you buy tickets without telling me?"

"I wanted to surprise you. I just hoped you would be able to come for ten days, dear Mary. It is so beautiful there. It will be so good. Please come, dear Mary. Please, I am begging you to come," he was using words he never used before. He never begged. He never insisted. He never pushed. He never assumed. I didn't know what to do.

"My dear Haile, I don't know what to say."

"Just say you will come, sweet Mary."

"I can't do that, Haile. I can't just go off and leave these kids. Christmastime is our time together. Can you understand?"

"Mary, please, just this once come stay with me," he wasn't giving up.

My stomach was in knots. Why was he being so insistent? Why was this so different? We had made plans. We knew we would be together. We knew we would someday work together. We had shared all of our thoughts. We both had felt comfortable with the idea of waiting for Anno to get older before I planned on traveling to another country for a significant amount of time. My job was to take care of these kids until the proper time. I could never give that up. That was and always had been first.

"Haile, I just can't come this Christmas. I feel awful that you have already bought tickets. I love to do things on the spur of the moment but I am not the only one involved here. You know, it's the kids too."

"Are you sure you won't reconsider, dear Mary?"

My God, I thought, why is he making this so hard? This was a Haile I did not know. "Dear Haile-Yesus, I cannot come and meet you in Bali. We will have to do it another time."

"Okay, dear Mary, I am sorry you will not come. Love to you and the kids," his voice was sad and low.

"Love to you too, beautiful Haile," I barely heard the little chuckle I could always count on when I called him "beautiful." I hung up the receiver and sat there as if in a trance. Fly off to Bali for ten days? It was more than just a crazy whim. He was a man I deeply loved and who loved me back. It felt good inside. I wished I could have gone to him. I just couldn't see how it would've worked out. I had to make that choice, didn't I? I told myself that Haile-Yesus had understood. Tony came around the corner, looking for me. I told him about the conversation.

"I didn't know what to do, Tony. I just couldn't go off now and leave you guys, but that doesn't mean I don't love him because I do. I guess I'll just have to write to him and tell him that maybe we could do it this June. I'll tell him how sorry I am and how much I love him and hope he understands."

"Sounds like a good plan," Tony sounded concerned and I noticed he was watching my hands fidget. He stayed and held me while I cried.

I knew that my obsession with wanting our Christmases to be wonderful stemmed from the memories of when I was a kid. We reveled in the opportunity to be together as a family and just "be." There was excitement twenty-four hours a day when we were all together. If any housework or chores were left undone or forgotten, I would get a little irritated but kept quiet and picked up the slack until a couple days after Xmas it would all have built up and I'd explode.

That meant me getting really mad and screaming all sorts of nasty things at whoever was within earshot. I never quite knew how it happened but my "moment" had become part of our Christmas traditions also, even though no one talked about it in the open. I still wanted everything perfect. And even though each year that desire diminished a little, it still consumed me at times.

Tony was the first to leave that year and, as tradition had it, as many people went to the airport as could fit into the car. There was a sort of quiet solemnness that came over everyone as soon as the first person packed up to leave. It would probably be another entire year before we would be able to all be together again. When we stopped at a red light the man in a car next to us rolled down his window and shouted, "Hey lady, your back tire is almost flat!"

"Thank you," I said forcing a smile as I rolled my window back up. Suddenly, I became so angry on the inside that I had to pull off the street into a parking lot. I knew I shouldn't drive in that kind of emotional condition. I had asked someone to check the tires over the holidays, but no one had. It was all that was needed to set me off. I immediately began screaming and cursing at the kids.

"Why do you guys do that? Why can't you help me? Huh? Why do I have to be the maid? Why do you take advantage of me...huh? Answer me...somebody answer me! Will you? Where is your father? Where has he been all these years? Huh? Who do you come to when you want or need anything? Who helps you out...huh? Me! It's always me! That's who! And who helps me? Nobody!" All my words seemed to run together as the sobs began and I started shaking. I took a deep breath and tried to stop my tears. I felt a hand on my shoulder.

"Don't! Don't touch me! Don't even bother!" I screamed, "Why? Why can't anyone help me? Why can't you? Why can't you? Huh? Can anyone tell me that? Can you? It's so damn hard to raise kids alone!" My face was in my hands. My nose was stopped up and the tears were burning my cheeks as they ran down towards the wet spot that was now on my jacket. "Dammit...anyway. Shit. Don't you know how hard it is? Or do you even care? No, you don't care. Obviously, you don't care about me at all. I hate this....why can't you guys help me? Why do I have to....beg....for everything? Why do I...have to be....responsible for every....single....thing?" I sobbed between my words. I was slowing down. There were more tears and less words.

The kids sat staring straight ahead; no one moved a muscle when this happened. Finally, I stopped. Everyone felt pretty lousy, especially me. Tony had missed his plane. After a long silence, a suggestion was softly offered.

"I guess we need to talk and work this out," Tony said with pained eyes.

"I'm sorry, Mom. I know I said I'd look at the tires and I didn't," Joe mumbled.

"Me too, Mom. I feel terrible. I'm sorry I didn't do it either," Tony said.

"I feel terrible too. I hate it when I do this. It feels so horrible on the inside. I hate myself when this happens but I still do it," I whispered sadly.

Together we sat and talked in the car. The kids apologized and I finally stopped crying. Later, Tony caught a cab for the rest of his trip to the airport. I knew I still wanted everything perfect at Christmastime—this traditional explosion was more than enough proof of that.

This had been was the third Christmas that my mother didn't come to visit. She wouldn't as long as I "remained a sinner," she said. Although I missed her terribly, I did not miss the verbal abuse that had been a constant in my life. Everyone who met the kids always found them to be so wonderful. Everyone, that is, except for my mother. I felt so sad that she could not experience that and enjoy them. Her continuous calls were just to remind me of my sinful ways. But I had now begun to believe that maybe I had something of a brain. I believed that the kids were great and that I had something to do with that. And I also knew, at least some of the time, that men actually did like me. Men as gentle and noble as Haile-Yesus. That felt like a miracle to me. Simple things like that felt so good.

30

Chris was already about to graduate from high school and Anno was going into seventh grade. It felt really weird for a while since there were only three of us living together now. They were my two partners to enjoy life with. When friends came to visit for the first time, their mouths literally hung open, and when Chris and Anno were not around they would question me about what they witnessed inside our home. Even Helen still questioned me when she came by.

"Instead of her acting like a baby, she acts like an old lady," Helen laughed at her observation about Anno. "Tell me again," she said, "How did she get that way?"

"Her responsibilities just grew as she did. It's a natural life process. Our kids need us for love, encouragement, and direction, but not for the nagging. She learned about responsibilities from our actions instead of our words," I responded, looking at her.

"Explain it to me again, if you wouldn't mind," Helen asked.

"Well, it was always the little things, which you and I both know are not really *little* things. When she started learning how to put her pajamas on someone would say, 'Let's have a race tonight to see who can get ready for bed the quickest!' We made up games. They weren't big games, but they were always important. The other part, and we've talked about this in our study group, is that when she'd put her P.J.'s on backwards, squeeze too much toothpaste out of the tube, or put on clothes that didn't match when she got dressed, we never said a word to try to correct her or get her to do it perfectly. Instead, we just let it be. That was the encouragement part."

"Yes, I remember being here one day when she put her shoes on the wrong feet and how amazed I was that you didn't say a word," Helen chuckled as she recalled the incident.

"That's a good example. For what does the parent usually say when their child has their shoes on the wrong feet? 'Your shoes are on the wrong feet. Sit down and put them on right.' And in some cases, the parents will say it day after day, demanding in frustration, 'When will you ever learn?'"

"How well I know that," Helen answered, nodding her head.

"When Anno learned how to make her own lunch, there was lots of extra peanut butter and jelly all over the knife, but when she watched the other kids scrape their knives on the inside edge of the jar, she learned to do it also. She watched them use the sponge to wipe up after themselves and soon she was doing it like they did. Sure, there were some pretty big hunks of peanut butter to wipe up some days, but those are the times when we need to close our eyes to the mistakes and point out something positive that happened during the making of the lunch.

"People who watch Anno and Chris in action seem to think that they are geniuses or something. It's so difficult for people to understand that if kids feel confident in little things when they are small, they will feel confident in big things when they are grown." I looked at my friend. "You're smiling, Helen, what is it?"

Her eyes flashed as she fired her climatic question, "Do you think Chris and Anno are geniuses?"

I leaned forward, "Of course they are geniuses. We are all geniuses. We just don't know it. We just haven't been encouraged in our strengths. I truly believe that most of us are geniuses and my belief has grown as I have continued to work with kids through the years."

"Well, my kids haven't shown their genius yet," Helen laughed nervously as she spoke.

"They have, Helen. You know they have," I answered with conviction.

"Well okay," she looked down, apparently in deep thought before continuing, "actually, the real reason I stopped by was to tell you that I ran into the principal of Lincolnwood School yesterday. He asked me if I thought you would consider speaking to the P.T.A. on parents' night at his school. I told him that I would ask you and see what you had to say. What do you think? Would you do it? I told you they loved your talk last week at Haven School but you wouldn't believe me," she paused and looked at me.

"I can't believe it. They want me to speak again? Wow, I already feel nervous."

"Yes, they want you to speak again. I know it's scary for you but please do it, will you? It's desperately needed." She sounded serious.

"Hey, you're starting to sound like me with that 'desperately needed' phrase," I laughed.

"Will you do it?" Helen wanted an answer before the jokes.

"Okay, I'll do it, I'll do it," I answered.

"Thank you very much. I have to run but I'll talk to you tomorrow and tell you the details," she said as she grabbed her purse from the table.

"Okay, thanks, Helen," I smiled.

"Thank *you*, Marydalton!" Helen said hurrying for the door, "Speaking at schools could really turn into something big as far as the number of parents you could reach."

It seemed impossible, but it was true. Chris graduated from high school and was accepted into college. He had won several awards and scholarships for his art. Between them and financial aid, he was ready to enter the next phase of his life completely on his own. He learned well from watching his brothers and sister. Anno and I were happy for him but it was with mixed emotions that we looked forward to the day he would leave for college. We felt lost at the thought of living without him.

Maria also graduated in June, from college this time. She had carried twenty-one hours her last semester and also worked part-time, keeping herself in a constant state of stress. To say she was ready to get her degree and be out of there was an understatement. It had been a long and hard financial struggle for her and she made one last call to me as a college student.

"Mom, you know how you've always said we can really learn a lot from being poor and having to work for things?"

"I remember," I chuckled.

"Okay, we know all about the poor part now. I think we've got it down. So, can we get on to the rich part?"

"Amen," I agreed wholeheartedly as we laughed together.

In August, Jenny graduated from college. John interviewed for a position at Chicago's Marshall Fields department store as he would graduate in January. And if we encouraged Joe to take that math class he needed to finish, he'd graduate too.

Four college graduates and the fifth kid leaving home for college all within six months. It was difficult, exciting, and I considered it quite an accomplishment. There were many times I felt like I couldn't keep up with the whole bunch of them. That summer also brought the wonderful news that Joe and Jenny were getting engaged and planned on marrying the following summer. Jenny had been in the family for so long that she was part of us already.

Many times I thought how wonderful it would be to share these wonderful kids with a partner. My thoughts usually spoke to Haile:

Haile-Yesus...where were you this summer? Have you gotten my letters? Why haven't you answered them?...I know you are busy dear Haile, but please write...This is the first summer you haven't come to visit since we met in 1977....Seems more than strange...but I'm sure there is a good reason....yet I feel something is terribly wrong. I'm always thinking of you...but I don't talk about it with anyone. I guess I should ask Sonste but I haven't told him about 'us' yet. What has happened? I am loving you from afar but prance the kitchen floor at night wondering if you are okay. I go over and over in my head, thinking what could have happened. I don't like my scary thoughts. What has happened dear Haile, what has happened? Every day I am questioning the silence. Each day my heart aches for you. I have no one to call. No one to contact. I am waiting to hear from you. Waiting for you to come. Be gentle to yourself, gentle one.

31

Everyone arrived a few minutes early for the study group and Helen questioned me first thing.

"So how did John's interview at Marshall Fields go?" she asked as she put the kettle on the stove.

I put my books down on the table and saw that everyone was waiting for my answer.

"He says he really wants the job at Fields so I told him not to worry because he would get the job. He immediately jumped at me, 'Oh sure it's easy for you to say. You're my Mom and you're prejudiced!' But it's true," I continued, "I know he'll get the job. Yes, I am their mom but I also know that whatever these kids want, they have the qualities to get." I paused and looked around the room before I continued, "They are normal and regular but in today's world their normality makes them seem outstanding to people they meet. I'm not trying to take away from them the compliment of being outstanding, but rather I'm trying to explain it to you in terms of what is considered 'normal' today. If that makes any sense..."

"Just tell us what happened, Mary," Helen interrupted me, but I barely noticed.

"Most people, for example, think it's normal for teenagers to rebel. That's a major myth that we have been brainwashed to believe. Teenagers do not really have to rebel." I poured some sugar into my coffee and continued talking, "Anyway, I know John will get the job if he wants it. It's him that doesn't know that for sure," I rested my case as I stubbed out my cigarette. I lit another one and breathed in deeply, "Sometimes I wish they would believe me. They really don't know how wonderful they are. In a sense, it's great. Because if they ever began feeling superior, I'd want to knock them off their high horse, if you know what I mean," I laughed. "But on the other hand, sometimes I wish they just knew a little bit how wonderful and encouraging they really are. Does that make sense?" I raised my eyebrows and waited for someone to respond.

"Oh Mary, get serious!" Helen said impatiently.

"Really, Mary," Lorie seconded the thought.

"They're all so level headed. I just can't see any of them flaunting their qualities," Helen said. "Is that what's really bothering you?"

"Yeah, I think so. I just get frustrated sometimes wanting them to believe in themselves and wanting them to realize how much they help others. It just seems like they should know that about themselves by now, but they don't. Then I wonder, if my kids don't know they're okay—even more than okay—because of the way they've been raised, how in the world could any other kids know that they are okay? And I'm not trying to brag about my parenting, but..."

"We know you're not trying to brag, Mary," Helen said. "Is there anyone here who thinks Mary is bragging?" Helen looked around the room and I watched everyone shake their head "no." they all smiled warmly at me and waited for me to continue.

"Okay, I'm sorry. I didn't mean it like that. It's just that sometimes it's kind of frustrating because I've worked so hard and given them so much of myself," I puffed that cigarette as fast as I talked, "and I want them to know how wonderful they are and I want them to know it now. I don't want them to go through life feeling the way I felt while I was growing up—like I was a total failure and complete mess in everything, you know?" There were tears in my eyes now.

Andrea, who seldom spoke, replied emphatically, "You must practice the words that you've learned from Dreikurs and now teach to others. 'Have the courage to be imperfect.' Your children will know that they're okay. Just give them a little time and don't be so hard on yourself."

"I know. I know. I get like that sometimes. I want them to know all their strong suits," I sighed.

"Take it easy, Mary," Helen's voice imitated my voice and made us both laugh.

"Time to get on with our lesson," I leaned back in my chair. "Okay, what chapters are we doing today?"

We planned the wedding that December during Christmas break. Our discussions were like smaller and more concentrated versions of the family meetings we had when the kids were growing up. Each of us chose a different area of responsibility to make it a great day. I was to be in charge of the flowers and the minister. The kids teased me by saying that I would do the best job of getting the minister since my second husband had been a Catholic priest and since we had heard that my first husband had now become a minister.

Planning the wedding excited our inner souls. The kids were paying for most of it themselves, so every little bit helped. I believed that the pieces would all fall together. We talked to a family friend who gladly offered to cater the wedding for a song and dance. Jenny's brother-in-law was a professional photographer. One of her sisters could get liquor at cost. The rehearsal dinner was going to be a picnic at the beautiful park on the lake behind our apartment. And Jenny had already found a beautiful dress.

I wrote to Haile again as soon as they picked the wedding date. I wanted to make sure that he knew plenty of time in advance and could make arrangements to come. Something was very strange about the fact that I had not gotten a letter from him for so long. Even though I had always sent ten letters to his one, this was so unlike Haile. *What's going on, Haile-Yesus?* I said inside my head week after week and month after month. I wondered if something had happened but refused to allow the thought to remain in my mind. I didn't know where to send my letter, though, because I wasn't sure where he was now. I wasn't sure about anything. So I sent a copy of my letter to Paris, Dacca, UNICEF and the United Nations. He had to be in one of those places.

"Dear Haile," I wrote, "Where are you?...Please come to visit soon...We have so much catching up to do...I miss you desperately and the children are getting married now...My heart hurts from missing you...Well, I know you will be here by the wedding, for sure...Love and kisses to you, my dear Haile."

It seemed I had sent this same letter at least a dozen times now over the past few months.

Ever since my divorce from Pat, Mother's contact with me diminished steadily. So with the wedding approaching, I decided to call her.

"Mother," I started, "I called to tell you that Joe is going to marry his high-school sweetheart and we want you to come."

"Will the wedding be in church or is it going to be some heathen affair? Because if it is, I won't be there."

"Well it's not going to be a 'heathen' affair, Mother, but..."

"I'm sorry. I just can't condone your actions or the actions of your children by my presence. Good-bye."

At least she said good-bye this time, I thought. That's progress in some weird sort of way. I think it had finally sunk into my head, even if it would never sink into my heart. Mother was never going to approve of anything I would say or do. Perhaps I didn't need her approval, but I would probably spend my life wanting it

When the Christmas holiday was over and it was time for everyone to leave, we got into the big huddle that had become another tradition. It was like one big hug. "Maybe it's from watching too many football games," somebody teased. With our arms around each other and heads in the middle, everyone looked at the floor. At first there was silence, then a giggle...silence again...then everyone tried to get in their two cents' worth:

"...No more seventeen-year-old girlfriends, okay, John...well, at least she had some class, Tony ...right, just keep kidding yourself...great spaghetti, Maria, thanks...thank you too...give my socks back before you go, Joe...I don't have your stinky socks...yeah sure, where's my sweatshirt that disappeared last year?...ask Tony, he has one that looks just like it...(silence)...I love you guys...yeah, me too...I love you guys, you're the greatest...this is the year...yep, this is the year, you guys...gonna be a great year...I love you guys...I love you all, too...me too...me three...love you...enough of this love stuff...got to go now...me too...yep...make me proud...I will, Mom...you too, Apple...make me proud, too...okay Kid, I will."

Powerful feelings filled our hearts. We all took a deep breath as if we could suck enough inside to last until the next time we would be together. We hugged each other in silence for what could never really be long enough and then it was over until our next meeting.

As I carried her suitcase to the car, Maria cried to me, "When am I going to get old enough so that I don't cry when I leave you guys?"

"I hope you don't ever get that old, sweetheart," I said as the tears ran down my cheeks too.

I always wanted them to stay just a day or two longer but that's not the way it worked when kids were grown up. Once they walked out that door and the tears had cleared, my head hit the pillow, exhausted. Immediately, I'd begin thinking and planning for the next time we would be together. The kids told me they did exactly the same thing.

The wedding drew near. Joe and Jenny decided they wanted the ceremony at a park off the lake near the big house where they had all grown up. And the reception was going to be in our apartment. Tony scrubbed and waxed the floors like he had no other purpose in life. John cleaned everything else until everything shined, including some windows that had not been opened, much less washed, in years. Chris designed the invitations. Maria cleaned all the furniture and made new couch covers. Anno was everyone's assistant. She was trying to avoid practicing the reading from "The Prophet" that Joe and Jenny wanted her to read during the ceremony. She kept saying in protest, "I can't do it, Joe. I don't read well."

"Yes, you can. I'll be your coach," he insisted.

"Oh, Joe!" she moaned.

"Oh, Anno!" he mimicked.

And so she read to him every day on the phone until he arrived home and then he coached her during the secret walks they took together.

The sun came up as the wedding day arrived. Everyone was up early, getting ready. All the guys were in one bedroom and all the girls were in another. Every second was bursting with excitement.

"Can you button this...how does this tie go...is my slip sticking out...no Anno...shouldn't Jenny be getting dressed now...better hurry up, Tony...how do I look, Mom...the groom isn't supposed to see the bride....he won't...we're going outside now....you guys, wait for me....you go in the other car...Mom, you wait for the limousine...somebody help me jam the rest of this stuff in Anno's bedroom...do you want those flowers over there...this collar is too tight...it's all that wrestling, Chris, your neck is too big...Joe, you look gorgeous...John, you look sensational...you all look gorgeous...wow...this place does sparkle...wipe up that bathroom...you better get dressed, Mom...your hair looks beautiful, Maria...got the book, Anno?...button this please, can you...oh, Jenny, how beautiful you are...wow...is Joe gone...yes the guys are going now...it's ten-thirty...the horse-drawn buggy is here...are you ready...hold her train up as you go down the stairs...turn the fan this way...it's not too hot yet...here comes the cake...put it here, I guess...we better go...is it really time already...where is my skirt...the apartment looks beautiful...no one would guess that five women and five men just got dressed here...look at all those flowers...sensational...marvelous!"

The lake was a bright and brilliant blue that day. It sparked like a sea of diamonds under the sun. The green leaves that hung from magnificent trees created a lush ceiling that swayed slowly in the calm breeze off the lake. The blue sky was sprinkled with small puffs of white clouds. I looked down on the beige sand. There were many days when we all sat on that same sand in our swimming suits. Today, it was the brilliant backdrop for the wedding.

Jenny was the new addition who seemed to have always been a part of the family. She was the "cute-as-a-button kid," as I called her affectionately. She was beautiful and courageous in many ways. It was wonderful when she peeked her head out of any room and asked, "What did I miss now? What's going on? Somebody tell me what's going on. Nobody ever tells me anything." She was loved by all of us and knew she was my favorite new kid on the block.

In her white dress, she walked gracefully through the grass. Joe, in his tux, stood waiting for his bride. Their eyes were brilliant and focused. The minister's dark skin looked like velvet against the brilliant blue background of the lake. They were surrounded by brothers, sisters, grandparents, and friends—everyone except Haile-Yesus.

Who was the most gorgeous? The bride and groom, of course. Yet, they all radiated. Everything they had learned, a whole life of working together, showed that day. Everything I had ever believed in was represented. It was not an elaborate wedding, not an expensive wedding, and yet it was a million-dollar wedding. I walked around through the crowd and watched the faces. Their brilliance had spread to all the guests. It showed and everyone felt it. The love, the caring, the kindness, the humor, the respect, and the courage were all there.

"I'd like to make a toast to the most beautiful woman in the world," Joe said.

Yes, I thought, she is a woman and he is a man. I had difficulty believing I was the mother of kids old enough to get married. I could've sworn that just yesterday they were toddlers playing in that sand over there. How quickly they had grown. My eyes filled with tears as I watched them play and joke with each other. I knew for sure that day. I knew for sure that they were definitely at the best ages that kids could ever be.

One Year Later

For years our friends and neighbors had joked (but were actually serious) about interviewing the kids sometime. They were curious to ask them questions about their experience of being raised so differently than their friends. Everyone knew that all the kids would be here for the wedding, so they asked if perhaps sometime during that week of the wedding—even though we'd be busy— they could come over for an evening and question the kids. It would be informal but the deal was that the kids, not me, would answer the questions. We agreed that it could be fun and picked a day. Even though I knew it would go fine, I was both nervous and excited.

I quickly walked to the back of the apartment where the kids were waiting for me before starting dinner.

"The whole apartment smells really good. A special new sauce, Maria?" I asked as I washed my hands at the sink.

"Nope, the same as always, Mom," Maria said, putting ice into seven glasses.

"Thanks for doing this, you guys," I said, drying my hands. I was nervous.

"You're welcome," Joe teased, taking the credit for cooking. "So Apple, tell us, what's this going to be like tonight?"

"Well, you know, people will be asking you questions and stuff. Probably the same questions you've been asked through the years. I doubt if there will be any new ones but who knows."

"So Apple, do we get to tell any family secrets?" Tony asked looking up from his book.

"I didn't know we had any, Tony!" I laughed.

"Oh I'm sure we could come up with a few spicy stories...like..."

"Don't embarrass me too much," I pleaded through laugher.

"I would never think of it, Apple," Joe clowned in.

"Right. I believe you, Joe!" I stared into his eyes as I heard the doorbell ring. "Come on now you guys and put a couple more of these chairs in the living room while I get the door. Darn, I had a feeling people would come early," I had excitement in my voice.

"We'll handle it, Mom, go open the door," Tony said closing his book.

"Thanks, guys!" I sighed as I reached for the buzzer.

"Mom?" Maria yelled from the kitchen.

"Yeah, Maria?" I yelled from the front hall before I opened the door.

"Don't worry, we'll only tell the truth," she promised.

"That's what I'm afraid of...." I gulped and laughed at the same time.

I opened the door and could hear them talking as they came up around the bend in the stairs. They continued their conversation until they reached the second floor.

"Come in, come in, you're early," I greeted them. "Let me take your coats."

I let everyone get comfortable and went back to the kitchen. The kids were just about finished with their dinners.

"I think I'll wait and eat after," I said, "Don't you want to come into the living room soon?"

"Sure, Mom, we're coming. We're just eating, remember? Maria cooked dinner! Besides they're not all here yet anyway, are they?" Tony said winking at me. He wanted me to relax. I stood in silence for a minute.

"Relax, Apple, this is going to be fun!" John urged.

"I know. I'm sorry. Just a little nervous, I guess. We don't have enough chairs," I said.

"That's okay, Mom. We've sat on the floor all our lives. We're not going to change that now because some people are over, are we? Remember we're going to have fun, Mom, and we're going to teach a few things also," Tony said as he continued eating.

"I know, thanks, you guys, I'm just nervous, you know," I said twisting my hands together.

"You're welcome, Mom," Joe was giving me a hug.

The doorbell rang again and I sped down the hall to answer it. But someone had already taken care of the next arrivals. John motioned to me from the hallway and I walked over to him.

"We're ready to start anytime, Mom."

I walked unnoticed into the living room and listened to the parents talk with each other. The kids tiptoed in one by one and sat on the floor. After a few minutes everyone was silent. I spoke softly.

"Okay, so are we all here?" I put my gum on the side of my mouth with my tongue. "Yes, we are all here but I'm still counting heads," I laughed nervously. "I'm always counting heads whenever we're together. It's something I started when we spent our summers at the beach when they were little bitty kids. I still do it. So, shall we start?" I catch my breath. The room is quiet for a moment and then Jeannie speaks.

"We've talked it over among ourselves and decided that we want to ask you questions and hear answers from you first hand. Would that be okay with you?

"Sure," Tony smiled.

"Fine," Joe nodded his head.

"Sure, whatever," Maria couldn't wait to get started.

"Could we start with things you remember and go from there? How about your high school years? Anyone remember anything? Anything they want to share anyway?"

TONY: "Sure, I remember high school. Who could forget 58 absences in my senior year? Who could forget being told that my job was school and if I didn't want to do my job, I didn't have to live at home anymore."

"She said that to you? That you didn't have to live there anymore?"

"She did. And I didn't miss another class that year either," he laughed hard as he recalled, "I also remember when grades didn't mean as much as how I must like such-and-such class or subject. I must like learning about this and reading about that. The idea was that learning, not grades, was the primary goal. A lesson I carry proudly and understand. It will be especially important when I begin to get paid to teach."

CHRIS: "Yeah, I remember it too, her saying, 'I have to go to work. That's my responsibility. If you want to live in this house, you have to go to school until you graduate—that's your job or responsibility.' She came down hard on Tony but gave him a clearly defined choice.

"There always were choices. For example, I learned how to make choices because she—as well as the group—showed belief in me that I had always been old enough to make choices for myself and be in on the general decision making for the family. Age was irrelevant. I had *always* been capable of making decisions and choices.

"It would be contradictory to say that I could remember when I *first* began taking responsibility for my actions. I can't remember. It always was. How did this come about? Did I 'learn' it? Was it 'taught' to me? It is always tricky to attempt to explain exactly how knowledge, responsibility, social awareness and social interest, and the sensitivity to show respect to one's fellow man is passed from 'teacher' to 'pupil,' 'parent' to 'child.'

"That is because when we attempt to explain this phenomenon in terms of either 'teaching' or 'learning'—which in reality are inseparable—we lose sight that this 'passing of knowledge' (for lack of a better term) is first sharing, and second showing by example."

"What about school?"

JOE: "School was our responsibility. Our homework and grades were not

Mom's responsibility. Responsibility at a very early age. Maturity comes quicker. No safety net, in other words. Our success and failures were just that: ours. When someone is riding your back like a jockey about grades, you as the horse get little credit. When's the last time you've seen a horse getting interviewed at the Kentucky Derby?

"We ran the race alone. The crowd (Mom) was always there cheering us on! 'You're neat, Kid,' she probably said more than anything besides, 'no you can't eat here today.' Always making you feel significant and that you had something to contribute. You felt just so neat."

"What about those famous family meetings? Anything you remember?"

JOHN: "The family council meetings made Sundays a pure uninterrupted day of hell-raising, bitching, and crying by as many members of the family as could be sufficiently embarrassed by the other vultures in the room. The family council meeting started off as a dreaded session that was usually over quickly and painlessly. Sometimes, though, actual reasoning was possible and agreement among all family members came about. Looking back, I realize it was a valuable group experience which no doubt has helped in any subsequent group meeting we've ever been involved with."

"What about your friends? Did they see your household as different from theirs?"

TONY: "I remember all the weird looks from friends when I told them it was my night to cook, or that I had to finish my jobs before I could go out. I never realized that we were different for doing these types of things. Family meetings would also be included in the 'weird' things we did. Talking about problems or planning the week's job list was not something my friends could understand. They could not understand why or what we did. She must have done some good talking at those first meetings, getting us to go from doing nothing to all the things we did. I remember when friends of mine or someone else would come over and they would not know how to pitch in and help, although most did when given clear directions and encouragement."

"You also shared cooking meals, right? Can you tell us about that?"

JOE: "Cooking? What a fiasco! Hot dogs, clumpy spaghetti, lots of liver burgers. Friends would ask, 'You cook dinner?' to which we'd respond, 'Yeah, my Mom's weird. Makes us do everything.' But we loved it. As long as we remembered to take something out to defrost. I remember trying to defrost hamburger at four o'clock with a thousand gallons of hot water. You always wondered why the heating bills were so high...."

JOHN: "We all had to take turns making dinner once a week, which would mean at 5:55 p.m. looking through the cabinets for something to quickly make. Sometimes it would be a dinner of starch and starch, while other times something edible actually came out of the kitchen. Along with this was the kitchen cleaning, which everyone hated. Many times it would be left until the morning, which would be the dreaded 'kitchen lockout' until the kitchen was cleaned with a toothbrush by everyone. This also involved the kitchen's Late Night Robberies, which we were famous for some times since the robberies all came at different times and each one would challenge the others on 'what you got to eat.'"

CHRIS: "Back in the days when we rotated cooking nights and there were still enough people living at home to fill all seven nights, I remember *many* times when I forgot to defrost meat in the morning before leaving for school. People even gave me suggestions on what to cook the night before, but still I would forget. The most sinking feeling came over me when, long after I had returned home from school, I would go to the kitchen to start dinner and have the cold realization that I had forgotten to defrost the chicken. 'Well that's it!

We just won't eat,' I said as panic overtook me. 'We simply won't eat tonight.'

Eventually, I figured something out. We'd eat tuna or hot dogs—some meal that requires no defrosting. Occasionally, my brothers and sisters would come to my rescue, but never Mom. And, of course, I loved that."

TONY: "Then there were the times we had to make lunches in the storage areas on the third floor...those were weird mornings trying to put lunches together, not quite understanding what the idea was or why we didn't have a Mom who did everything around the house like other mothers... Thank goodness we didn't have another regular mother, I wouldn't want to be like the untrained friends I had and have.

"Why were you making lunches in the storage areas?"

"Because we hadn't cleaned the kitchen so we'd sneak food upstairs for our lunches."

"Did she know what you were doing?"

"I don't think so! She might say she did now...hahaha...but I don't think she knew!"

"With my own kids, I find it hard to think of choices. What, if any, do any of you remember?"

JOE: "Choices. 'You can go upstairs on your own or I'll carry you,' that was a favorite one. Or 'Do the dishes or no dinner.' Or 'Finish jobs or stay inside.' The great thing about the choices is they were offered in such a way not to threaten but to state a fact. The key was carrying it out! Not just talk."

CHRIS: "Everyone sitting around the dinner table in our big house eating and talking. Anno begins to cause disturbances, acting up, etc. At first everyone ignores her, but finally it is impossible to carry on with her unruly behavior. Mom gives her a choice, warning her the first time. Something like, 'Anno, if you would like to sit here with us, you may not yell and scream; if you would like to do that you may go to your room and do it.' All said in a matter-of-fact, pleasant tone of voice. Anno smiles at the attention. Everyone stops momentarily, not being able to hold back from looking at Anno and letting a smile sneak out. Anno stops for a brief minute, but in no time she is at it again.

"Mom to Anno: 'Anno, would you like to walk to your room or would you like me to carry you?' Anno remains silent, hoping this will work. Nope. Mom gets up and carries her upstairs—-Anno yelling and kicking the whole way. Even real tears. Mom again: 'when you feel you are ready to join us, you may.' I always thought that was a silly question. What—is she going to sit down and ponder the ramification of the situation? Get serious. She's ready as soon as Mom lets her go.

"This time she cries five minutes loud enough so we can all hear and share a good laugh at the table. The crying stops. After a lapse of time, she mysteriously appears playing peek-a-boo with us. She returns and is at her old games. This time Mom takes her without warnings. This repeats a couple times."

TONY: "This is not about choices, but I have to say it. Best time to instantly anger your children. 'You can't leave until the kitchen (or whatever fits the situation) is clean.' My God, when she said those words I wanted to kill her. It felt like she was waiting around the corner until we got our jackets and baseball and we would be two steps away from the door and there she would be, saying, 'Don't leave until the dishes are done.' Every time, I hated you when you said that."

"And the bathroom, with the radio, tell us about the famous bathroom?"

MARIA: "'You made her leave.' The obvious statement uttered two seconds after the fight started and one second after Mom turned to leave. You knew when you got in a fight that it was over—she left for the bathroom. I remember 'taking over' after Mom left. I was Mom and 'the boys' did, or played all their games on me. It took me a long time to get over that! But, I guess I learned. Slowly—very slowly. It was so funny when we'd fight because we knew, or at least I knew, that she'd be gone. I knew in the back of my head."

TONY: "I remember when she began to use a radio and the bathroom to avoid becoming involved in our fights. One time we were fighting on the first floor but moved the fight to the second floor right outside the bathroom. The fight just kind of dissolved into nothing except shouting once we realized that she wasn't going to get involved or stop us. Then as the radio got louder, we just stopped. I know now and can explain why it happened but at the time it was like, 'ooh, the nerve of her just to ignore us when we are fighting for her attention.' "

JOHN: "After she met Dreikurs, anytime we would fight, it would immediately signal a race to the bathroom with the transistor radio for the Dreikurs Disciple. She would stay for five to fifteen minutes, depending on the fight or screaming occurring."

"Did she spank you after meeting Dreikurs?"

JOE: "Not that I can remember. There were a lot of trips to the bathroom with that little radio. I remember Pat spanking me once. For what, I don't remember, but I got revenge somehow. How, I don't remember either."

"What about when she put your things in a locked closet?"

TONY: "I remember being trained on leaving stuff around the house. It really sucked not being able to find the jacket I knew I left on the front stairs. Where was it? In Mom's closet, of course, to be returned at the end of the week. These little lessons seemed to work all the time. I don't remember how long the process took but it seemed like we were learning to take responsibility for ourselves all the time. The shock. The outrage we felt because she had the nerve to pick up after us in her own fashion, until we learned to do it right. God, how about the old dirty clothes business. 'What do you mean I don't have any clean clothes? Just because I left them lying all around my room and didn't put them in the dirty clothes basket doesn't mean Mom can't pick them up and wash them. What do you mean, start a load of clothes? Or fold the ones in the dryer? Those are Mom jobs.' "

MARIA: "When I think back about how I used to leave all my stuff around, I can't believe it! Or rather, I can see where or how I got where I am now! Anyway, I remember being so embarrassed when I didn't have my algebra book. I know I lied to my friends. I couldn't say, 'My Mom took it because I left it lying around.' Jeez! Boy, that was a quick learned lesson. 'I forgot my drumsticks' three days in a row??? That was horrible, but a good lesson!"

"So Chris, you and Anno being the younger ones of this group, was it even more different for you?"

CHRIS: "As a child growing up in a democratic household, I was never rewarded for doing chores, doing homework, or getting good grades. By the same token, I was never punished or grounded. We didn't have rewards and punishments as motivators in our house. Instead, we had 'encouragement and logical consequences.' I'll begin with encouragement as a replacement for rewards. As far back as I can remember, I used to draw. As soon as I finished a drawing, I'd run to Mom's room to show her my latest creation. She was all smiles. She appreciated anything I did. She always had some encouraging comment about the piece of artwork I happened to be working on at that time. As I grew older, I stopped running to Mom, but kept sketchbooks nonetheless because drawing and painting had become so pleasurable for me. And because I enjoyed it so much, I became a 'half-decent artist.'

"We're all artists inside. We just need someone to unconditionally encourage us. Mom never commented on 'me' or rewarded me for being such a good boy. Rather, she talked specifically about the work. Later, as I became 'sophisticated' and began to become acquainted with visual art terminology, I would tell her exactly what she liked about the piece, and why, based on her pedestrian comments... ha ha...!

"As far as school, subjects and grades are concerned, Mom wasn't concerned. It was our own business. I remember showing her report cards up to about seventh grade. She never commented on whether I got 'A's or 'B's or 'I's. She said she was happy we enjoyed that subject so much. And we would talk about why I enjoyed the class. Grades weren't even secondary. They simply weren't a concern. You say, 'but you might have been a naturally intelligent child.' Bullshit. All children are extremely intelligent—more so than adults—it's just a question of where they put their energies and for what purpose they use their 'intelligence.'

"By the time eighth grade rolled around, I stopped telling Mom about grades because I knew they would not interest her. In high school, I'd mention here and there that I had got (uh hum, cough, cough) all 'A's. Finally, she started encouraging me to get a few 'F's to become good at making mistakes. I'm glad she did, looking back on it now. And I almost took her up on it senior year...when she signed a big stack of blank sheets of paper so that I could go to school late if I needed or wanted to.

"And she would not have to be involved with perfunctory handling of parental notes, etc. That was my business and my responsibility. She was not in the least bit concerned that I'd take advantage of a 'privilege' that would shock most other high school seniors and their parents alike. Meanwhile, other seniors were ditching, fighting with their parents, and getting grounded or being given early curfews. Their phone, allowance, and car 'privileges' were being stripped. Mom and I had worked past all of that, but by very different means. She used natural and logical consequences in raising us. I feel that by the time it got down to Anno and me, we only learned 'democratic' ways because it was part of all our lives."

"Anno, do you remember any of this? Did you notice that you were being raised differently? What did you think about all of it?"

ANNO: "Well, to tell the truth, I had no idea that I was being raised any differently. It was the only environment I knew. I do realize our family's difference now though. When I talk with my friends, I find our experiences are very different. They can't believe that my mom excuses me from school if I need a 'mental health' day. That's just totally inconceivable for them. They are so distant from their parents. What is theirs is theirs and not their parents'. There's no sharing going on there. My mom and I share clothes. It's just very different.

"Responsibility is a big difference that I notice. I have a friend who told me a story about how she pretended to be asleep so she didn't have to help put away the groceries. It really bothers me to hear this since I have the responsibility of *going* to the store. Just putting the groceries away is such a small job now.

"Grades and housework are things I have a hard time talking about with some people. In our house, doing housework was always done because it needed to be done, not because we were getting paid. But some friends of mine get paid to do it. I can't even comprehend this. They also get paid for the grades that they get. You know, so much money for an 'A' so much for a 'B' and so on. But I've always done my schoolwork for my own satisfaction. That's the way it should be. If you're not doing it for yourself and the only motivation is money, how can you ever learn to do something just because it might please someone else? This has got to be part of the result that we live in such a 'me' society. How anybody can be that way, it can really frustrate me sometimes..."

I got up and went into the kitchen to refresh my tea. Pouring the hot water, I remembered all the times I would lay on my bed and listen to them talk to one another. Here, in the kitchen, it was déjà vu. These parents didn't know that these kids could go on all night telling stories if you let them. Ah yes, some things would never change. Weren't they all just in high school with all the doubts and fears, joys, competitions, girls and guys, and who likes who, dates, and jobs to make money?

They were constantly helping each other. "Bet you can get a job with me at the restaurant. Want me to ask for you?" Their voices became soft and convincing; their hearts learned to be truthful and yet gentle, and when the teenage years arrived I was convinced it was the best age they could be. I had five teenagers at once, no rebellion but loads of craziness. "Are you going to go out looking like that?" There was constant movement, exhausting at times, but courage coming out everywhere. I went to band concerts, swim meets, and wrestling tournaments. Were they really so little such a short time ago, with me lying on my bed in the late afternoon, stealing a couple extra minutes trying to get enough energy to spend a little more time listening and guiding that night?

Ever since they were tiny I loved those voices, sometimes tears, sometimes laughter,. "Can I have your trophies when you die, Joey?" All the trading of baseball cards, homework, getting answers. "You change her diaper this time; she just had a beamer." It was always there—that support and camaraderie, the creativity and love, the teasing after I won them over to my side way back when—then suddenly they seemed to have grown up overnight.

And they were in college struggling yet making it, bursting with courage and struggles. And when they came home for holidays, the talks resumed instantly as if we were never separated, even though many times it had been as long as a year. Sometimes whispering so no one else would hear, or open forum on the bedroom floor, until the wee hours. And I still do it. I lay on my bed right down the hall listening to them talk, plan, tease, and laugh. It is always one of my very favorite times of life. It will always be, listening to them solve the biggest problems and telling the greatest stories, explaining who is the worst villain and the greatest 'catch', discussing who is more protective of whom.

"Can I wear your shirt?"

"Not this time buddy."

"Did I tell you about my friend Robert doing drugs and then dying? Yep, he died, funeral just last week right before Christmas."

"That's a bummer."

They look at each other in silence, knowing full well that they all had another year of life and all of them were still alive. Knowing how fortunate they were; still all intact and life was full and rich. They had taken it in, the encouragement, the training, geniuses they are.

And most important of all, "If you rub my back first I'll rub yours longer."

"Oh no you don't. You said that the last time, you do mine first tonight!"

And Tony saying in a voice that can be heard down the block, "This is our year guys. This is it. I can feel it in my bones. This is our year. Mark my words. Joe, listen to me! Jenny! John! Chris! Anno are you ready? Maria, Apple? Are you listening? I'm telling you this is the year, for all of us. I'm telling ya...listen to me all of you so I don't have to say I told you so."

"Tony you said that last year...remember?"

"I know and it was, wasn't it?"

And my insides swell with good stuff running through my veins. And even though I've said it a dozen times before, I didn't have as much experience then and I was still learning but now it is different and I know for sure! This is the best age ever! This is the best age that kids can ever be.

Addendum: Their Thoughts on Each Other...

Tony...by Chris:

Tony is a giver. He'd give the shirt off his back to whoever happened to be with him at the moment. The last person Tony thinks of is Tony. The first person he thinks of is you. It seems material possessions and money mean nothing to him unless he can use them to make others happy. Tony gives you his brand new bicycle that he used not half a summer, so that your life will be easier, more enjoyable. Tony uses the 150 dollars won in a poker game to buy the family lunch, treats, snacks, and goodies. His generosity is unconditional. It is love. And for Tony it comes as second nature. Tony is a teacher. I remember my junior year in high school when I was preparing to look into colleges. His wise words on the importance of grades, financial aid, and scholarships guided me smoothly along the path of higher education. His guidance made all the difference in my life.

I remember all the times he helped me write English and history essays. I remember the flow of words highly organized yet gentle, coming out of his mouth as he edited my work. He was tactful and yet he instilled a confidence in me that "I could get it done!" if I worked at it.

Now he is going to touch the lives of about 150 people a year in his English teaching and basketball /baseball coaching. His teaching will have a tremendously positive effect on the world.

In a few years, Tony will find himself principal of a school. Then he will move on to teach teachers how to teach. He is the only one who can limit himself. He can do whatever he wants to achieve.

As brothers, we've always been close. I remember when we were young. There was a rivalry between us. I never felt any between John or Joe. But that ended in our teenage years. I've always been able to tell him anything, like a best friend. We can always have a good time together. I couldn't ask for a best friend better than Ton-Ton.

Tony...by Joe:

He's a friend, a good friend. He does little things that friends do for each other. Writes a note, makes a call. He's a thinker. I'd say he thinks more than anyone I know. New ideas are always coming out of his head. Most neat, some weird, like the time he came up with the idea to have a baseball hitting station in the dark. Sometimes I worry about these ideas.

Tony's passion for life is easy to see. He gets involved in many things and commits his waking hours to doing whatever it is he's involved in to the best of his ability. Another thing that impresses me about Tony is his ability to take a great deal of pride in whatever he's doing—from school work to collecting garbage to pay his way through college. Tony has been working for the Grounds Dept. at C.S.U, "You see that ice over there?"

"No, Tony, I don't."

"Right, because we spent four hours yesterday chipping it away. It's in our area, you know."

He's got his act so together that those he comes in contact with "catch" this attitude. Some people are parts of groups. Tony stands out and leads in groups.

I have spent more time together with Tony than any of my siblings in the last five years. We have spent many hours coaching together. Together we make a hell of a team. We also consider ourselves very close friends. There's nothing we wouldn't do for each other. Tony has the knack of taking you out of the dumps with his incredible sense of humor. This humor is rather wild, rather unique but always hilarious.

Chris...by Maria:

Chris is so funny in the way he acts around me sometimes. He is sometimes afraid to say stuff and yet he says more to me than any of my brothers. I mean, he may be afraid, but he does it anyway. We have the best talks. Talks about life, you know, religion, God, war, doing stuff, things you can only talk about with someone you really like.

I love seeing how different he is from me. Where he is in his life and where

I was at the same age. Sometimes I feel a lot older than him and other times it's like he is older than me. That is natural, I know.

Chris has the ability to get almost anyone to do anything for him. He can really get me, that's for sure, although I have caught on in these past few years. I know that I could get the "boys" to do stuff for me, but Chris can get me to do stuff for him.

When he was a student teacher he would call, upset and asking for help. He did want help, but he would really have preferred it if I would just solve it all. I tried to do just that before I caught on.

One of my favorite stories about Chris is the broken window in the car. He was supposed to fix it and it was about a million degrees below zero. So, he went downstairs and was gone for about 20 minutes. I don't know how he could stand it. It was so cold. Then he came upstairs and said, I just don't know how to fix this!! I've tried everything. Seconds, really, seconds later Joe, John, and Tony ran for their coats, grabbed tools, discussed possibilities, went out the door and down to the car all in the time it took Chris to get his coat off. Jenny and I were on the couch laughing until I thought our sides would burst.

Chris is so funny, capable, sensitive, gorgeous, hanging on whoever is standing next to him, intelligent, caring. I see myself in him and it helps me. I remember dressing him up. Getting him ready for school. Taking care of him, my own baby!

Chris is one of the most intuitive people I have ever met. He can tell at a glance if you are alright. He wants, as we all do, for everything to be alright for everybody in the family. He quietly snuggles up to you just to check you out.

Chris loves to have "intellectual" conversations. He loves to discuss life and all its aspects. He analyzes, thinks, converses, and really puts himself in your shoes, trying to see all sides of the issue. He loves to think of the odd angle, the odd side of the issue to see what your reaction will be.

Chris is a realistic idealist. He knows what he wants and how he thinks things should be. He also knows how to work in the real world to get what he wants. As a teacher, Chris has many ambitions and ideas about how he wants to teach. He works so hard to balance what he is told he must do with what he knows is the best way to teach.

Chris is the wiggler. He wiggles his way into the middle of everything. Conversations, beds, chairs, anything, as long as he can be in the middle.

Christopher by Anno:

Snoogie, Butkus, Scruffler, Soupy, or whatever you want to call him, he's my bro'. The other half of the "Chris and Anno Show." Chris is the one I've spent the most time with in my family. Therefore, we have the most jokes with each other. I love to tell stories about Chris because, well, I just do. Usually when I tell about a fun time we had together or something crazy that he did, the person I am talking to wants to know his age. When I tell them that he is twenty-three, they laugh because they expect it to be a younger brother. I guess that's what's so special about Chris: his fun-loving attitude about life and other. He's young at heart (and in age) but I think he will always be that way. It's part of him.

If I had to describe Chris in a word, I would have to say: incredibly fun. Okay, that's two words but so what? It's true. Chris is also very respectful to others and beneath his fun exterior he is wise (if I may take a "mom" word) and very knowledgeable about life and people. He's just an all around "neat" guy, and I love him bunches!! (Okay, you can commence crying and saying AWW!) No, just kidding again. I just have to say that Chris is the best— there's no way around it.

John...by Anno:

There is something unique and special about each of my brothers. The thing that stands out in my mind about John is his sense of humor. It is one of the best of anyone I know. He is usually subtle with his jokes, and once someone else laughs, he laughs too. I always love to hear his little "hee hee" laugh.

John is the kind of guy who has fun all the time. He works very hard at his job and is serious about it. But I also think he enjoys it and understands that it should be fun as well as hard work. John's got style too. Not just "fashion" style, although he does have that. He always looks nice no matter what he's wearing. I think that shows something about his personality. He is kind and carefree and fun and "cute." He thinks it's funny when I say "cute." With each of my brothers, I have a nickname of some sort. John calls me Peanut. I love it when he calls me that. Although it is just a name, I enjoy it because it is something just between the two of us. I am proud to be seen with John and to talk about him to people, just like all of my brothers.

John...by Chris:

John is independent, confident, solid, practical, proud, generous, respectful, and successful. John has big shoulders, tough on the outside but loving, soft, and sweet on the inside. He is a natural leader. When he speaks, people listen.

He's an organizer of household chores, desktop files, all the knickknacks in the pantry, thoughts, people. He wins people over with his magnetism, optimism, his keen sense of where to play it safe, and when to take a risk, and his charisma—which he gets from me.

He is an extremely hard worker. He knows how to get what he wants. He seems to know exactly what it is that he wants, which is perhaps mysterious about him. Then he goes out and gets it. He's dedicated to that which is dear to him: his work, his family, and his friends. He always gives one hundred percent.

I believe that he gets one hundred percent out of the people who work with and under him because he encourages them, shows them respect, and expects one hundred percent from them as well. I remember when he was head coach of my eighth grade YMCA club. He set the tone for the club: hard work, team work, and have fun. We all trusted him. I guess he won some award because of it. As an older brother, he's always helped me to be the best I could be. He basically wrote the resume that got me my first job.

Something very important that I learned about John this past Christmas was that although John shows his affection differently than I do, it doesn't mean he doesn't love and care about his siblings just as much as I do. I have learned to stop judging and comparing him, and others for that matter, by the way he shows his affection. This realization has made me extremely happy although John may not realize it yet. I am now completely at ease when I talk to him or with him. It feels great.

John single-handedly clothed me with first class hand-me downs since as far back as I can remember. This has meant a savings of $1,300.00 for yours truly. How could I complain? Finally, John knows how to make the group laugh when all else might seem gloomy. He keeps our home full of stupid-ass toys from Vegas toy stores.

Maria...by Joe:

She's the ultimate friend. Every quality you would list that relates to friendship... Maria possesses. She's always there when the chips are down to provide a hug and words of encouragement. I know she's done this for me many times. Having her near is a source of strength... a support system. You're never alone. When you need a favor Maria is usually there before you even ask. She'll go to the wall for you.

Maria is in her fifth year of teaching and teaches as though she were a twenty-year vet and a rookie at the same time. She's wise beyond her years and exudes so much enthusiasm you'd think it was her first year of teaching. Her future has to include the classroom but she would also be very invaluable to new teachers, she would affect thousands more!

As hard as she works she keeps most things in perspective and isn't afraid to be an ornery person. She can be one of the most fun individuals around. In the classroom, she starts with a lump of clay and turns it into a marvelously creative group of individuals. Some of the activities she accomplishes in class surprise some of her colleagues. But her family and those she works closely with have come to expect these "miracles" yearly. We're supposedly a "Nation at Risk" as far as our education is concerned. If the teachers in America had the enthusiasm, drive, creativity, and love that Maria has we would be a "Nation at its Best." Maria continuously strives to make herself the best teacher and person she can be.

Maria...by Tony:

Maria is the one who can tell me if my ideas are great or just a little too much. Probably doesn't sound like much, but ask her about some of the ideas I've bounced off her since we've been sharing a home. She is also the one who can always get me on track when I'm having trouble writing. She just patiently reads everything I hand her, and helps me get it right. It is also very nice living with her, especially since I'm still going to school. Many of my friends don't have a quiet house life; they are always fighting about something. With Maria, we can usually work out any living problems that we have quickly and without it taking a lot of energy.

Working in her classroom last year was something else. I can always identify her class because they are usually the loudest. At the same time, they are the ones who are enjoying school most, and doing the most learning. She seems to flow right through class, aware of everything that she needs to be aware of, minding her business otherwise. I guess she just fits in the class, and I'd like to be able to establish the same kind of presence in the class, leading without seeming to.

Let's see, what else? Well, Maria, is Maria. It's just very nice to be able to come home and discuss things, or be left alone at this time in my life, and almost a perfect roommate. That doesn't sound very exciting, but it's like a pillar of strength that I can lean on everyday, whether she is aware of it or not. And I'm sure that I'll lean on her even more as I get into the classroom full time.

Anno...by John:

A real spark plug here, I have a lot of great times with her. I can remember helping Anno with her homework when she was in sixth and seventh grade. She would wait until 8:30 at night before starting and then as I watched TV she would start. By 9:30 we would be finished and then we'd watch the "Honeymooners" until 10:00 and she would go to bed.

Anno has a great presence. She can come into a room and get you to smile by just watching her. It's scary how far advanced in self-confidence she is. She thinks she can do anything, she doesn't seem to let little things bother her and she can handle a crowd, like a politician. Since she grew up with people older than her she knows "grown-ups" and can deal with them very easily.

Anno...by Maria:

Anno is my sister. I love to be able to say that. She is one of the funniest, most intellectual, most beautiful people I know. She is the consummate actress. Her face is mobile like clay.

When Anno was little we used to joke about her being Dreikurs reincarnated. She is so right on with people. Anno is very respectful and so encouraging. She believes we can do anything. She sees through the games and dishonesty and understands so well why people do what they do. She is so beautiful that many times she may not be perceived as being as intelligent as she is.

It is amazing to me that she doesn't realize how wonderful she is. She is special because she is a sister. Someone I can talk to about things only a sister would understand. The older she gets the closer we get. I love being with her and I count her as one of my best friends.

Anno will take this world by storm. She has already started but only a few of us know that. Just you wait!

Joe...by Tony:

If it weren't for Joe, it's highly likely I wouldn't be coaching. It is certain that I wouldn't be as good as I am. A lot of my technique, philosophy, style, etc., are imitations and things I saw Joe do. I repeat his phrases, with ease now. Also, I coach because I get to be with him. It was great doing basketball together, because we could show the kids how to play hard, and work together—especially when the two of us beat the five of them, because we worked together.

Baseball is the same way— I wouldn't be doing it if not for Joe. I like the fact that we can bounce ideas off each other, and if one of us feels strongly, we go with that decision. I know you're thinking this is just an example of mutual respect, but we're also living it, if you know what I mean.

Coaching basketball is completely different now. I have to make all the decisions and have learned a lot, but it was more fun with Joe, and I could learn just from watching Joe. Anyway, that's one of the obvious areas that Joe has been a factor. He's my buddy out here.

We like playing catch and talking baseball. Watching him in the classroom, watching his classes, was also a reflection of all I see in Joe and want to be. It seemed to me he had a group of people working together on different parts of the same project, all with a common goal— it blew me away.

I mean, I knew he was good, but seeing is something else. He does things, he accomplishes things that I want to do. I guess that's why we're so alike in so many ways. And why I find myself doing the same things and activities that he does.

Basically Joe is being himself and doing the things he does has and continues to play a large role in the way I try to do certain things. It feels good, and means something, when Joe makes a positive comment about something I've done, or the way the basketball team plays. Anyway, I guess I've stuck to the coaching/teaching aspect, but those are two of the important things in my life, and where he has had the most affect in my life.

Joe...by John:
Joe is someone who is destined to be on top of his profession, he is still gaining confidence in his teaching abilities and needs one or two years and

then he will excel quickly. His coaching skills have obviously been noticed, and with good reason. Watching him run a practice with high-school freshmen was like a professional sports clinic. His team listened to him carefully and they improved a lot over the short time I was there. I see someone who could be an N.B.A. coach or a college president.

We've had a pretty good relationship in our lives, one that started very competitively and now one that is pretty good from mutual respect. A very caring, strong and smart guy and I can't wait to see his next game.

Jenny...by John:

Jenny joined our family in her senior year in high school. She is more of a sister than a sister-in-law. She was adopted into the family and accepted by us warmly. Back when Joe and Jenny first started college no one where they were going to end up—I don't think they even knew—but they finally made it to Colorado.

Jenny's wedding to Joe in August of 1985 was a very happy day in everyone's life. It was a chance for this family to shine. I've never seen us so in tune with everyone. That wedding really clicked and we were stars. Stars. I remember that day very well and always will. Of course, Joe and Jenny did not do the planning for the wedding. Oh sure, they did the stuff that was seen, but the rest of us were really doing it. I think the planning started back in December of 1984. One step at a time was planned. One more step wouldn't be planned until we finished the one before. Joe never would agree to too many things at once. It was our family meeting at our best.

Jenny on entering the family:

It's been almost ten years since I first met Joe and the rest of the guys and in all honesty, I believe that in this time I have grown up for a second time. First, with my own family, second with you dudes. It's hard to think of a time in my life that I didn't know them. In the beginning, my relationship with Joe's family was primarily based on my relationship with Joe. My first impressions of Joe's family was that they had camaraderie in their relationships with each other and Mary, "the mom," was different from a lot of the other moms that I knew. She was a friend to her kids but not in the sense that she was trying to relive her own childhood through them or that she was running their lives... she just treated kids as her equals. As if she liked them for who they were.

After my mom died, I lived with them for a summer. That summer relationships began to change. Up until 1980 I had been the youngest of six children in my parents' house. Although I had been away at college it was scary to think I had no home to go back to after spring semester, but Mary offered to let me stay with them for the summer.

At first I was nervous. It felt like I was starting all over. The second part of my development started that summer—the Adlerian years. Now, I could tell you guys operated under a different philosophy. You were so close, open, positive, equal, cooperative.

I thought it would be hard trying to fit in. Afraid I'd mess up and make a mistake, but soon I discovered that mistakes weren't such a big thing in this family. I remember saying to Chris once something like, "How do you guys like this to be done?" Chris answered back saying, "What do you mean **you** guys? You live here just like we do." I think at this point my insecurity of where I belonged was lifted. These people accepted me for who I am and I am part of the group. I learned a lot that summer. How a family works better as a team than in constant opposition and that everyone contributes to be the most effective.

Some of the things this family has done for me over the years, encouraged me to major in art and in my teaching, taught me about equality and democracy, provided an important support system, became my friends and confidants, helped to build my self-confidence, and showed me a different way to live life. I am starting to realize that I need to be responsible for this kind of living in my own household.

Every week Joe and I have a meeting. Sometimes we say a lot and sometimes we don't, but it keeps the line of communication open. Mary has done a great job of training her children democratically, but unless we practice it outside of her influence we lose the principles of democracy in our own lives.

And finally I really appreciate how Mary Dalton and I have developed a relationship, separate from my relationship with Joe. She is a good friend.

Where They Are Now

Maria: Teacher Extraordinaire: Ninth Year Teacher. Whole Language Reading and Life Studies.

"During the course of a principals' professional experience he becomes blessed when he encounters that one teacher who can "do it all." The teacher who is not only an expert in curriculum and instructional techniques but is totally understanding of how children best learn. For me, Maria is that one teacher. Not only is she a gifted skillful instructor, she is an outstanding role model for both her children and her peers. Her incredible strong work ethic, her ability to motivate children, her understanding of the importance of shared student responsibility and classroom climate help to make her so very special. Maria has helped me value being a principal."
Avi Poster, Principal, Homes Jr. High School, Wheeling, Ill. November, 1992

"Maria has the talent of making people believe in themselves more than they ever had before. She as an infectious self-confidence that makes everything seem possible. She is a leader who as many followers. And the beauty of it all is that Maria is as human and vulnerable as the people she leads. I would still be wandering without her help. I admire and love her deeply."
Tonia Ekstedt, 2nd year teacher and friend. November, 1992

Joe: Teacher Extraordinaire: Seventh Year Teacher. World History, Social Studies, Student Council and Life Studies.

"Joe is the most courageous teacher I have ever met. He stands up for what he believes is best for kids and holds true on his convictions and commitment to education. He takes risks in his teaching but plans for these risks, making them very calculated and precise, leaving no room for error in achieving his ultimate goal of touching and changing the lives of the youth of our school and America. Joe is gifted with the true ability to empower people

to be the best they can be. I've never seen a teacher motivate kids to achieve their goals and set lofty goals to reach for, as Joe."
Steve Johnson, Science Teacher, Thompson Valley High School, Loveland, Colorado. November, 1992.

John: Businessman Extraordinaire: Eighth Year in Business.

"It is well known within our company that John is a very dedicated and conscientious character who has made major contributions, not only on a general basis, but in his dynamic and "get things done" approach and management style. He is admired by his colleagues and continually strives for quality as well as excellence. John is a team player as well as key management leader who has never left a job undone nor allowed anything to detour him from his responsibilities. His integrity, respect, and humor are always intact. He remains a highly respected and much admired man within this community, a reputation he truly deserves."
Rick Eastwick, THE GAP, Inc. San Francisco, California

Tony: Teacher Extraordinaire: Fourth Year Teacher of English Literature, Writing and Life Studies.

"I hope that whatever my children do that they do it as well as Tony teaches. He makes such an impact on children's lives not just in the classroom but in everything he does. The quality of instruction, his ideas and how much I've learned from him is incredible. He's the best teacher I've ever seen in the classroom.

I think the world of your son as an educator, as a human being and hopefully as a friend!"
Dale Krueger, Principal, Kenneth Henderson School, Garden City, Kansas. November, 1993

Chris: Teacher Extraordinaire: Fifth Year Teacher of Spanish and Life Studies.

"Rarely have I known a teacher as caring and committed both to his students and his subject as Chris. He has an empathy that makes them respond in a positive way to whatever transpires in the educative process. I am particularly impressed by his strong work ethic and extremely effective interpersonal skills. Most of all, Chris sees teaching in its broadest context; he prepares his students to be responsible citizens capable of thriving in a multicultural world."

Roger Stein, Director of English and Foreign Language, Niles West H.S., Skokie, Ill. November, 1992

Anno: College Student. University of Wisconsin, Madison, Wis.

"I knew I loved a special person when Anno and I worked side by side as waitresses. Bored at work one morning, Anno spit her gum out into the empty restaurant for no apparent reason and sent me laughing for quite some time. It seems an odd memory to hold so close, but I do believe that in committing such a harmless and unrestrained act, she set out to relieve me of whatever worried me that day. Anno, through her irony and strong sense of humor, lavishes me with a much-needed positive perspective and outlook. Because of the loving and supportive family that surrounded her, she has taught me of unselfish love; that love can be pure in itself and ALWAYS a lesson."

Jenny Hey, friend. November, 1992

My dear friend, Haile-Yesus, died of stomach cancer the spring following that Xmas he begged me to visit him in Bali. I'm sure he knew he was sick and that's why he begged me to come despite my 'No,' which was so out of character for him. None of my letters to him ever came back from UNICEF or the United Nations and although I knew something had happened to him, I had no confirmation of my thoughts until two years later. It was then that Sonste and I learned that he had gone to Washington, D.C. to seek medical help. But it was too late to save him because the cancer had become too advanced at that point. There are no words to express how deeply I miss him. He was a pure love, full of kindness and all good things. I will always long to be able to see him and talk with him just once more.

Afterword: 22 Years Later

I do not have the words to describe what has happened over the last 25 years inside this family. As I work with families, I re-read the same chapters I assign them from *Children: the Challenge*. The book continues to teach me.

There are been more mountaintops in our family than I could ever have imagined and, conversely, there have been more valleys than I'd like to admit. "All my children are prodigies"--a proverb that hung in our home throughout their childhood. I believed it and experienced it. They lived it. My kids never met a lemon that they could not turn into lemonade. For me, it was like seeing little miracles throughout life. Each in his or her own way, my children could win over the devil if necessary and then play with him.

I know that we are an exceptional family. We will carry on the work we have learned to do, both in our communities and inside our homes. I know we will look into the mirror and see the greatness inside of us. I look forward to the mountaintops at the end of each of our valleys, when we will renew the great gift we have been given.

A month after I met Dreikurs, I remember sitting back with my Coke and cigarette feeling quite good because, "boy was I democratic now" with my kids. It makes me laugh aloud and shake my head because I really believed I was. Now I know that I am always learning. I know we can change things and break unhealthy cycles in our families and our lives. We'll make a million mistakes along the way but if we believe that "it's a law of nature: what we feed grows", like my daddy use to say, "then we've got a chance."

In their professional lives my children are all outstanding. Sonste told me, after witnessing Maria teach, that she was the greatest teacher he had ever seen. Those words meant a lot to me because Sonste (as well as Dreikurs) taught all over the world for over 50 years. The Principals at Maria's schools Principals describe her as "a once-in-lifetime teacher." As one parent told me, "She is the light, the beacon, the love, the center of the universe. Everyone in the school district wants his or her kid to be in Maria's classroom." Her students love her to death.

I know that if Sonste could have had the opportunity to see my other children in the classroom and the work world, he would have used some of the same words to describe them.

Joe is known as a master teacher who can work kids and parents alike to draw them in. He gets people involved who have never been involved before. Those who "never had the time" now have the time. It would take lots of pages to list his accomplishments and the lives he has touched. He is humble in his work. Joe has three boys and lives in Colorado with his wife across the street from his brother Tony and his family.

Tony was a master teacher and then master Principal of Peak to Peak School in Colorado and made the school into one of the 100 best schools in the US as described in *Time* magazine. He knew every child's name in the whole school. He is the center of the universe where he teaches. He is now a consultant, continuing his work with teachers and administrators. Tony is married and has two girls adopted from China.

Chris was a master teacher in the classroom, involving the community and kids in projects never dreamed of before. After leaving the actual classroom and literally taking his classroom into the world (co-founding Global Visionaries with his brother Joe), he has made an impact on kids from both the U.S. and Guatemala. His work has been tireless, endless, and not without pain as he has integrated low and high-income kids into the program training teenagers to become leaders and global citizens. His work is admired. To quote the parents, "This program is DIFFERENT. It's not like the other programs of which there are many." He and his partner have a beautiful daughter.

They didn't all go in the classroom. John went into business and became far more successful than anyone could wish for. John is a superstar in business world. The people he works for and those who work for him realize they are not working with an ordinary businessperson. His caring and understanding set him apart from others and his staff love working for him. And when he has started a new job, his people follow him, even when it means moving to another city. They pick up their family and follow him. John has three girls and lives in California.

Anne's creativity and brilliance comes to life in her Chip and Moo characters and books. Having registered in art school and attended one semester, she realized she had it all inside and didn't need more schooling to make her art and express her creativity. Anne has a daughter and she and her partner are general managers of a new restaurant near Los Angeles.

Over the years I have been so touched to hear people comment on the impact my children have made in their child's life or in their own life. And then they ask, "What are your other kids like?"

"Well, the same," I answer, "The same yet different with their own personalities."

I am moved by my children's passion for their work and their families, as well as their passion for shining a light on the possibilities for their fellow man.

My children are exciting and crazy. They are mine and they are the world's. I truly believe that we can all raise children like I did. The most profound thing that I have learned in my work with parents, families, and schools is that our children are our greatest resource and we have it in our power to provide them with the tools to be exceptional, passionate people.

Acknowledgments

Rudolf Dreikurs, thank you for the fire you lit under me that never went out. It was truly the beginning of a new life for my children and me. Manford Sonstegard, or "Sonste", as we fondly called you, thank you for becoming my mentor after Dreikurs died. You took me under your wing as your student and your friend. You were my mentor until the day you died and an unbelievable source of encouragement and wisdom. Your quiet and brilliant manner is always with me. Haile-Yesus Abeje, thank you for your humor, gentleness, love, wisdom, laughter, and encouragement. Thank you for your never-ending inspiration. Maria Sadelak, thank you for never once ever doubting my abilities and intelligence.

Lisa Querido, thank you for reading and giving feedback on the book. Special thanks for your fresh eyes and encouragement. Helen Townsend Carleton, thank you for being dependable and thoughtful throughout the editing process. You were always sensitive, uplifting and caring with every suggestion and correction. All your comments were given with love and tenderness. You are and continue to be vital and refreshing. Eddie Brown, thank you for your total belief in me and your acceptance of me no matter what I attempted to accomplish. Jim Stricklin, thank you for laughter and wisdom and for being a great teacher and always making me question what I believe. Thank you for your encouragement, enlightenment, and love and not being afraid to share your beliefs with me. Max Kelly, thank you for the beautiful cover design and the love you put into your work.

For my two daughters, Maria and Anne, there are no words to describe how much you've helped me, encouraged me, teased me, edited and corrected me. To Maria, who is always inspiring, loving, loyal and wise-- thanks for your optimistic and honest help. You are always right-on even though it's difficult for me to accept sometimes. To Anno, who is always reassuring when I'm doubtful and creatively helpful in stressful times--you are so exceptionally funny, organized, refreshing, and always encouraging and influential. To my son, Christopher, thank you for your encouragement and for always pushing me onward and upward. You are empathetic, positive and stimulating in your approach. Your faith in me is unending and contagious.

About the Author

Mary Dalton, author, activist, lecturer and educator, has worked with thousands of parents, grandparents, teachers, students, and kids concerning the struggles and challenges of raising our children. With her common sense and encouraging and down-to-earth attitude, she supports parents to become proficient in the art of parenting and teachers to become leaders in the classroom. Dalton has lectured all over the country. She continues to work with parents and teachers counseling families in open demonstrations and training parents and teachers to lead study groups. Born in Perryville, Missouri, she is the mother of six and grandmother of twelve. She now lives in Seattle, Washington.